WOLVERINE

ENEMY OF THE STATE

WRITER: MARK MILLAR
PENCILS: JOHN ROMITA JR.
& KAARE ANDREWS (ISSUE #32)
INKS: KLAUS JANSON
& KAARE ANDREWS (ISSUE #32)

COLORS: PAUL MOUNTS & JOSE VILLARRUBIA (ISSUE #32)
LETTERS: VIRTUAL CALLIGRAPHY'S RANDY GENTILE
COVER ART: GREG LAND, JOE QUESADA, JOHN ROMITA JR.
& KAARE ANDREWS
ASSISTANT EDITOR: CORY SEDLMEIER
EDITOR: JENNIFER LEE
EXECUTIVE EDITOR: AXEL ALONSO
SPECIAL THANKS TO NATHAN COSBY, ANDREW DEVENNEY
& ANDREW WICLIFFE

COLLECTION EDITOR: JENNIFER GRÜNWALD
SENIOR EDITOR, SPECIAL PROJECTS: JEFF YOUNGQUIST
DIRECTOR OF SALES: DAVID GABRIEL
PRODUCTION: JERRY KALINOWSKI
BOOK DESIGNER: JEOF VITA
CREATIVE DIRECTOR: TOM MARVELLI

EDITOR IN CHIEF: JOE QUESADA
PUBLISHER: DAN BUCKLEY

ERINE: ENEMY OF THE STATE VOL. 2. Contains material originally published in magazine form as WOLVERINE #26-32. First printing 2005. ISBN# 0-7851-1926-4. Published by MARVEL COMICS, a division of MARVEL ENTERTAINMENT ?, INC. OFFICE OF PUBLICATION: 417 5th Avenue, New York, NY 10016. Copyright © 2005 Marvel Characters, Inc. All rights reserved. $19.99 per copy in the U.S. and $32.00 in Canada (GST #R127032852); Canadian Agreement 8537. All characters featured in this issue and the distinctive names and likenesses thereof, and all related indicia are trademarks of Marvel Characters, Inc. No similarity between any of the names, characters, persons, and/or tions in this magazine with those of any living or dead person or institution is intended, and any such similarity which may exist is purely coincidental. **Printed in the U.S.A.** AVI ARAD, Chief Creative Officer; ALAN FINE, President & ? Toy Biz and Marvel Publishing; DAVID BOGART, VP of Editorial Operations; DAN CARR, Director of Production; ELAINE CALLENDER, Director of Manufacturing; JUSTIN F. GABRIE, Managing Editor; STAN LEE, Chairman Emeritus. For ation regarding advertising in Marvel Comics or on Marvel.com, please contact Joe Maimone, Advertising Director, at jmaimone@marvel.com or 212-576-8534.

7 6 5 4 3 2 1

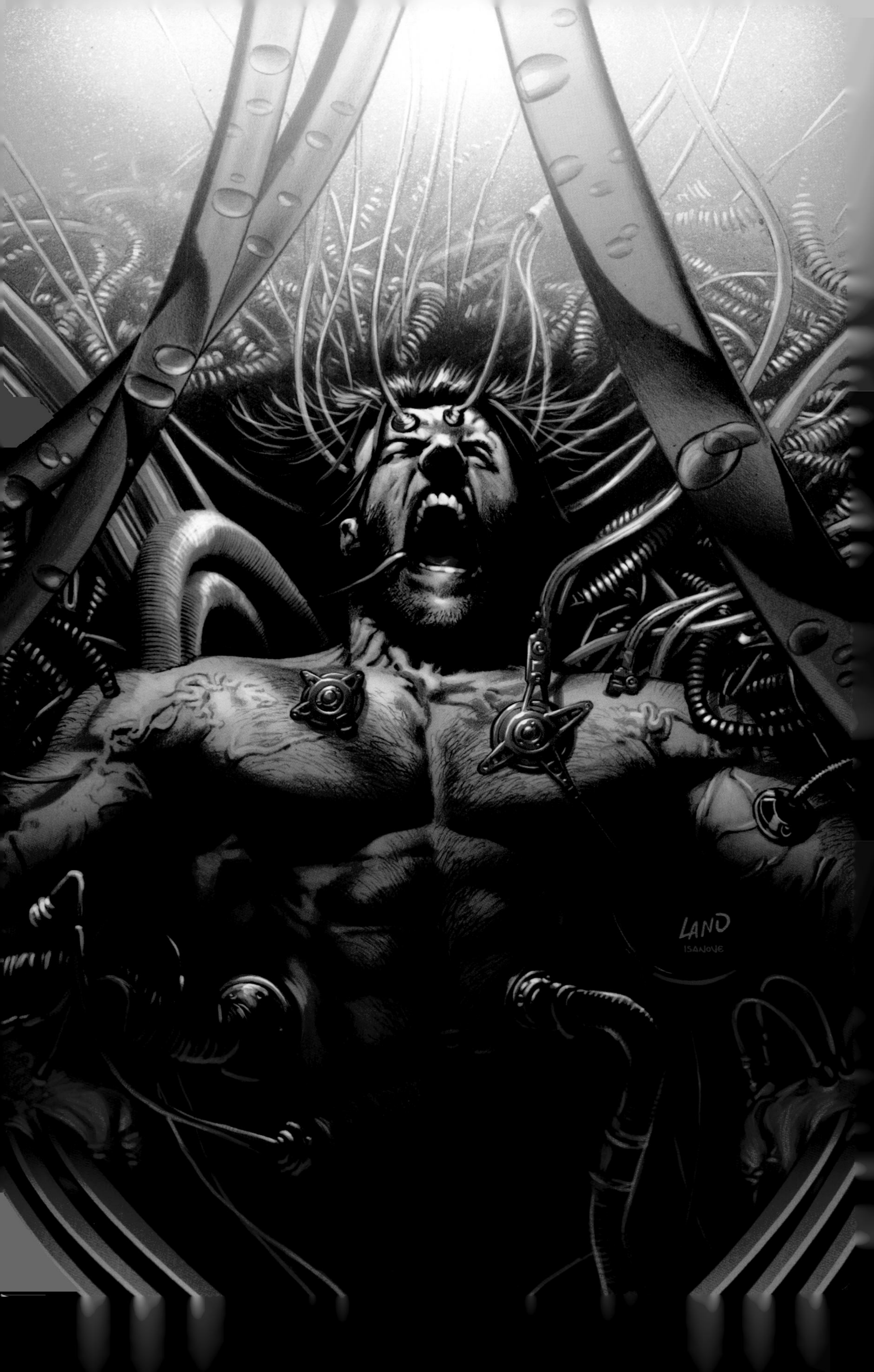
LAND
ISANOVE

AKAMATU, JAPAN.
EIGHTEEN MONTHS AGO

omi shishido said his first
ords when he was two weeks
d. He was walking at three
onths and reading and
riting by his first birthday.

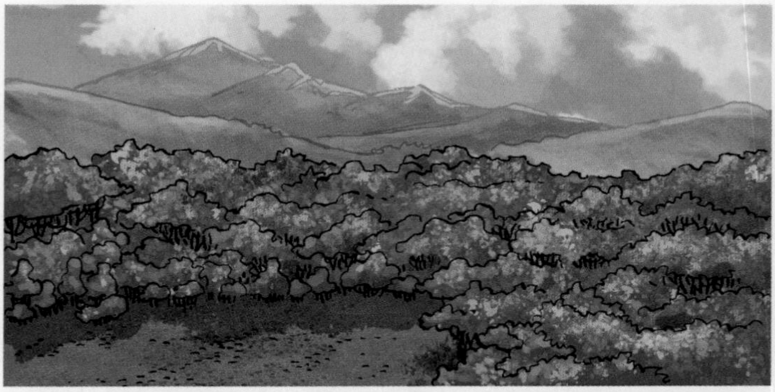

y the age of four, he had
stablished himself as one
f the five best painters in
odern Japan.

y his sixth birthday, he had
omposed his first opera and
ttempted suicide for the
econd time.

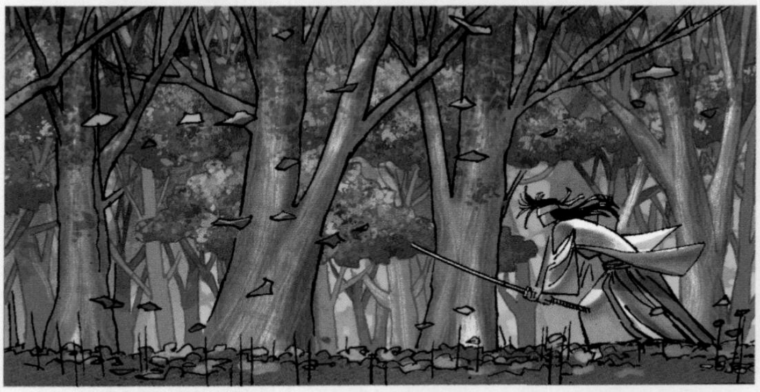

ged thirteen, Tomi devised
mathematical formula that
roved, without question, the
xistence of God and discovered
hat everyone else knew from
e moment he was born.

omi was a mutant. One of
e gifted ones. He discovered he
ould turn people to stone just
looking at them and the TV
etworks dubbed him
he Gorgon.

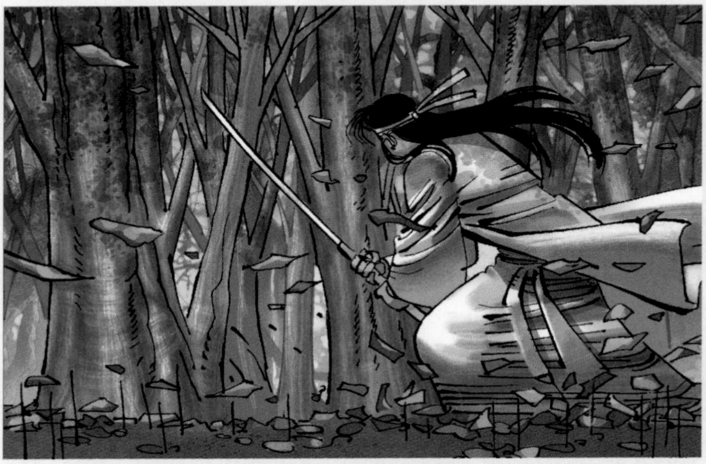

er the next four years,
e Gorgon ran a mutant
ath-cult called The Dawn
the White Light and
bjected Japan to a relentless
ries of **terrorist attacks.**

ed eighteen, he went
search of something
arker...

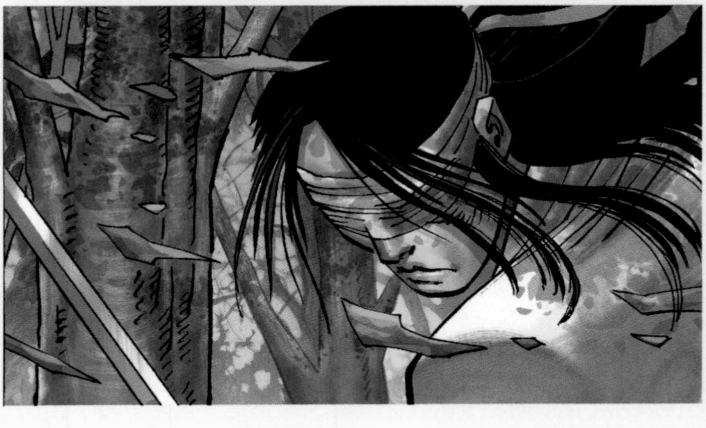

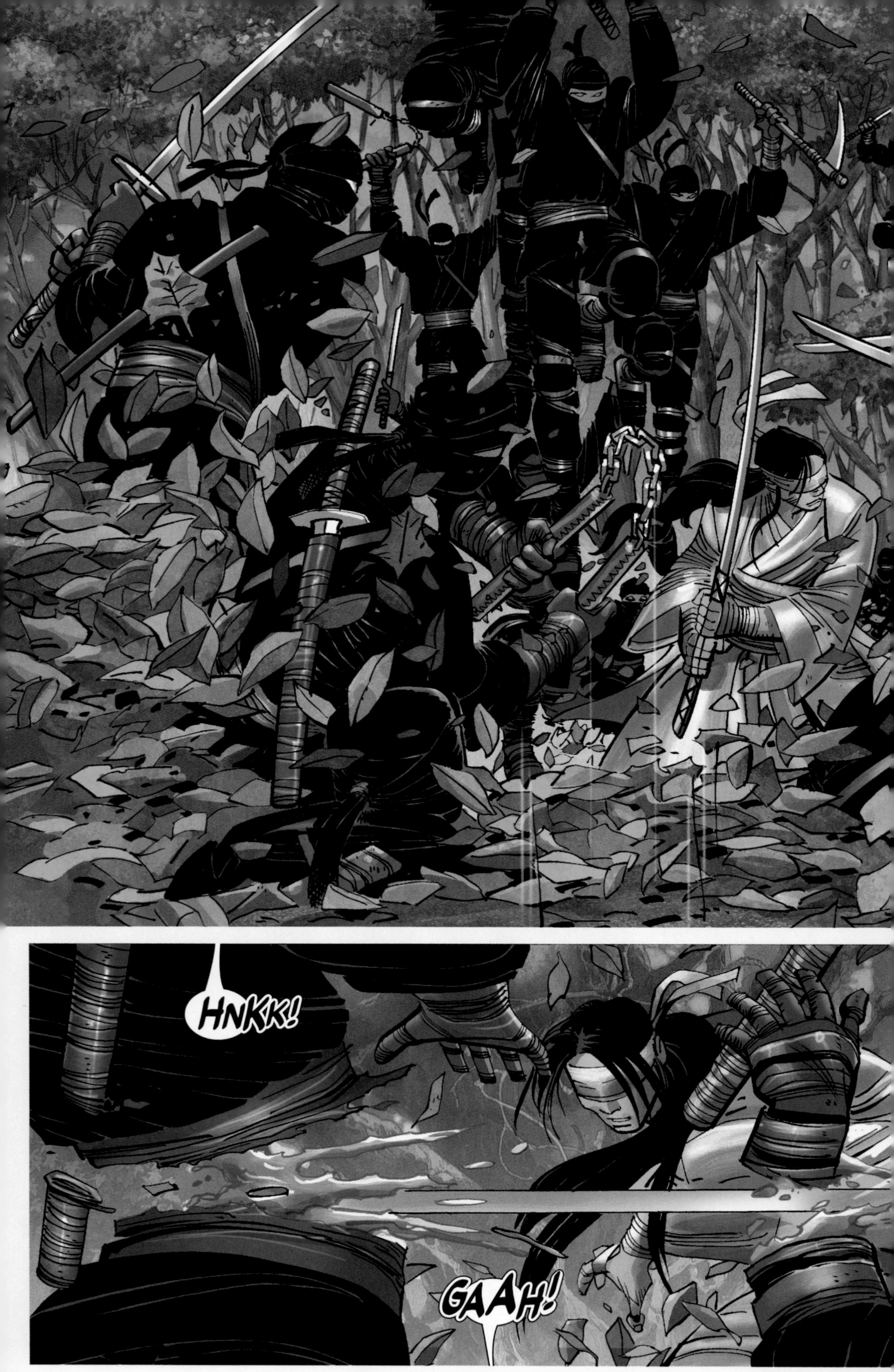
HNKK!
GAAH!

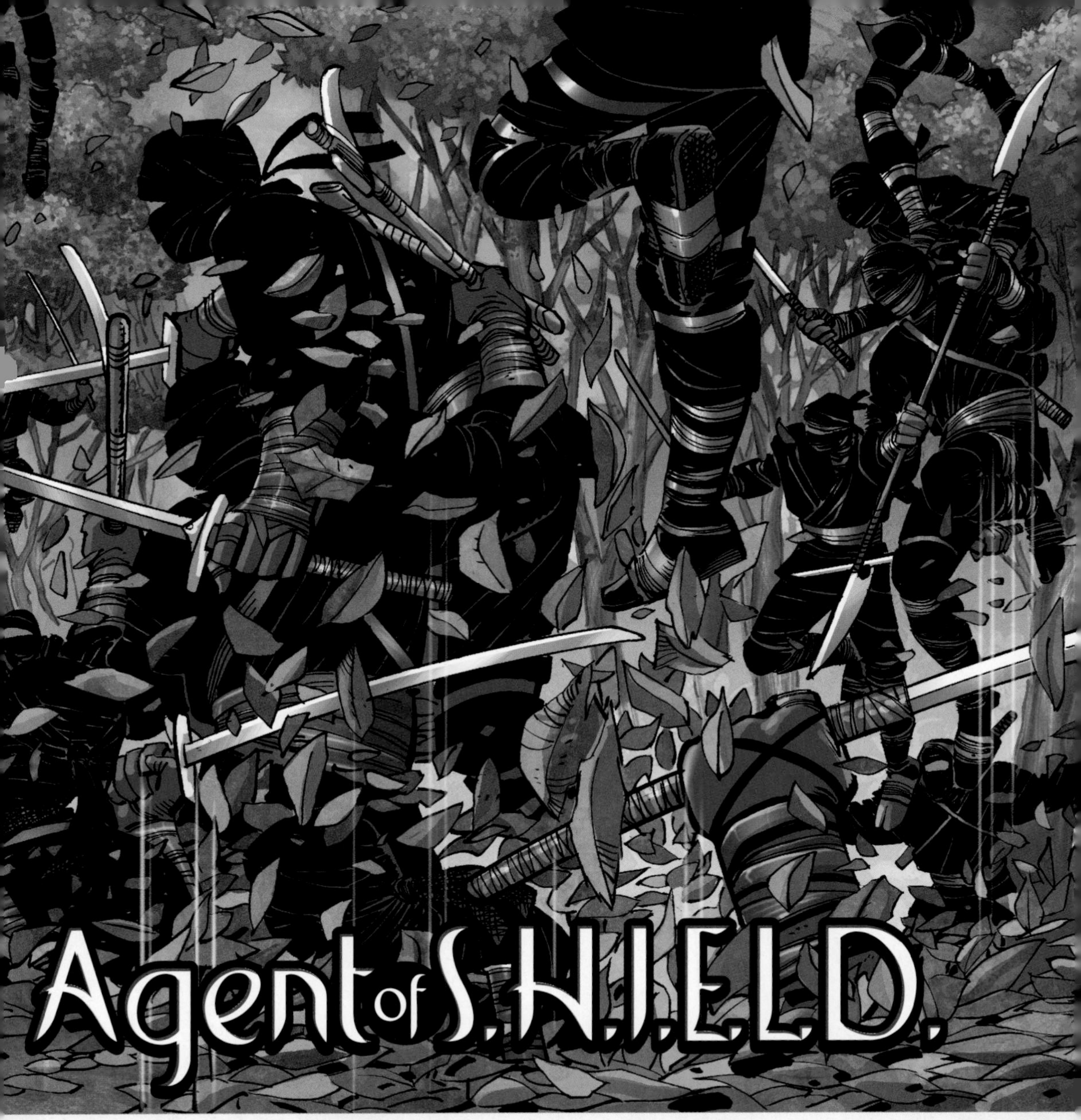
Agent of S.H.I.E.L.D.

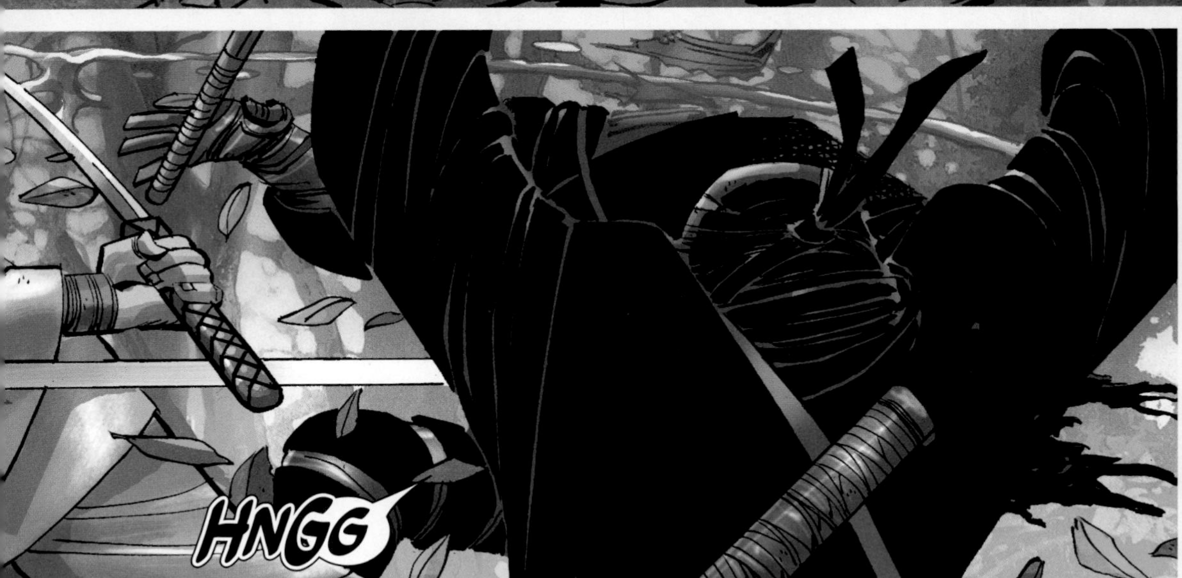
HNGG

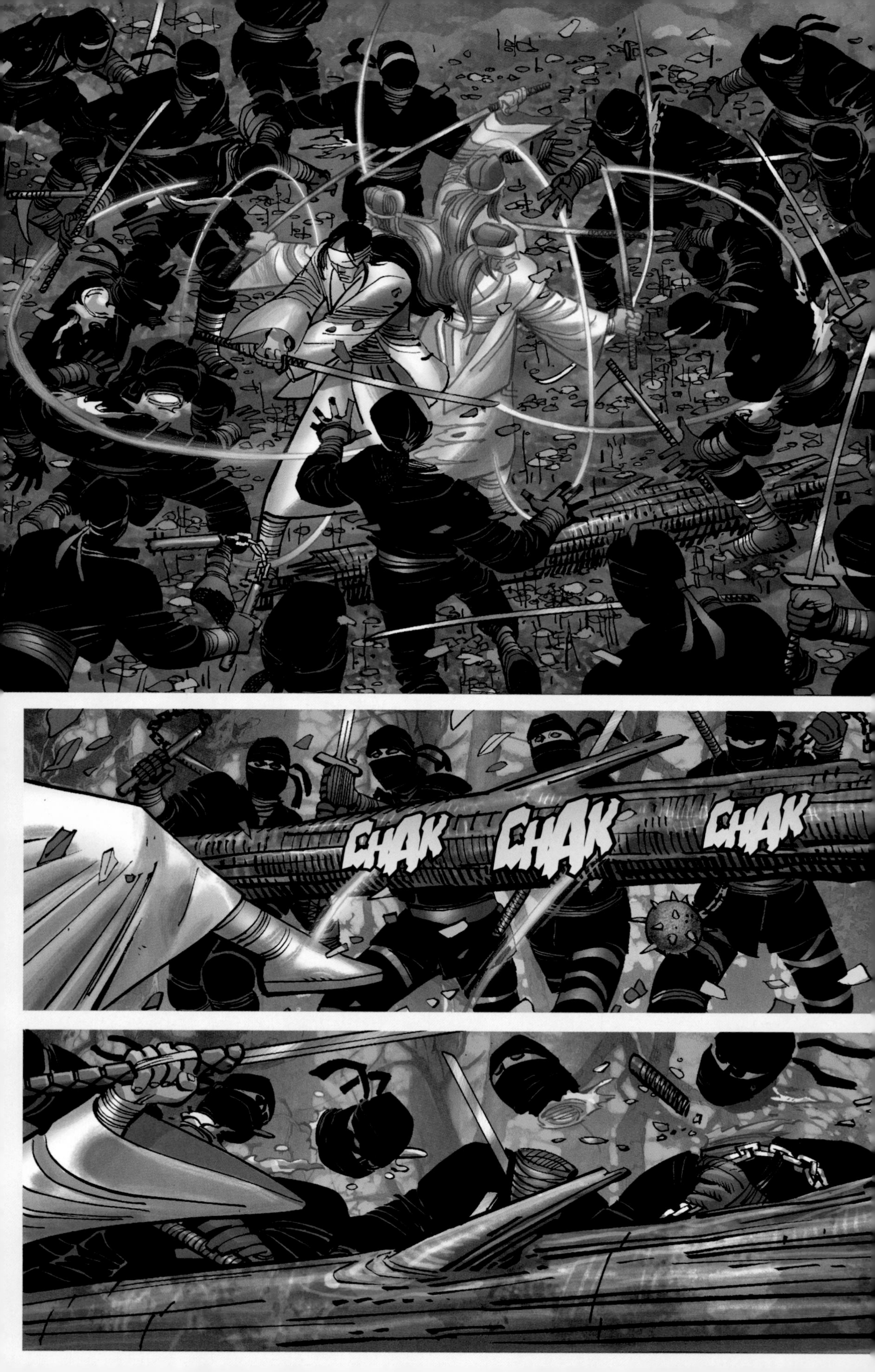
CHAK
CHAK
CHAK

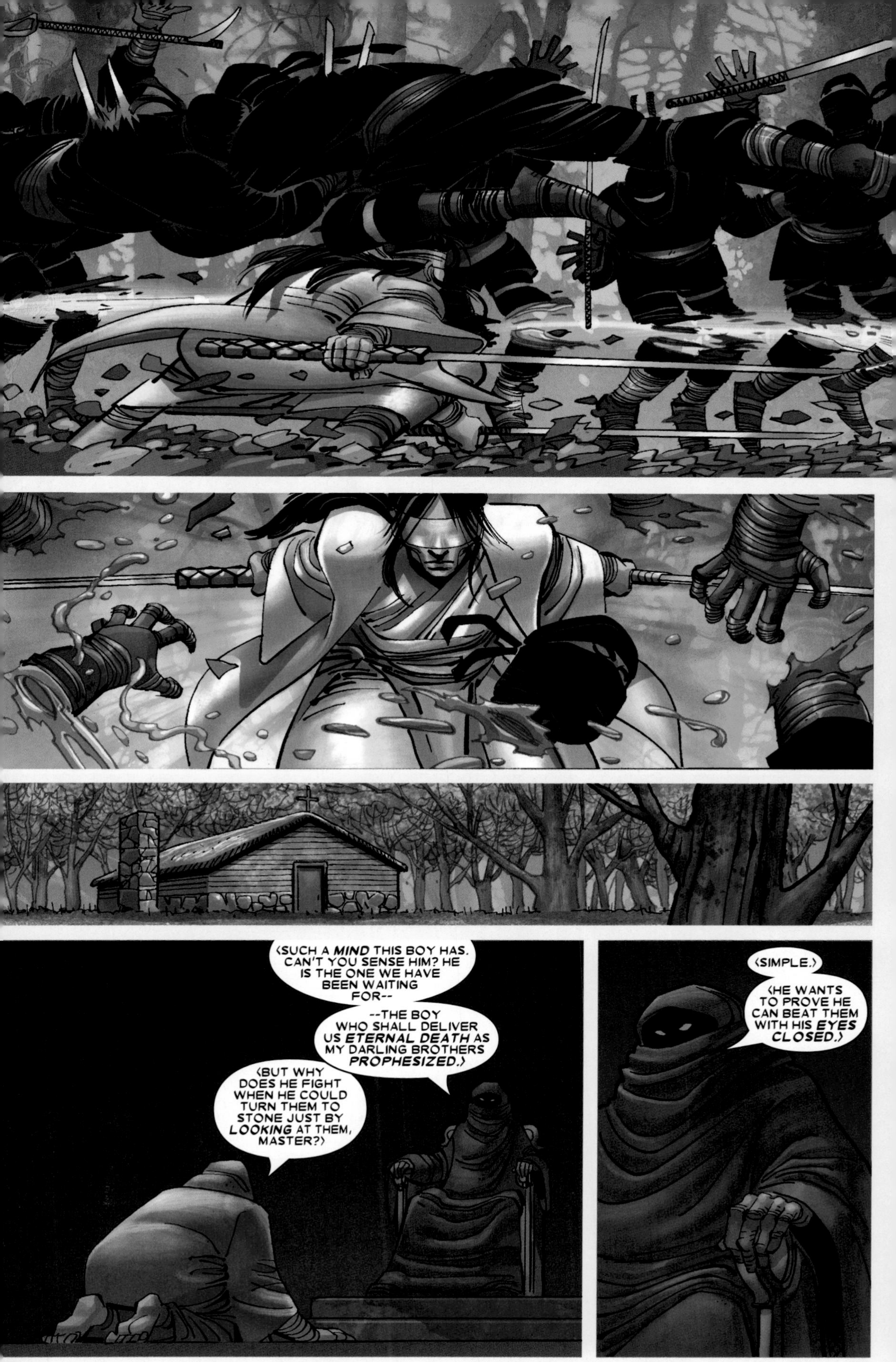
‹SUCH A MIND THIS BOY HAS. CAN'T YOU SENSE HIM? HE IS THE ONE WE HAVE BEEN WAITING FOR--
--THE BOY WHO SHALL DELIVER US ETERNAL DEATH AS MY DARLING BROTHERS PROPHESIZED.›
‹BUT WHY DOES HE FIGHT WHEN HE COULD TURN THEM TO STONE JUST BY LOOKING AT THEM, MASTER?›
‹SIMPLE.›
‹HE WANTS TO PROVE HE CAN BEAT THEM WITH HIS EYES CLOSED.›

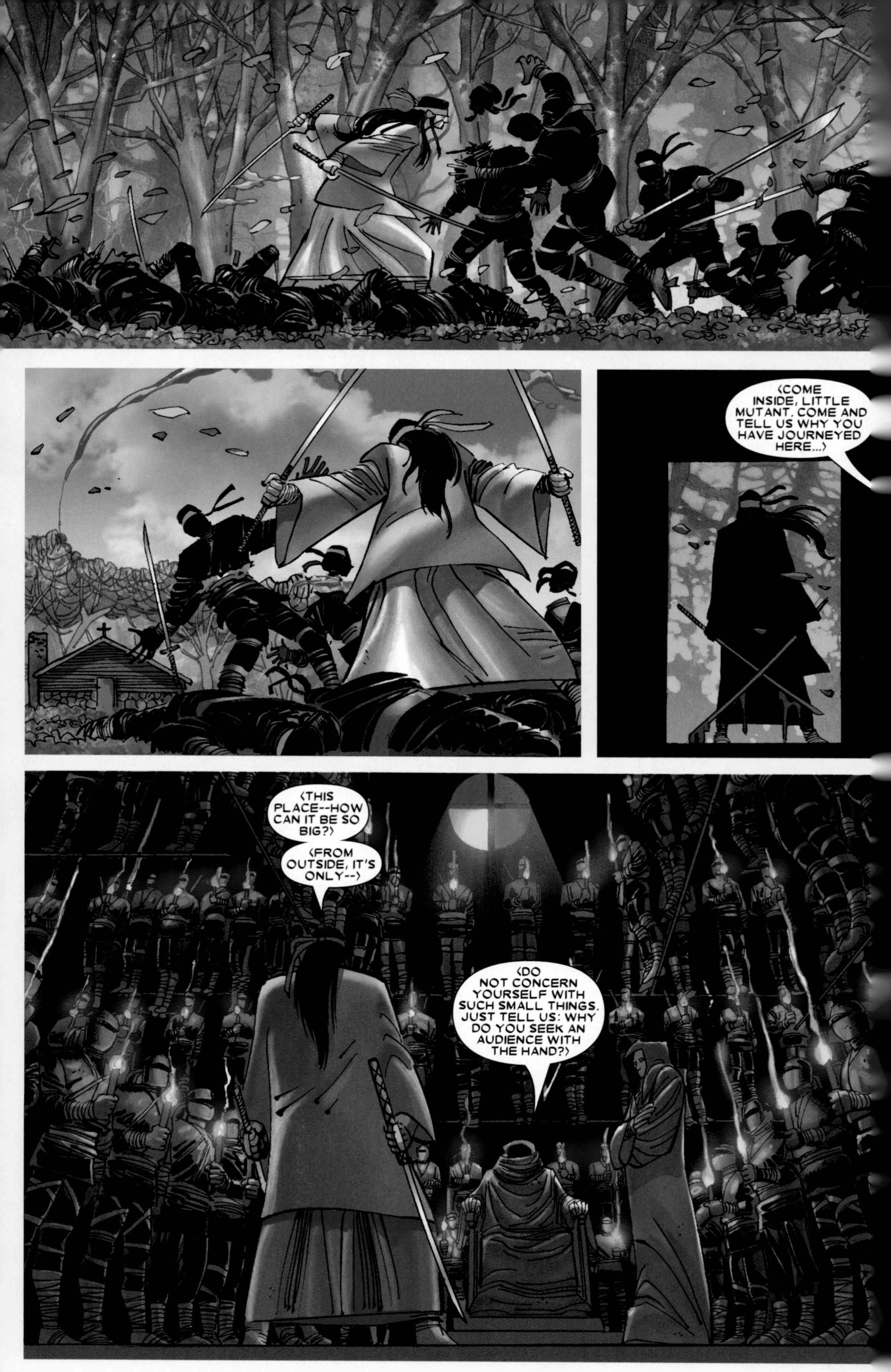
‹COME INSIDE, LITTLE MUTANT. COME AND TELL US WHY YOU HAVE JOURNEYED HERE...›
‹THIS PLACE--HOW CAN IT BE SO BIG?›
‹FROM OUTSIDE, IT'S ONLY--›
‹DO NOT CONCERN YOURSELF WITH SUCH SMALL THINGS. JUST TELL US: WHY DO YOU SEEK AN AUDIENCE WITH THE HAND?›

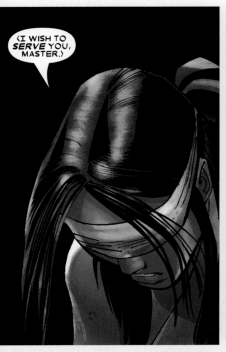

〈I WISH TO **SERVE** YOU, MASTER.〉

〈AND THIS IS HOW YOU WOULD IMPRESS? BY KILLING ALL OUR GUARDS?〉

〈I AM WORTH A THOUSAND OF YOUR GUARDS. A MILLION, EVEN.〉

〈SKILLED, YES. BUT THE HAND PROTECTS A COLD HEART. ARE YOU RUTHLESS ENOUGH FOR OUR PURPOSES, LITTLE MUTANT?〉

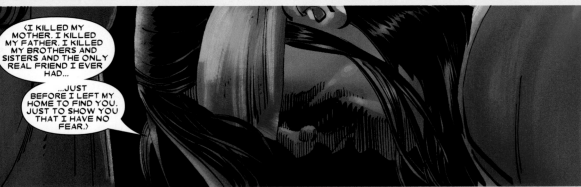

〈I KILLED MY MOTHER. I KILLED MY FATHER. I KILLED MY BROTHERS AND SISTERS AND THE ONLY REAL FRIEND I EVER HAD...〉

〈...JUST BEFORE I LEFT MY HOME TO FIND YOU. JUST TO SHOW YOU THAT I HAVE NO FEAR.〉

〈AMBITION IS ONE THING. DEDICATION, ANOTHER.〉

〈YOU WISH TO SEE MY DEDICATION TO YOUR CULT?〉

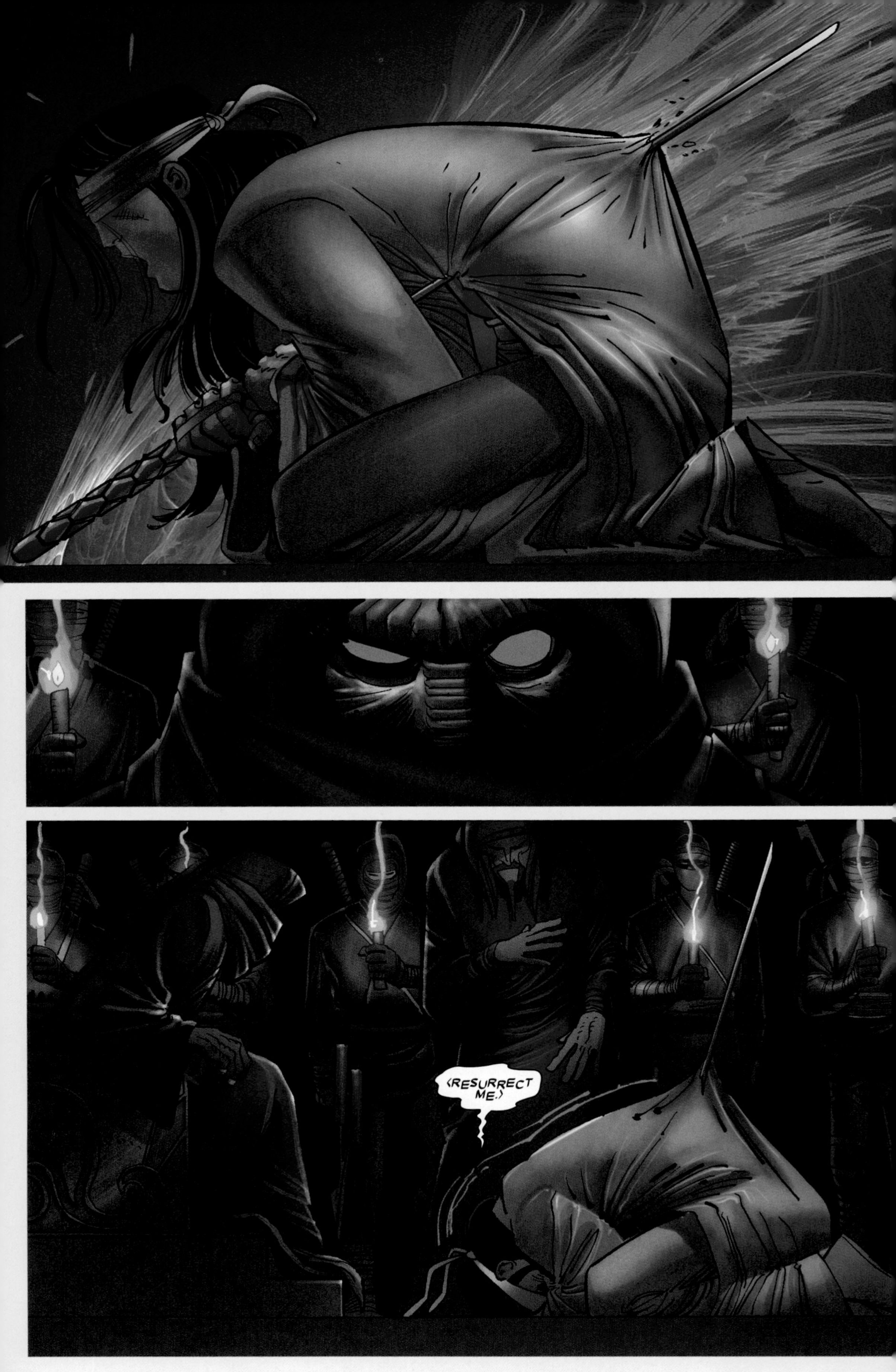
‹RESURRECT ME.›

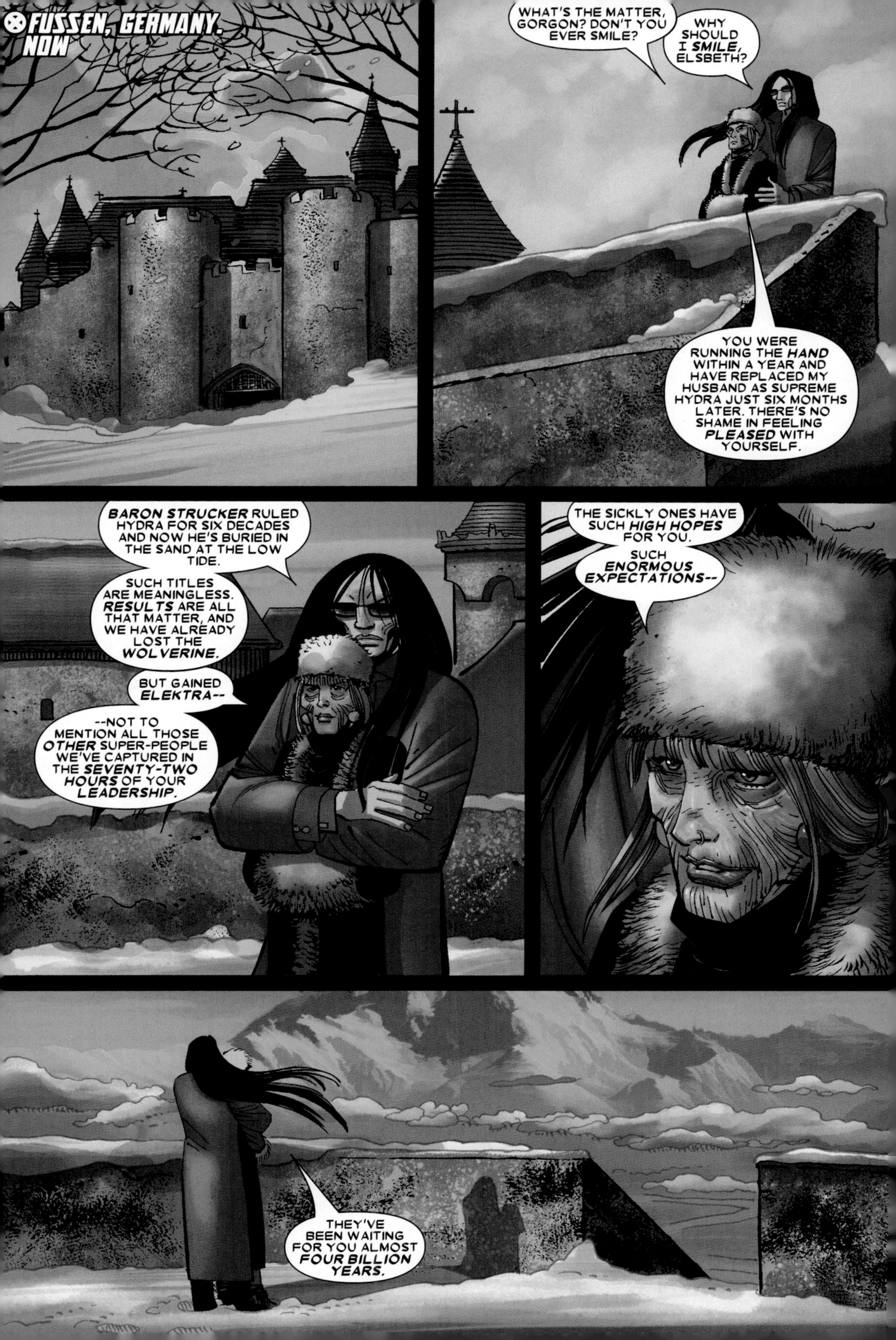
FUSSEN, GERMANY. NOW
WHAT'S THE MATTER, GORGON? DON'T YOU EVER SMILE?
WHY SHOULD I SMILE, ELSBETH?
YOU WERE RUNNING THE HAND WITHIN A YEAR AND HAVE REPLACED MY HUSBAND AS SUPREME HYDRA JUST SIX MONTHS LATER. THERE'S NO SHAME IN FEELING PLEASED WITH YOURSELF.
BARON STRUCKER RULED HYDRA FOR SIX DECADES AND NOW HE'S BURIED IN THE SAND AT THE LOW TIDE.
SUCH TITLES ARE MEANINGLESS. RESULTS ARE ALL THAT MATTER, AND WE HAVE ALREADY LOST THE WOLVERINE.
BUT GAINED ELEKTRA--
--NOT TO MENTION ALL THOSE OTHER SUPER-PEOPLE WE'VE CAPTURED IN THE SEVENTY-TWO HOURS OF YOUR LEADERSHIP.
THE SICKLY ONES HAVE SUCH HIGH HOPES FOR YOU.
SUCH ENORMOUS EXPECTATIONS--
THEY'VE BEEN WAITING FOR YOU ALMOST FOUR BILLION YEARS.

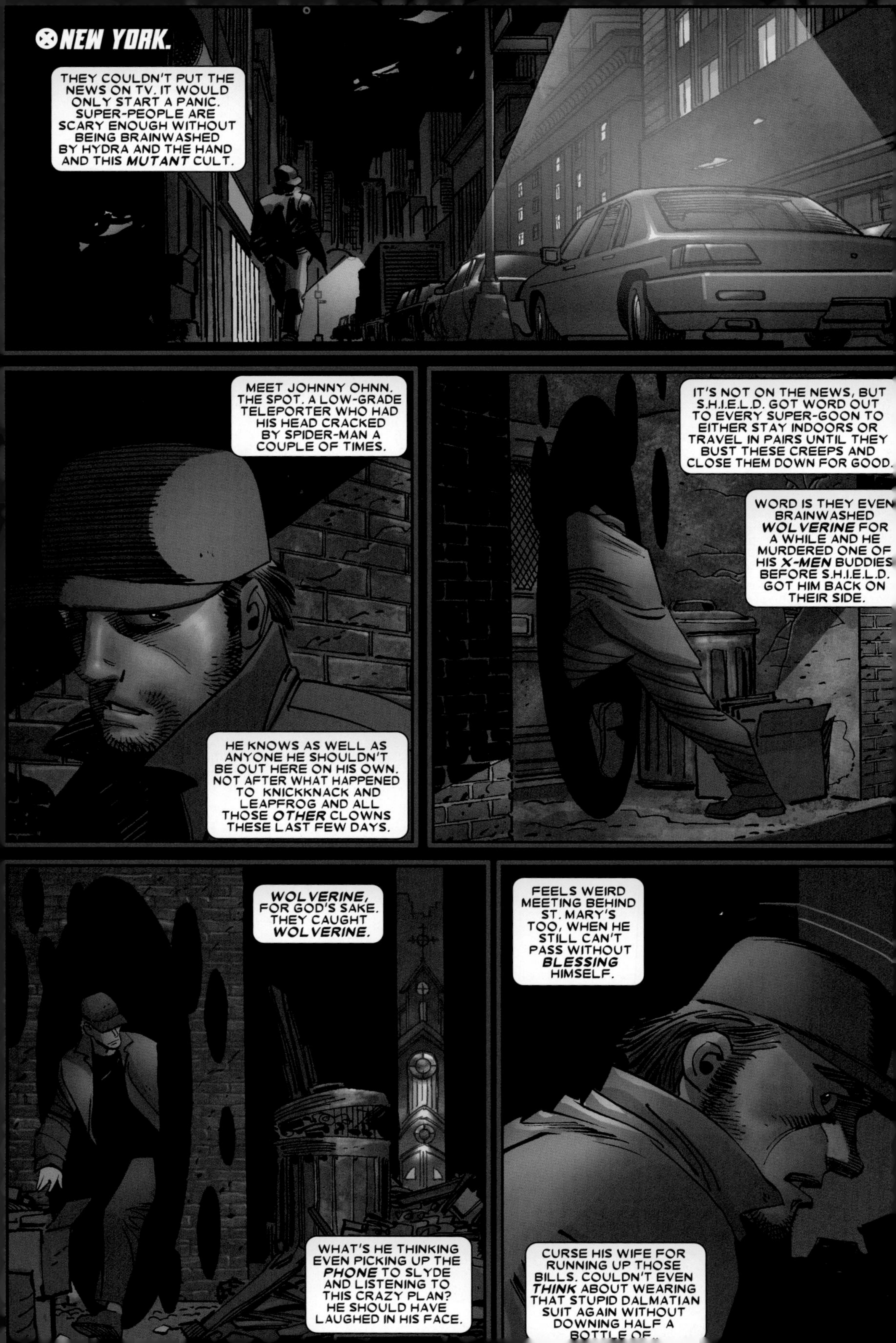
NEW YORK.
THEY COULDN'T PUT THE NEWS ON TV. IT WOULD ONLY START A PANIC. SUPER-PEOPLE ARE SCARY ENOUGH WITHOUT BEING BRAINWASHED BY HYDRA AND THE HAND AND THIS MUTANT CULT.
MEET JOHNNY OHNN. THE SPOT. A LOW-GRADE TELEPORTER WHO HAD HIS HEAD CRACKED BY SPIDER-MAN A COUPLE OF TIMES.
HE KNOWS AS WELL AS ANYONE HE SHOULDN'T BE OUT HERE ON HIS OWN. NOT AFTER WHAT HAPPENED TO KNICKKNACK AND LEAPFROG AND ALL THOSE OTHER CLOWNS THESE LAST FEW DAYS.
IT'S NOT ON THE NEWS, BUT S.H.I.E.L.D. GOT WORD OUT TO EVERY SUPER-GOON TO EITHER STAY INDOORS OR TRAVEL IN PAIRS UNTIL THEY BUST THESE CREEPS AND CLOSE THEM DOWN FOR GOOD.
WORD IS THEY EVEN BRAINWASHED WOLVERINE FOR A WHILE AND HE MURDERED ONE OF HIS X-MEN BUDDIES BEFORE S.H.I.E.L.D. GOT HIM BACK ON THEIR SIDE.
WOLVERINE, FOR GOD'S SAKE. THEY CAUGHT WOLVERINE.
WHAT'S HE THINKING EVEN PICKING UP THE PHONE TO SLYDE AND LISTENING TO THIS CRAZY PLAN? HE SHOULD HAVE LAUGHED IN HIS FACE.
FEELS WEIRD MEETING BEHIND ST. MARY'S TOO, WHEN HE STILL CAN'T PASS WITHOUT BLESSING HIMSELF.
CURSE HIS WIFE FOR RUNNING UP THOSE BILLS. COULDN'T EVEN THINK ABOUT WEARING THAT STUPID DALMATIAN SUIT AGAIN WITHOUT DOWNING HALF A BOTTLE OF...

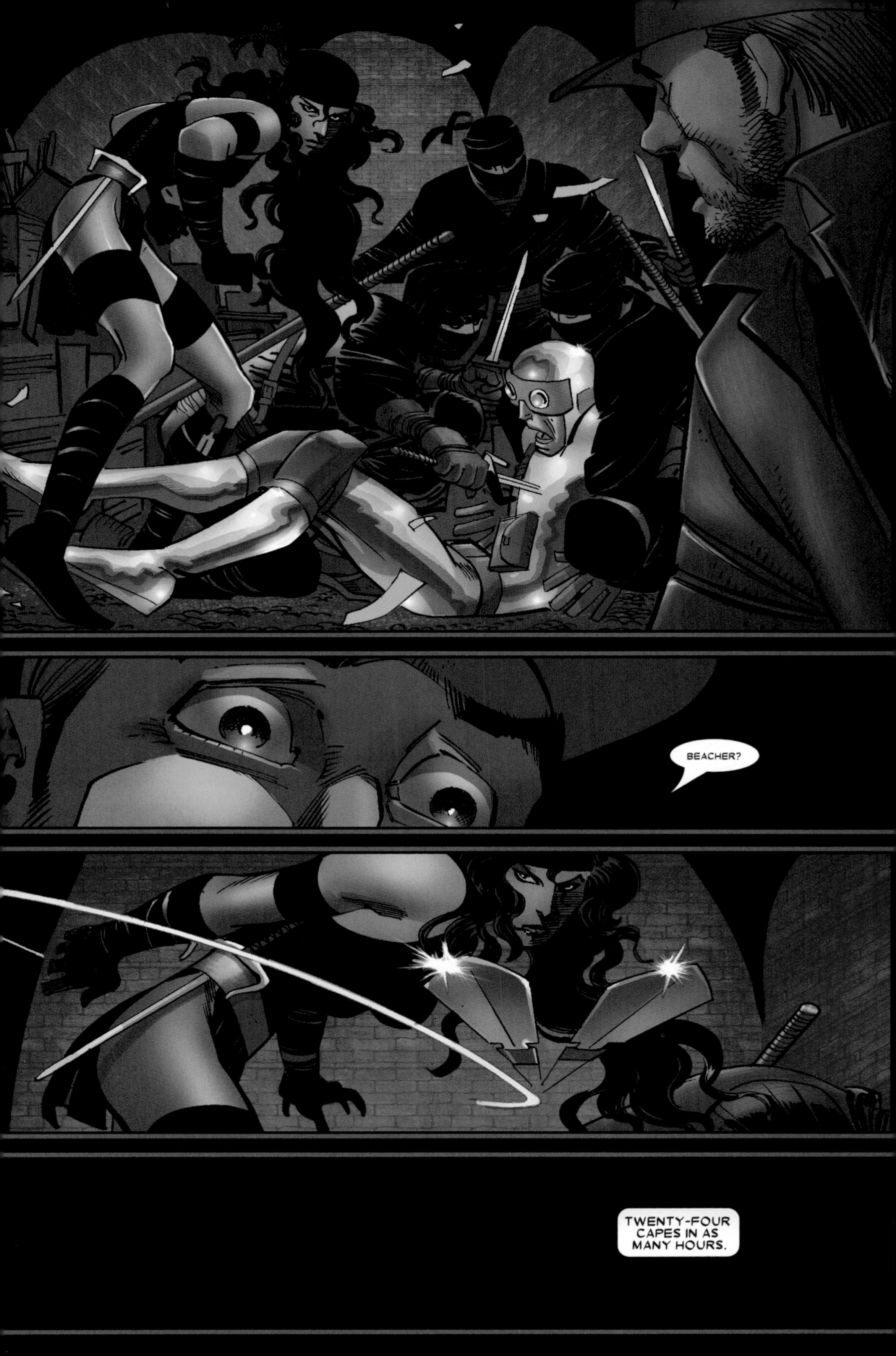
BEACHER?
TWENTY-FOUR CAPES IN AS MANY HOURS.

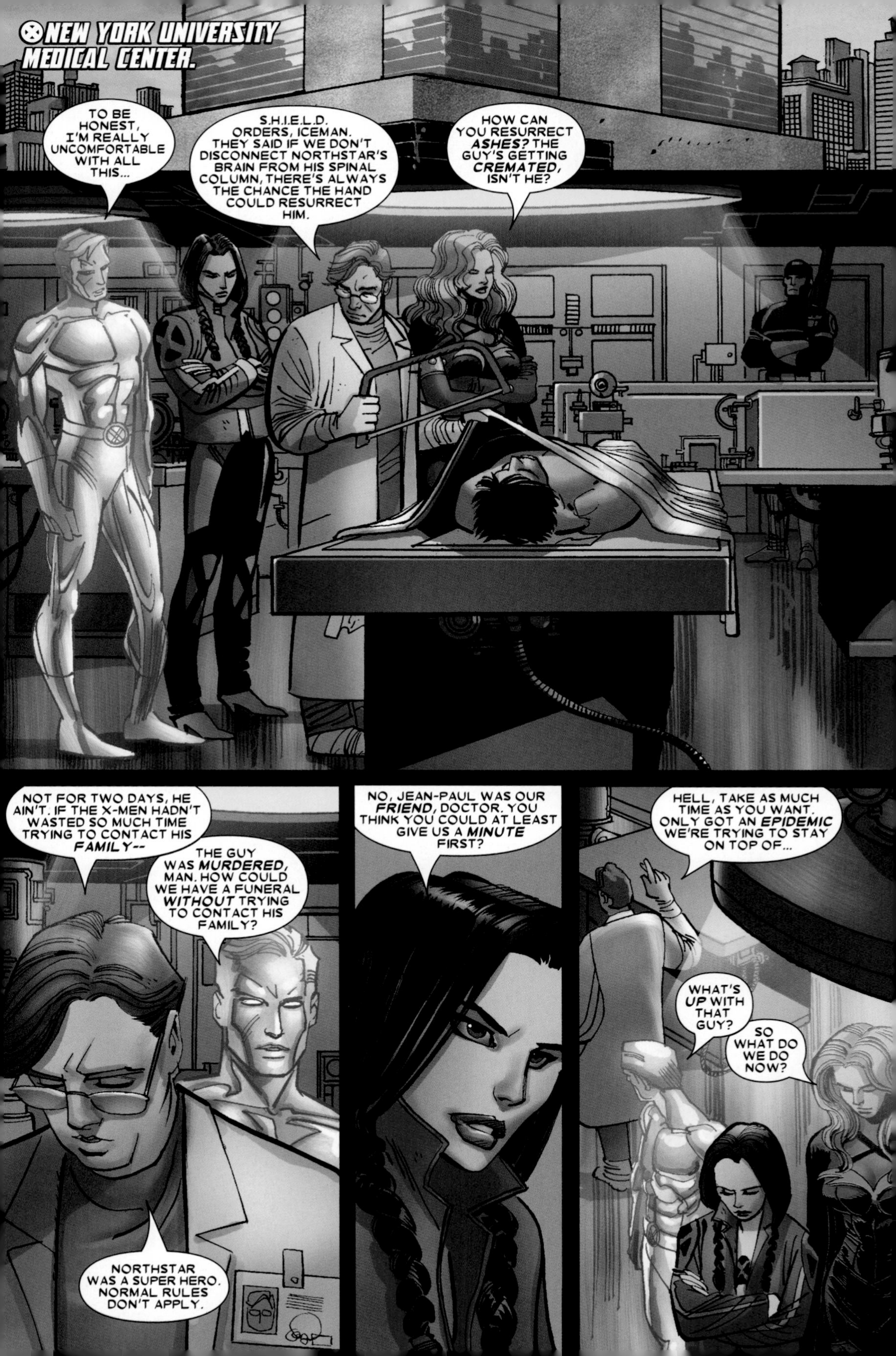
NEW YORK UNIVERSITY MEDICAL CENTER.
TO BE HONEST, I'M REALLY UNCOMFORTABLE WITH ALL THIS...
S.H.I.E.L.D. ORDERS, ICEMAN. THEY SAID IF WE DON'T DISCONNECT NORTHSTAR'S BRAIN FROM HIS SPINAL COLUMN, THERE'S ALWAYS THE CHANCE THE HAND COULD RESURRECT HIM.
HOW CAN YOU RESURRECT ASHES? THE GUY'S GETTING CREMATED, ISN'T HE?
NOT FOR TWO DAYS, HE AIN'T. IF THE X-MEN HADN'T WASTED SO MUCH TIME TRYING TO CONTACT HIS FAMILY--
THE GUY WAS MURDERED, MAN. HOW COULD WE HAVE A FUNERAL WITHOUT TRYING TO CONTACT HIS FAMILY?
NORTHSTAR WAS A SUPER HERO. NORMAL RULES DON'T APPLY.
NO, JEAN-PAUL WAS OUR FRIEND, DOCTOR. YOU THINK YOU COULD AT LEAST GIVE US A MINUTE FIRST?
HELL, TAKE AS MUCH TIME AS YOU WANT. ONLY GOT AN EPIDEMIC WE'RE TRYING TO STAY ON TOP OF...
WHAT'S UP WITH THAT GUY?
SO WHAT DO WE DO NOW?

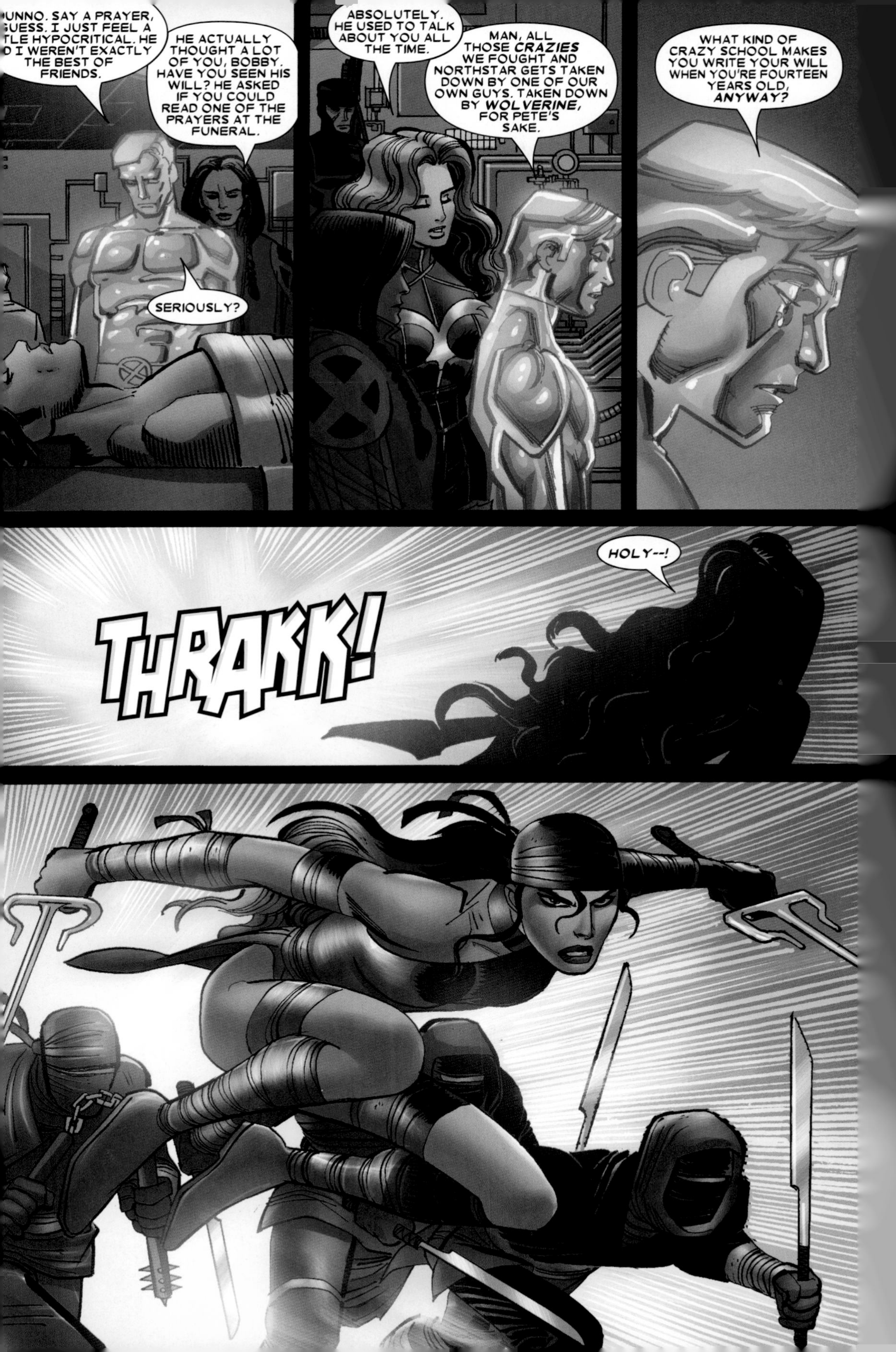
DUNNO. SAY A PRAYER, I GUESS. I JUST FEEL A LITTLE HYPOCRITICAL. HE AND I WEREN'T EXACTLY THE BEST OF FRIENDS.
HE ACTUALLY THOUGHT A LOT OF YOU, BOBBY. HAVE YOU SEEN HIS WILL? HE ASKED IF YOU COULD READ ONE OF THE PRAYERS AT THE FUNERAL.
SERIOUSLY?
ABSOLUTELY. HE USED TO TALK ABOUT YOU ALL THE TIME.
MAN, ALL THOSE CRAZIES WE FOUGHT AND NORTHSTAR GETS TAKEN DOWN BY ONE OF OUR OWN GUYS. TAKEN DOWN BY WOLVERINE, FOR PETE'S SAKE.
WHAT KIND OF CRAZY SCHOOL MAKES YOU WRITE YOUR WILL WHEN YOU'RE FOURTEEN YEARS OLD, ANYWAY?
HOLY--!
THRAKK!

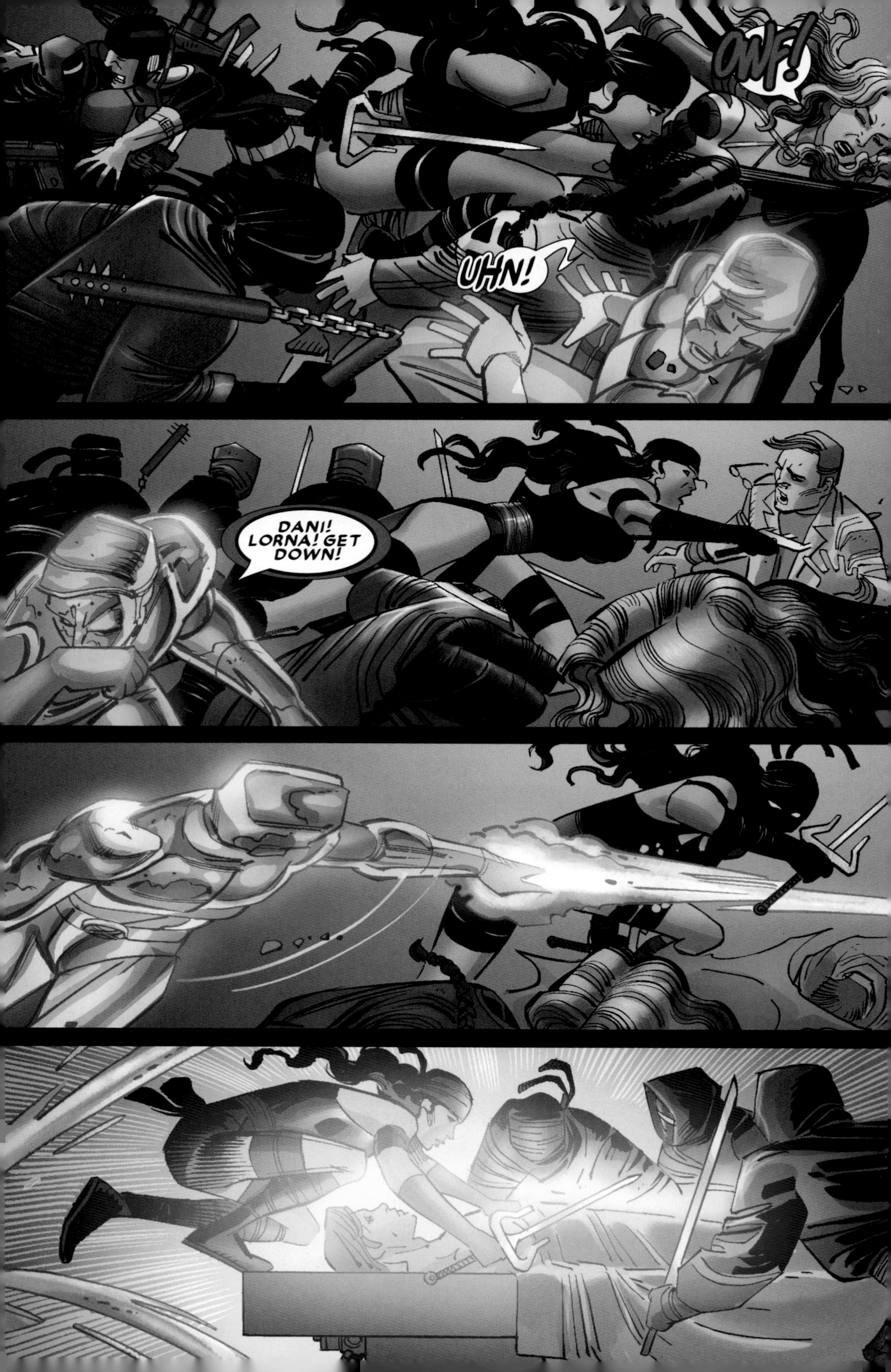
OWF!
UHN!
DANI! LORNA! GET DOWN!

WHAT THE *HELL* WAS *THAT*--?

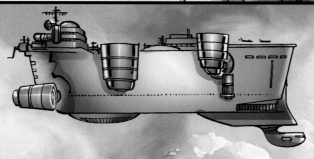

⊗**THE S.H.I.E.L.D. HELICARRIER BLACK HAWK**

THEY GOT *NORTHSTAR.*

WHAT? I THOUGHT THE *X-MEN* WERE GUARDING HIM.

NO GUARANTEE--

THAT BRINGS THE TOTAL TO FORTY-ONE STEALS THIS WEEK: FOUR HEROES AND THIRTY-SEVEN VILLAINS. JUST CURIOUS WHY THEY SWITCHED *TACTICS* ALL OF A SUDDEN...

VILLAINS ARE HARDER TO ORGANIZE AND EASIER TO PICK OFF. NOW *PIPE DOWN*, HUH? I'M TRYING TO GET A SIT-REP ON *WOLVERINE* FROM DOWNSTAIRS...

LORD KNOWS I'VE HAD *EASIER* JOBS, BUT THE DEPROGRAMMING'S WORKING OUT *SO FAR*, COLONEL FURY.

WE'RE RUNNING FIFTY THOUSAND SIMULATIONS A MINUTE AT THE MOMENT, AND YOUR LITTLE FRIEND HERE *APPEARS* TO BE RESPONDING.

ANESTHETIC'S THE *TRICKY* PART. THAT HEALING FACTOR OF HIS MEANS IT'S OUT AS QUICKLY AS IT'S GOING IN.

JUST STAY AT *EIGHTY* MILLS A MINUTE AND WE REACH AN EQUILIBRIUM, DUDE.

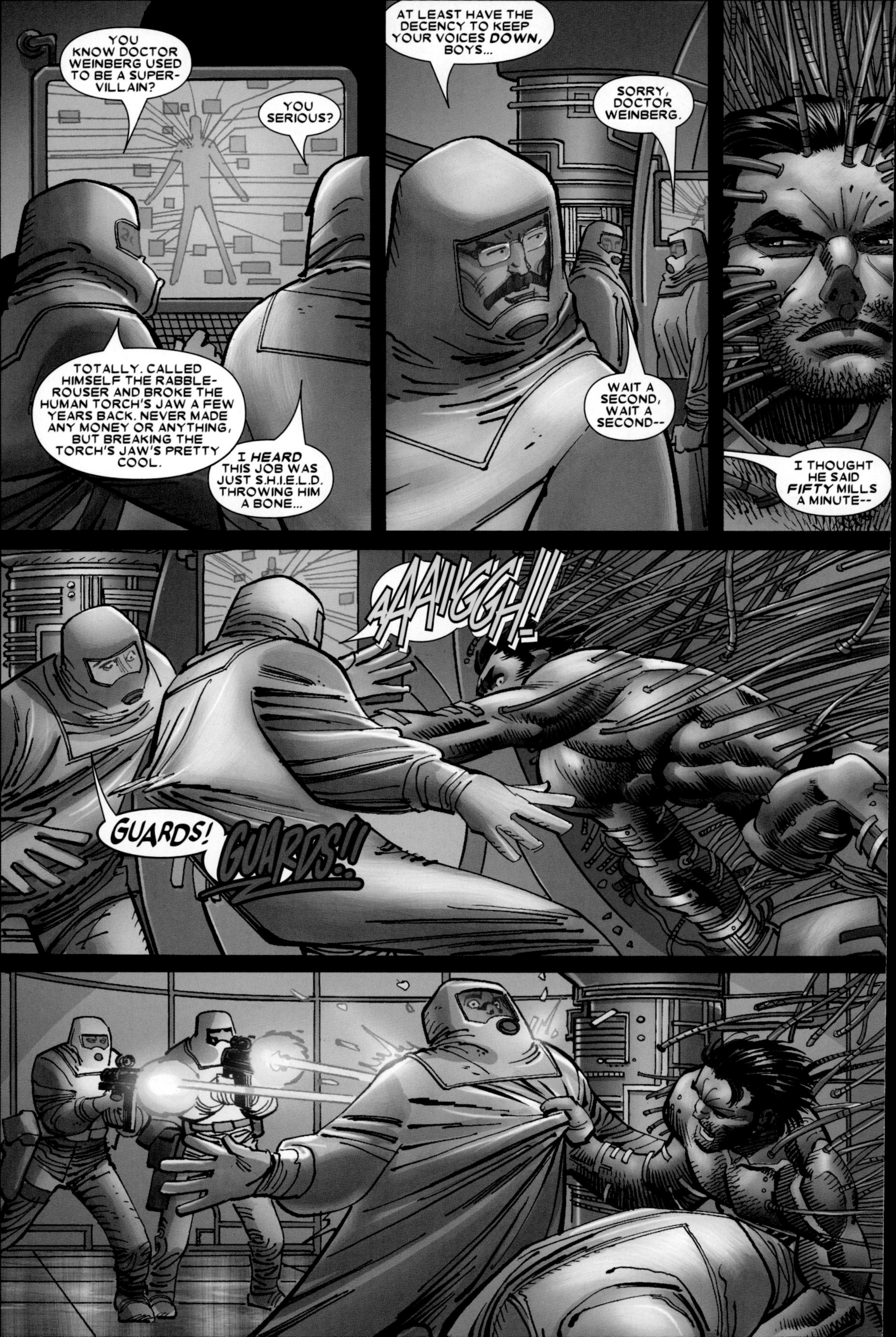
YOU KNOW DOCTOR WEINBERG USED TO BE A SUPER-VILLAIN?
YOU SERIOUS?
TOTALLY. CALLED HIMSELF THE RABBLE-ROUSER AND BROKE THE HUMAN TORCH'S JAW A FEW YEARS BACK. NEVER MADE ANY MONEY OR ANYTHING, BUT BREAKING THE TORCH'S JAW'S PRETTY COOL.
I HEARD THIS JOB WAS JUST S.H.I.E.L.D. THROWING HIM A BONE...
AT LEAST HAVE THE DECENCY TO KEEP YOUR VOICES DOWN, BOYS...
SORRY, DOCTOR WEINBERG.
WAIT A SECOND, WAIT A SECOND--
I THOUGHT HE SAID FIFTY MILLS A MINUTE--
AAAIGGH!!
GUARDS!
GUARDS!!

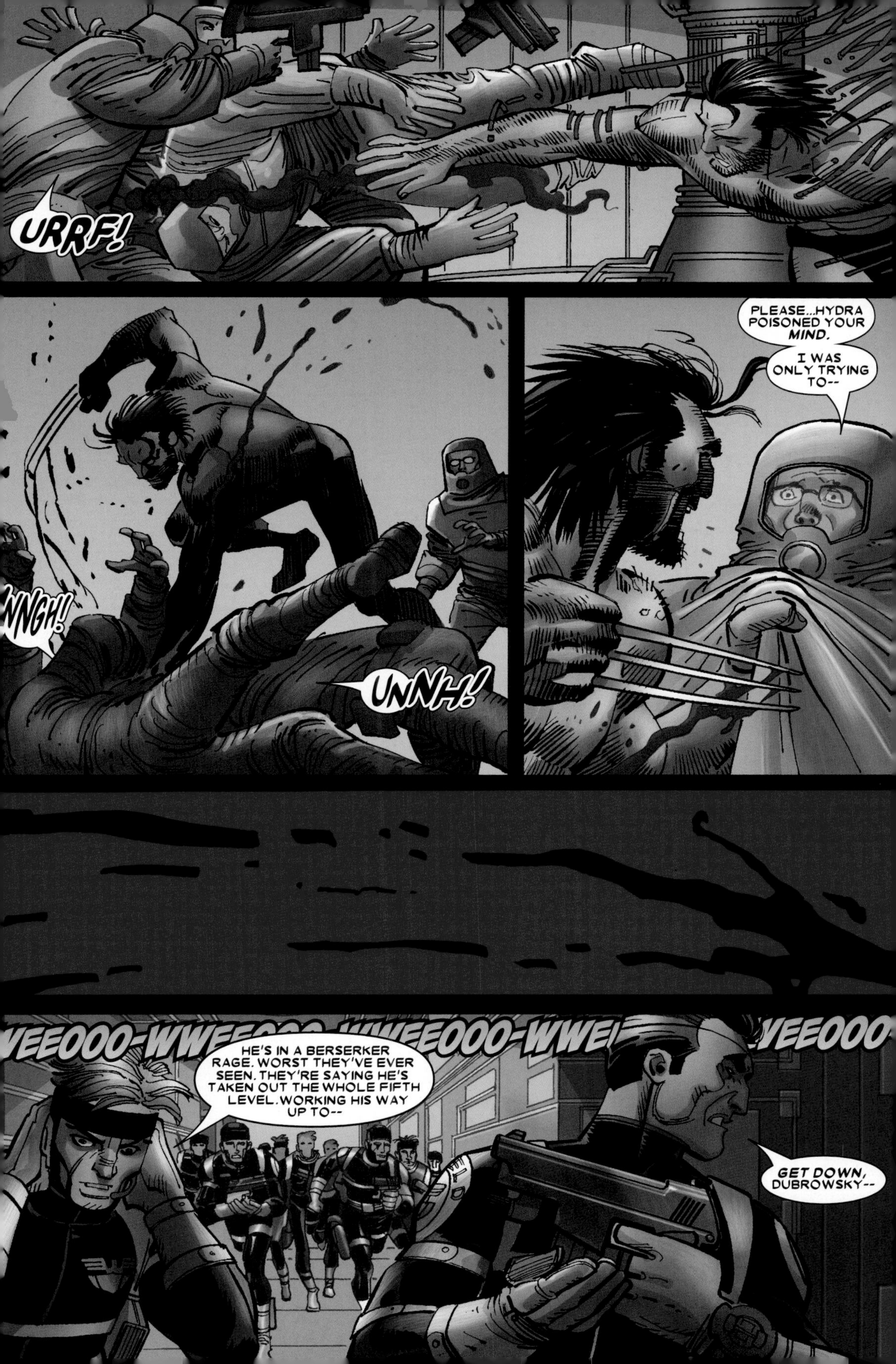

URRF!
NNGH!
UNNH!
PLEASE...HYDRA POISONED YOUR MIND.
I WAS ONLY TRYING TO--
WEEOOO-WWEEOOO-WWEEOOO-WWEE
HE'S IN A BERSERKER RAGE. WORST THEY'VE EVER SEEN. THEY'RE SAYING HE'S TAKEN OUT THE WHOLE FIFTH LEVEL. WORKING HIS WAY UP TO--
GET DOWN, DUBROWSKY--

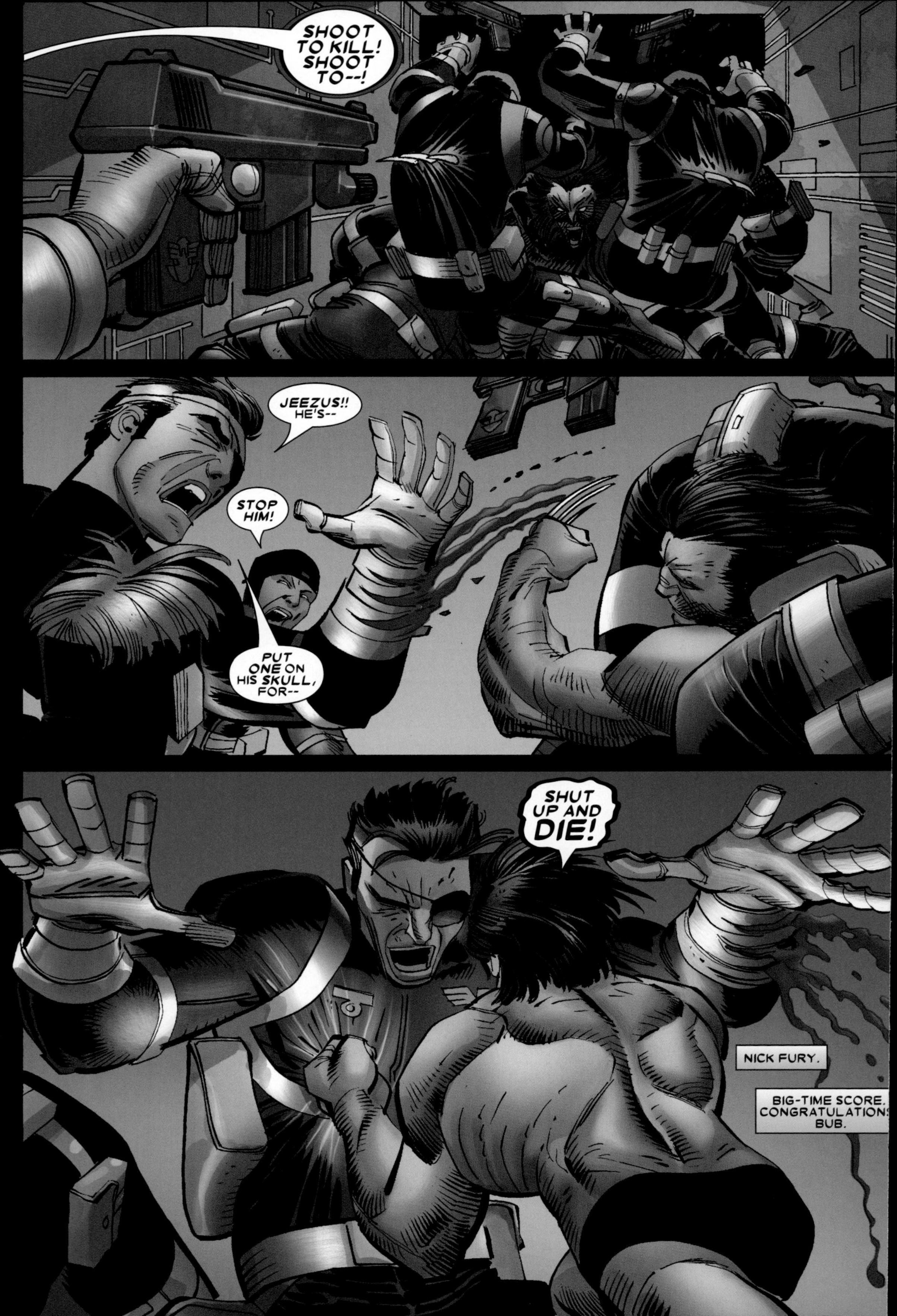
SHOOT TO KILL! SHOOT TO--!
JEEZUS!! HE'S--
STOP HIM!
PUT ONE ON HIS SKULL, FOR--
SHUT UP AND DIE!
NICK FURY.
BIG-TIME SCORE. CONGRATULATIONS BUB.

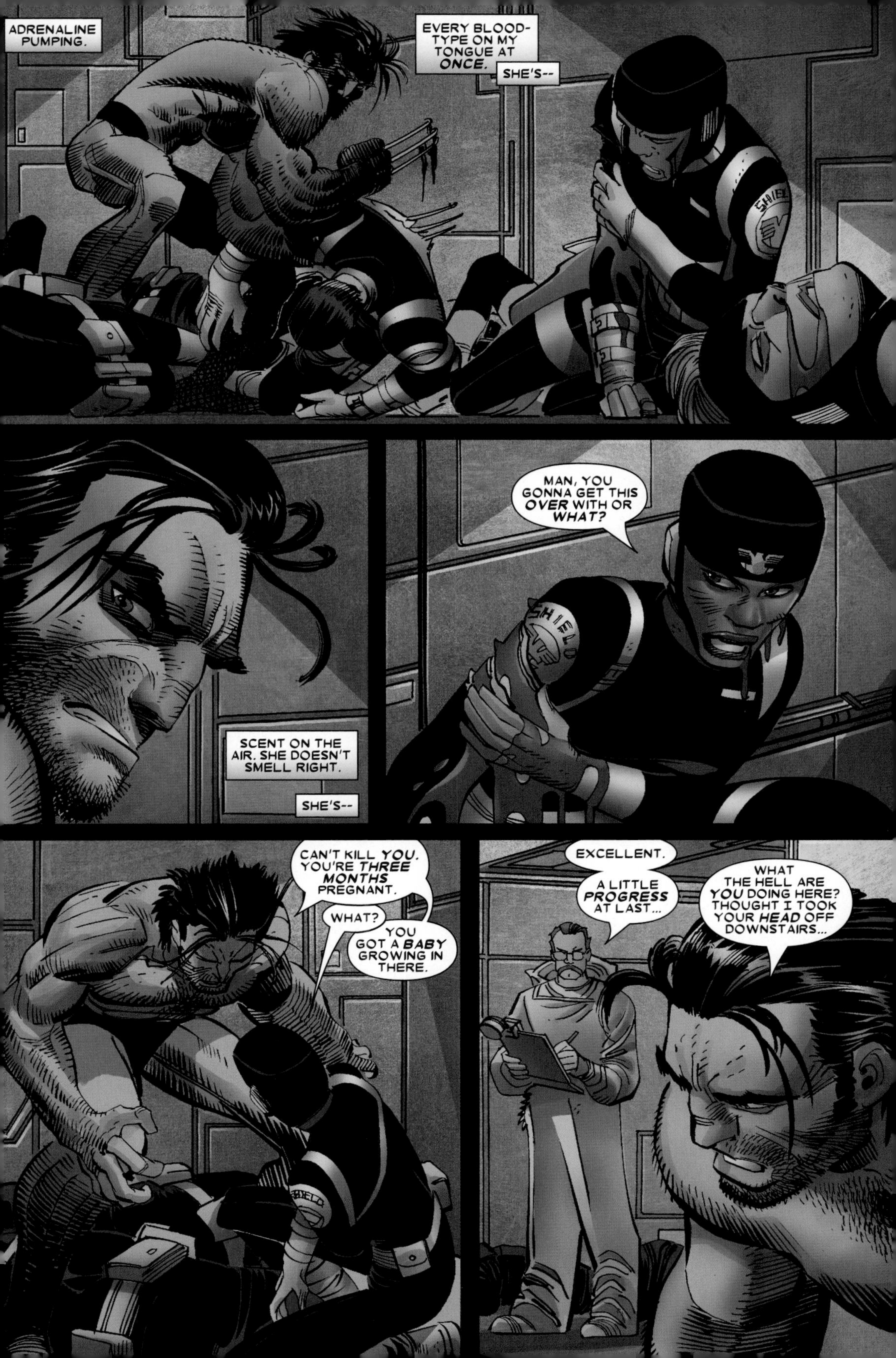
ADRENALINE PUMPING.
EVERY BLOOD-TYPE ON MY TONGUE AT ONCE.
SHE'S--
MAN, YOU GONNA GET THIS OVER WITH OR WHAT?
SCENT ON THE AIR. SHE DOESN'T SMELL RIGHT.
SHE'S--
CAN'T KILL YOU. YOU'RE THREE MONTHS PREGNANT.
WHAT?
YOU GOT A BABY GROWING IN THERE.
EXCELLENT.
A LITTLE PROGRESS AT LAST...
WHAT THE HELL ARE YOU DOING HERE? THOUGHT I TOOK YOUR HEAD OFF DOWNSTAIRS...

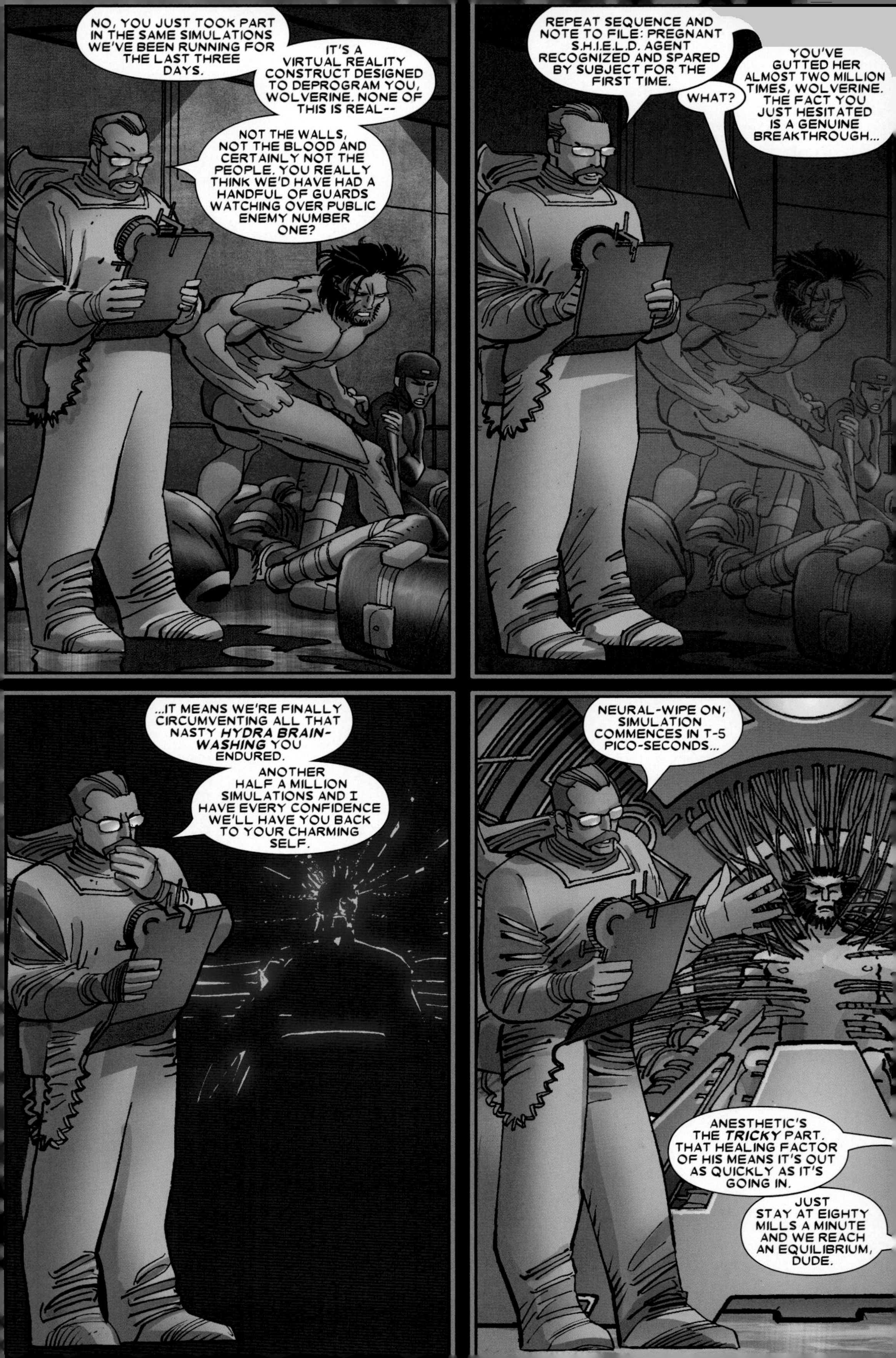
NO, YOU JUST TOOK PART IN THE SAME SIMULATIONS WE'VE BEEN RUNNING FOR THE LAST THREE DAYS.
IT'S A VIRTUAL REALITY CONSTRUCT DESIGNED TO DEPROGRAM YOU, WOLVERINE. NONE OF THIS IS REAL--
NOT THE WALLS, NOT THE BLOOD AND CERTAINLY NOT THE PEOPLE. YOU REALLY THINK WE'D HAVE HAD A HANDFUL OF GUARDS WATCHING OVER PUBLIC ENEMY NUMBER ONE?
REPEAT SEQUENCE AND NOTE TO FILE: PREGNANT S.H.I.E.L.D. AGENT RECOGNIZED AND SPARED BY SUBJECT FOR THE FIRST TIME.
WHAT?
YOU'VE GUTTED HER ALMOST TWO MILLION TIMES, WOLVERINE. THE FACT YOU JUST HESITATED IS A GENUINE BREAKTHROUGH...
...IT MEANS WE'RE FINALLY CIRCUMVENTING ALL THAT NASTY *HYDRA BRAIN-WASHING* YOU ENDURED.
ANOTHER HALF A MILLION SIMULATIONS AND I HAVE EVERY CONFIDENCE WE'LL HAVE YOU BACK TO YOUR CHARMING SELF.
NEURAL-WIPE ON; SIMULATION COMMENCES IN T-5 PICO-SECONDS...
ANESTHETIC'S THE *TRICKY* PART. THAT HEALING FACTOR OF HIS MEANS IT'S OUT AS QUICKLY AS IT'S GOING IN.
JUST STAY AT EIGHTY MILLS A MINUTE AND WE REACH AN EQUILIBRIUM, DUDE.

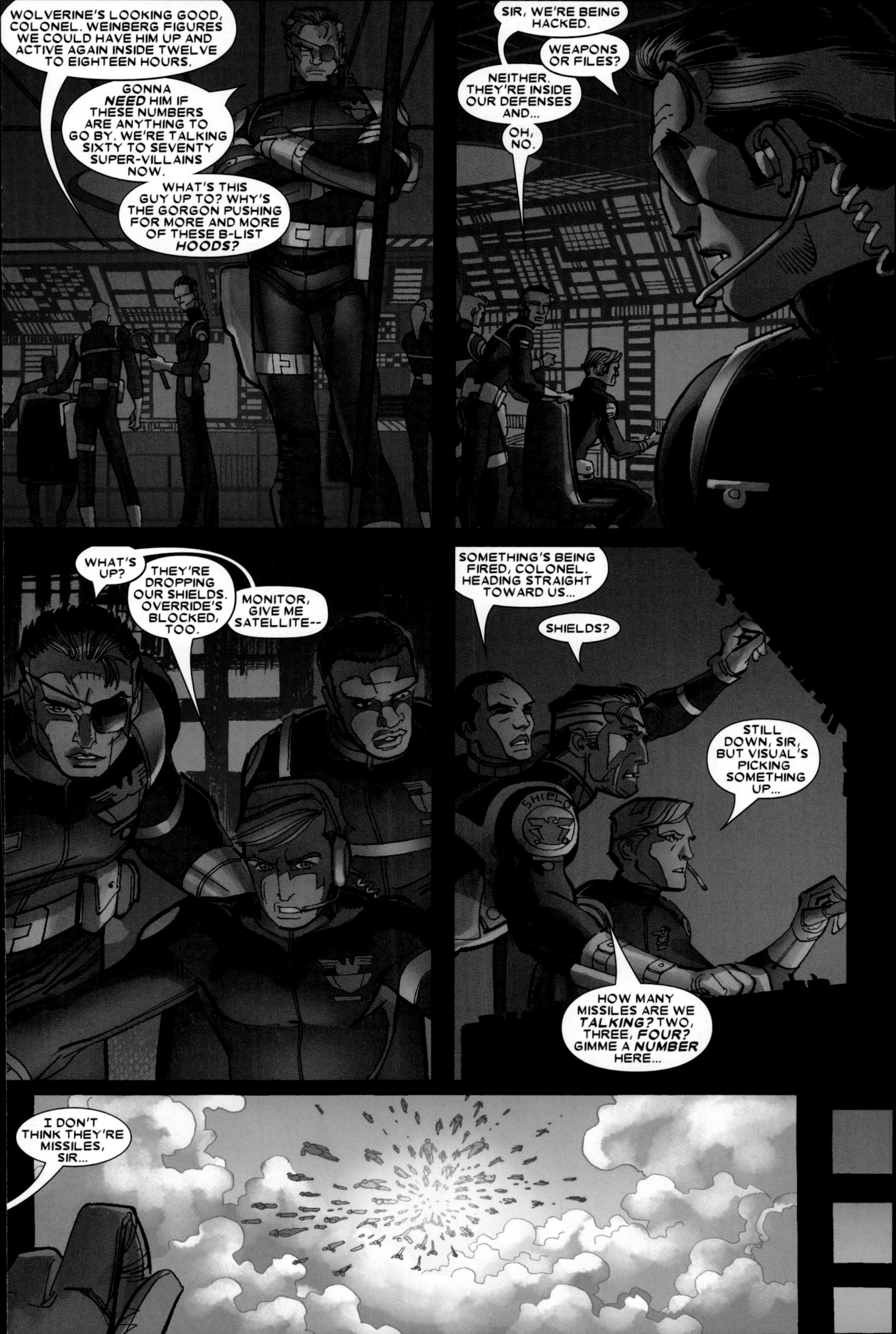

WOLVERINE'S LOOKING GOOD, COLONEL. WEINBERG FIGURES WE COULD HAVE HIM UP AND ACTIVE AGAIN INSIDE TWELVE TO EIGHTEEN HOURS.
GONNA *NEED* HIM IF THESE NUMBERS ARE ANYTHING TO GO BY. WE'RE TALKING SIXTY TO SEVENTY SUPER-VILLAINS NOW.
WHAT'S THIS GUY UP TO? WHY'S THE GORGON PUSHING FOR MORE AND MORE OF THESE B-LIST *HOODS?*
SIR, WE'RE BEING HACKED.
WEAPONS OR FILES?
NEITHER. THEY'RE INSIDE OUR DEFENSES AND...
OH, NO.
WHAT'S UP?
THEY'RE DROPPING OUR SHIELDS. OVERRIDE'S BLOCKED, TOO.
MONITOR, GIVE ME SATELLITE--
SOMETHING'S BEING FIRED, COLONEL. HEADING STRAIGHT TOWARD US...
SHIELDS?
STILL DOWN, SIR, BUT VISUAL'S PICKING SOMETHING UP...
HOW MANY MISSILES ARE WE *TALKING?* TWO, THREE, *FOUR?* GIMME A *NUMBER* HERE...
I DON'T THINK THEY'RE MISSILES, SIR...

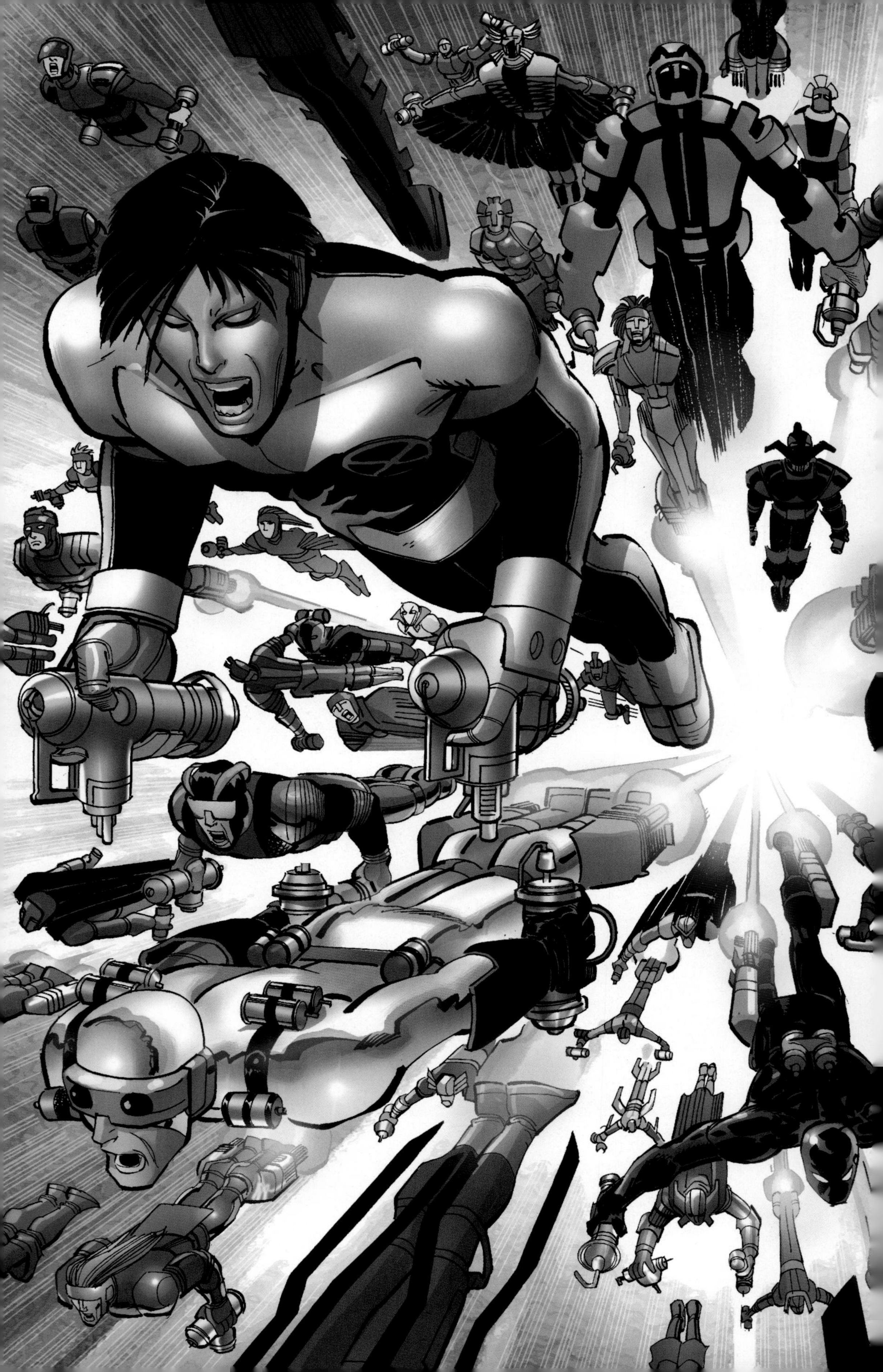

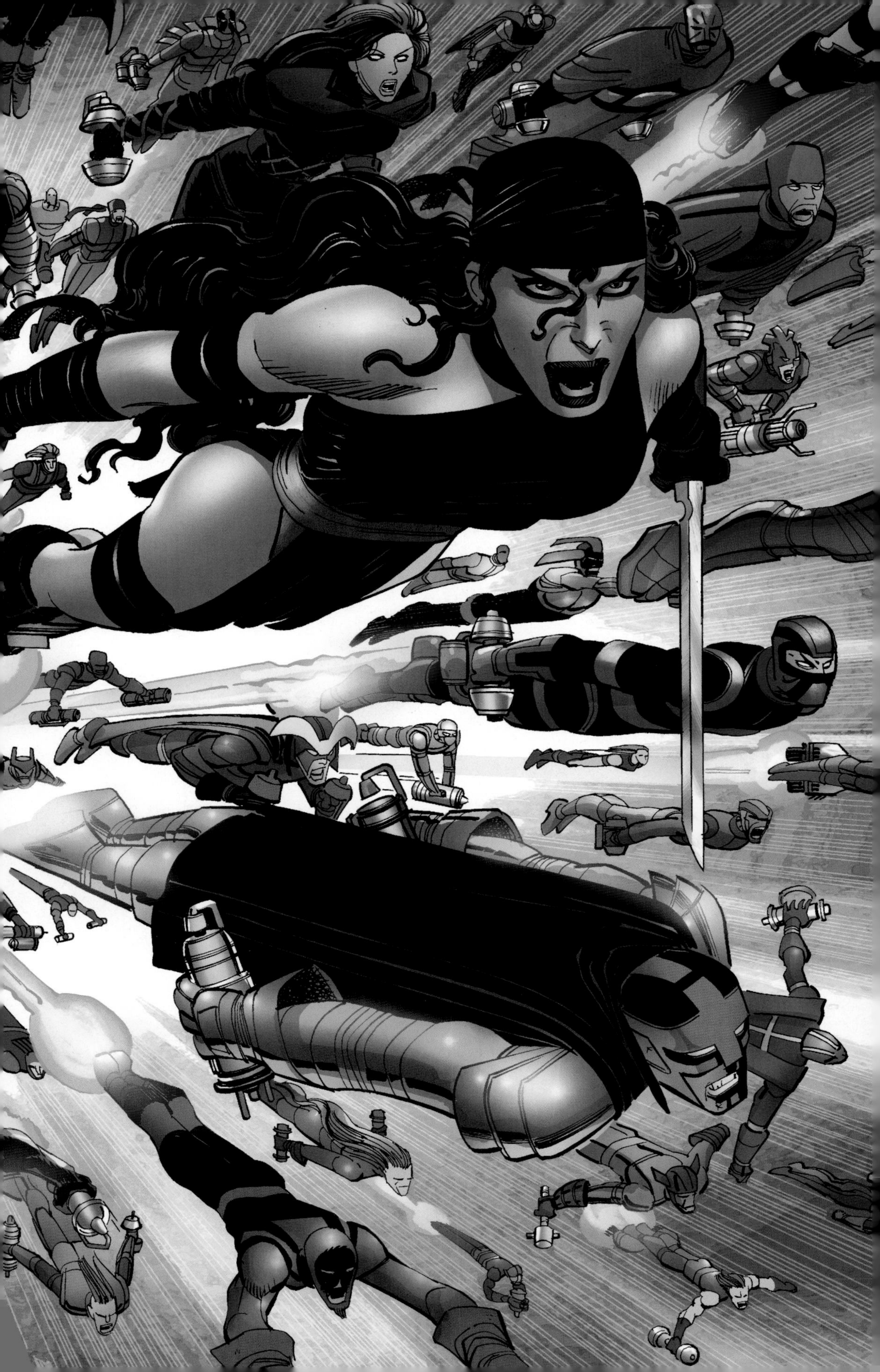

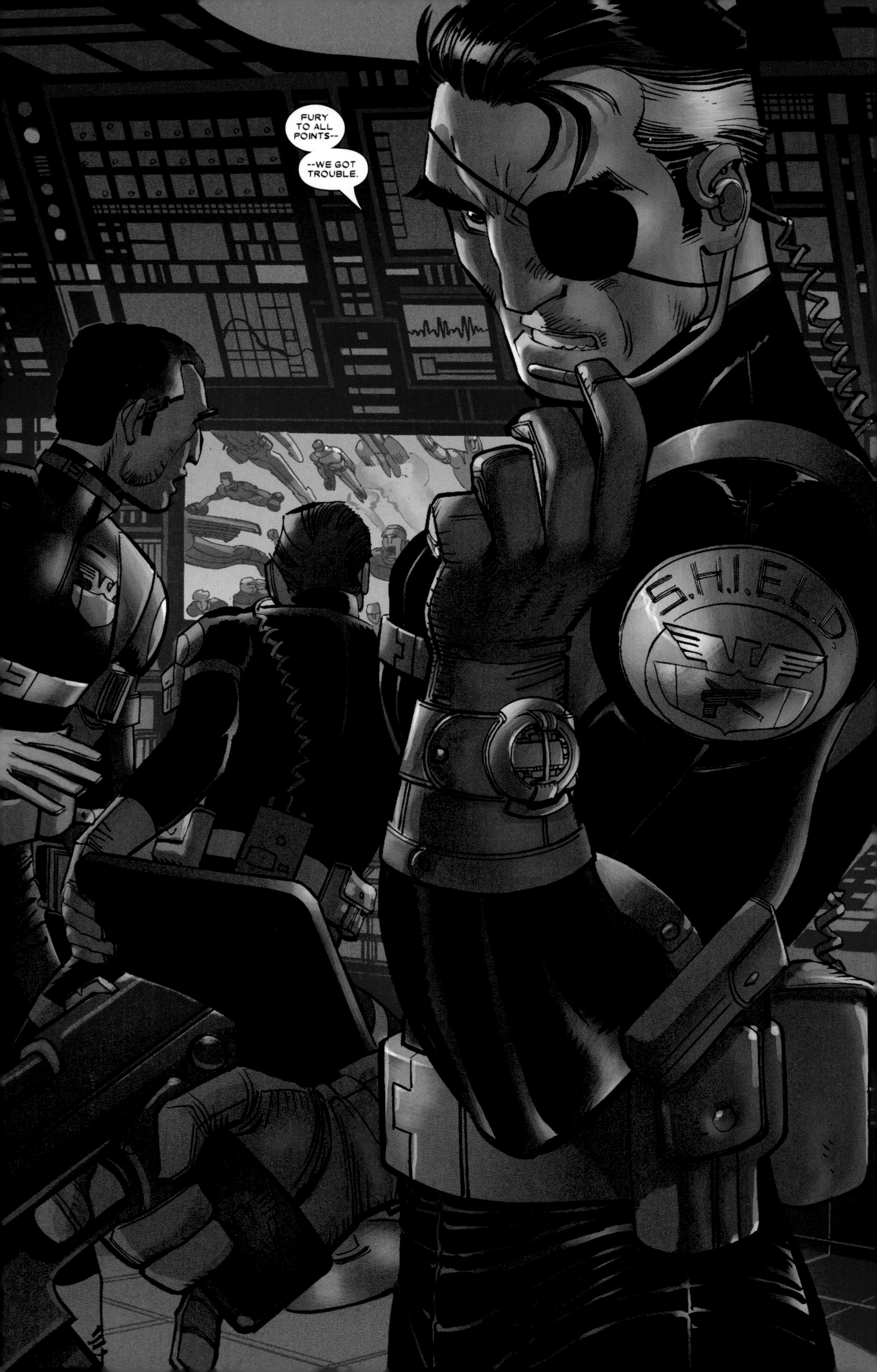
FURY TO ALL POINTS--
--WE GOT TROUBLE.
S.H.I.E.L.D

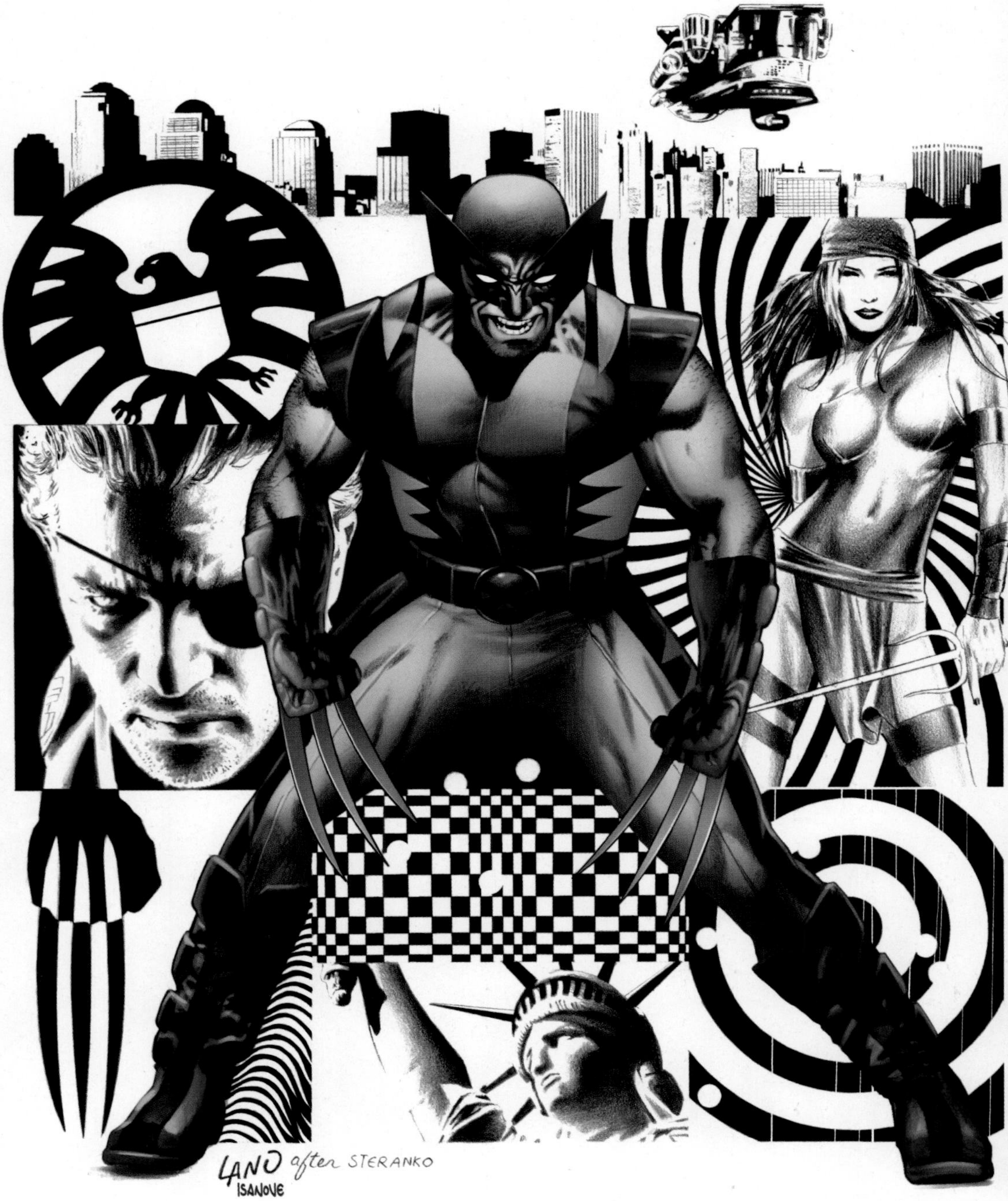
LAND after STERANKO
ISANOVE

#27

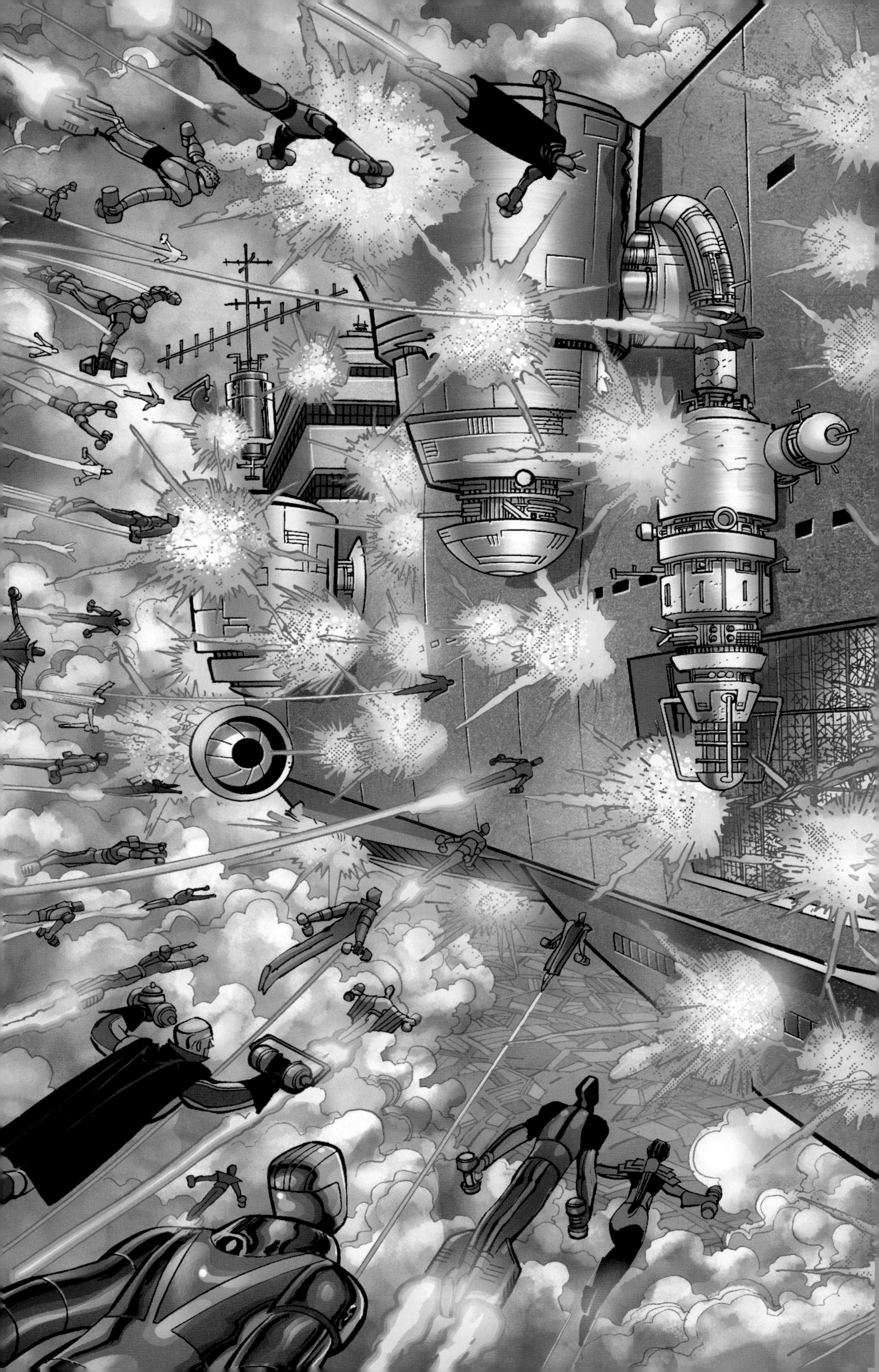

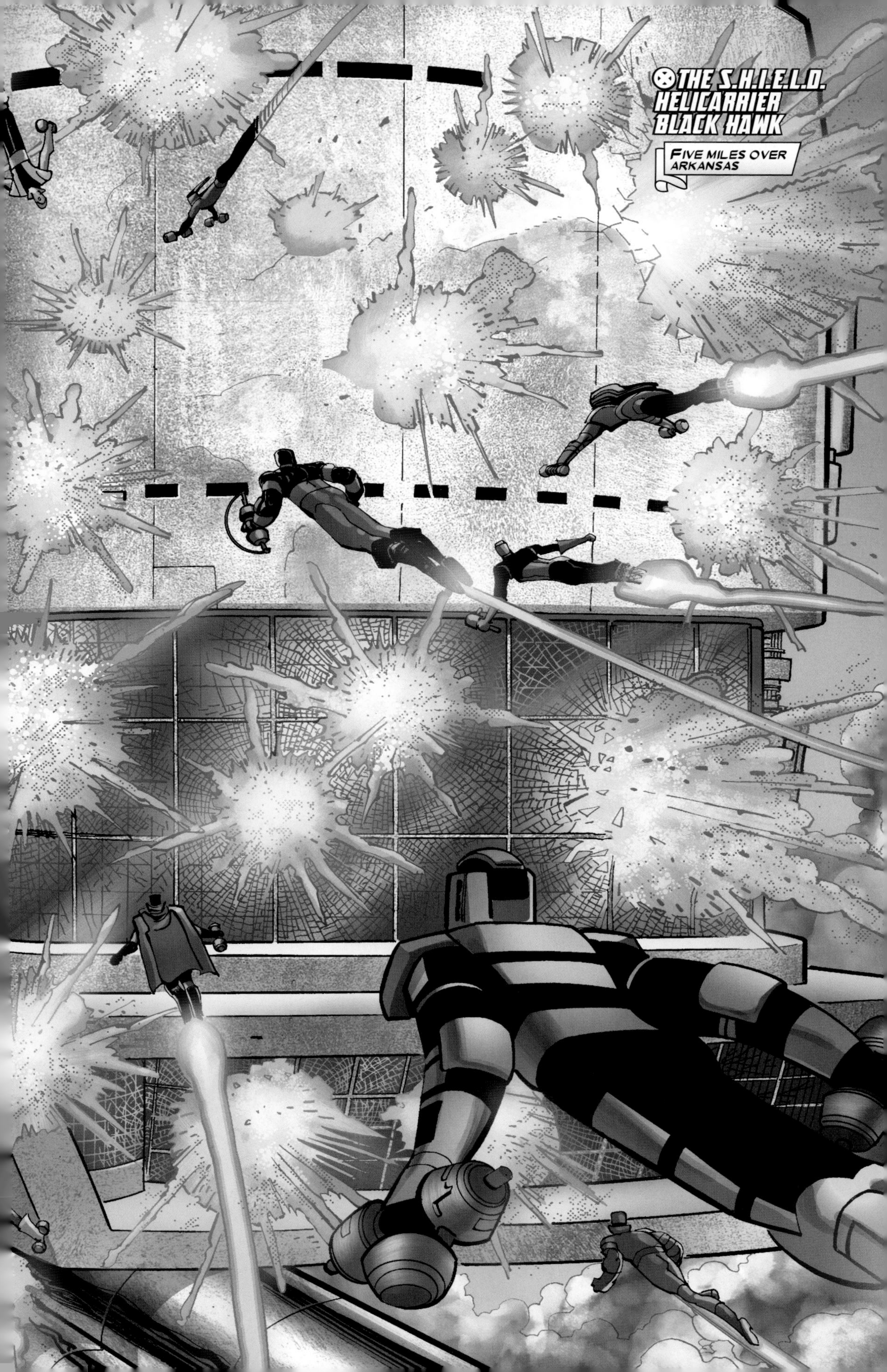
THE S.H.I.E.L.D. HELICARRIER BLACK HAWK
FIVE MILES OVER ARKANSAS

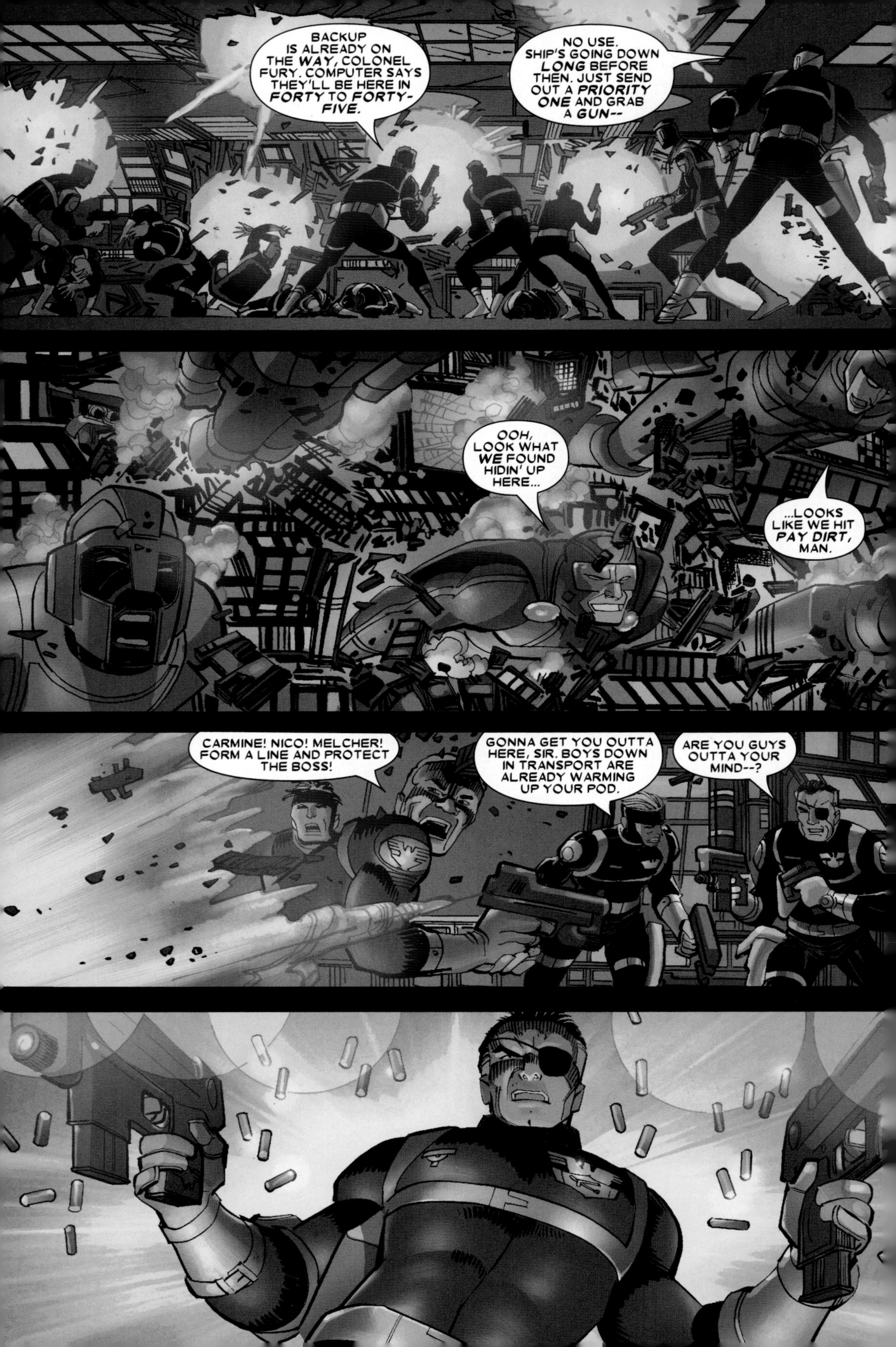
BACKUP IS ALREADY ON THE WAY, COLONEL FURY. COMPUTER SAYS THEY'LL BE HERE IN FORTY TO FORTY-FIVE.
NO USE. SHIP'S GOING DOWN LONG BEFORE THEN. JUST SEND OUT A PRIORITY ONE AND GRAB A GUN--
OOH, LOOK WHAT WE FOUND HIDIN' UP HERE...
...LOOKS LIKE WE HIT PAY DIRT, MAN.
CARMINE! NICO! MELCHER! FORM A LINE AND PROTECT THE BOSS!
GONNA GET YOU OUTTA HERE, SIR. BOYS DOWN IN TRANSPORT ARE ALREADY WARMING UP YOUR POD.
ARE YOU GUYS OUTTA YOUR MIND--?

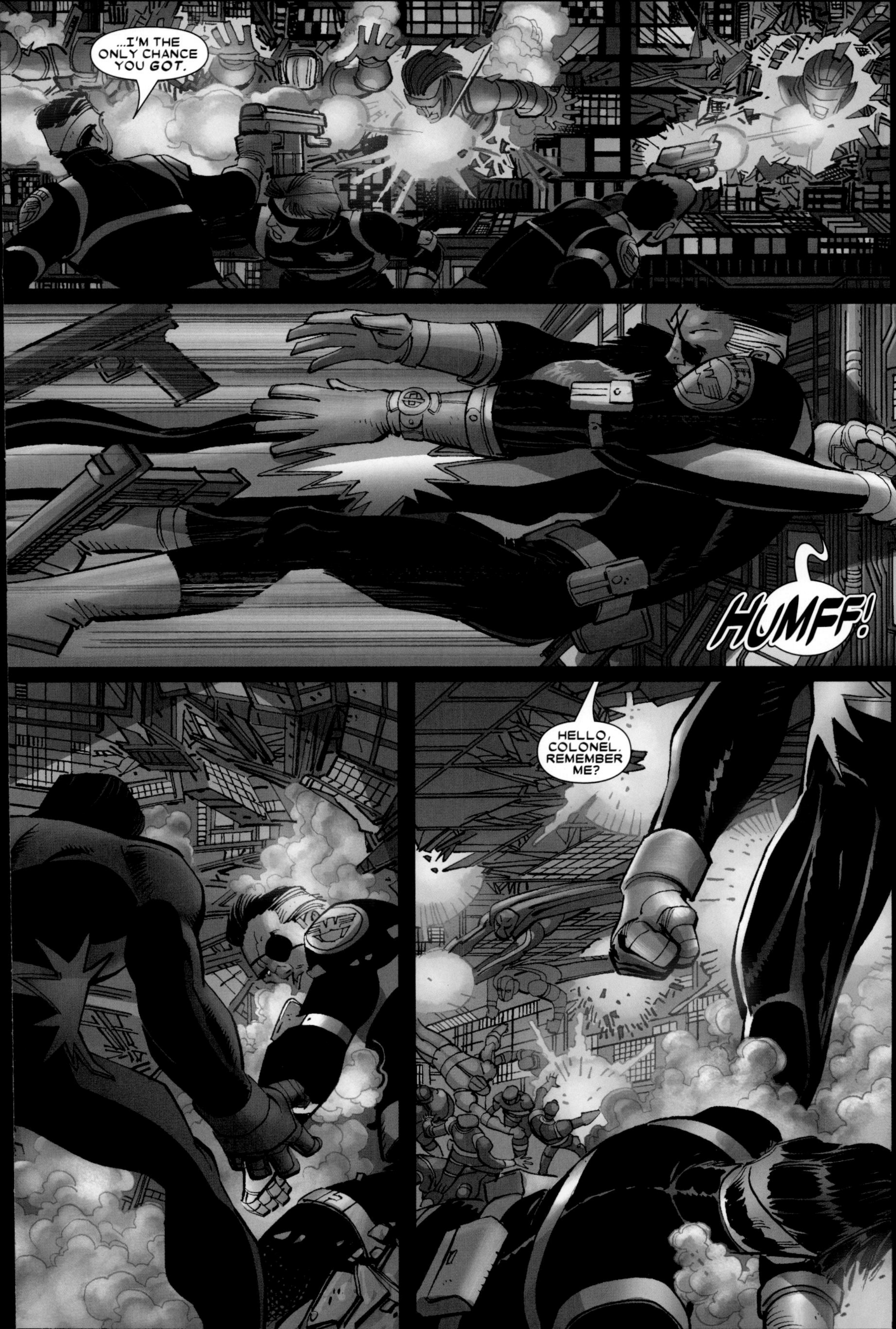
...I'M THE ONLY CHANCE YOU GOT.
HUMFF!
HELLO, COLONEL. REMEMBER ME?

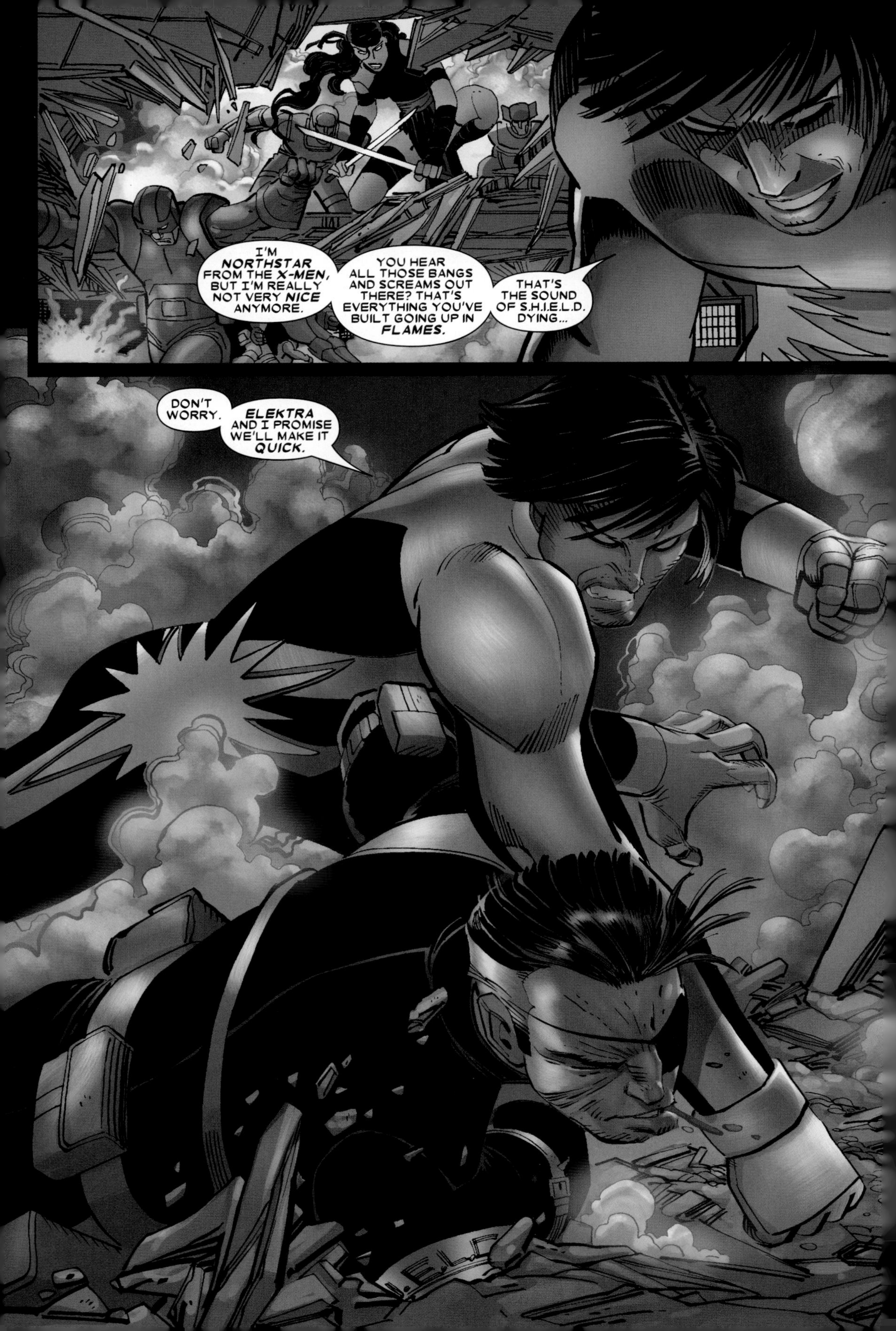

I'M NORTHSTAR FROM THE X-MEN, BUT I'M REALLY NOT VERY NICE ANYMORE.
YOU HEAR ALL THOSE BANGS AND SCREAMS OUT THERE? THAT'S EVERYTHING YOU'VE BUILT GOING UP IN FLAMES.
THAT'S THE SOUND OF S.H.I.E.L.D. DYING...
DON'T WORRY.
ELEKTRA AND I PROMISE WE'LL MAKE IT QUICK.

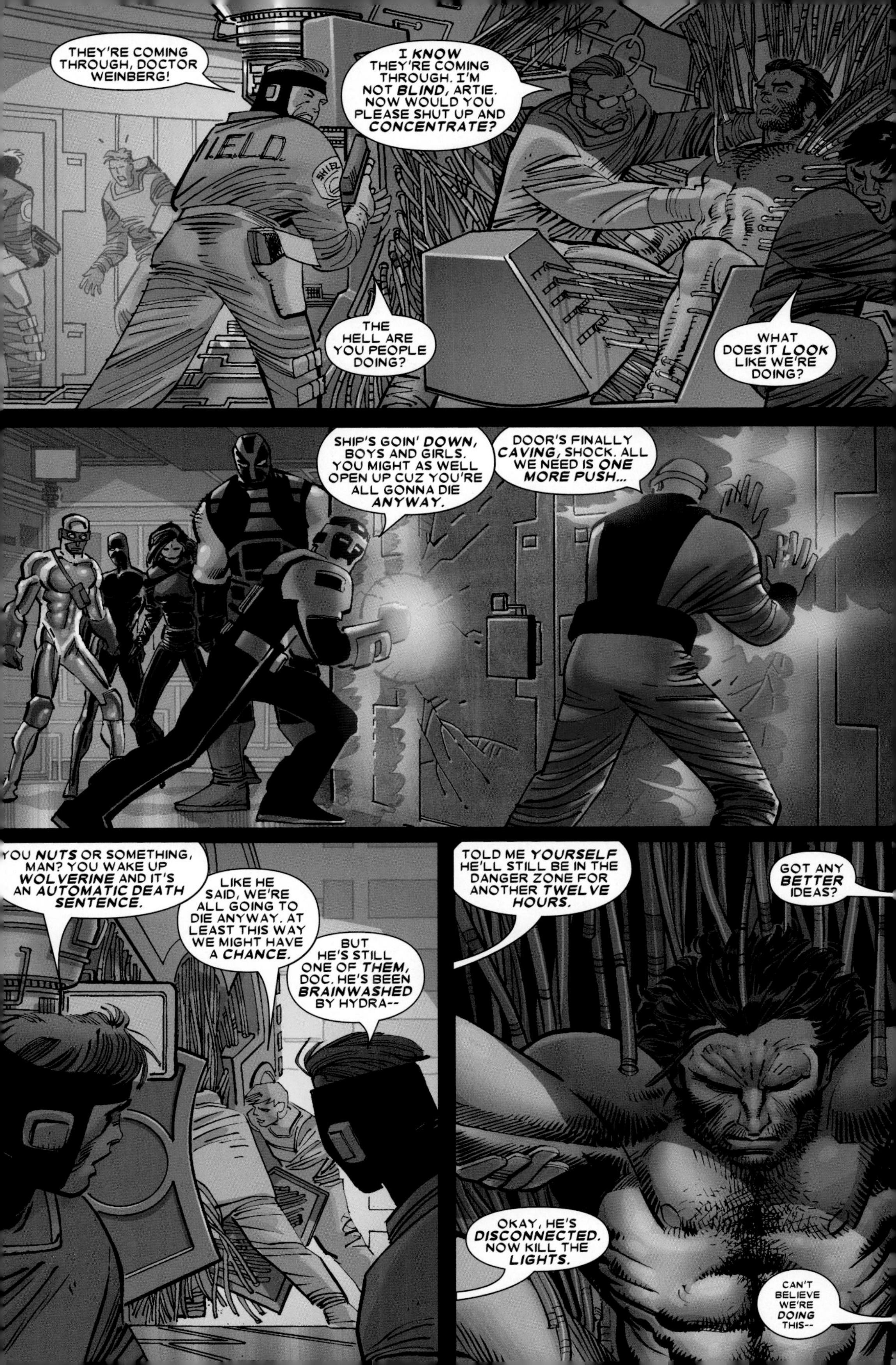
THEY'RE COMING THROUGH, DOCTOR WEINBERG!
I KNOW THEY'RE COMING THROUGH. I'M NOT BLIND, ARTIE. NOW WOULD YOU PLEASE SHUT UP AND CONCENTRATE?
THE HELL ARE YOU PEOPLE DOING?
WHAT DOES IT LOOK LIKE WE'RE DOING?
SHIP'S GOIN' DOWN, BOYS AND GIRLS. YOU MIGHT AS WELL OPEN UP CUZ YOU'RE ALL GONNA DIE ANYWAY.
DOOR'S FINALLY CAVING, SHOCK. ALL WE NEED IS ONE MORE PUSH...
YOU NUTS OR SOMETHING, MAN? YOU WAKE UP WOLVERINE AND IT'S AN AUTOMATIC DEATH SENTENCE.
LIKE HE SAID, WE'RE ALL GOING TO DIE ANYWAY. AT LEAST THIS WAY WE MIGHT HAVE A CHANCE.
BUT HE'S STILL ONE OF THEM, DOC. HE'S BEEN BRAINWASHED BY HYDRA--
TOLD ME YOURSELF HE'LL STILL BE IN THE DANGER ZONE FOR ANOTHER TWELVE HOURS.
GOT ANY BETTER IDEAS?
OKAY, HE'S DISCONNECTED. NOW KILL THE LIGHTS.
CAN'T BELIEVE WE'RE DOING THIS--

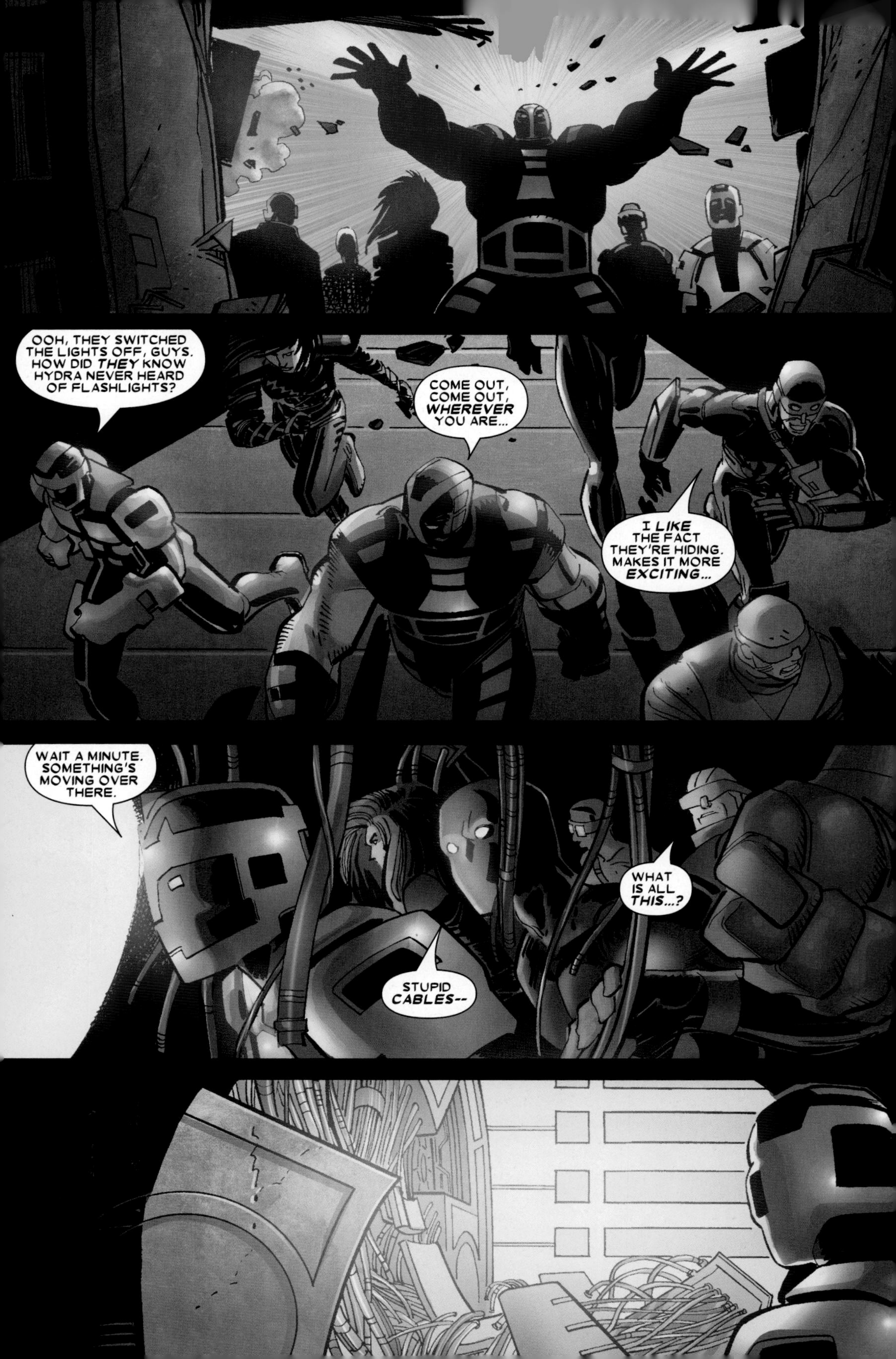
OOH, THEY SWITCHED THE LIGHTS OFF, GUYS. HOW DID *THEY* KNOW HYDRA NEVER HEARD OF FLASHLIGHTS?
COME OUT, COME OUT, *WHEREVER* YOU ARE...
I *LIKE* THE FACT THEY'RE HIDING. MAKES IT MORE *EXCITING*...
WAIT A MINUTE. SOMETHING'S MOVING OVER THERE.
STUPID *CABLES*--
WHAT IS ALL *THIS*...?

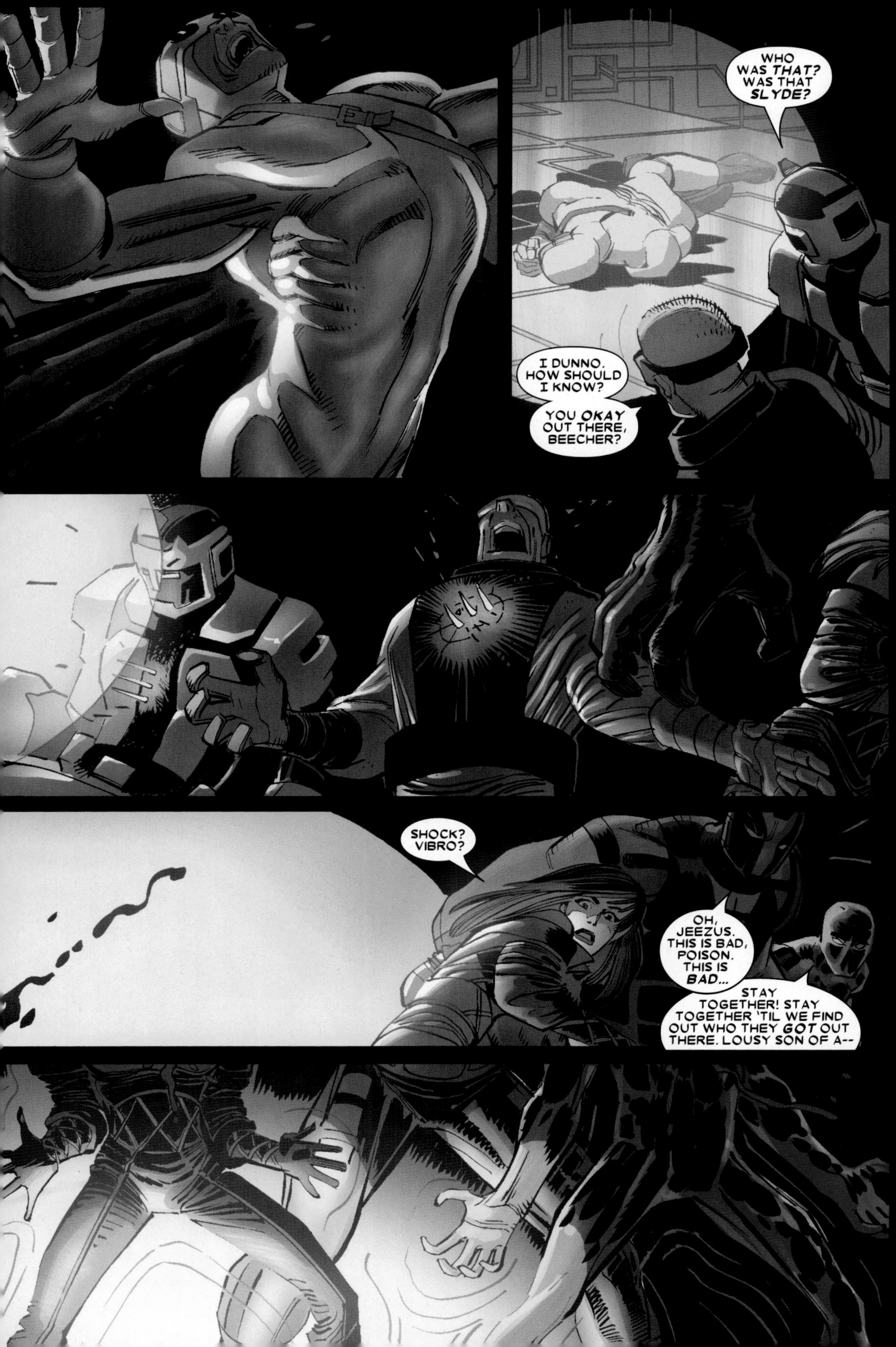
WHO WAS THAT? WAS THAT SLYDE?
I DUNNO. HOW SHOULD I KNOW?
YOU OKAY OUT THERE, BEECHER?
SHOCK? VIBRO?
OH, JEEZUS. THIS IS BAD, POISON. THIS IS BAD...
STAY TOGETHER! STAY TOGETHER 'TIL WE FIND OUT WHO THEY GOT OUT THERE. LOUSY SON OF A--

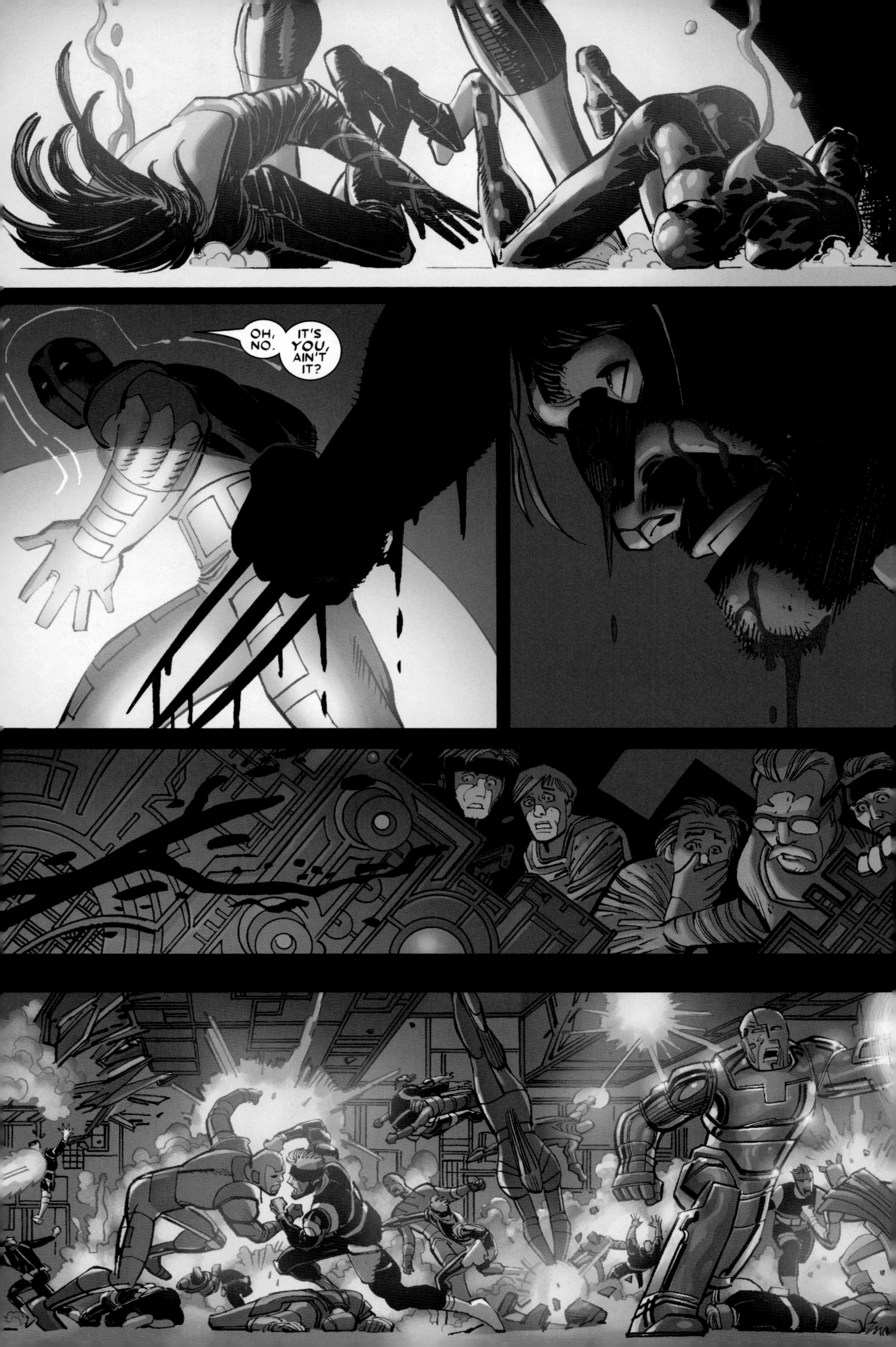
OH, NO.
IT'S YOU, AIN'T IT?

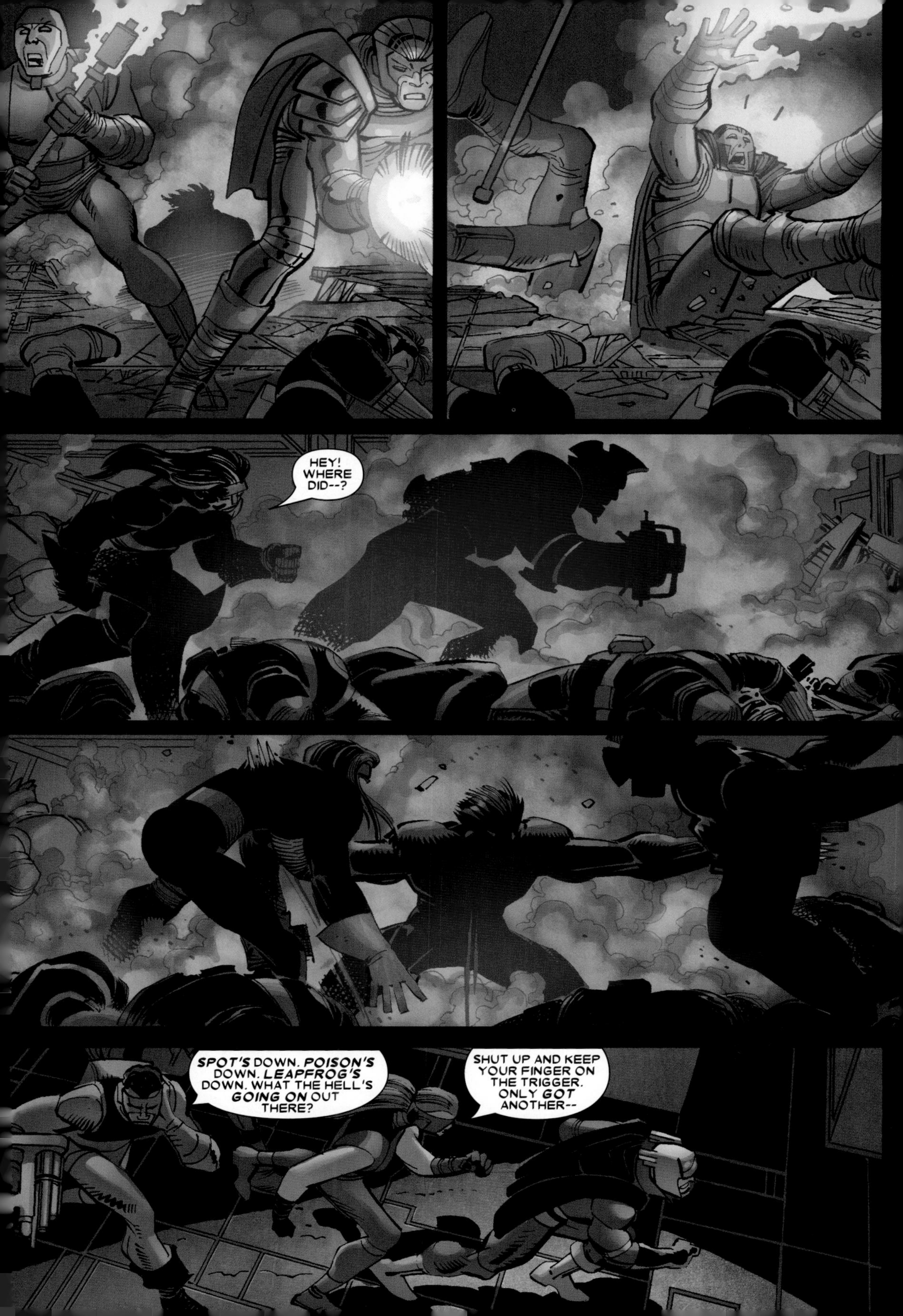
HEY! WHERE DID--?
SPOT'S DOWN. POISON'S DOWN. LEAPFROG'S DOWN. WHAT THE HELL'S GOING ON OUT THERE?
SHUT UP AND KEEP YOUR FINGER ON THE TRIGGER. ONLY GOT ANOTHER--

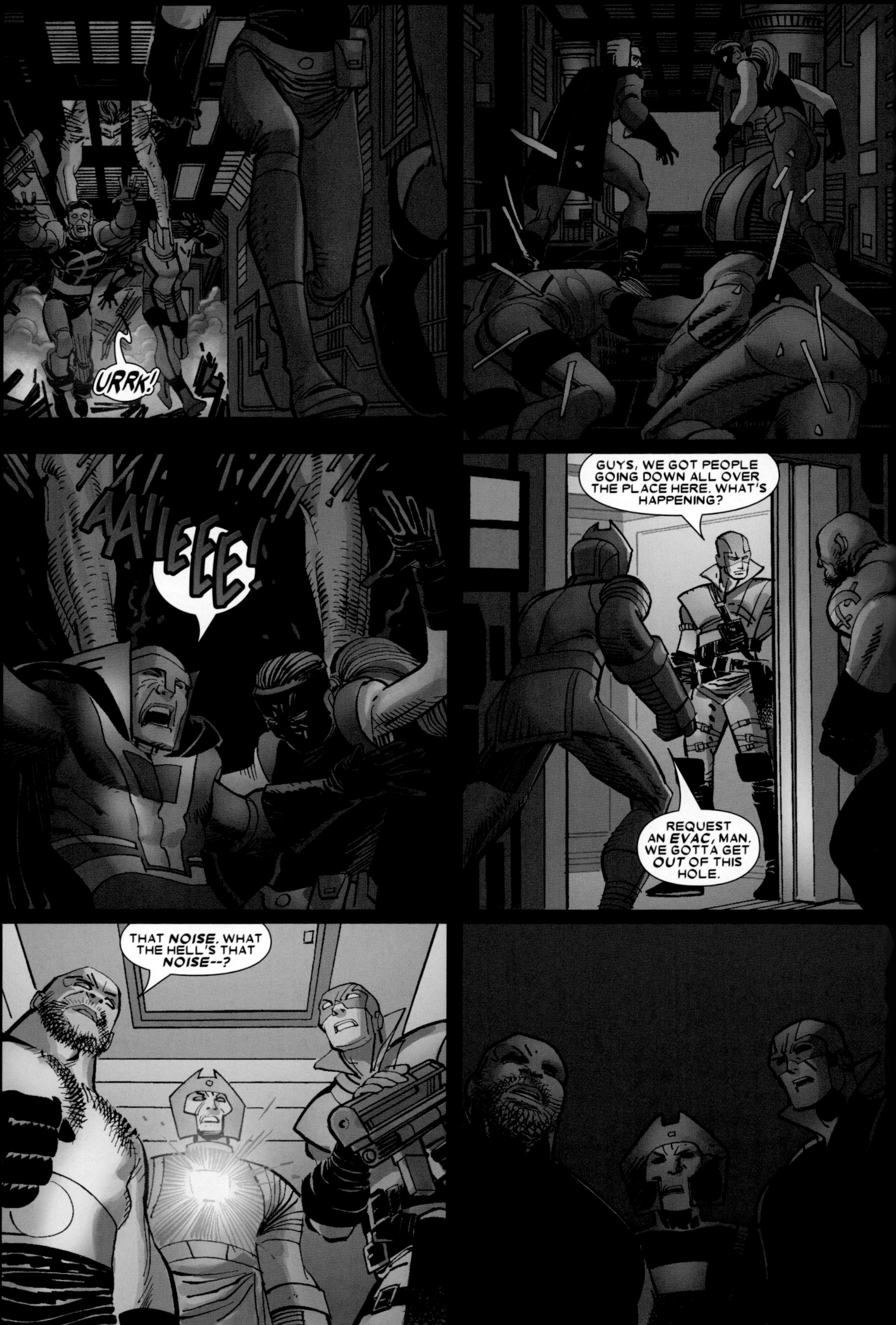
URRK!
AAIIEEEE!
GUYS, WE GOT PEOPLE GOING DOWN ALL OVER THE PLACE HERE. WHAT'S HAPPENING?
REQUEST AN EVAC, MAN. WE GOTTA GET OUT OF THIS HOLE.
THAT NOISE. WHAT THE HELL'S THAT NOISE--?

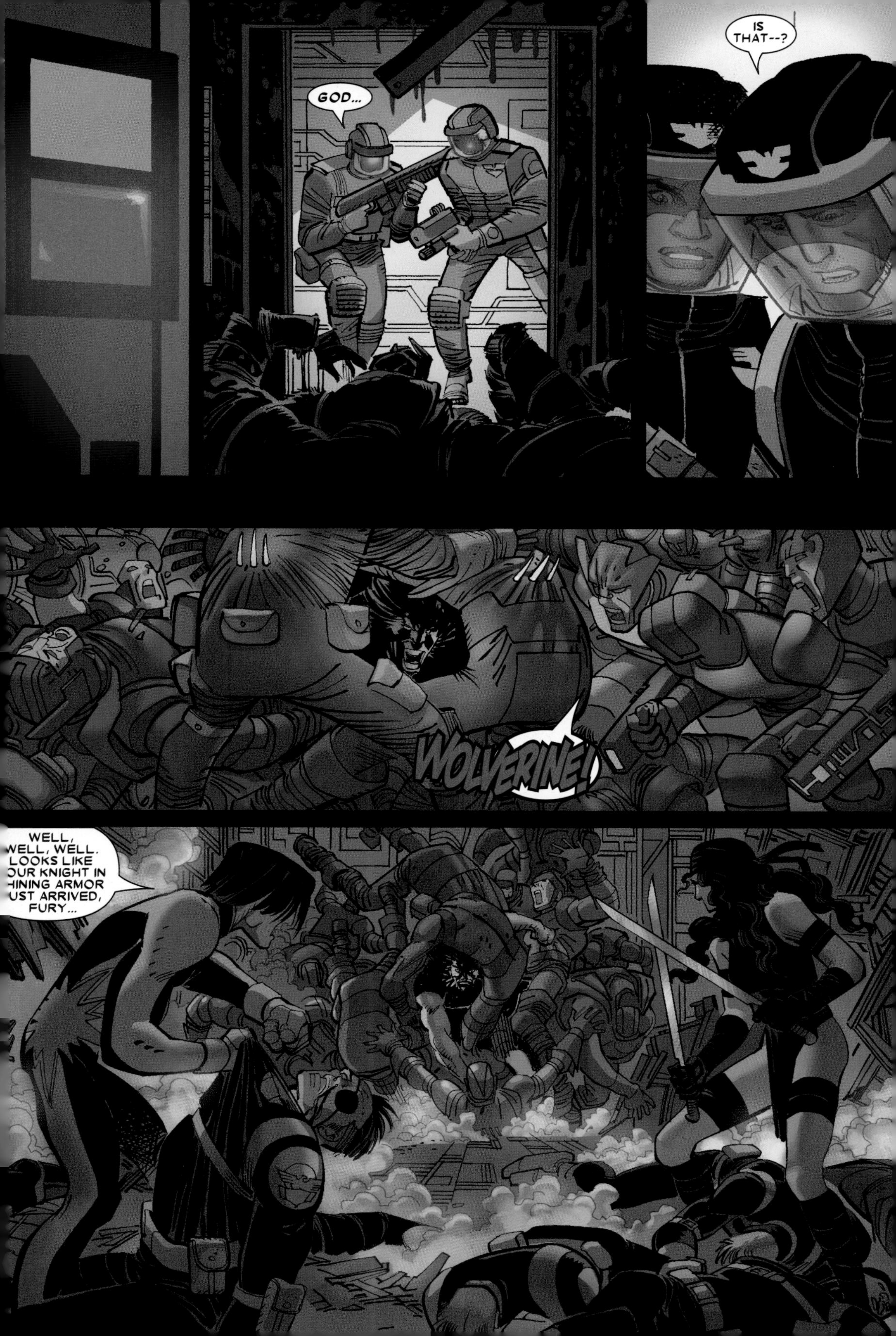
GOD...
IS THAT--?
WOLVERINE!
WELL, WELL, WELL. LOOKS LIKE OUR KNIGHT IN HINING ARMOR UST ARRIVED, FURY...

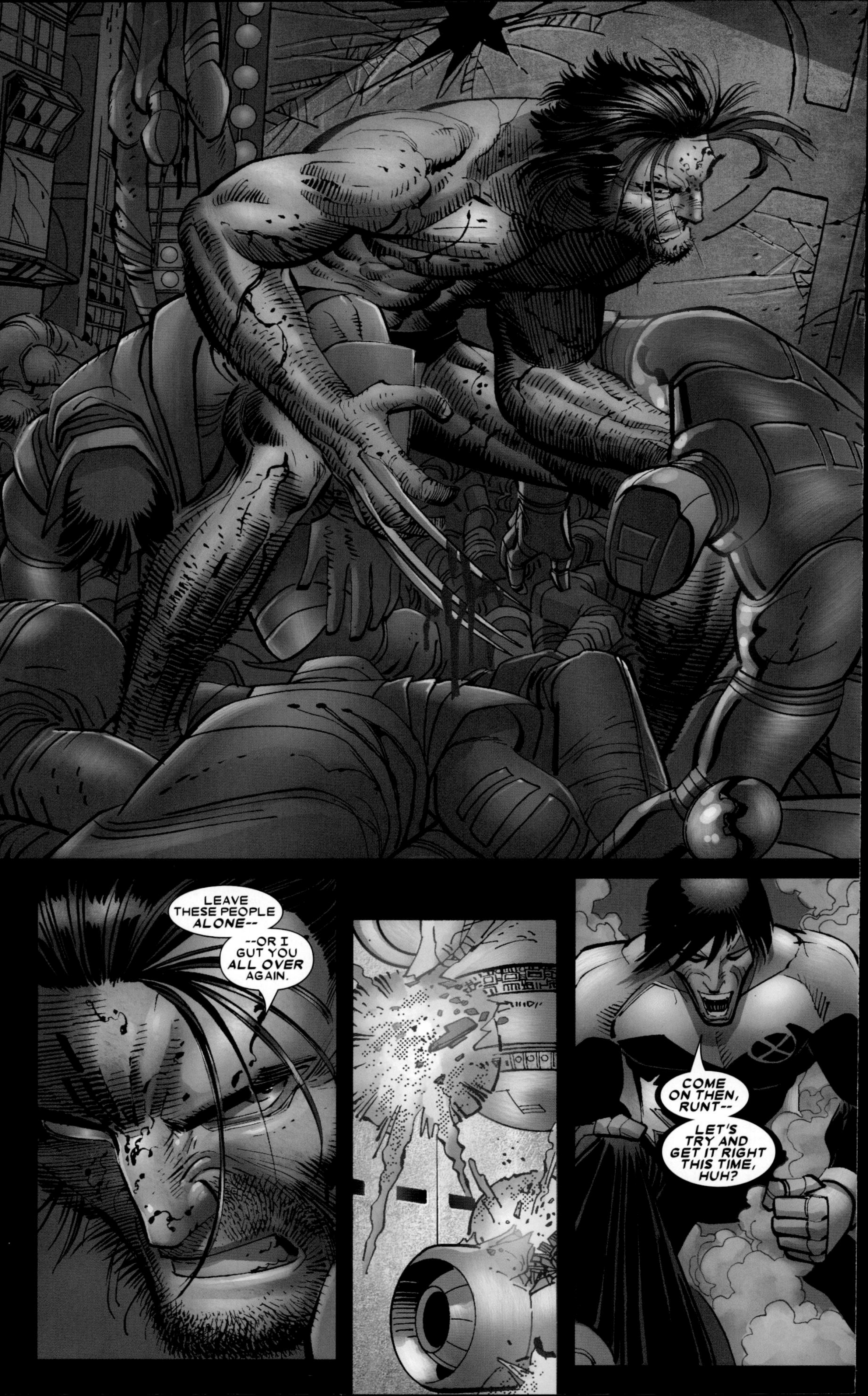
LEAVE THESE PEOPLE ALONE--
--OR I GUT YOU ALL OVER AGAIN.
COME ON THEN, RUNT--
LET'S TRY AND GET IT RIGHT THIS TIME, HUH?

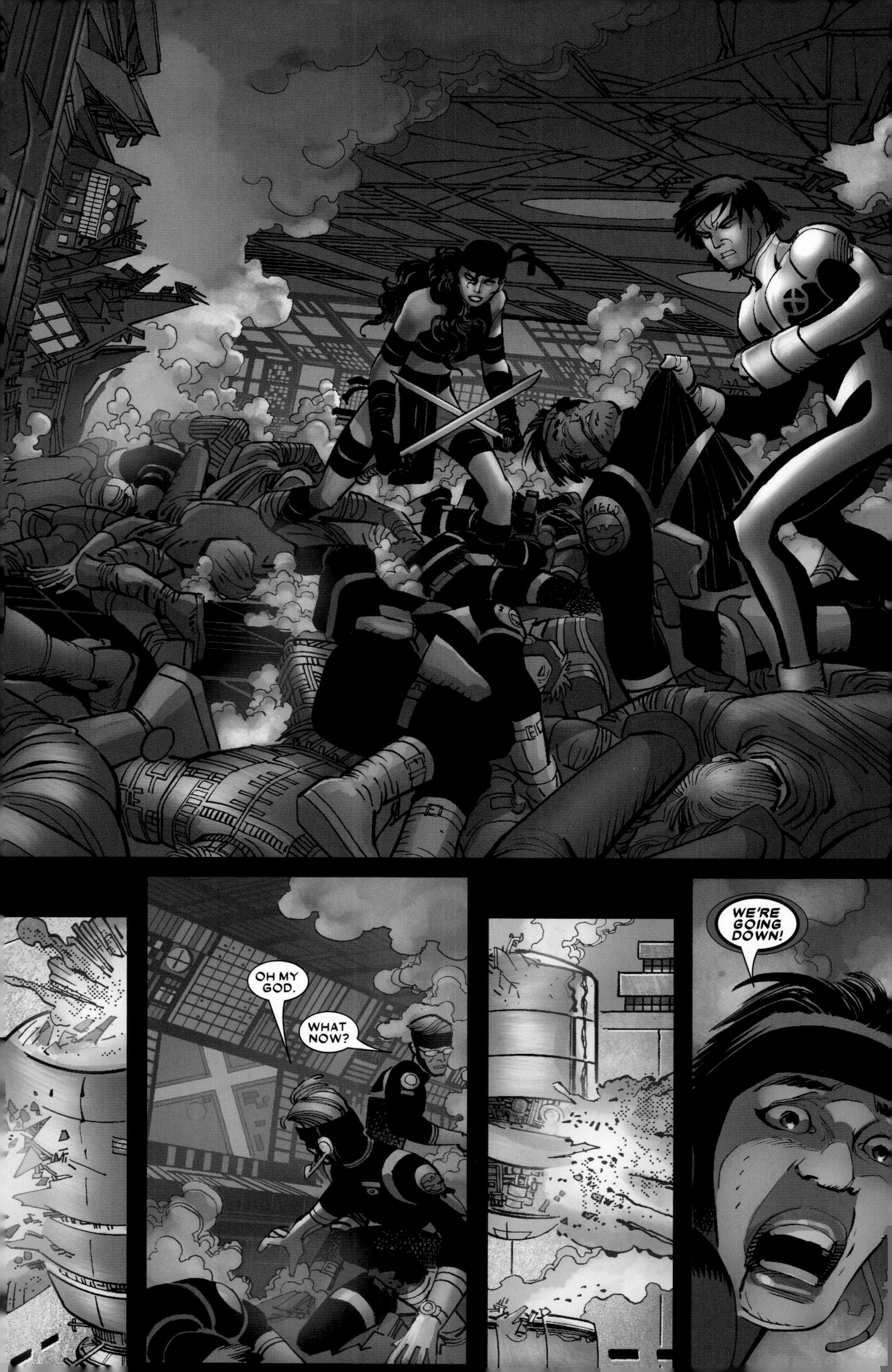
OH MY GOD.
WHAT NOW?
WE'RE GOING DOWN!

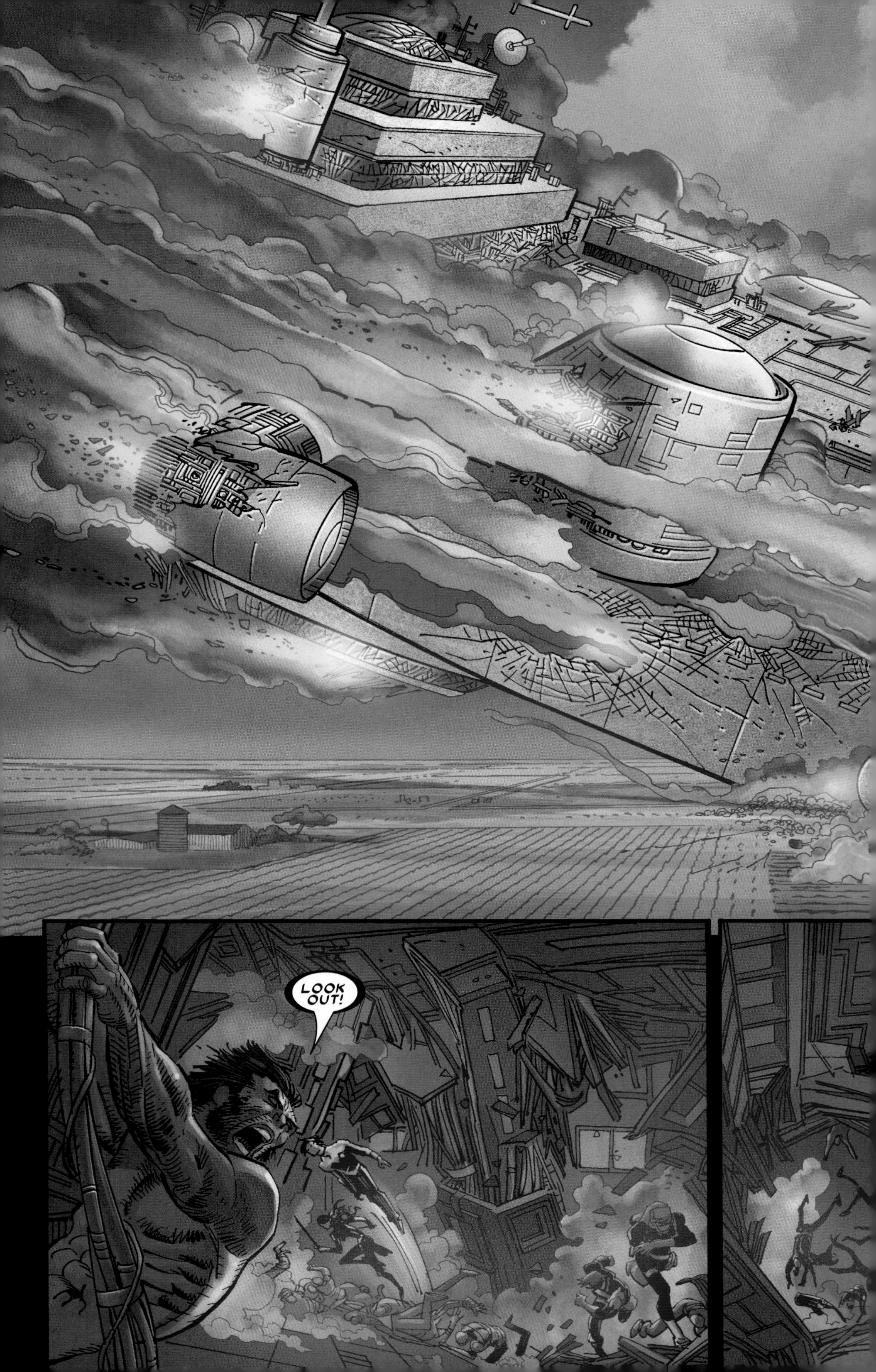
LOOK OUT!

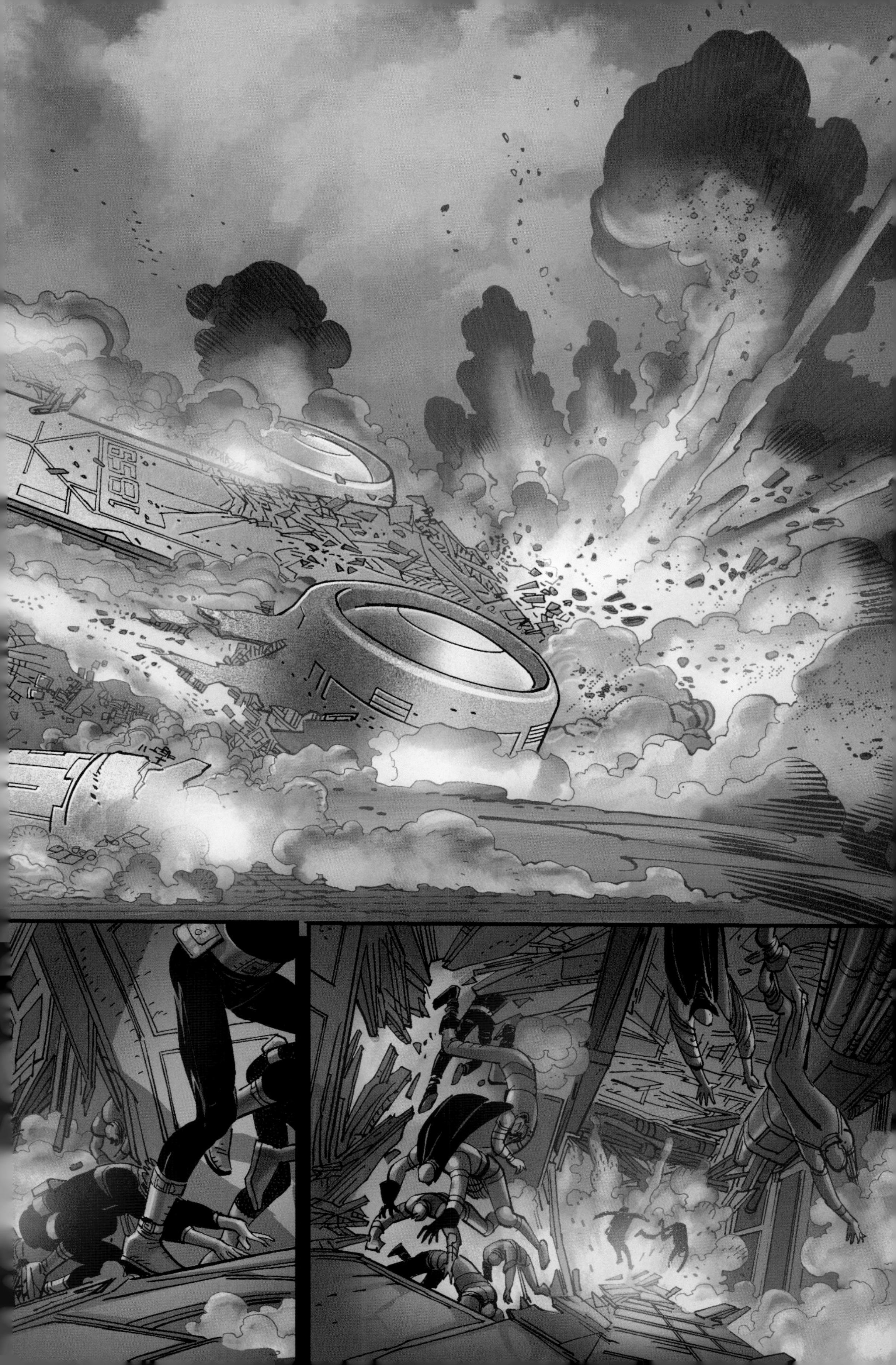

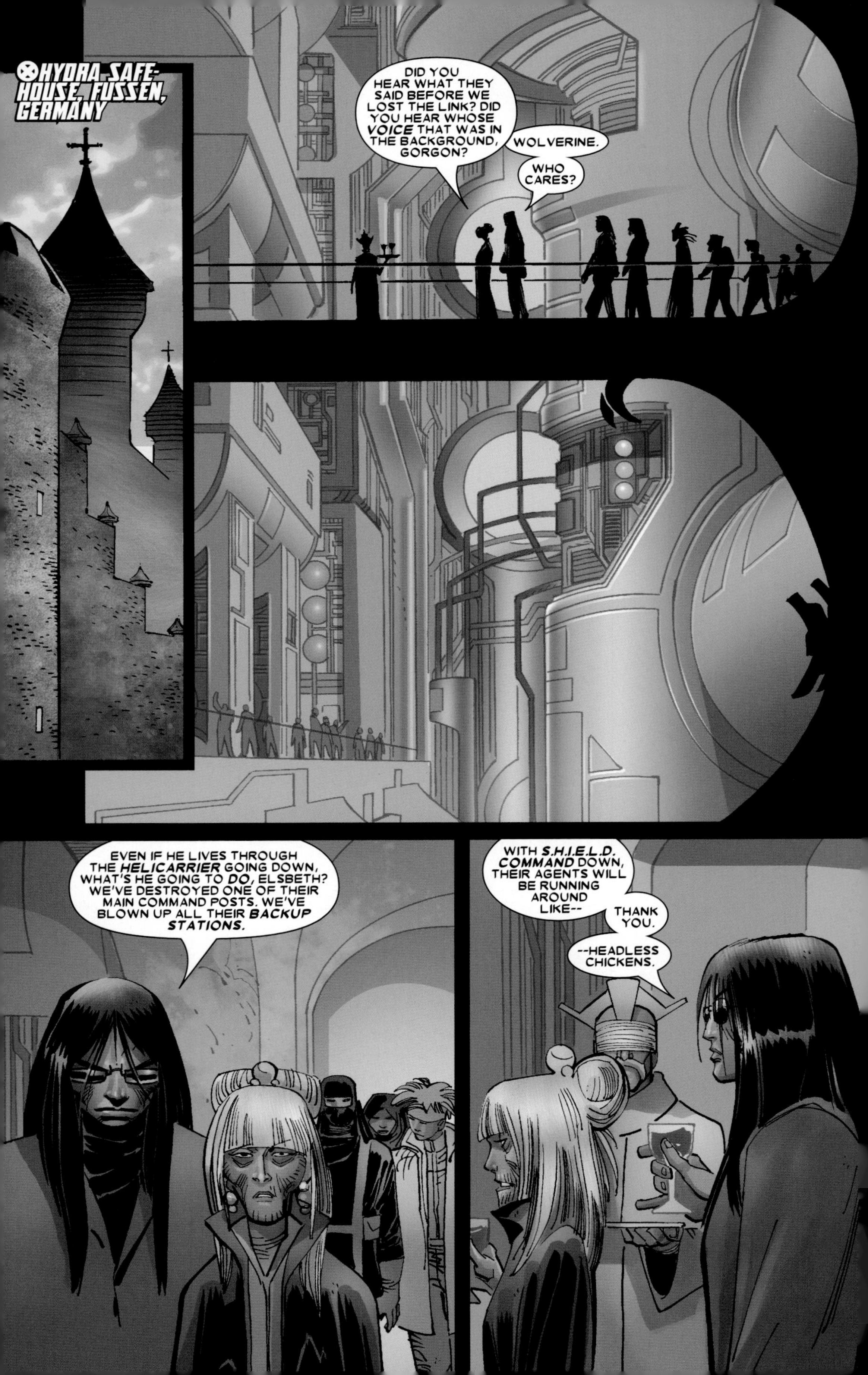
HYDRA SAFE-HOUSE, FUSSEN, GERMANY
DID YOU HEAR WHAT THEY SAID BEFORE WE LOST THE LINK? DID YOU HEAR WHOSE VOICE THAT WAS IN THE BACKGROUND, GORGON?
WOLVERINE.
WHO CARES?
EVEN IF HE LIVES THROUGH THE HELICARRIER GOING DOWN, WHAT'S HE GOING TO DO, ELSBETH? WE'VE DESTROYED ONE OF THEIR MAIN COMMAND POSTS. WE'VE BLOWN UP ALL THEIR BACKUP STATIONS.
WITH S.H.I.E.L.D. COMMAND DOWN, THEIR AGENTS WILL BE RUNNING AROUND LIKE--
THANK YOU.
--HEADLESS CHICKENS.

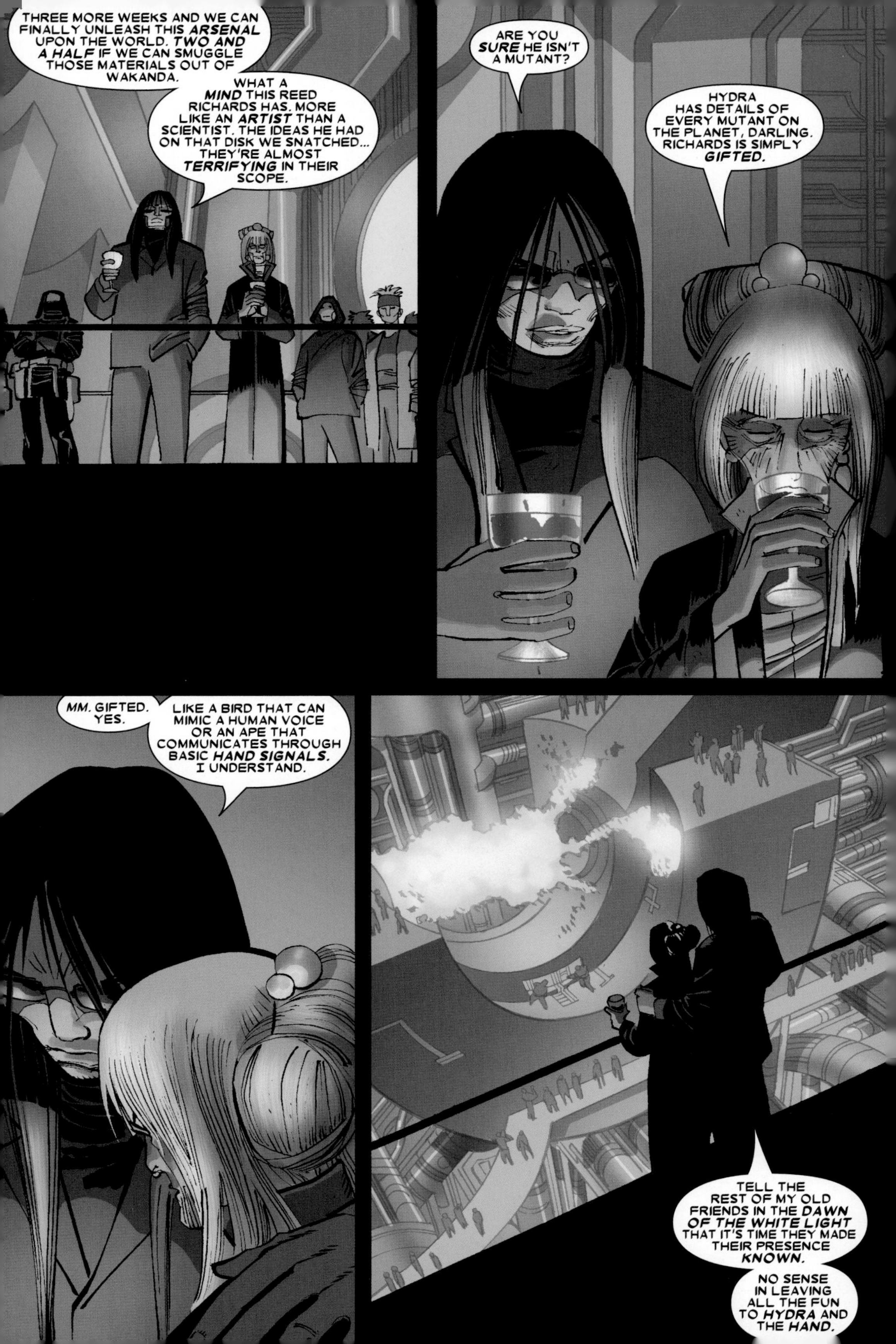
THREE MORE WEEKS AND WE CAN FINALLY UNLEASH THIS ARSENAL UPON THE WORLD. TWO AND A HALF IF WE CAN SMUGGLE THOSE MATERIALS OUT OF WAKANDA.
WHAT A MIND THIS REED RICHARDS HAS. MORE LIKE AN ARTIST THAN A SCIENTIST. THE IDEAS HE HAD ON THAT DISK WE SNATCHED... THEY'RE ALMOST TERRIFYING IN THEIR SCOPE.
ARE YOU SURE HE ISN'T A MUTANT?
HYDRA HAS DETAILS OF EVERY MUTANT ON THE PLANET, DARLING. RICHARDS IS SIMPLY GIFTED.
MM. GIFTED. YES.
LIKE A BIRD THAT CAN MIMIC A HUMAN VOICE OR AN APE THAT COMMUNICATES THROUGH BASIC HAND SIGNALS. I UNDERSTAND.
TELL THE REST OF MY OLD FRIENDS IN THE DAWN OF THE WHITE LIGHT THAT IT'S TIME THEY MADE THEIR PRESENCE KNOWN.
NO SENSE IN LEAVING ALL THE FUN TO HYDRA AND THE HAND.

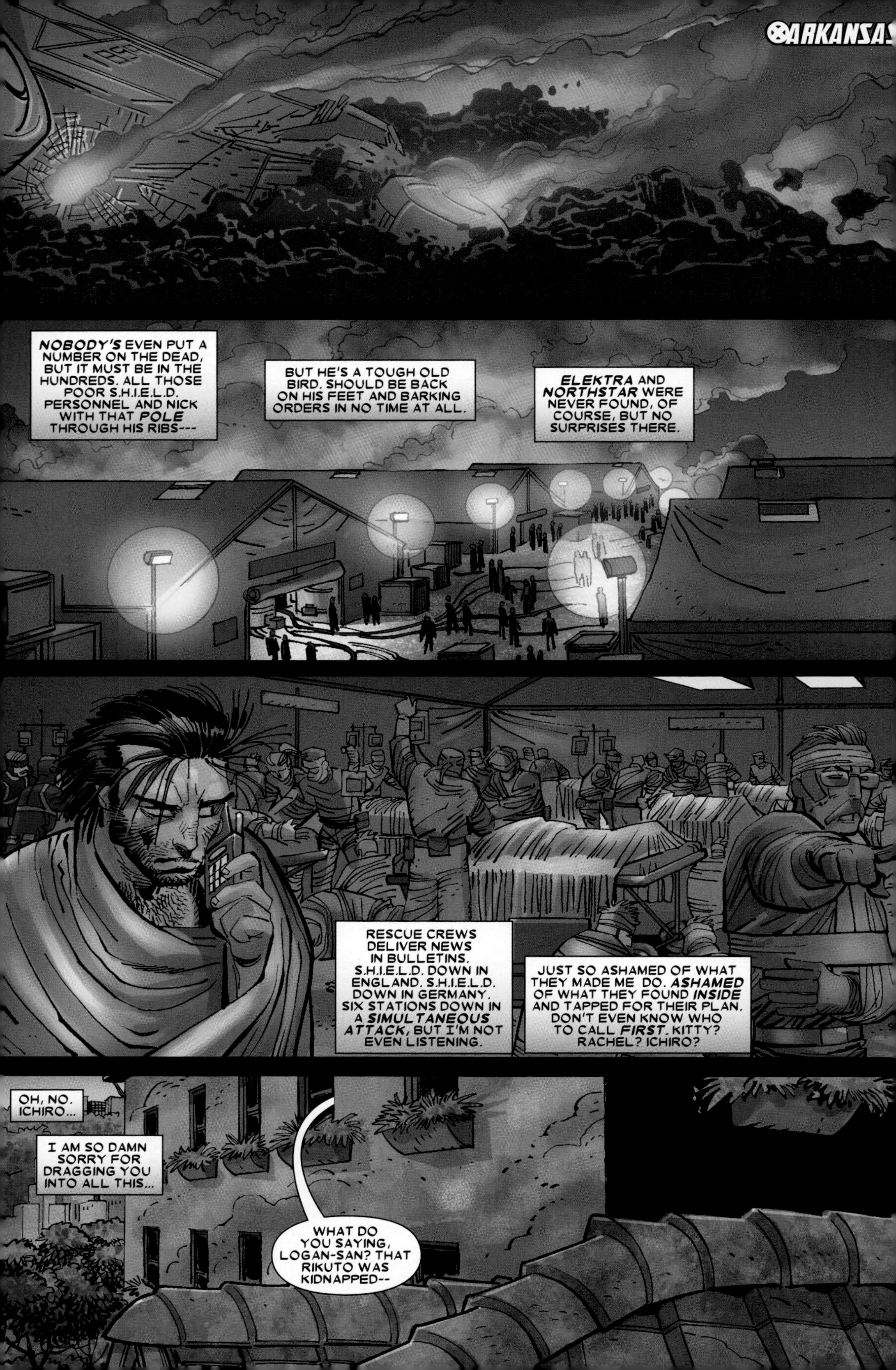
ARKANSAS
NOBODY'S EVEN PUT A NUMBER ON THE DEAD, BUT IT MUST BE IN THE HUNDREDS. ALL THOSE POOR S.H.I.E.L.D. PERSONNEL AND NICK WITH THAT POLE THROUGH HIS RIBS---
BUT HE'S A TOUGH OLD BIRD. SHOULD BE BACK ON HIS FEET AND BARKING ORDERS IN NO TIME AT ALL.
ELEKTRA AND NORTHSTAR WERE NEVER FOUND, OF COURSE, BUT NO SURPRISES THERE.
RESCUE CREWS DELIVER NEWS IN BULLETINS. S.H.I.E.L.D. DOWN IN ENGLAND. S.H.I.E.L.D. DOWN IN GERMANY. SIX STATIONS DOWN IN A SIMULTANEOUS ATTACK, BUT I'M NOT EVEN LISTENING.
JUST SO ASHAMED OF WHAT THEY MADE ME DO. ASHAMED OF WHAT THEY FOUND INSIDE AND TAPPED FOR THEIR PLAN. DON'T EVEN KNOW WHO TO CALL FIRST. KITTY? RACHEL? ICHIRO?
OH, NO. ICHIRO...
I AM SO DAMN SORRY FOR DRAGGING YOU INTO ALL THIS...
WHAT DO YOU SAYING, LOGAN-SAN? THAT RIKUTO WAS KIDNAPPED--

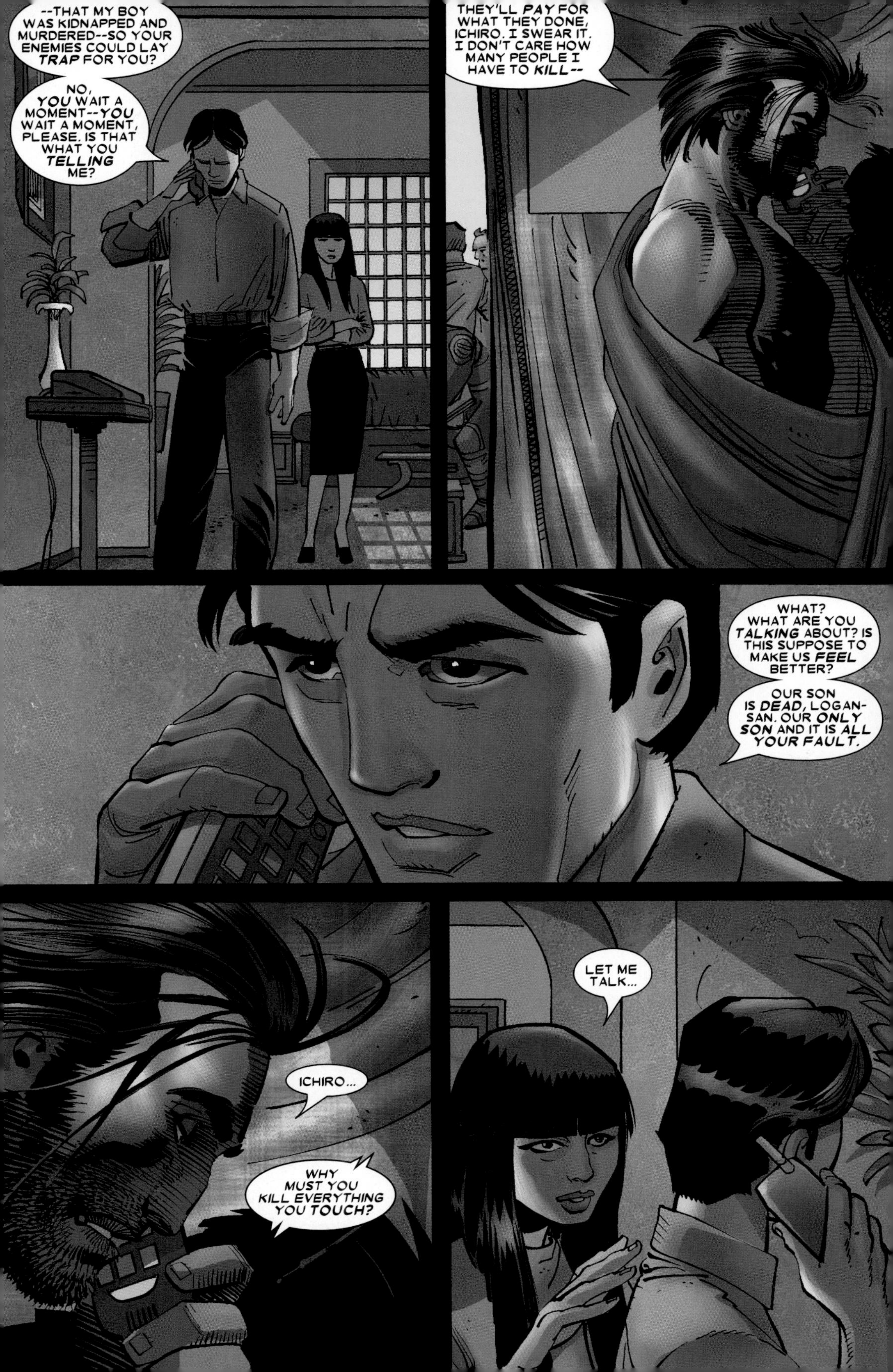
--THAT MY BOY WAS KIDNAPPED AND MURDERED--SO YOUR ENEMIES COULD LAY TRAP FOR YOU?
NO, YOU WAIT A MOMENT--YOU WAIT A MOMENT, PLEASE. IS THAT WHAT YOU TELLING ME?
THEY'LL PAY FOR WHAT THEY DONE, ICHIRO. I SWEAR IT. I DON'T CARE HOW MANY PEOPLE I HAVE TO KILL--
WHAT? WHAT ARE YOU TALKING ABOUT? IS THIS SUPPOSE TO MAKE US FEEL BETTER?
OUR SON IS DEAD, LOGAN-SAN. OUR ONLY SON AND IT IS ALL YOUR FAULT.
ICHIRO...
WHY MUST YOU KILL EVERYTHING YOU TOUCH?
LET ME TALK...

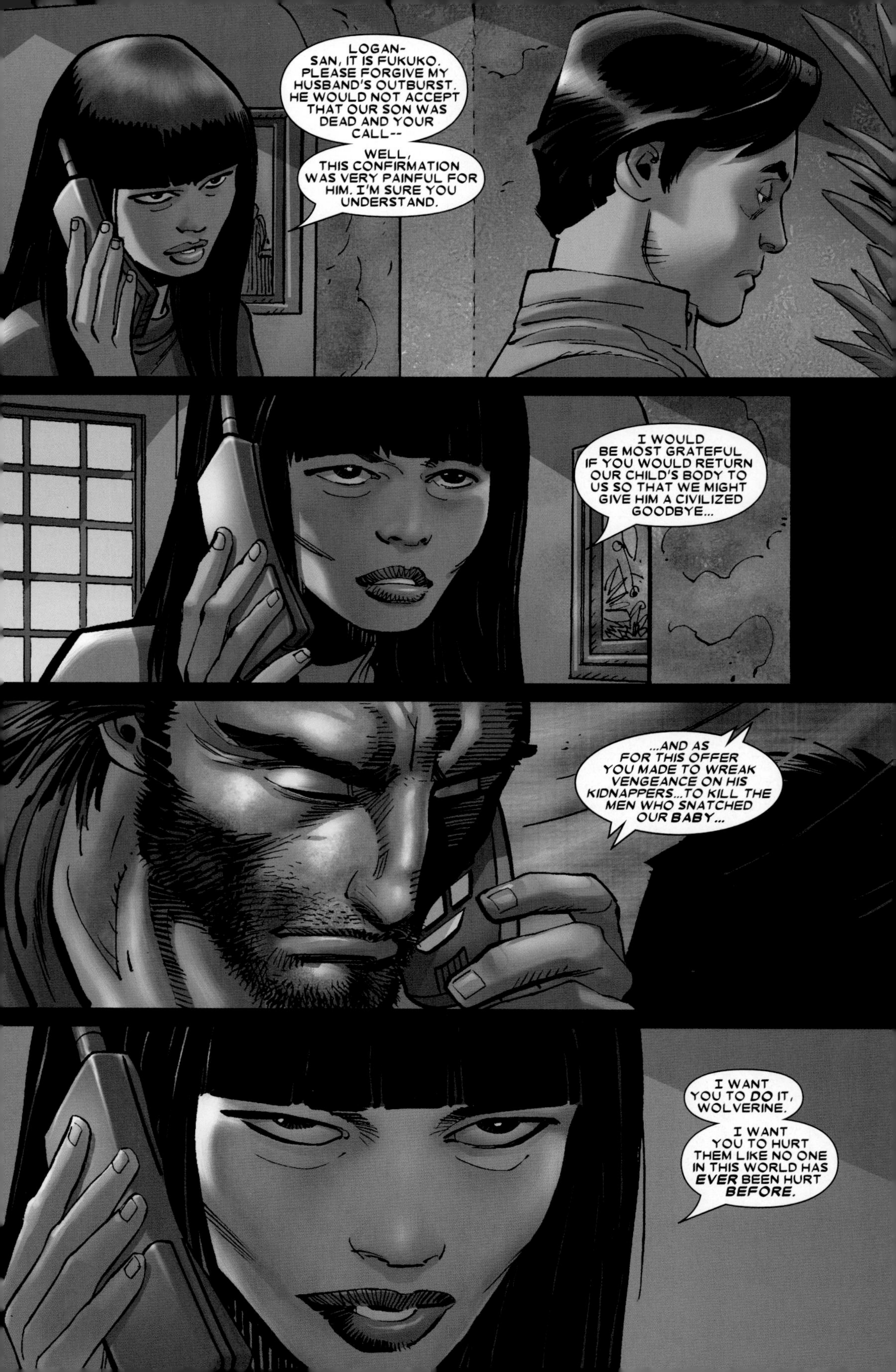
LOGAN-SAN, IT IS FUKUKO. PLEASE FORGIVE MY HUSBAND'S OUTBURST. HE WOULD NOT ACCEPT THAT OUR SON WAS DEAD AND YOUR CALL--
WELL, THIS CONFIRMATION WAS VERY PAINFUL FOR HIM. I'M SURE YOU UNDERSTAND.
I WOULD BE MOST GRATEFUL IF YOU WOULD RETURN OUR CHILD'S BODY TO US SO THAT WE MIGHT GIVE HIM A CIVILIZED GOODBYE...
...AND AS FOR THIS OFFER YOU MADE TO WREAK VENGEANCE ON HIS KIDNAPPERS...TO KILL THE MEN WHO SNATCHED OUR BABY...
I WANT YOU TO DO IT, WOLVERINE.
I WANT YOU TO HURT THEM LIKE NO ONE IN THIS WORLD HAS EVER BEEN HURT BEFORE.

WOLVERINE IN HERE?

SUITING UP INSIDE. TRIED TO *TELL* HIM WE WANTED TO RUN MORE TESTS, BUT--

JUST WHAT DO YOU THINK YOU'RE DOING? *YOU'RE* IN NO CONDITION TO PUT THAT ON.

HOW MANY PEOPLE ARE *ACTIVE* IN *THE HAND*, DOC?

WHAT?

HOW MANY PEOPLE ARE IN *HYDRA* AND *THE HAND?*

UH, LAST ESTIMATE I SAW WAS EIGHTEEN HUNDRED PEOPLE IN THE HAND AND FORTY-NINE THOUSAND *HYDRA* AGENTS.

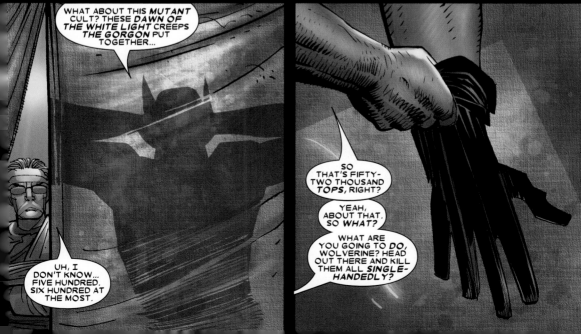

WHAT ABOUT THIS *MUTANT* CULT? THESE *DAWN OF THE WHITE LIGHT* CREEPS *THE GORGON* PUT TOGETHER...

UH, I DON'T KNOW... FIVE HUNDRED, SIX HUNDRED AT THE MOST.

SO THAT'S FIFTY-TWO THOUSAND *TOPS*, RIGHT?

YEAH, ABOUT THAT. SO *WHAT*?

WHAT ARE YOU GOING TO *DO*, WOLVERINE? HEAD OUT THERE AND KILL THEM ALL *SINGLE-HANDEDLY*?

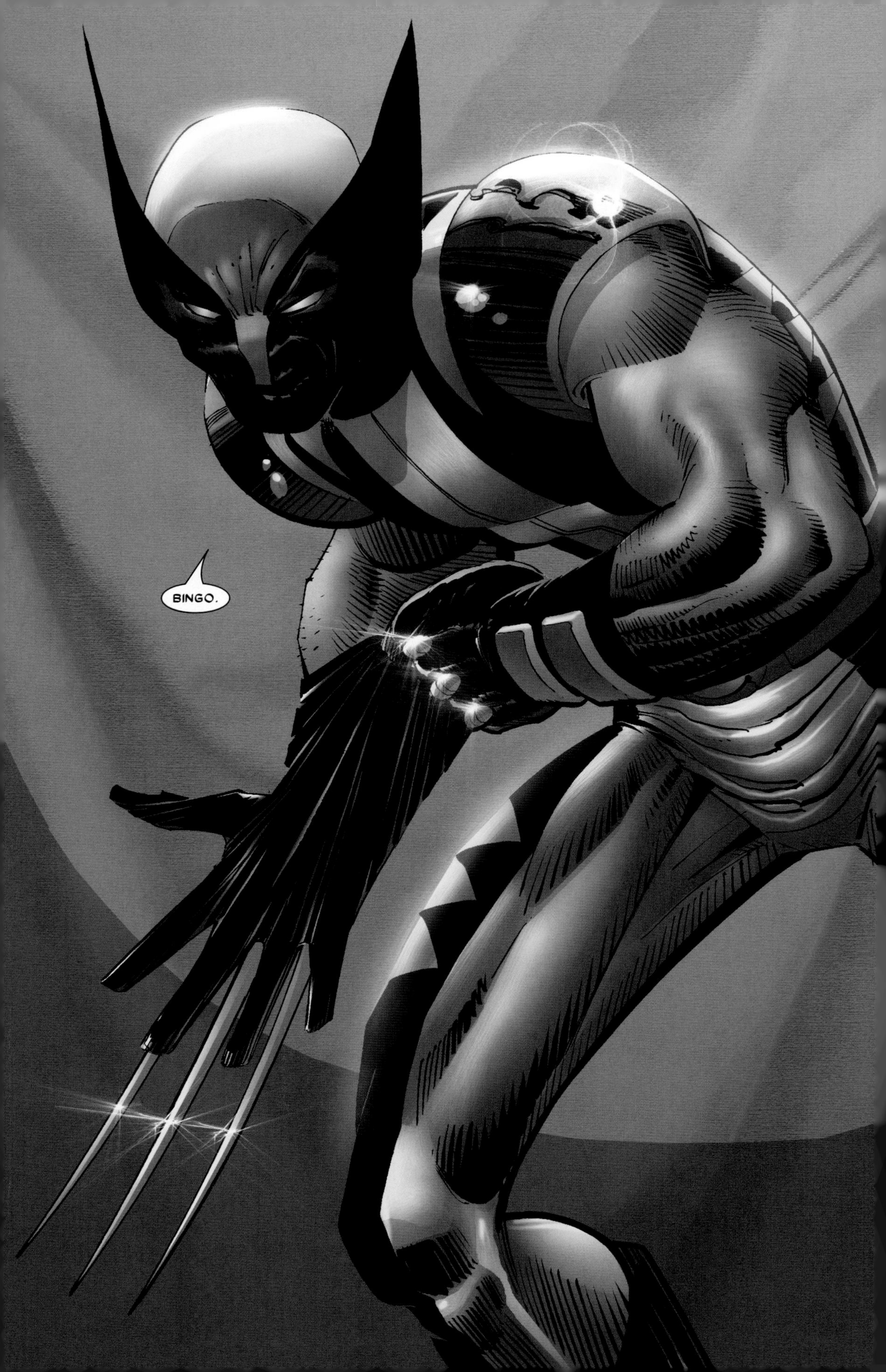
BINGO.

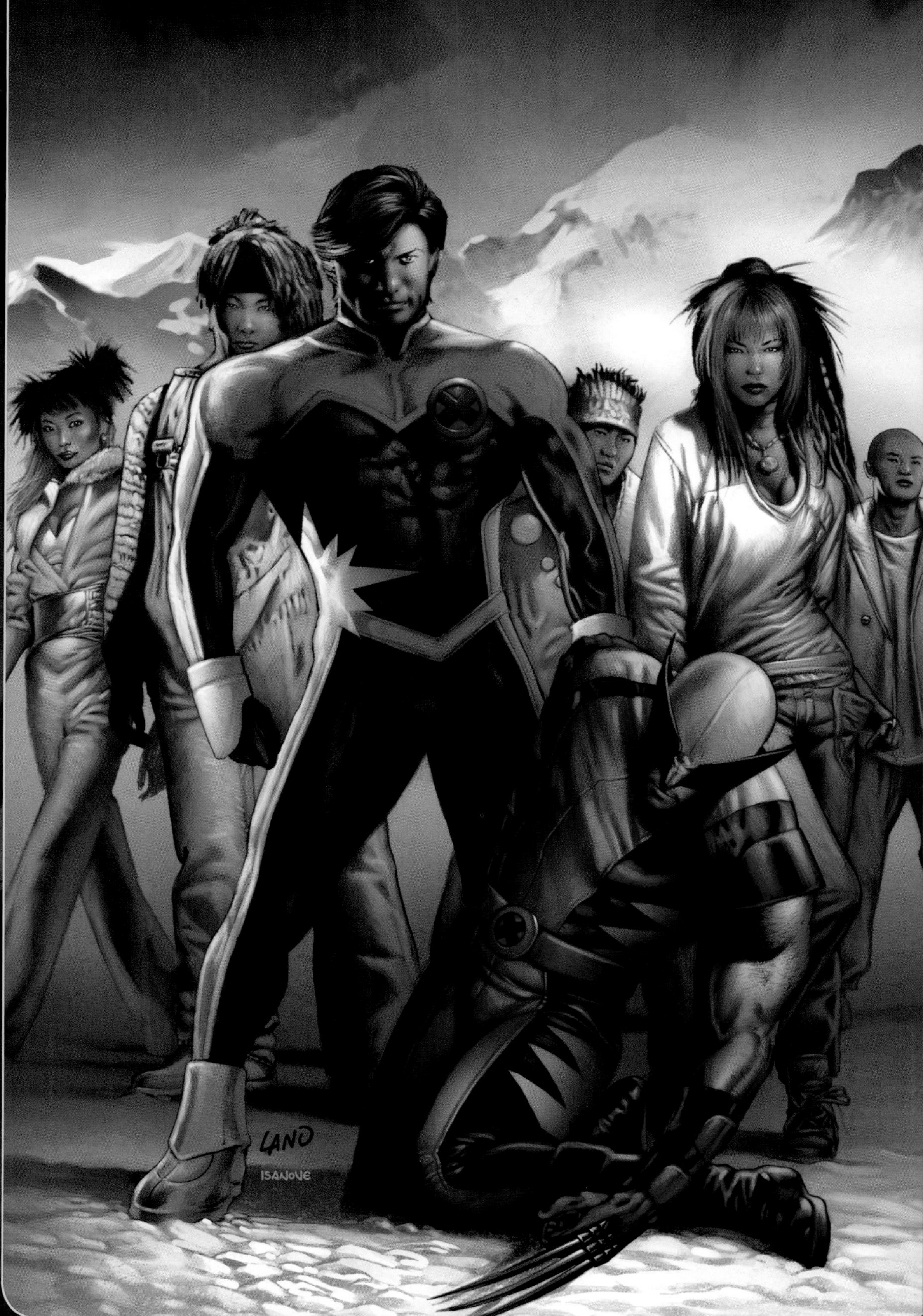
LAND
ISANOVE

#28

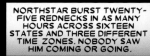

YOU KNOW WHAT HAPPENS WHEN A SUPER-GUY HITS A NORM AT MACH THREE? THE NORM EXPLODES LIKE A WATERMELON AND EVEN *DENTAL* I.D. BECOMES IMPOSSIBLE.

THE COPS CAN'T FIND ENOUGH TO FILL A *PLASTIC BAG.*

NORTHSTAR BURST TWENTY-FIVE REDNECKS IN AS MANY HOURS ACROSS SIXTEEN STATES AND THREE DIFFERENT TIME ZONES. NOBODY SAW HIM COMING OR GOING.

ONLY THING THEY KNOW FOR SURE IS THAT HE'S HEADING UP THE DAWN OF THE WHITE LIGHT AND THEY'RE HAVING A LITTLE FUN WHILE *S.H.I.E.L.D.* COMMAND IS DOWN.

THE DAWN IS A *DEATH CULT,* A GANG OF MUTANTS PUT TOGETHER BY THE GORGON BEFORE HE MOVED ON TO *BIGGER AND BETTER THINGS.*

THEY'RE HITTING TOWN AFTER TOWN WITH NO *PATTERN* OR *STRATEGY* EXCEPT POPPING THE KINDS OF FOLKS NORTHSTAR HAD A *PROBLEM* WITH.

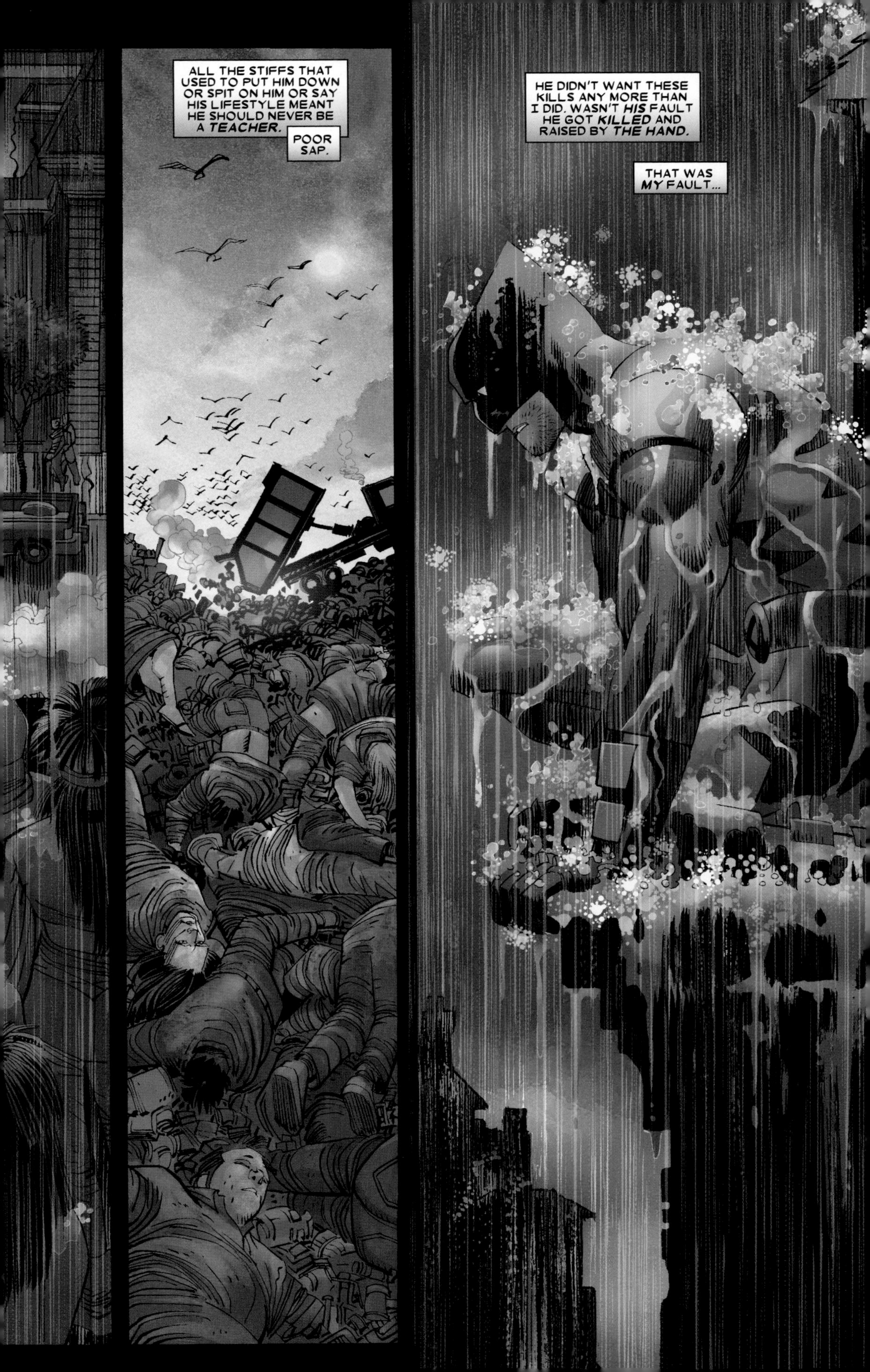
ALL THE STIFFS THAT USED TO PUT HIM DOWN OR SPIT ON HIM OR SAY HIS LIFESTYLE MEANT HE SHOULD NEVER BE A TEACHER.
POOR SAP.
HE DIDN'T WANT THESE KILLS ANY MORE THAN I DID. WASN'T HIS FAULT HE GOT KILLED AND RAISED BY THE HAND.
THAT WAS MY FAULT...

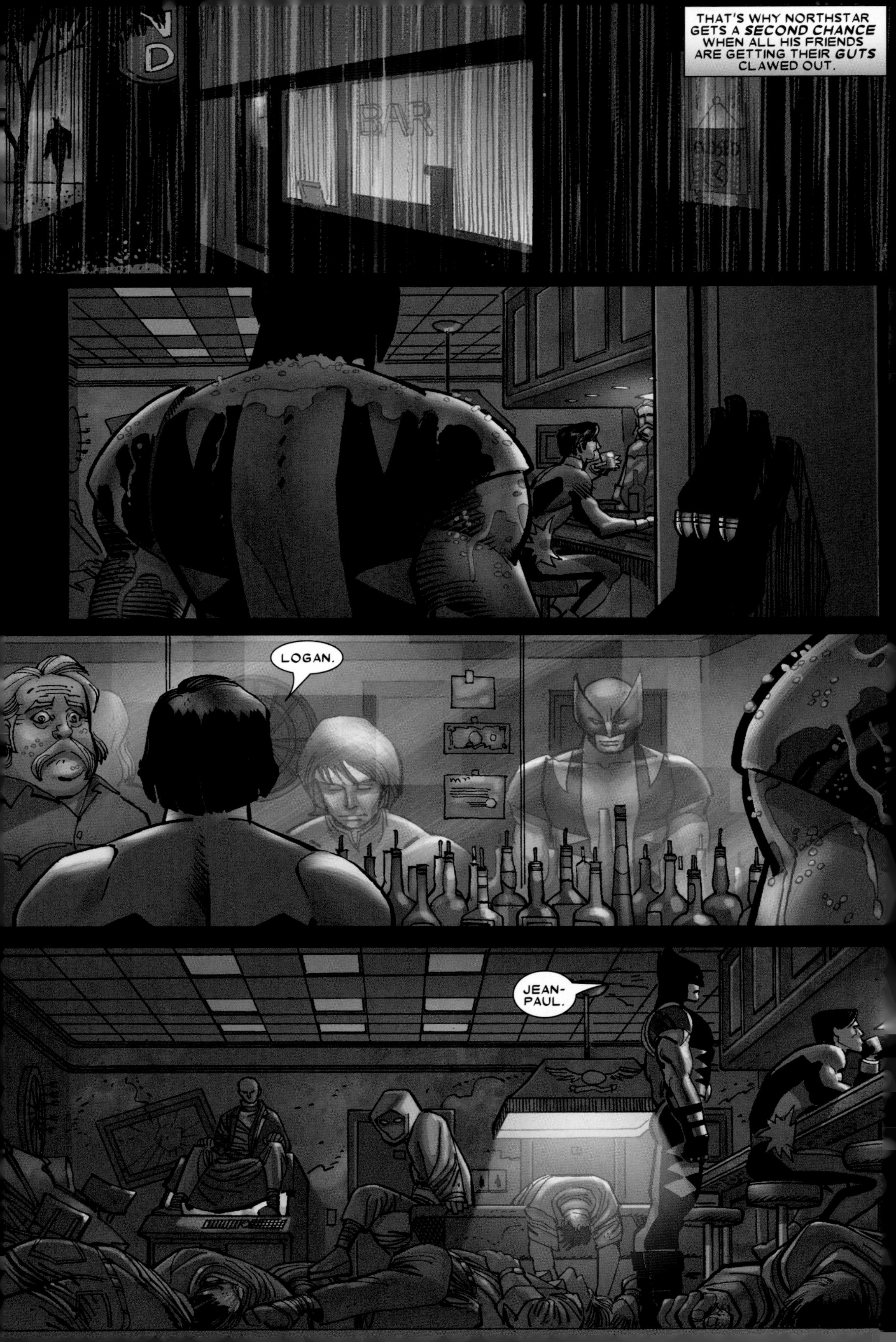
THAT'S WHY NORTHSTAR GETS A SECOND CHANCE WHEN ALL HIS FRIENDS ARE GETTING THEIR GUTS CLAWED OUT.
BAR
LOGAN.
JEAN-PAUL.

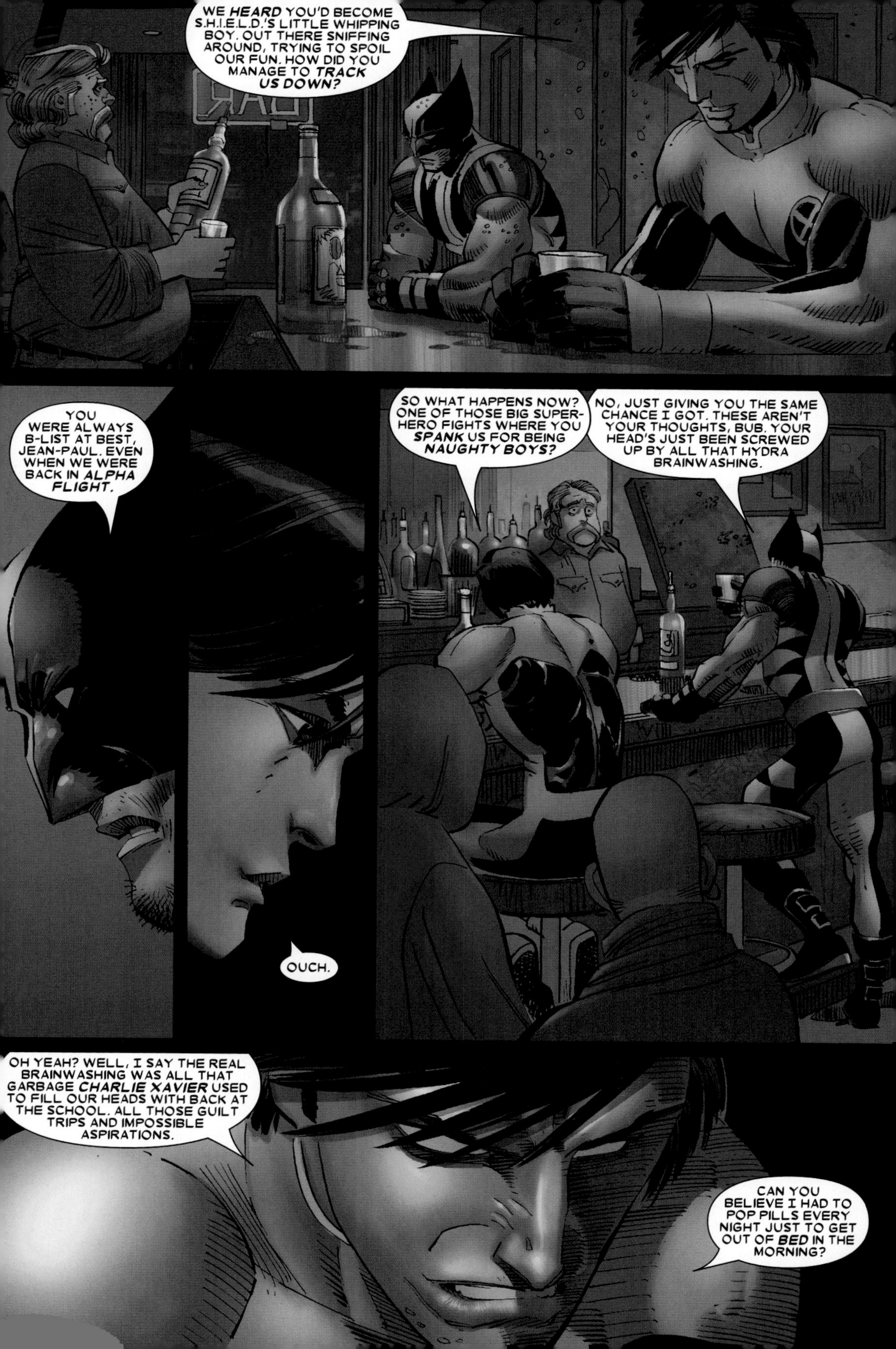
WE HEARD YOU'D BECOME S.H.I.E.L.D.'S LITTLE WHIPPING BOY. OUT THERE SNIFFING AROUND, TRYING TO SPOIL OUR FUN. HOW DID YOU MANAGE TO TRACK US DOWN?
YOU WERE ALWAYS B-LIST AT BEST, JEAN-PAUL. EVEN WHEN WE WERE BACK IN ALPHA FLIGHT.
OUCH.
SO WHAT HAPPENS NOW? ONE OF THOSE BIG SUPER-HERO FIGHTS WHERE YOU SPANK US FOR BEING NAUGHTY BOYS?
NO, JUST GIVING YOU THE SAME CHANCE I GOT. THESE AREN'T YOUR THOUGHTS, BUB. YOUR HEAD'S JUST BEEN SCREWED UP BY ALL THAT HYDRA BRAINWASHING.
OH YEAH? WELL, I SAY THE REAL BRAINWASHING WAS ALL THAT GARBAGE CHARLIE XAVIER USED TO FILL OUR HEADS WITH BACK AT THE SCHOOL. ALL THOSE GUILT TRIPS AND IMPOSSIBLE ASPIRATIONS.
CAN YOU BELIEVE I HAD TO POP PILLS EVERY NIGHT JUST TO GET OUT OF BED IN THE MORNING?

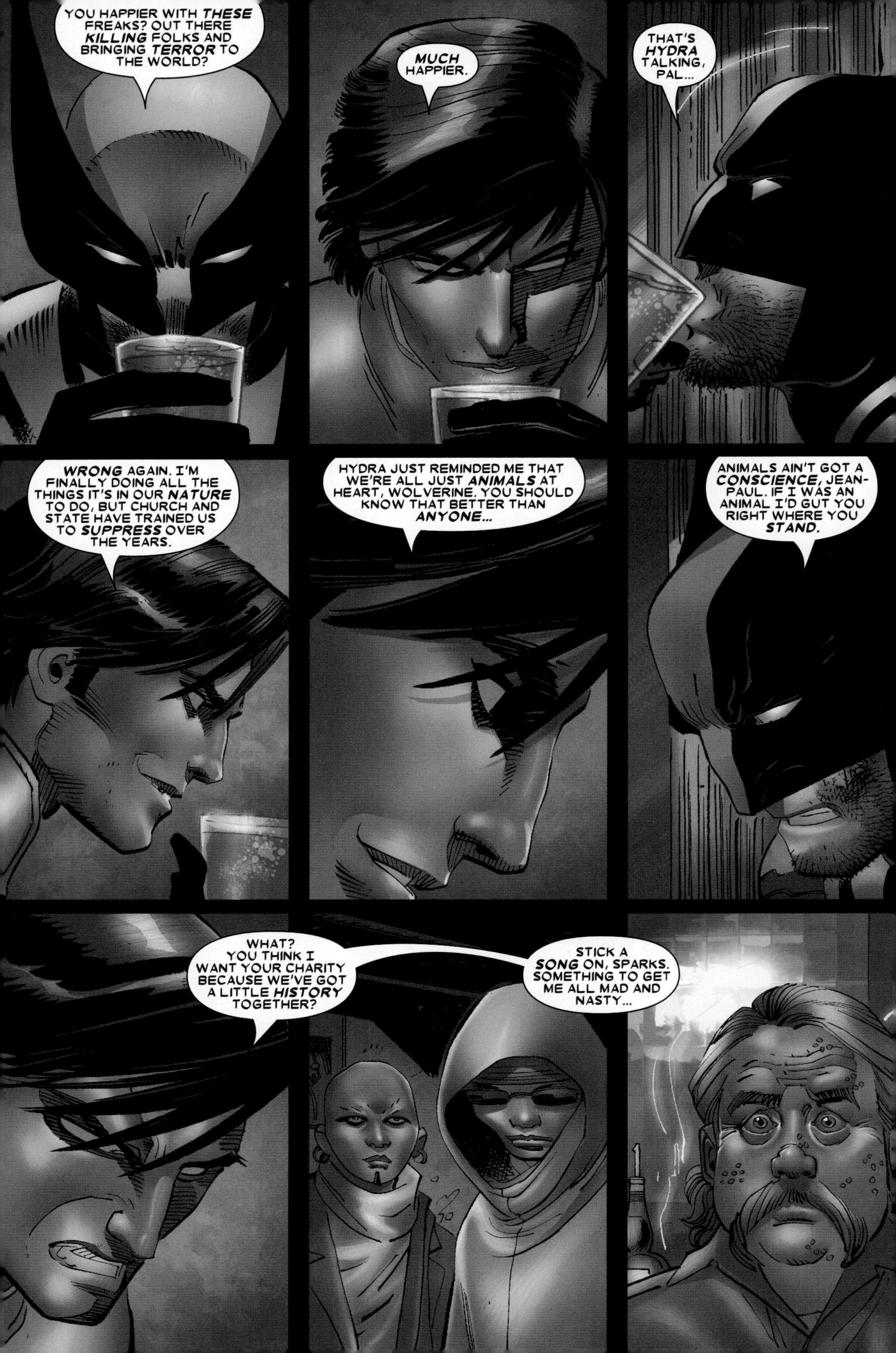
YOU HAPPIER WITH THESE FREAKS? OUT THERE KILLING FOLKS AND BRINGING TERROR TO THE WORLD?
MUCH HAPPIER.
THAT'S HYDRA TALKING, PAL...
WRONG AGAIN. I'M FINALLY DOING ALL THE THINGS IT'S IN OUR NATURE TO DO, BUT CHURCH AND STATE HAVE TRAINED US TO SUPPRESS OVER THE YEARS.
HYDRA JUST REMINDED ME THAT WE'RE ALL JUST ANIMALS AT HEART, WOLVERINE. YOU SHOULD KNOW THAT BETTER THAN ANYONE...
ANIMALS AIN'T GOT A CONSCIENCE, JEAN-PAUL. IF I WAS AN ANIMAL I'D GUT YOU RIGHT WHERE YOU STAND.
WHAT? YOU THINK I WANT YOUR CHARITY BECAUSE WE'VE GOT A LITTLE HISTORY TOGETHER?
STICK A SONG ON, SPARKS. SOMETHING TO GET ME ALL MAD AND NASTY...

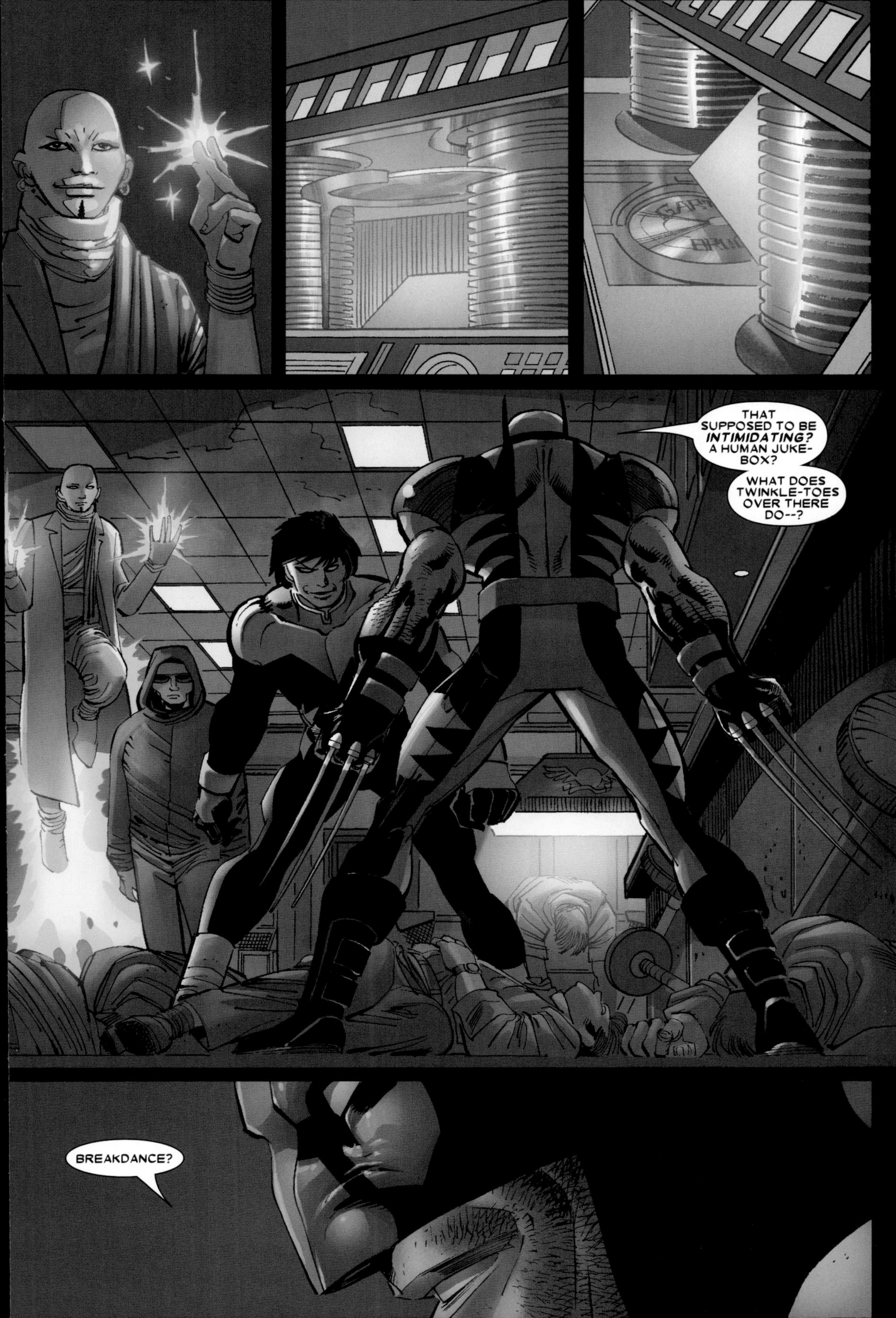
THAT SUPPOSED TO BE *INTIMIDATING?* A HUMAN JUKE-BOX?
WHAT DOES TWINKLE-TOES OVER THERE DO--?
BREAKDANCE?

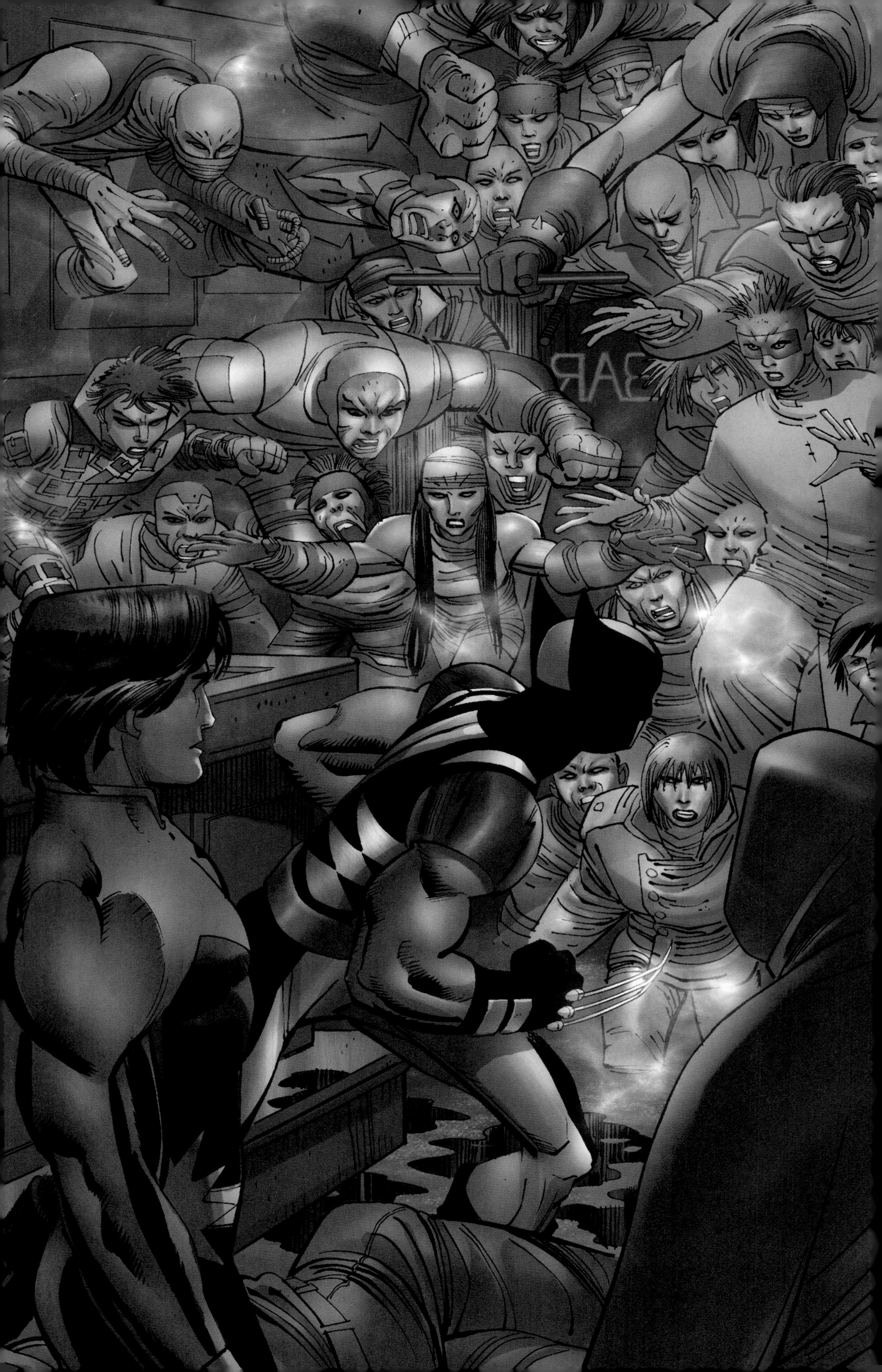

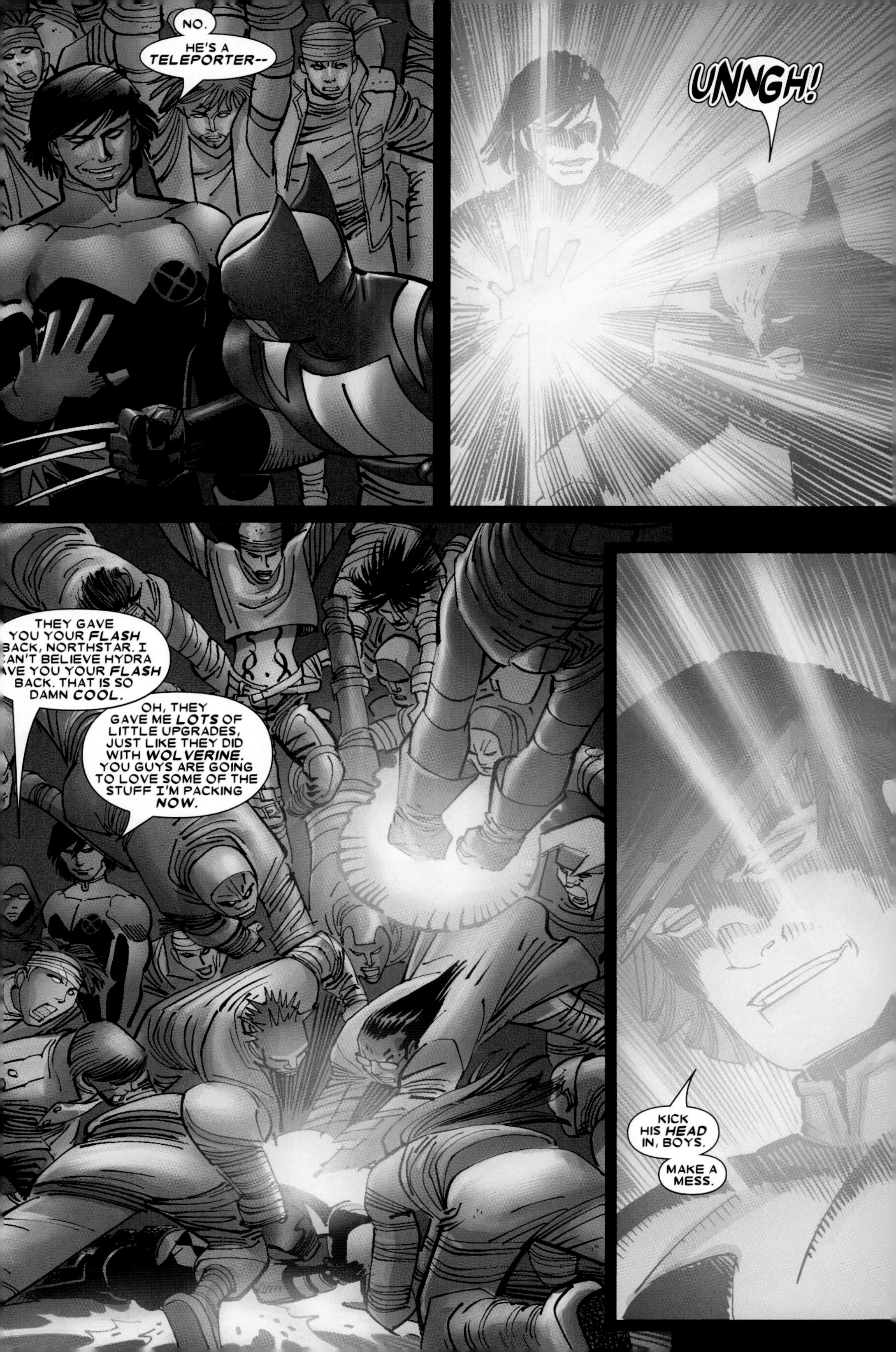

NO.
HE'S A TELEPORTER--
UNNGH!
THEY GAVE YOU YOUR FLASH BACK, NORTHSTAR. I AN'T BELIEVE HYDRA AVE YOU YOUR FLASH BACK. THAT IS SO DAMN COOL.
OH, THEY GAVE ME LOTS OF LITTLE UPGRADES, JUST LIKE THEY DID WITH WOLVERINE. YOU GUYS ARE GOING TO LOVE SOME OF THE STUFF I'M PACKING NOW.
KICK HIS HEAD IN, BOYS.
MAKE A MESS.

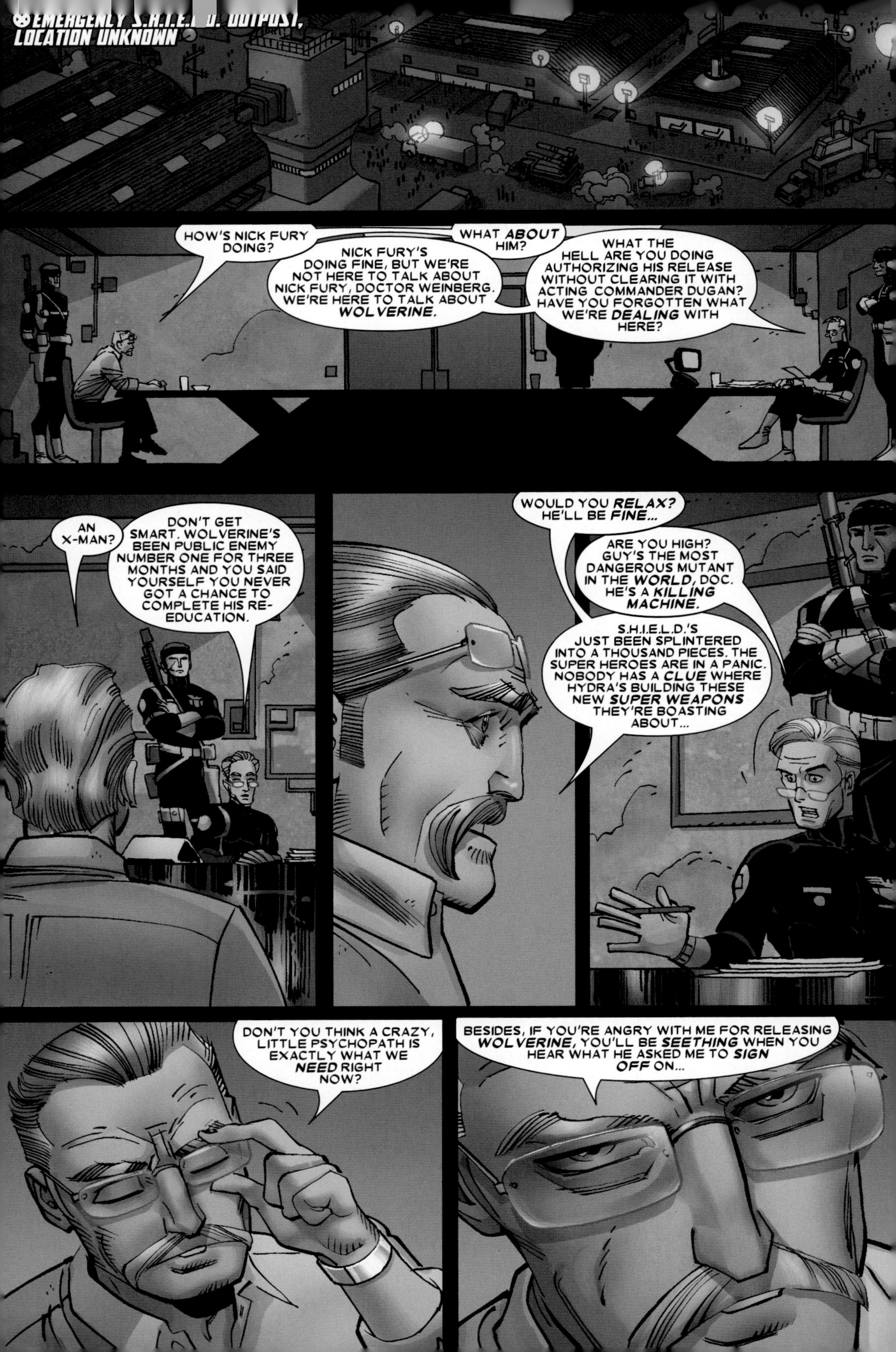
EMERGENCY S.H.I.E.L.D. OUTPOST,
LOCATION UNKNOWN
HOW'S NICK FURY DOING?
WHAT ABOUT HIM?
NICK FURY'S DOING FINE, BUT WE'RE NOT HERE TO TALK ABOUT NICK FURY, DOCTOR WEINBERG. WE'RE HERE TO TALK ABOUT WOLVERINE.
WHAT THE HELL ARE YOU DOING AUTHORIZING HIS RELEASE WITHOUT CLEARING IT WITH ACTING COMMANDER DUGAN? HAVE YOU FORGOTTEN WHAT WE'RE DEALING WITH HERE?
AN X-MAN?
DON'T GET SMART. WOLVERINE'S BEEN PUBLIC ENEMY NUMBER ONE FOR THREE MONTHS AND YOU SAID YOURSELF YOU NEVER GOT A CHANCE TO COMPLETE HIS RE-EDUCATION.
WOULD YOU RELAX? HE'LL BE FINE...
ARE YOU HIGH? GUY'S THE MOST DANGEROUS MUTANT IN THE WORLD, DOC. HE'S A KILLING MACHINE.
S.H.I.E.L.D.'S JUST BEEN SPLINTERED INTO A THOUSAND PIECES. THE SUPER HEROES ARE IN A PANIC. NOBODY HAS A CLUE WHERE HYDRA'S BUILDING THESE NEW SUPER WEAPONS THEY'RE BOASTING ABOUT...
DON'T YOU THINK A CRAZY, LITTLE PSYCHOPATH IS EXACTLY WHAT WE NEED RIGHT NOW?
BESIDES, IF YOU'RE ANGRY WITH ME FOR RELEASING WOLVERINE, YOU'LL BE SEETHING WHEN YOU HEAR WHAT HE ASKED ME TO SIGN OFF ON...

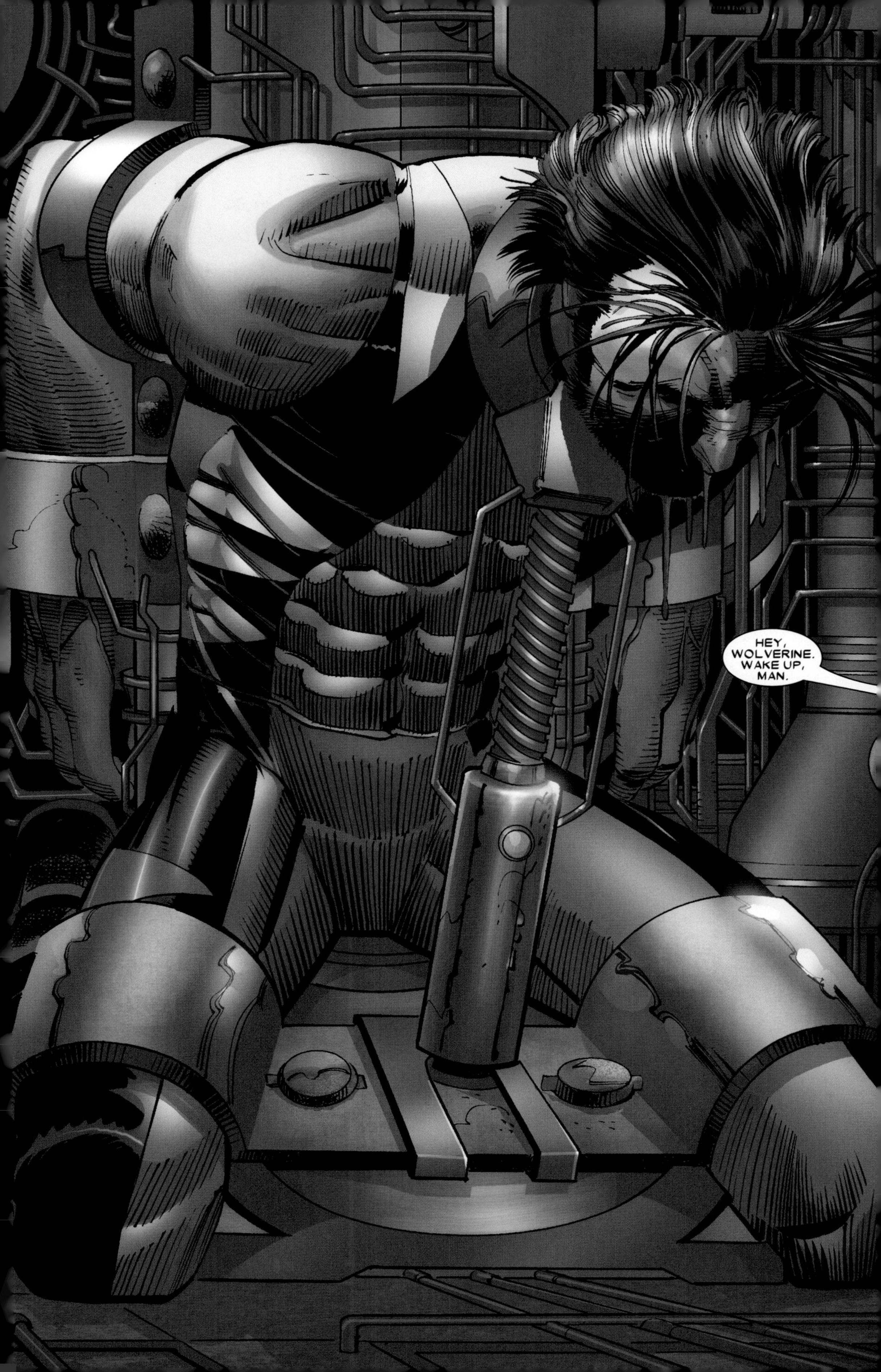
HEY, WOLVERINE. WAKE UP, MAN.

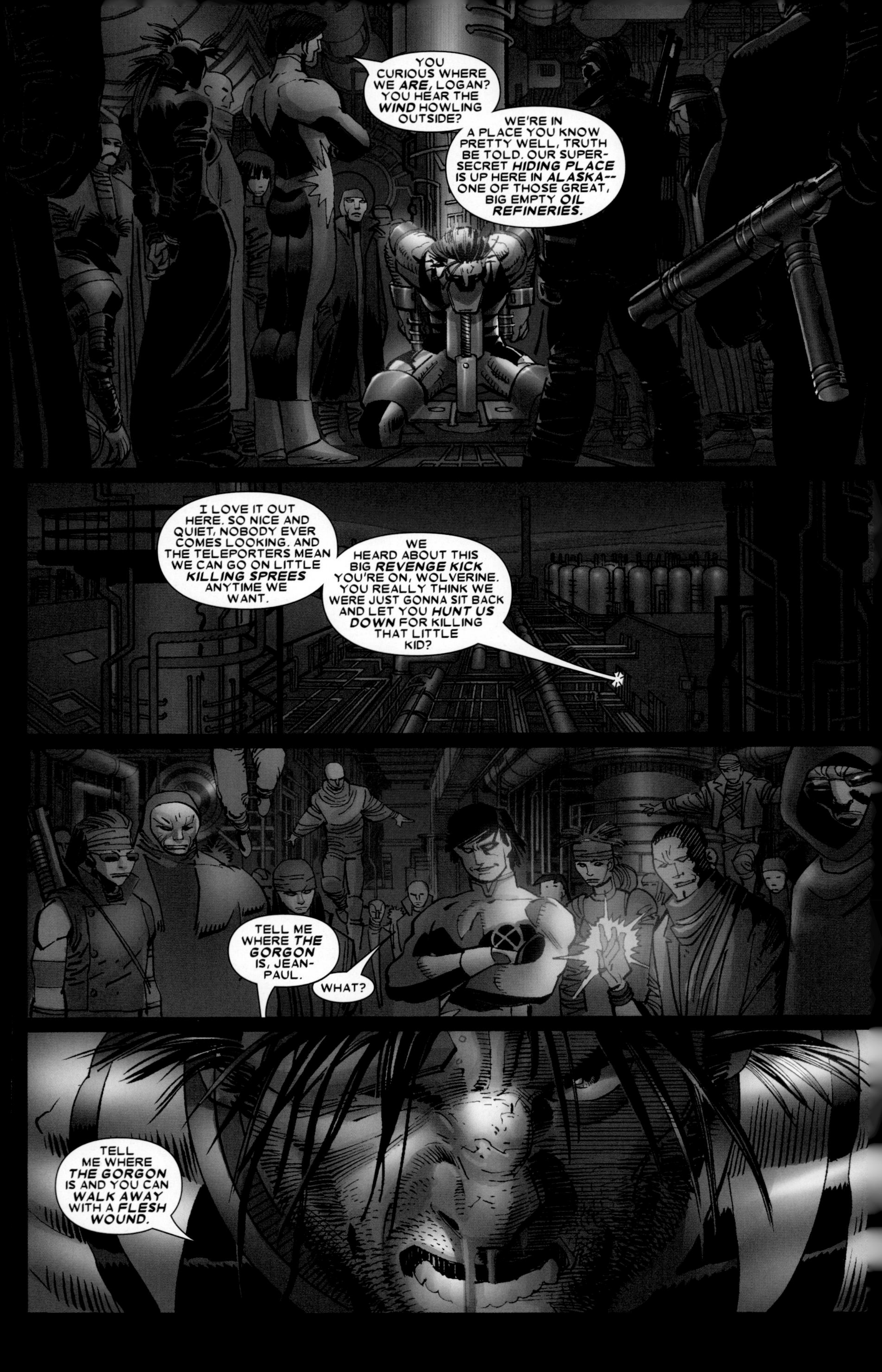
YOU CURIOUS WHERE WE *ARE*, LOGAN? YOU HEAR THE *WIND* HOWLING OUTSIDE?
WE'RE IN A PLACE YOU KNOW PRETTY WELL, TRUTH BE TOLD. OUR SUPER-SECRET *HIDING PLACE* IS UP HERE IN *ALASKA*-- ONE OF THOSE GREAT, BIG EMPTY *OIL REFINERIES.*
I LOVE IT OUT HERE. SO NICE AND QUIET, NOBODY EVER COMES LOOKING. AND THE TELEPORTERS MEAN WE CAN GO ON LITTLE *KILLING SPREES* ANYTIME WE WANT.
WE HEARD ABOUT THIS BIG *REVENGE KICK* YOU'RE ON, WOLVERINE. YOU REALLY THINK WE WERE JUST GONNA SIT BACK AND LET YOU *HUNT US DOWN* FOR KILLING THAT LITTLE KID?
TELL ME WHERE *THE GORGON* IS, JEAN-PAUL.
WHAT?
TELL ME WHERE *THE GORGON* IS AND YOU CAN *WALK AWAY* WITH A *FLESH WOUND.*

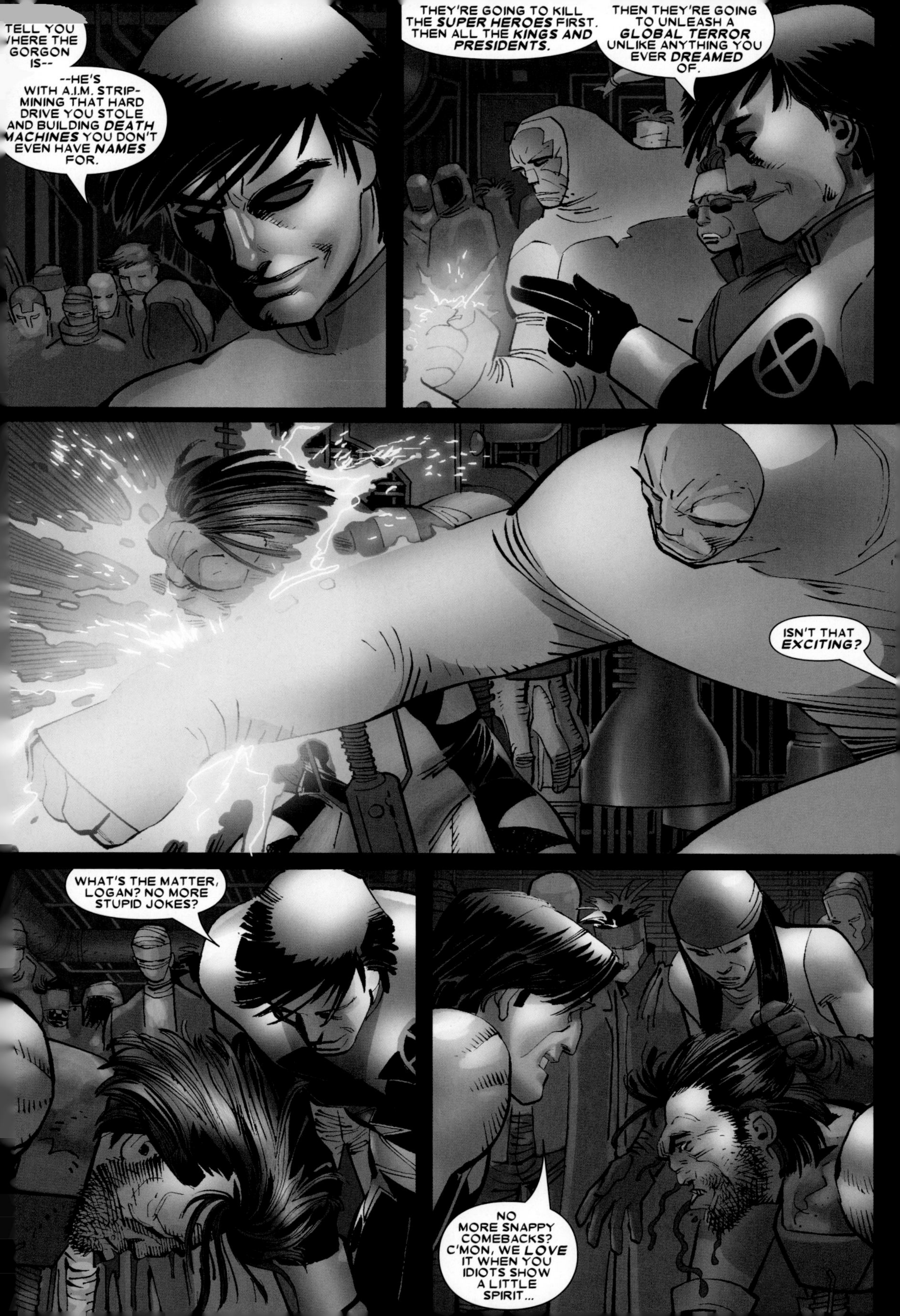
TELL YOU WHERE THE GORGON IS--
--HE'S WITH A.I.M. STRIP-MINING THAT HARD DRIVE YOU STOLE AND BUILDING *DEATH MACHINES* YOU DON'T EVEN HAVE *NAMES* FOR.
THEY'RE GOING TO KILL THE *SUPER HEROES* FIRST. THEN ALL THE *KINGS AND PRESIDENTS.*
THEN THEY'RE GOING TO UNLEASH A *GLOBAL TERROR* UNLIKE ANYTHING YOU EVER *DREAMED* OF.
ISN'T THAT *EXCITING?*
WHAT'S THE MATTER, LOGAN? NO MORE STUPID JOKES?
NO MORE SNAPPY COMEBACKS? C'MON, WE *LOVE* IT WHEN YOU IDIOTS SHOW A LITTLE SPIRIT...

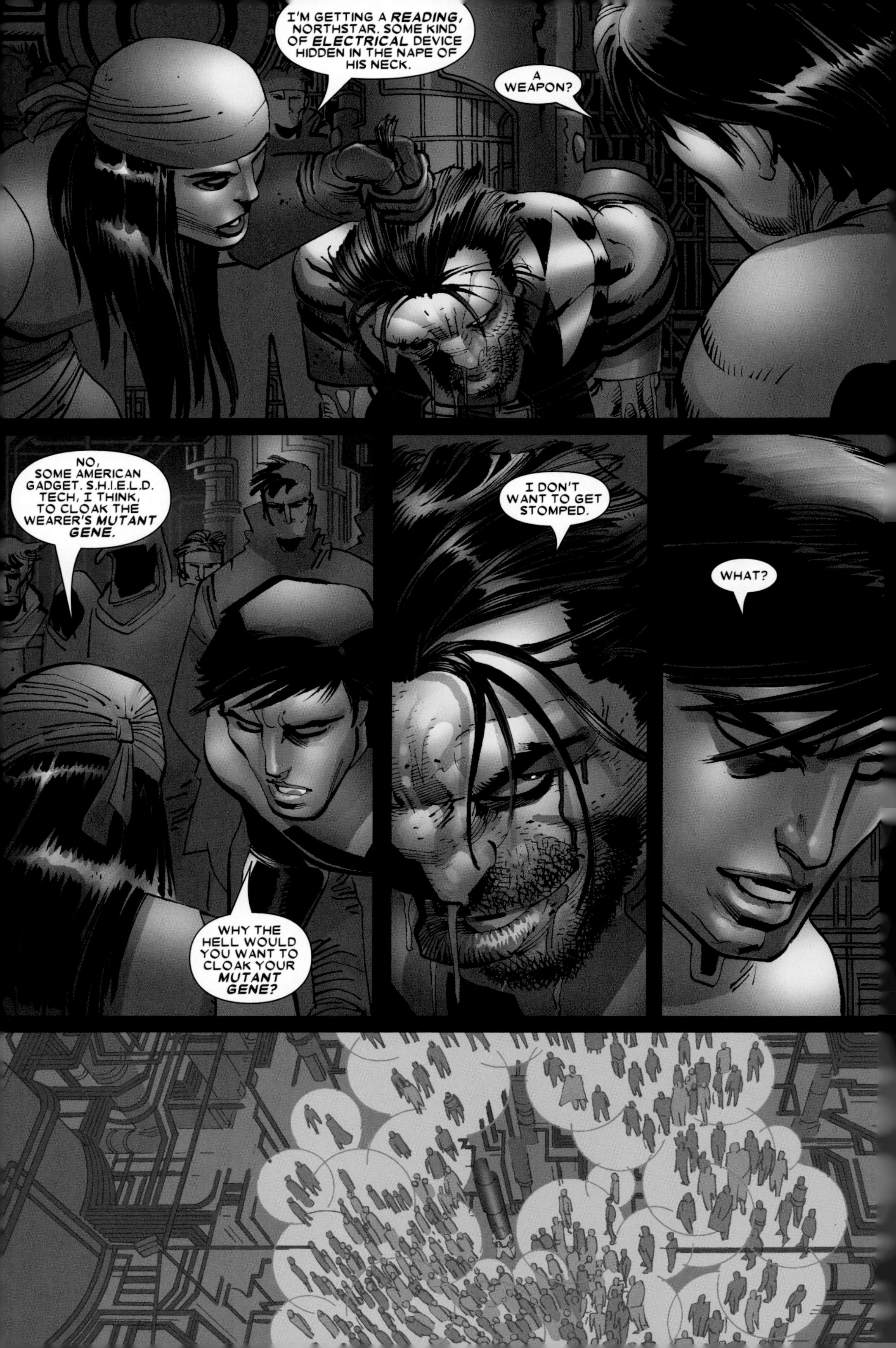
I'M GETTING A *READING*, NORTHSTAR. SOME KIND OF *ELECTRICAL* DEVICE HIDDEN IN THE NAPE OF HIS NECK.
A WEAPON?
NO, SOME AMERICAN GADGET. S.H.I.E.L.D. TECH, I THINK, TO CLOAK THE WEARER'S *MUTANT GENE.*
WHY THE HELL WOULD YOU WANT TO CLOAK YOUR *MUTANT GENE?*
I DON'T WANT TO GET STOMPED.
WHAT?

I HEARD THESE THINGS CRASH-LANDED IN RUSSIA AFTER SOME BIG FIGHT WITH THE AVENGERS.

AVENGERS. AVENGERS *CLASSIC.*

S.H.I.E.L.D. STEPPED IN WHEN THE RUSSIAN MOB TRIED TO SELL THEM TO THE IRAQIS A MONTH BEFORE THE WAR.

CAN YOU BELIEVE THE *NERVE* OF THOSE CLOWNS?

ALL THREE HAVE BEEN IN STORAGE EVER SINCE.

GATHERING DUST--

WAITING FOR SOME CRAZY GUY LIKE DOCTOR WEINBERG TO SIGN A FEW *RELEASE FORMS--*

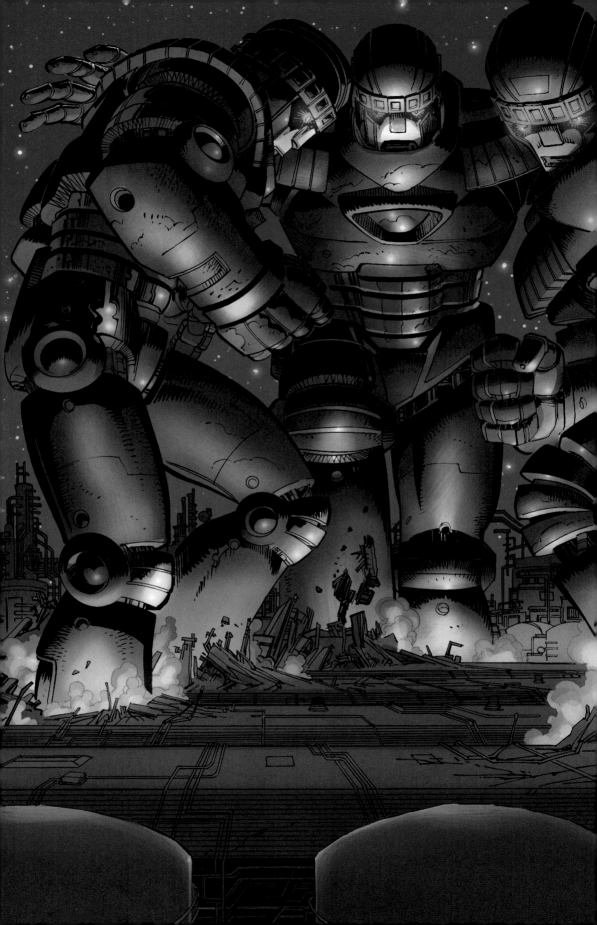

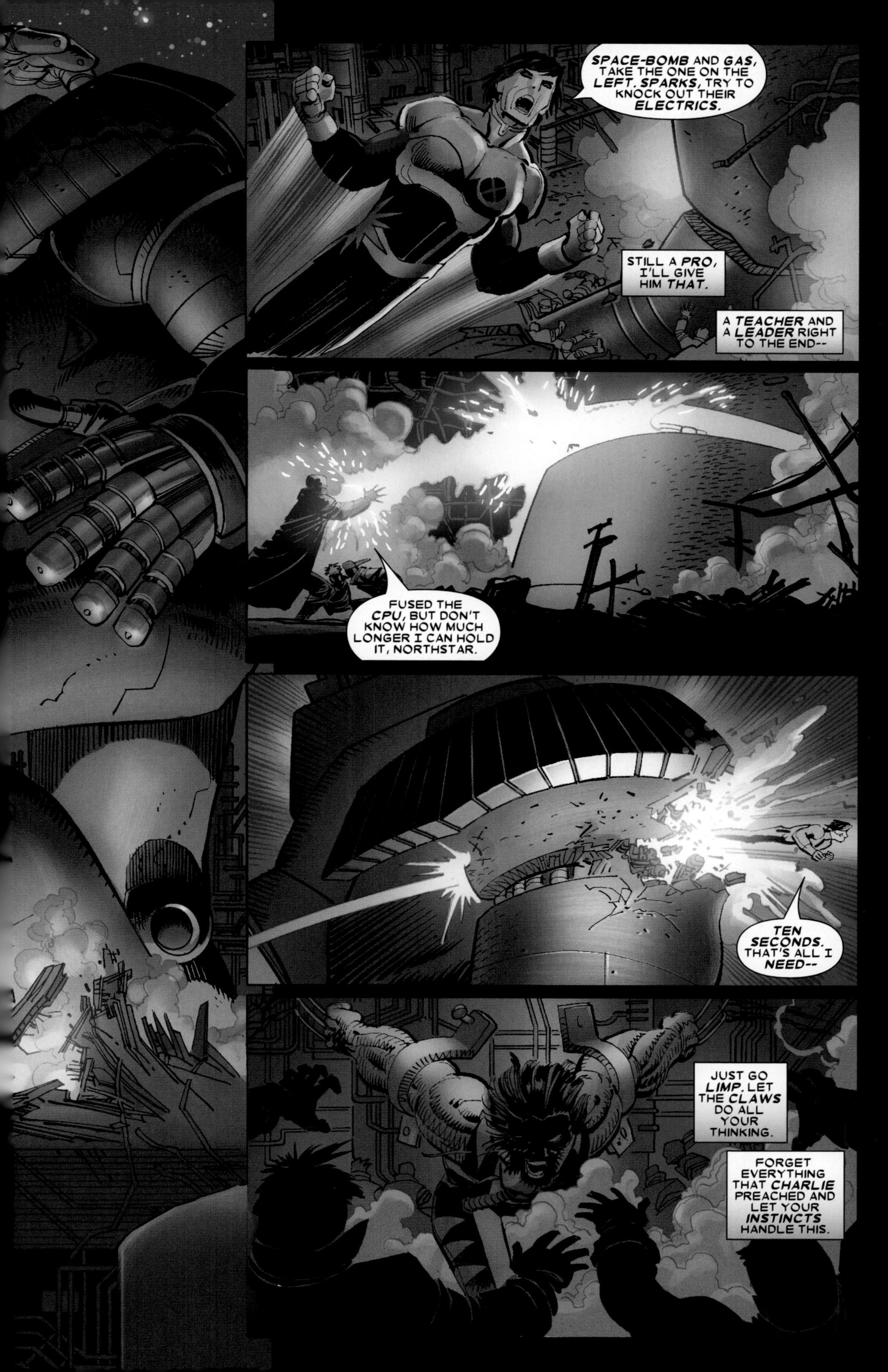
SPACE-BOMB AND GAS, TAKE THE ONE ON THE LEFT. SPARKS, TRY TO KNOCK OUT THEIR ELECTRICS.
STILL A PRO, I'LL GIVE HIM THAT.
A TEACHER AND A LEADER RIGHT TO THE END--
FUSED THE CPU, BUT DON'T KNOW HOW MUCH LONGER I CAN HOLD IT, NORTHSTAR.
TEN SECONDS. THAT'S ALL I NEED--
JUST GO LIMP. LET THE CLAWS DO ALL YOUR THINKING.
FORGET EVERYTHING THAT CHARLIE PREACHED AND LET YOUR INSTINCTS HANDLE THIS.

THERE'S NO *TIME* TO TAKE THE HIGH ROAD. TOO MUCH AT *STAKE* FOR THAT UTOPIAN BALONEY.

JUST SIZE THEM UP LIKE SIDES OF *BEEF*--

--AND MAKE YOUR *CUTS.*

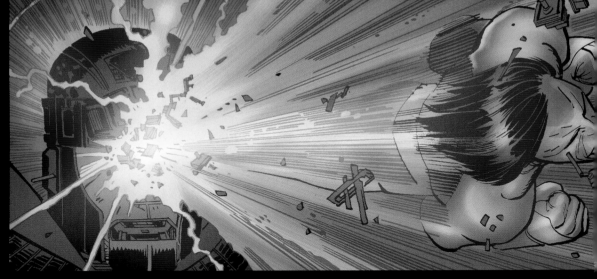

THERMOS, TURN THE LEGS AS BRITTLE AS YOU CAN! *ROCKSLIDE* AND *QUAKE,* FOLLOW THROUGH AND SHATTER THEIR *HULLS!*

WE CAN *DO* THIS! JUST STAY *FOCUSED!*

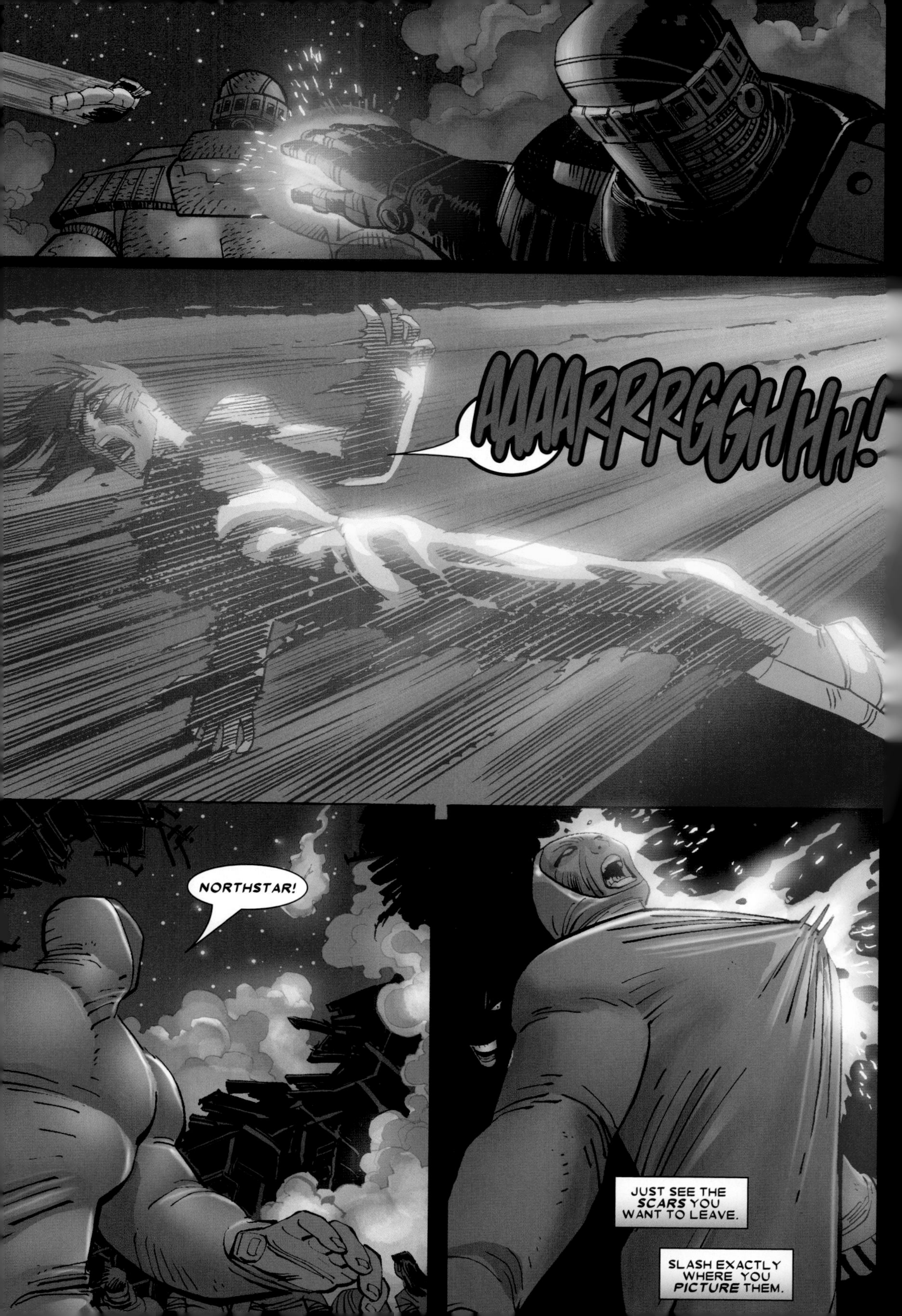
AAAARRRGGHHH!
NORTHSTAR!
JUST SEE THE SCARS YOU WANT TO LEAVE.
SLASH EXACTLY WHERE YOU PICTURE THEM.

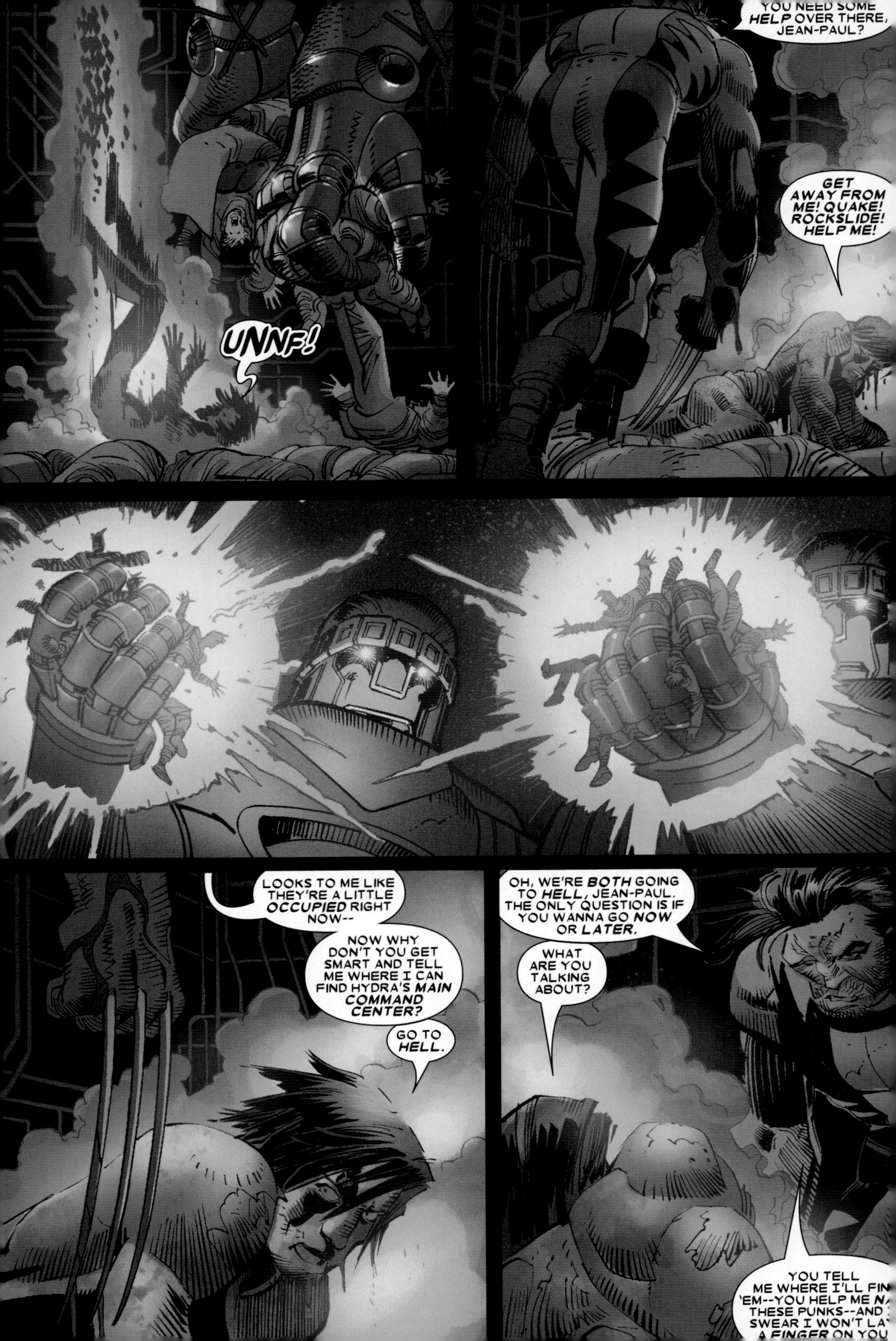
UNNF!
YOU NEED SOME HELP OVER THERE, JEAN-PAUL?
GET AWAY FROM ME! QUAKE! ROCKSLIDE! HELP ME!
LOOKS TO ME LIKE THEY'RE A LITTLE OCCUPIED RIGHT NOW--
NOW WHY DON'T YOU GET SMART AND TELL ME WHERE I CAN FIND HYDRA'S MAIN COMMAND CENTER?
GO TO HELL.
OH, WE'RE BOTH GOING TO HELL, JEAN-PAUL. THE ONLY QUESTION IS IF YOU WANNA GO NOW OR LATER.
WHAT ARE YOU TALKING ABOUT?
YOU TELL ME WHERE I'LL FIN 'EM--YOU HELP ME NA THESE PUNKS--AND I SWEAR I WON'T LA A FINGER ON YOU

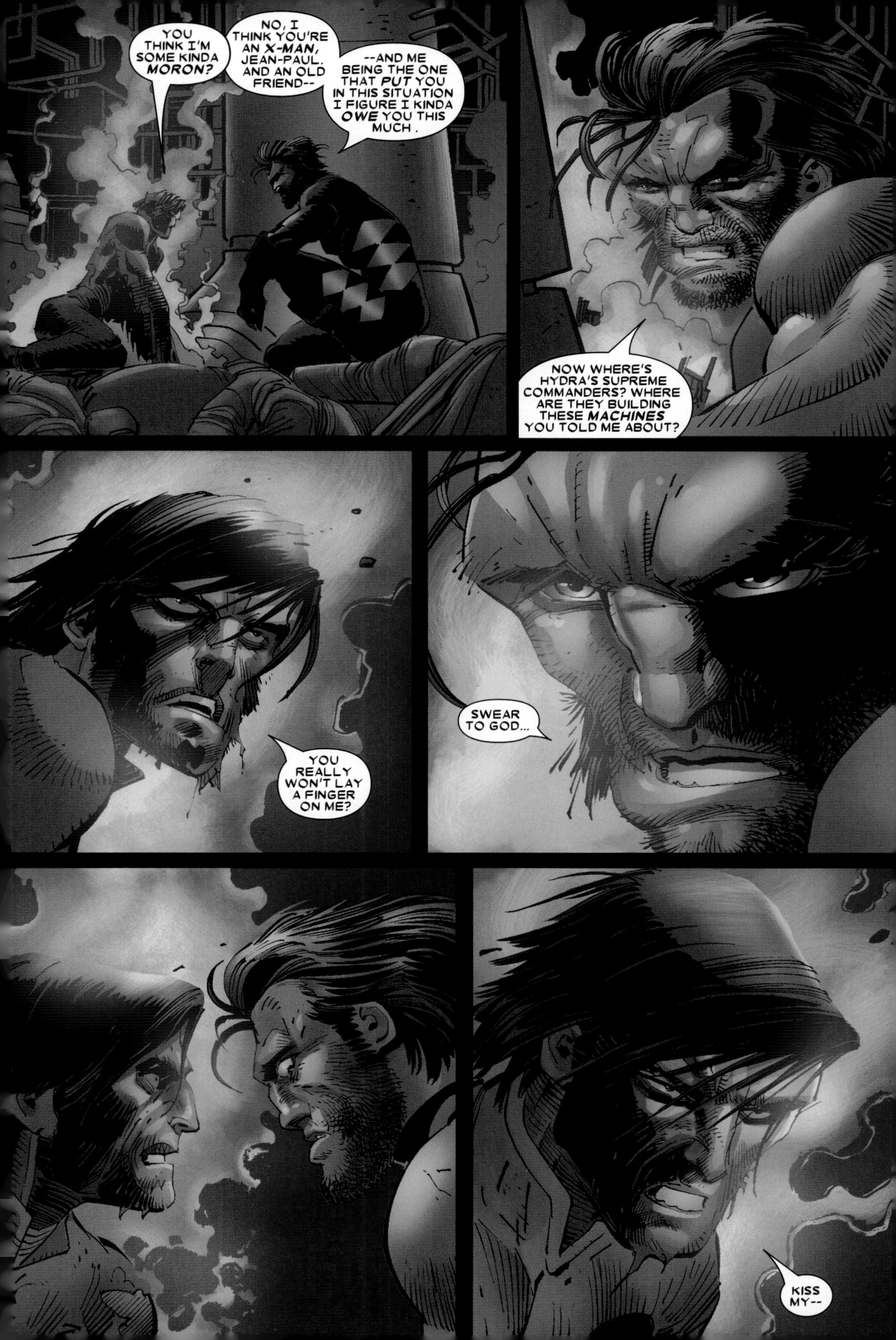
YOU THINK I'M SOME KINDA MORON?
NO, I THINK YOU'RE AN X-MAN, JEAN-PAUL. AND AN OLD FRIEND--
--AND ME BEING THE ONE THAT PUT YOU IN THIS SITUATION I FIGURE I KINDA OWE YOU THIS MUCH.
NOW WHERE'S HYDRA'S SUPREME COMMANDERS? WHERE ARE THEY BUILDING THESE MACHINES YOU TOLD ME ABOUT?
YOU REALLY WON'T LAY A FINGER ON ME?
SWEAR TO GOD...
KISS MY--

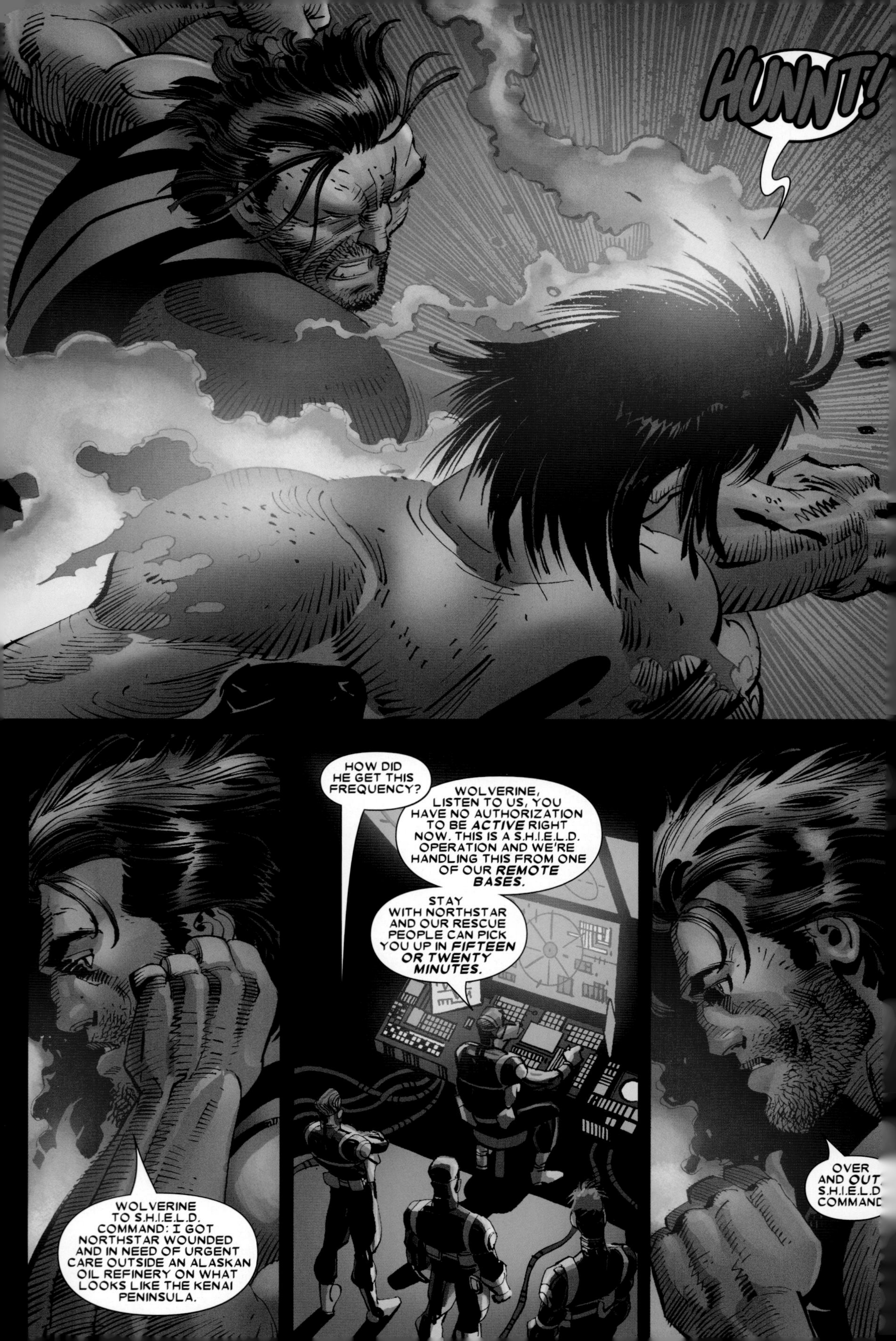
HUNNT!
WOLVERINE TO S.H.I.E.L.D. COMMAND: I GOT NORTHSTAR WOUNDED AND IN NEED OF URGENT CARE OUTSIDE AN ALASKAN OIL REFINERY ON WHAT LOOKS LIKE THE KENAI PENINSULA.
HOW DID HE GET THIS FREQUENCY?
WOLVERINE, LISTEN TO US, YOU HAVE NO AUTHORIZATION TO BE *ACTIVE* RIGHT NOW. THIS IS A S.H.I.E.L.D. OPERATION AND WE'RE HANDLING THIS FROM ONE OF OUR *REMOTE BASES.*
STAY WITH NORTHSTAR AND OUR RESCUE PEOPLE CAN PICK YOU UP IN *FIFTEEN OR TWENTY MINUTES.*
OVER AND *OUT,* S.H.I.E.L.D. COMMAND

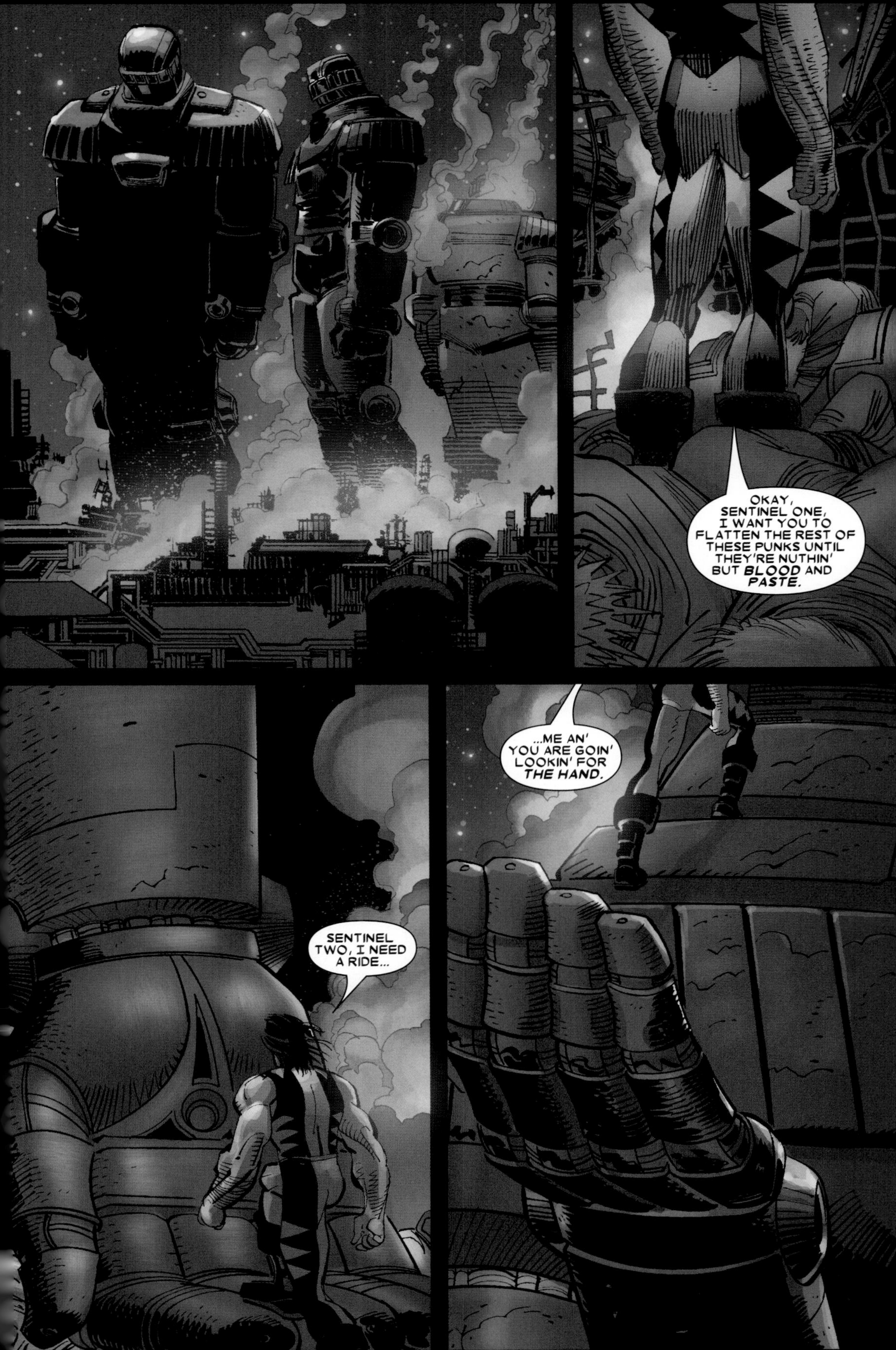
OKAY, SENTINEL ONE, I WANT YOU TO FLATTEN THE REST OF THESE PUNKS UNTIL THEY'RE NUTHIN' BUT *BLOOD* AND *PASTE.*
SENTINEL TWO, I NEED A RIDE...
...ME AN' YOU ARE GOIN' LOOKIN' FOR *THE HAND.*

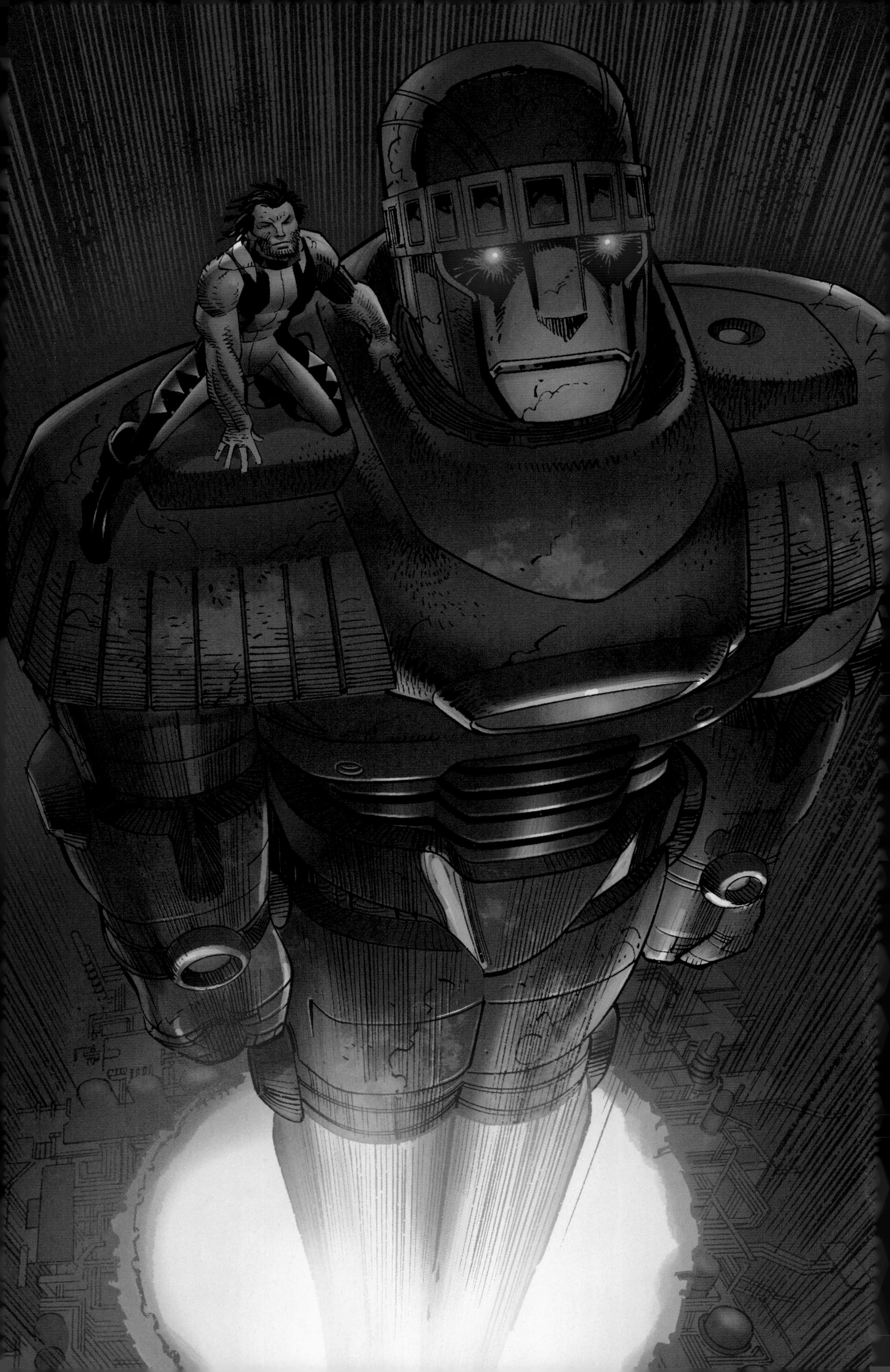

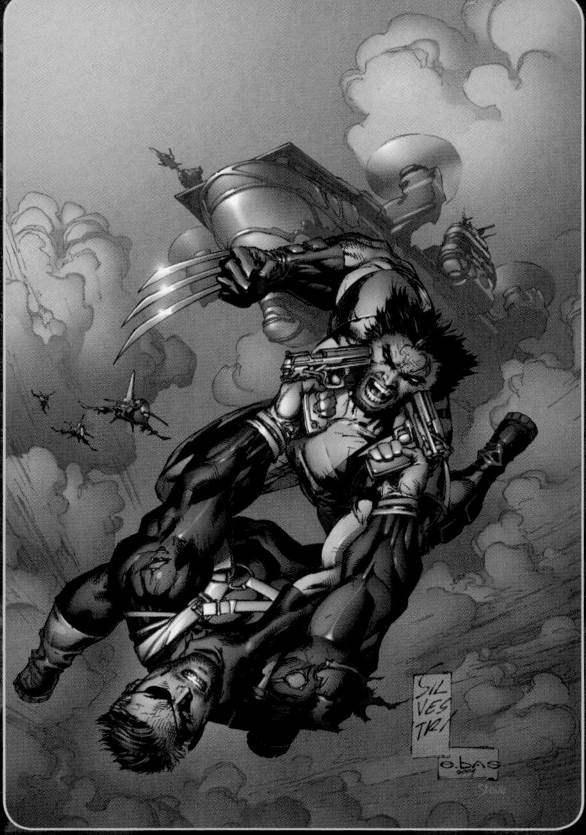

ISSUE #26 VARIANT

ISSUE #27 VARIANT

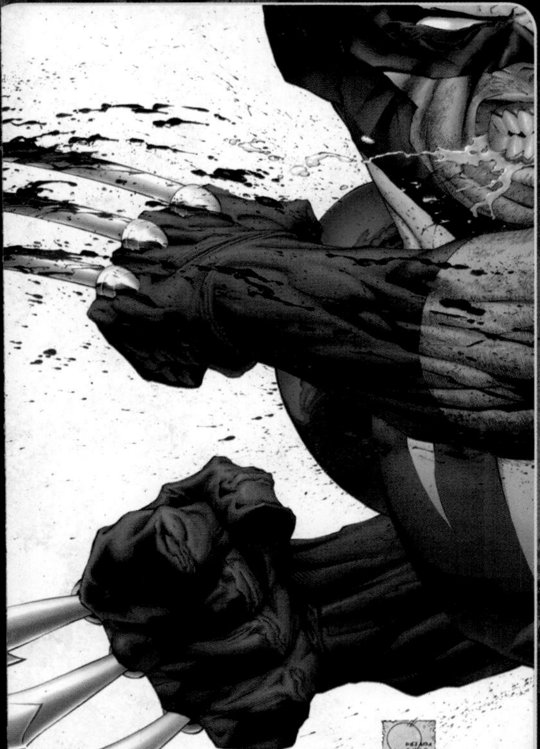

ISSUE #32 VARIANT

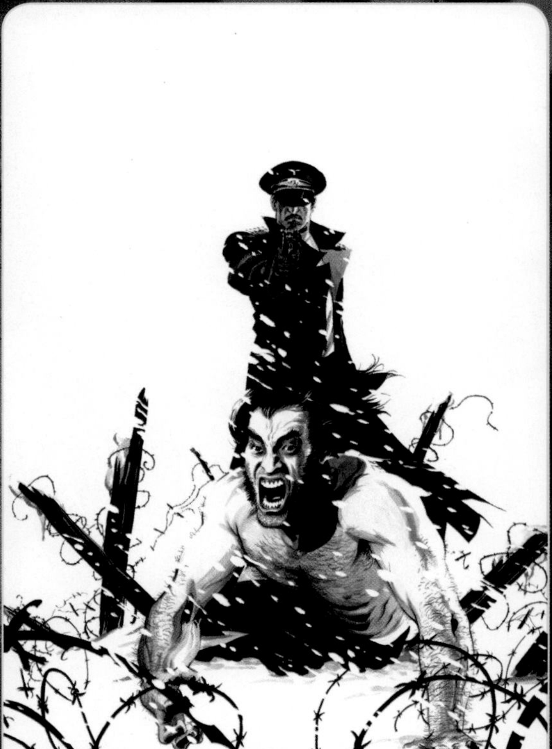

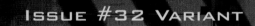

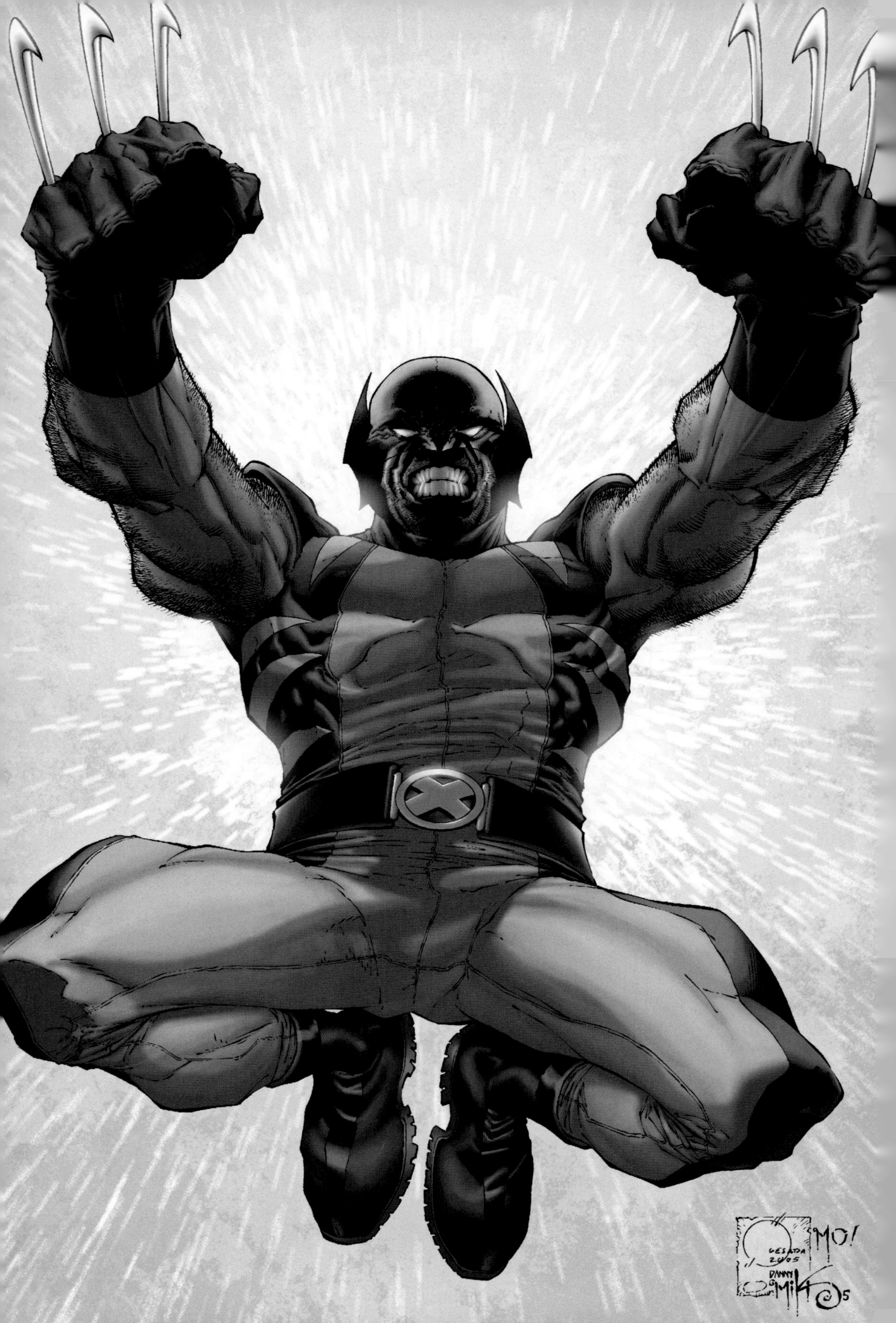

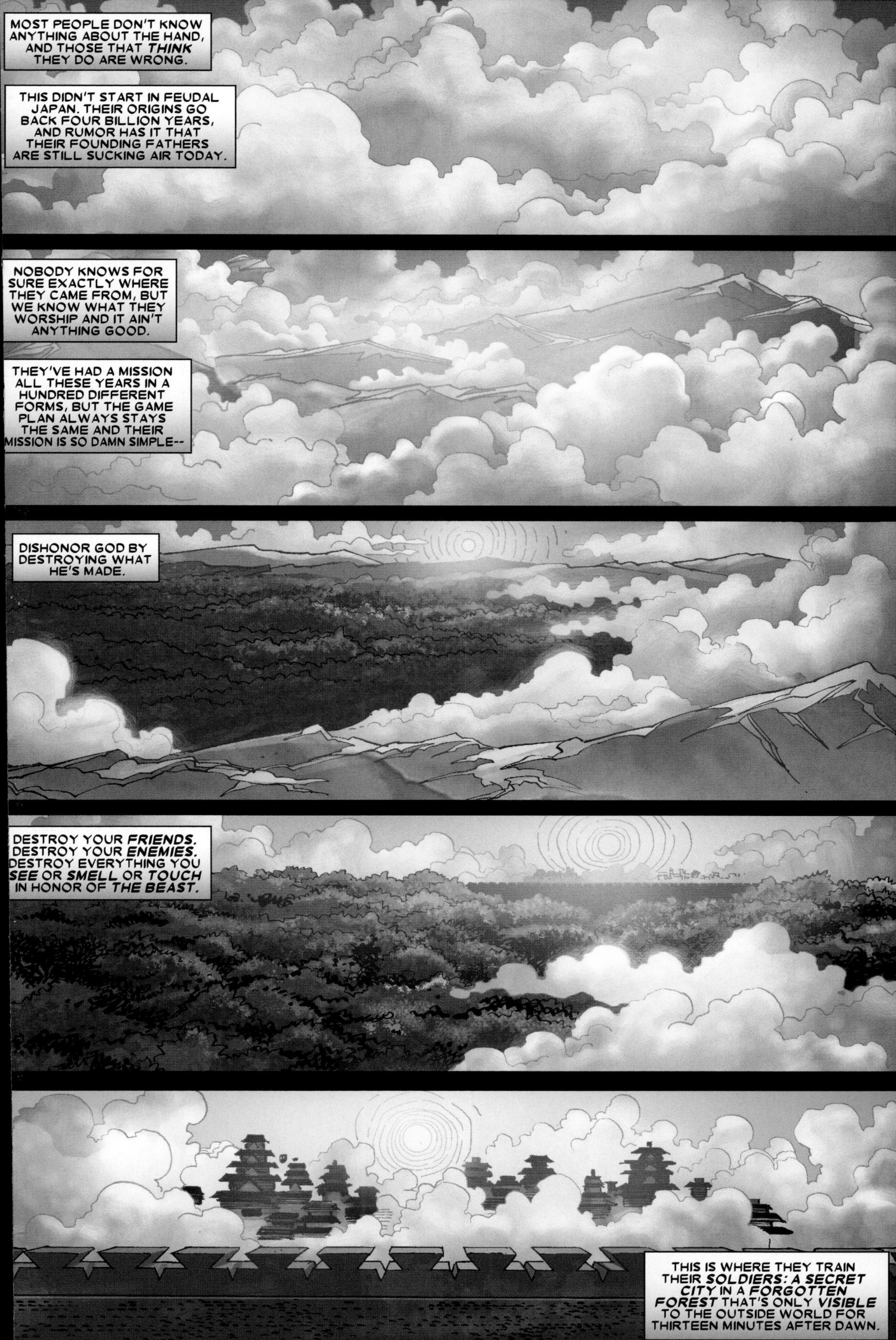
MOST PEOPLE DON'T KNOW ANYTHING ABOUT THE HAND, AND THOSE THAT *THINK* THEY DO ARE WRONG.
THIS DIDN'T START IN FEUDAL JAPAN. THEIR ORIGINS GO BACK FOUR BILLION YEARS, AND RUMOR HAS IT THAT THEIR FOUNDING FATHERS ARE STILL SUCKING AIR TODAY.
NOBODY KNOWS FOR SURE EXACTLY WHERE THEY CAME FROM, BUT WE KNOW WHAT THEY WORSHIP AND IT AIN'T ANYTHING GOOD.
THEY'VE HAD A MISSION ALL THESE YEARS IN A HUNDRED DIFFERENT FORMS, BUT THE GAME PLAN ALWAYS STAYS THE SAME AND THEIR MISSION IS SO DAMN SIMPLE--
DISHONOR GOD BY DESTROYING WHAT HE'S MADE.
DESTROY YOUR *FRIENDS*. DESTROY YOUR *ENEMIES*. DESTROY EVERYTHING YOU *SEE* OR *SMELL* OR *TOUCH* IN HONOR OF *THE BEAST*.
THIS IS WHERE THEY TRAIN THEIR *SOLDIERS: A SECRET CITY* IN A *FORGOTTEN FOREST* THAT'S ONLY *VISIBLE* TO THE OUTSIDE WORLD FOR THIRTEEN MINUTES AFTER DAWN.

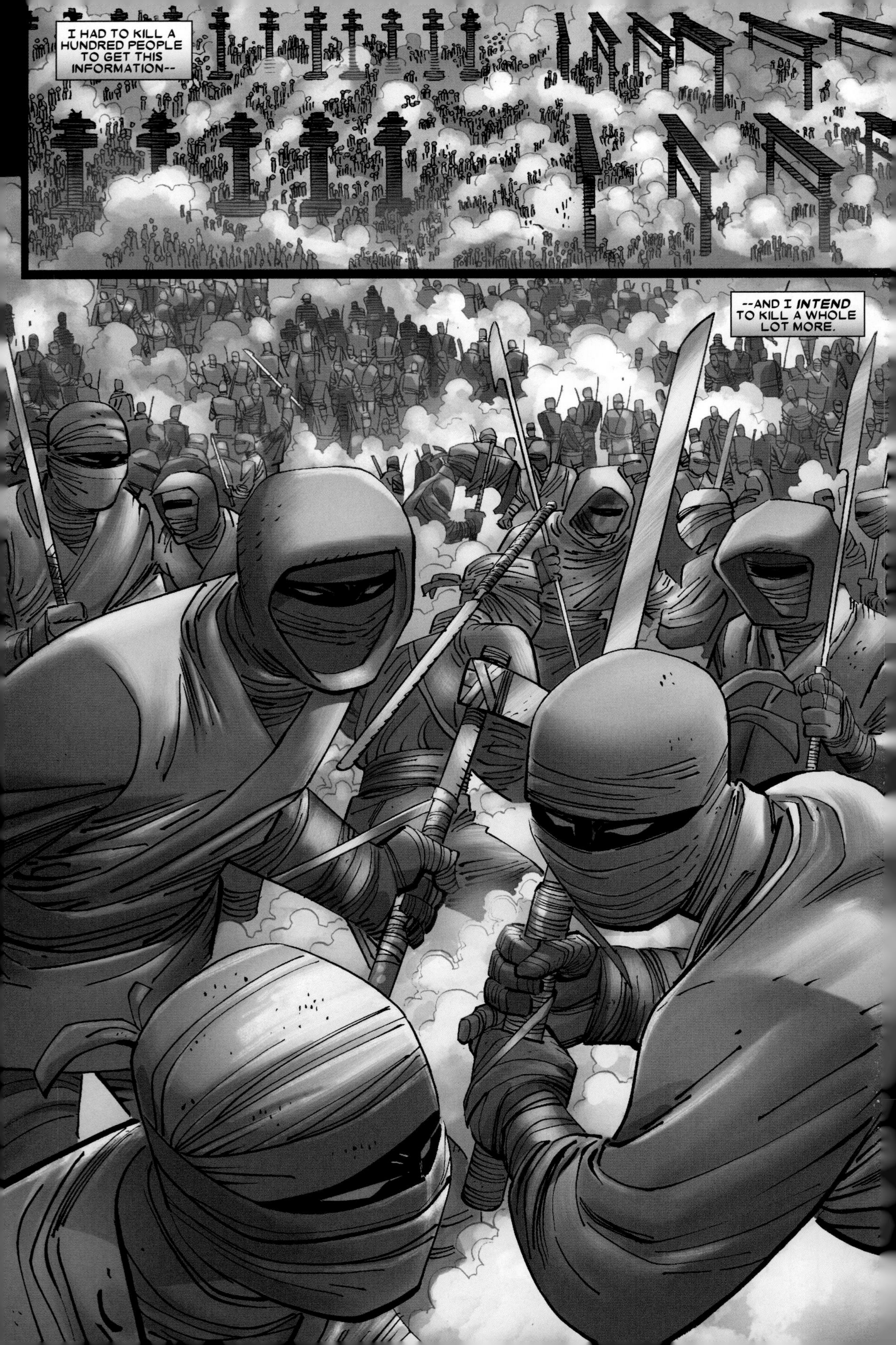
I HAD TO KILL A HUNDRED PEOPLE TO GET THIS INFORMATION--
--AND I *INTEND* TO KILL A WHOLE LOT MORE.

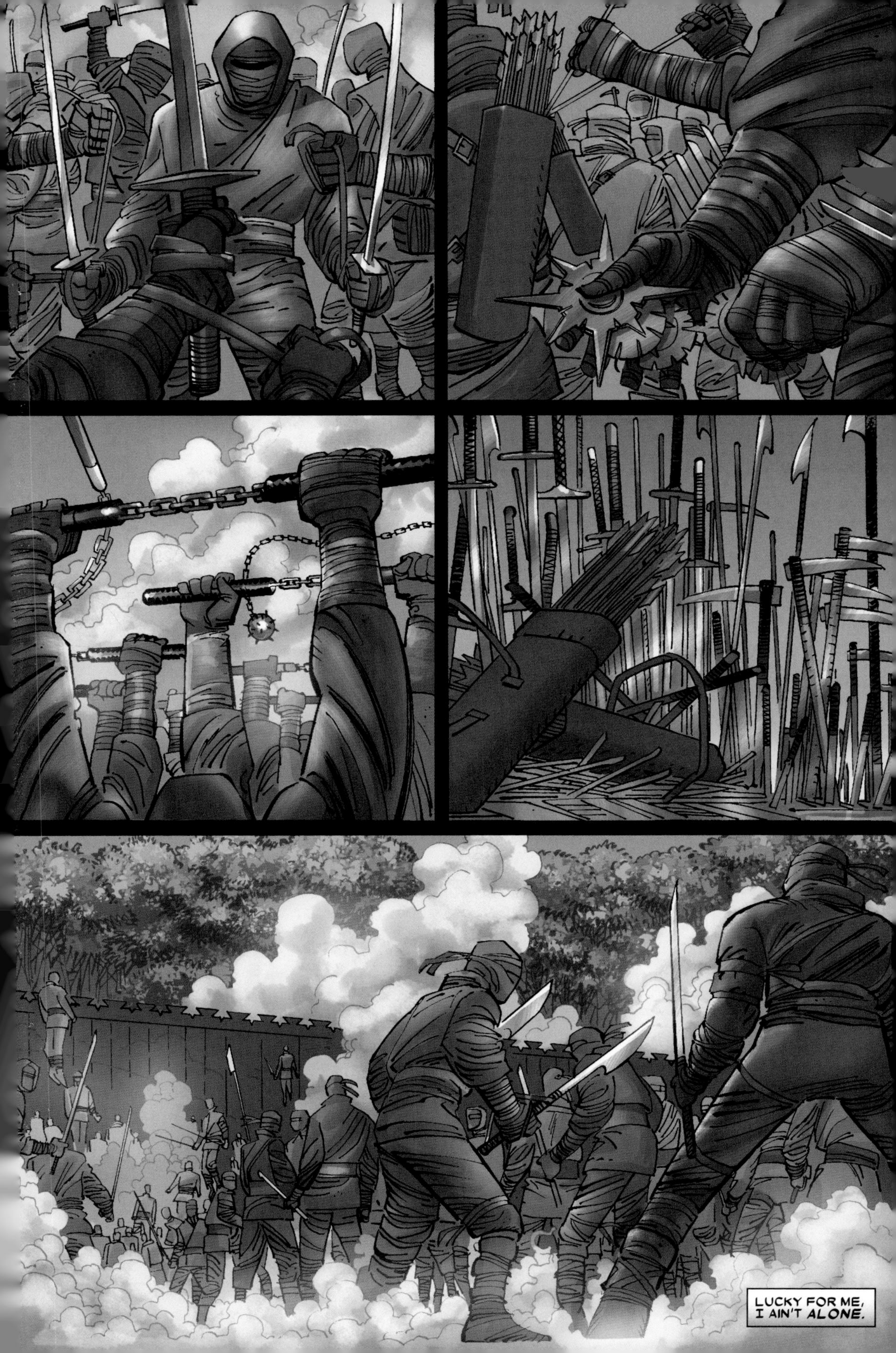
LUCKY FOR ME, I AIN'T ALONE.

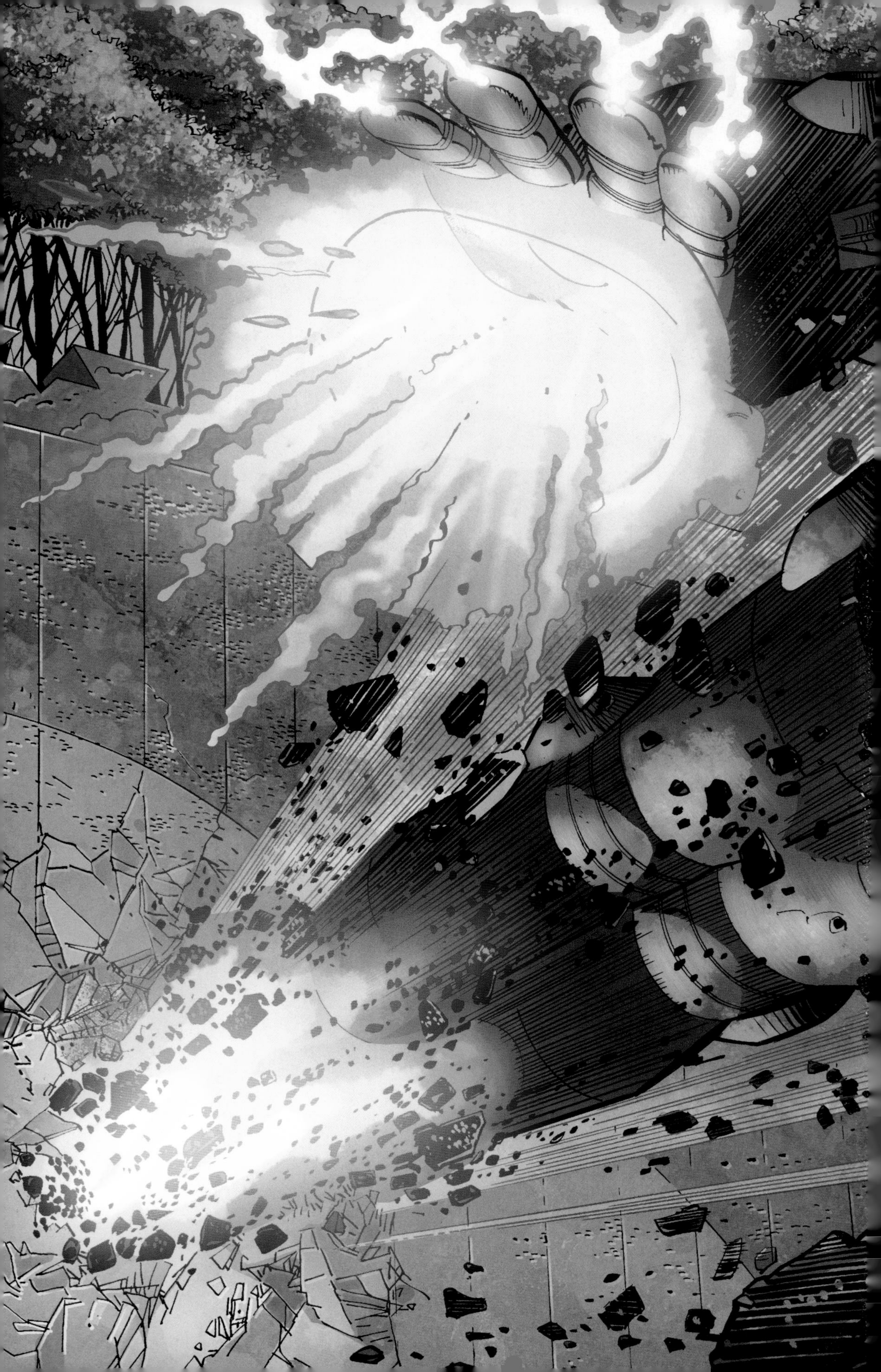

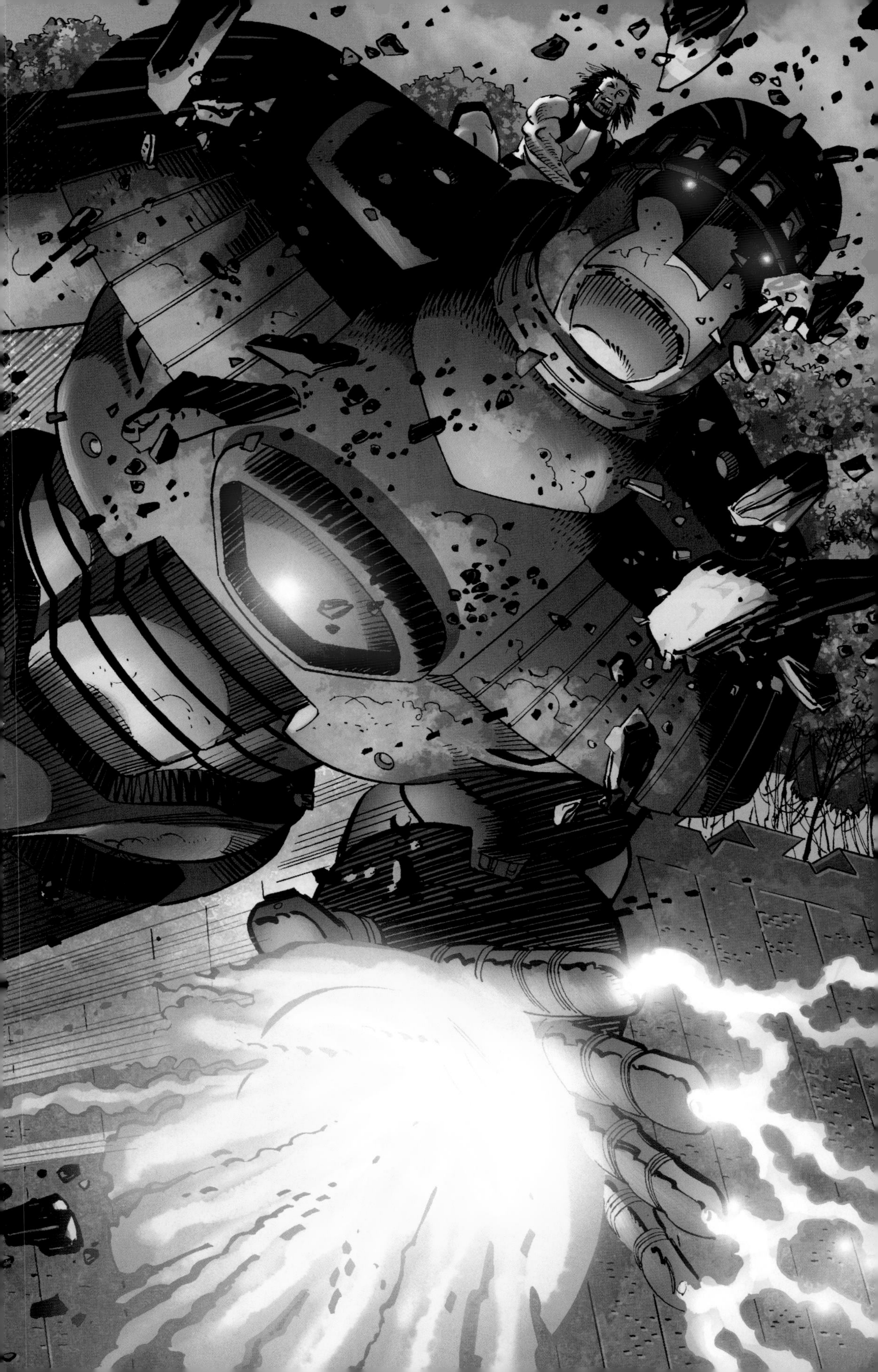

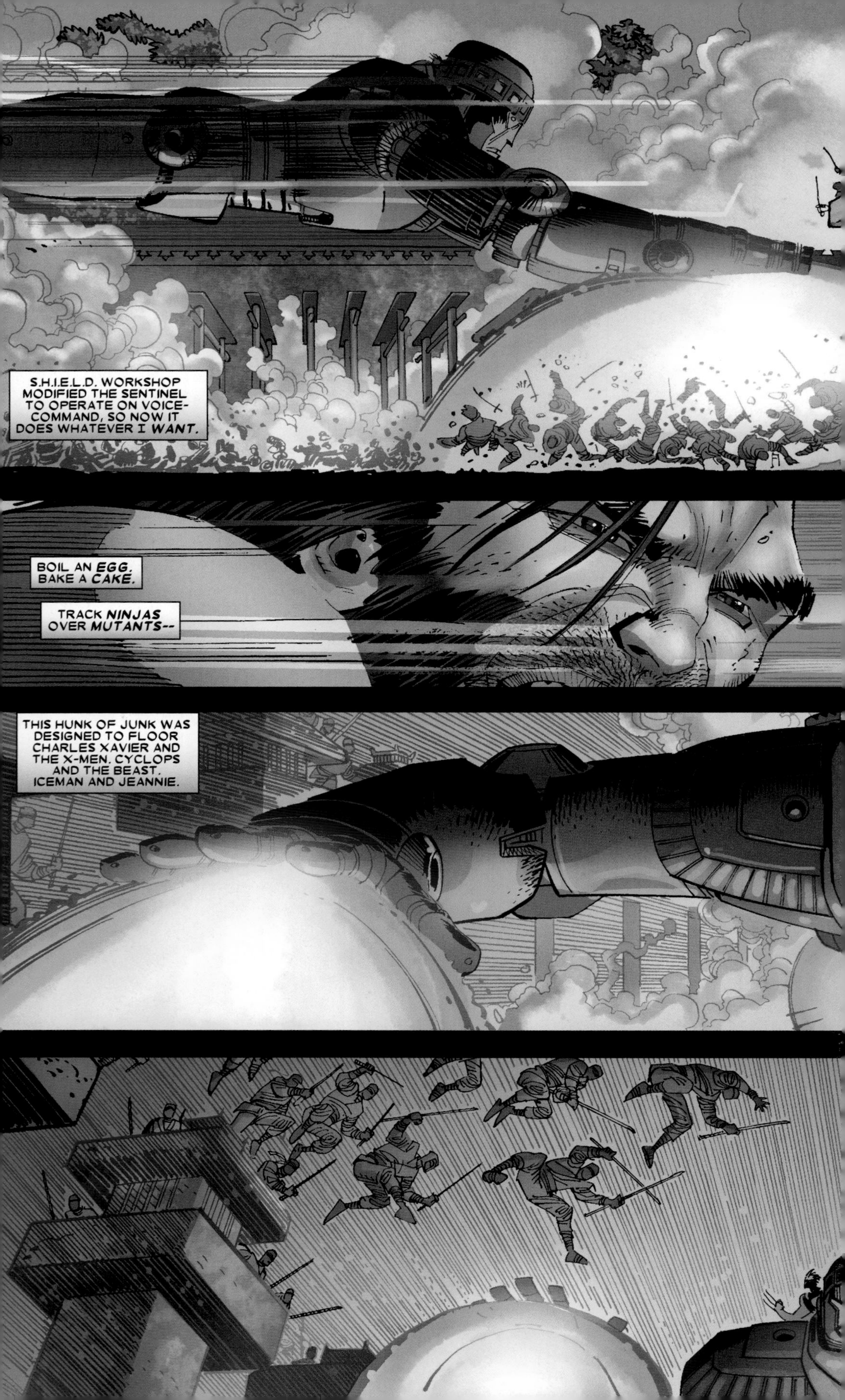
S.H.I.E.L.D. WORKSHOP MODIFIED THE SENTINEL TO OPERATE ON VOICE-COMMAND, SO NOW IT DOES WHATEVER I WANT.
BOIL AN EGG. BAKE A CAKE.
TRACK NINJAS OVER MUTANTS--
THIS HUNK OF JUNK WAS DESIGNED TO FLOOR CHARLES XAVIER AND THE X-MEN. CYCLOPS AND THE BEAST. ICEMAN AND JEANNIE.

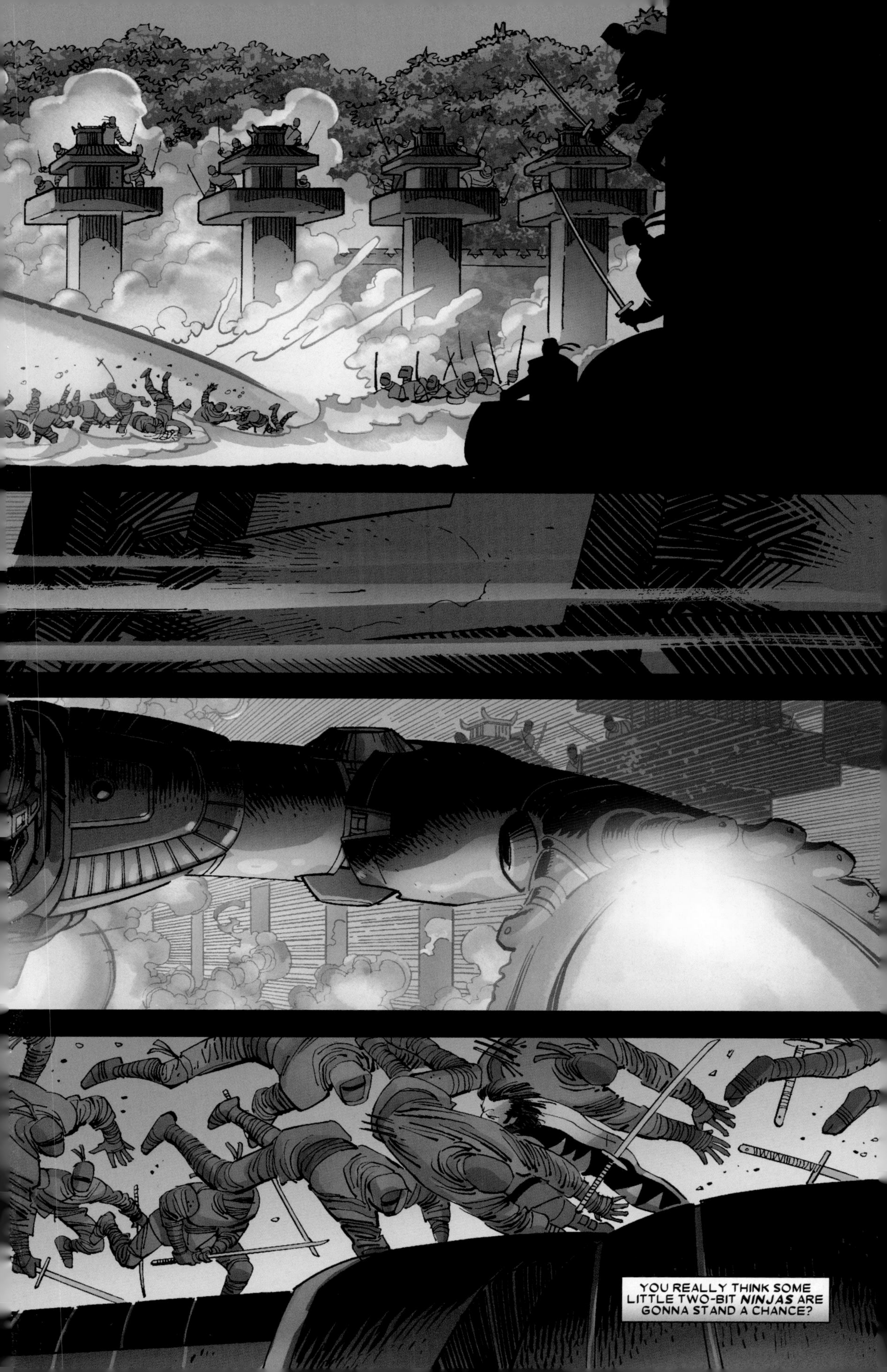
YOU REALLY THINK SOME LITTLE TWO-BIT NINJAS ARE GONNA STAND A CHANCE?

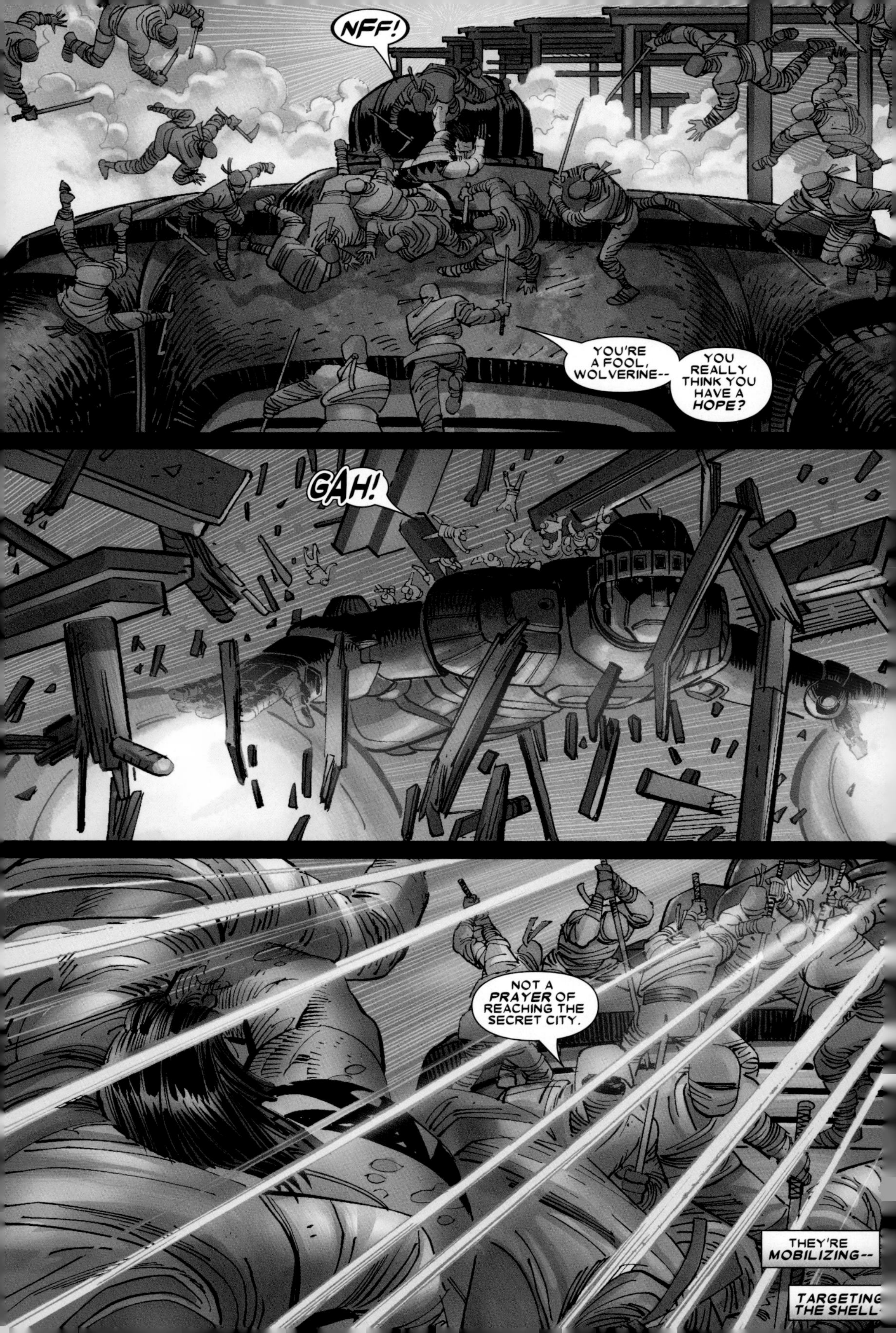
NFF!
YOU'RE A FOOL, WOLVERINE--
YOU REALLY THINK YOU HAVE A HOPE?
GAH!
NOT A PRAYER OF REACHING THE SECRET CITY.
THEY'RE MOBILIZING--
TARGETING THE SHELL--

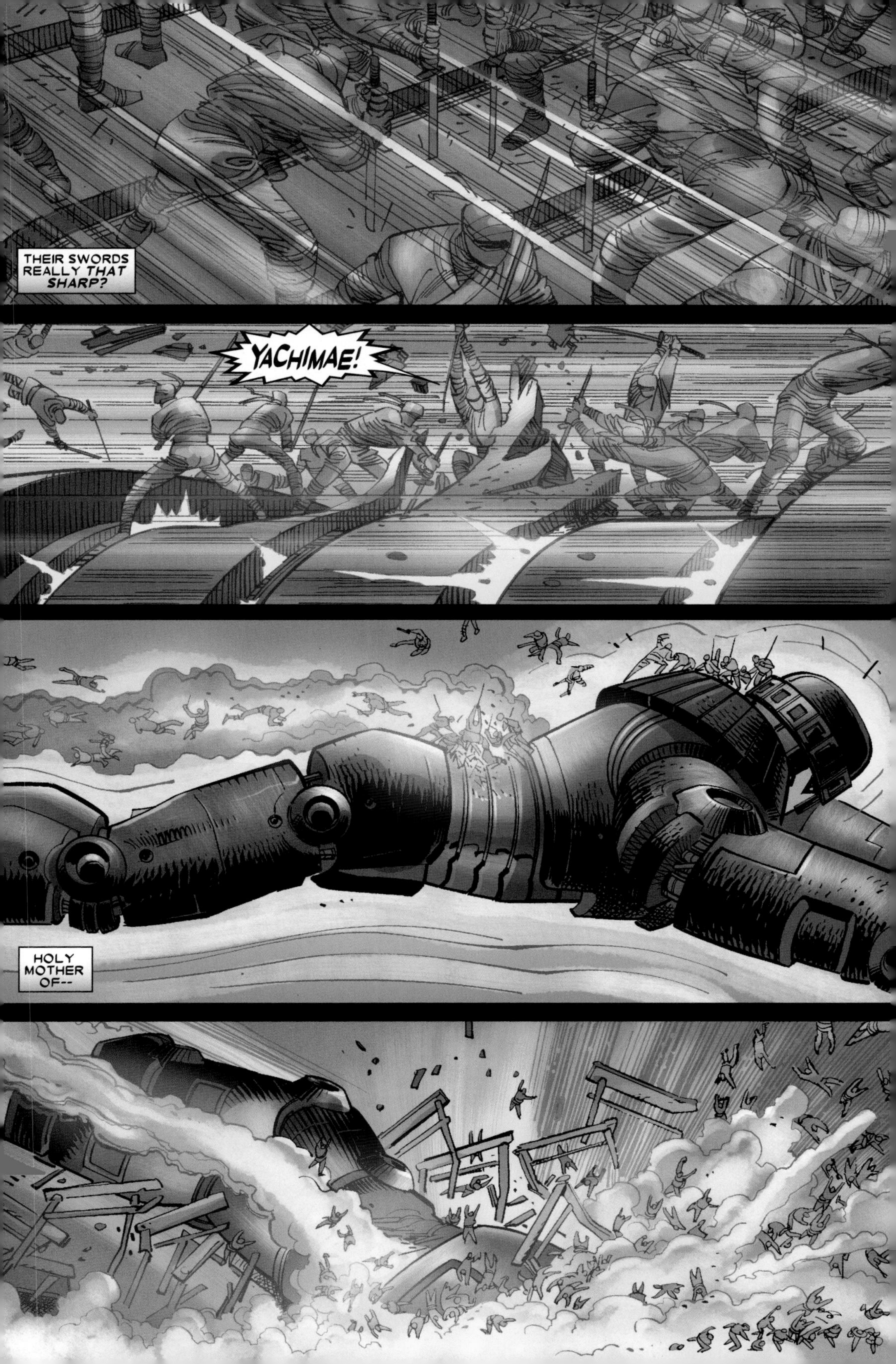
THEIR SWORDS REALLY THAT SHARP?
YACHIMAE!
HOLY MOTHER OF--

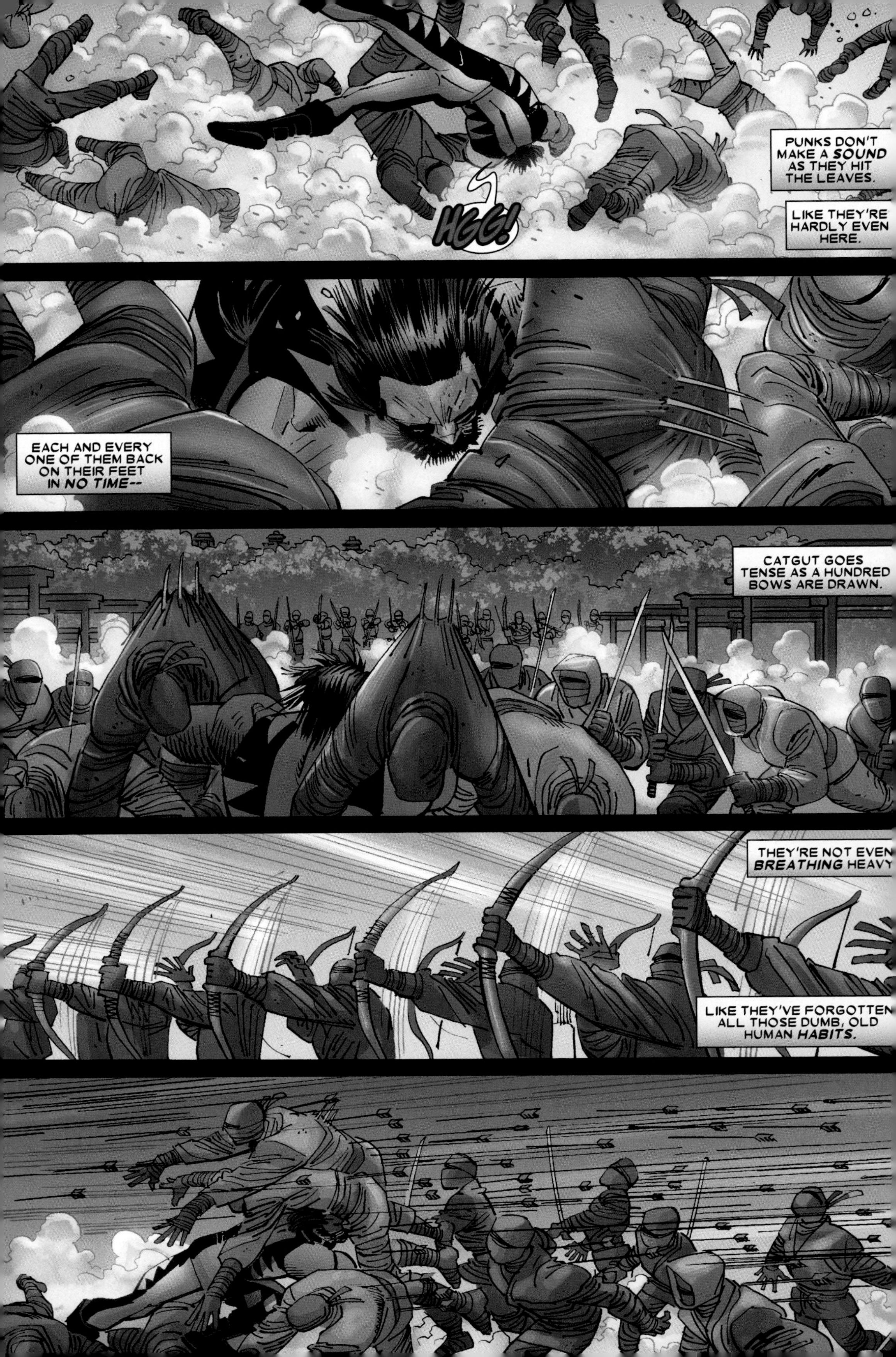
HGG!
PUNKS DON'T MAKE A SOUND AS THEY HIT THE LEAVES.
LIKE THEY'RE HARDLY EVEN HERE.
EACH AND EVERY ONE OF THEM BACK ON THEIR FEET IN NO TIME--
CATGUT GOES TENSE AS A HUNDRED BOWS ARE DRAWN.
THEY'RE NOT EVEN BREATHING HEAVY
LIKE THEY'VE FORGOTTEN ALL THOSE DUMB, OLD HUMAN HABITS.

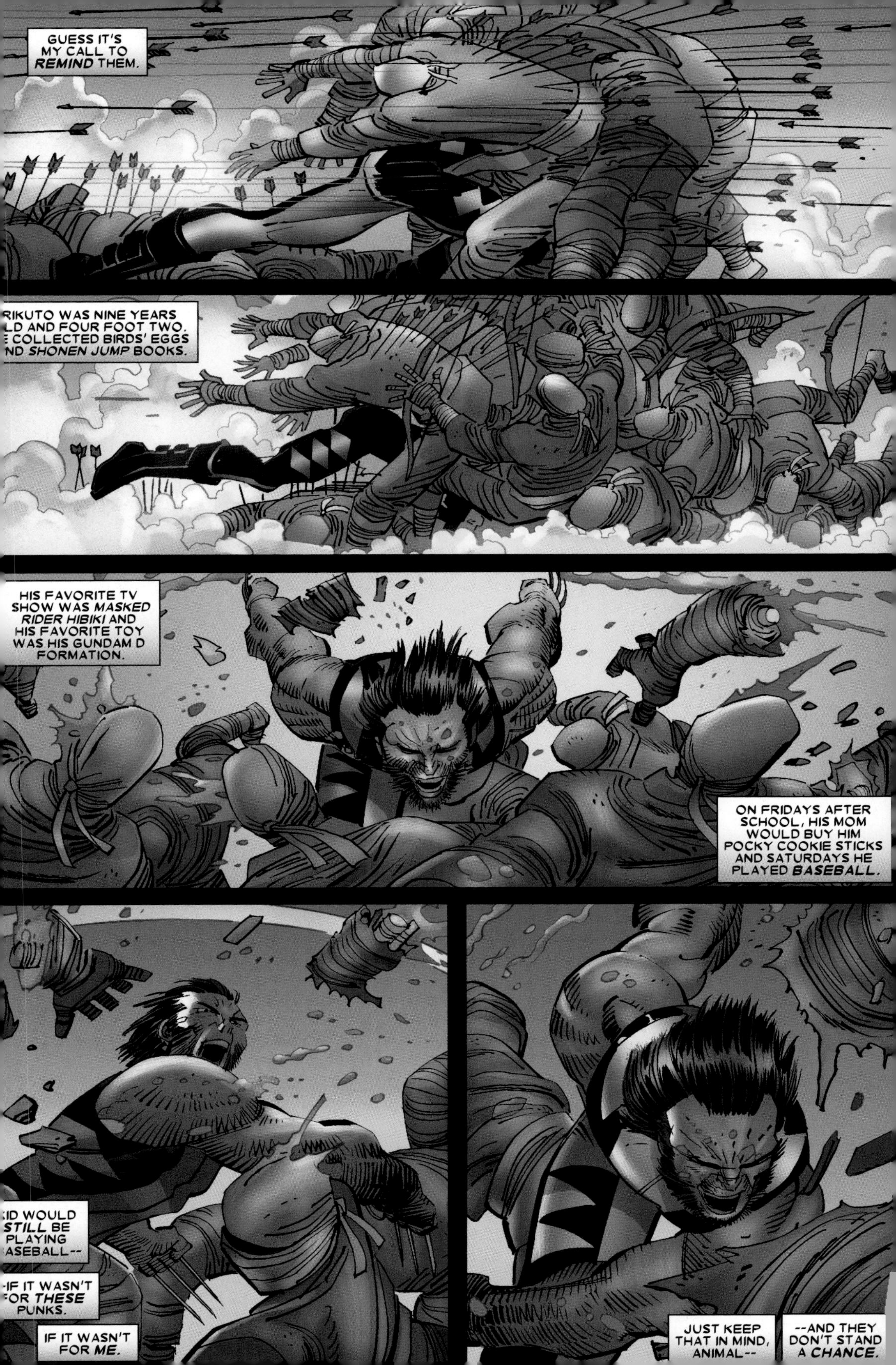
GUESS IT'S MY CALL TO *REMIND* THEM.
RIKUTO WAS NINE YEARS LD AND FOUR FOOT TWO. E COLLECTED BIRDS' EGGS ND *SHONEN JUMP* BOOKS.
HIS FAVORITE TV SHOW WAS *MASKED RIDER HIBIKI* AND HIS FAVORITE TOY WAS HIS GUNDAM D FORMATION.
ON FRIDAYS AFTER SCHOOL, HIS MOM WOULD BUY HIM POCKY COOKIE STICKS AND SATURDAYS HE PLAYED *BASEBALL*.
ID WOULD *STILL* BE PLAYING ASEBALL--
-IF IT WASN'T FOR *THESE* PUNKS.
IF IT WASN'T FOR *ME*.
JUST KEEP THAT IN MIND, ANIMAL--
--AND THEY DON'T STAND A *CHANCE*.

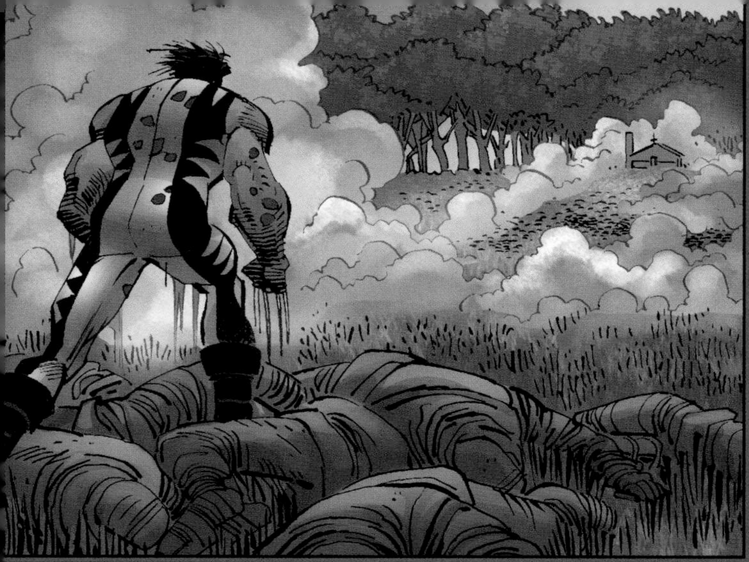

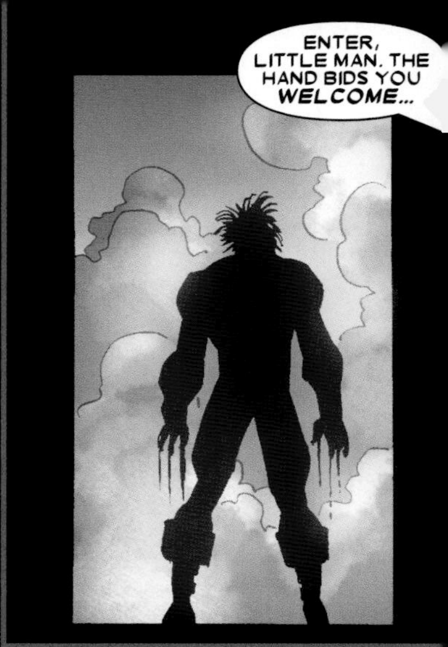
ENTER, LITTLE MAN. THE HAND BIDS YOU WELCOME...

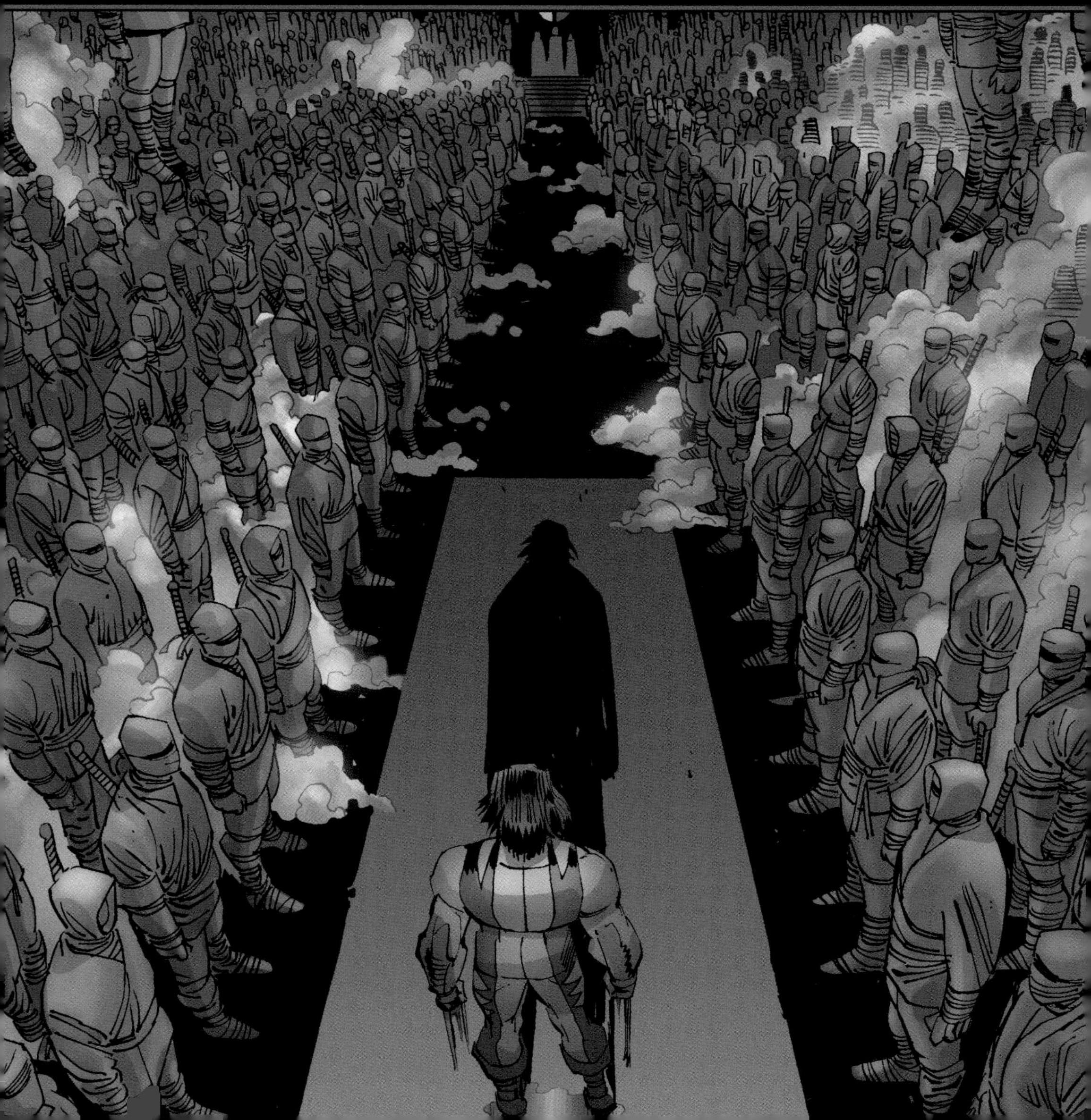

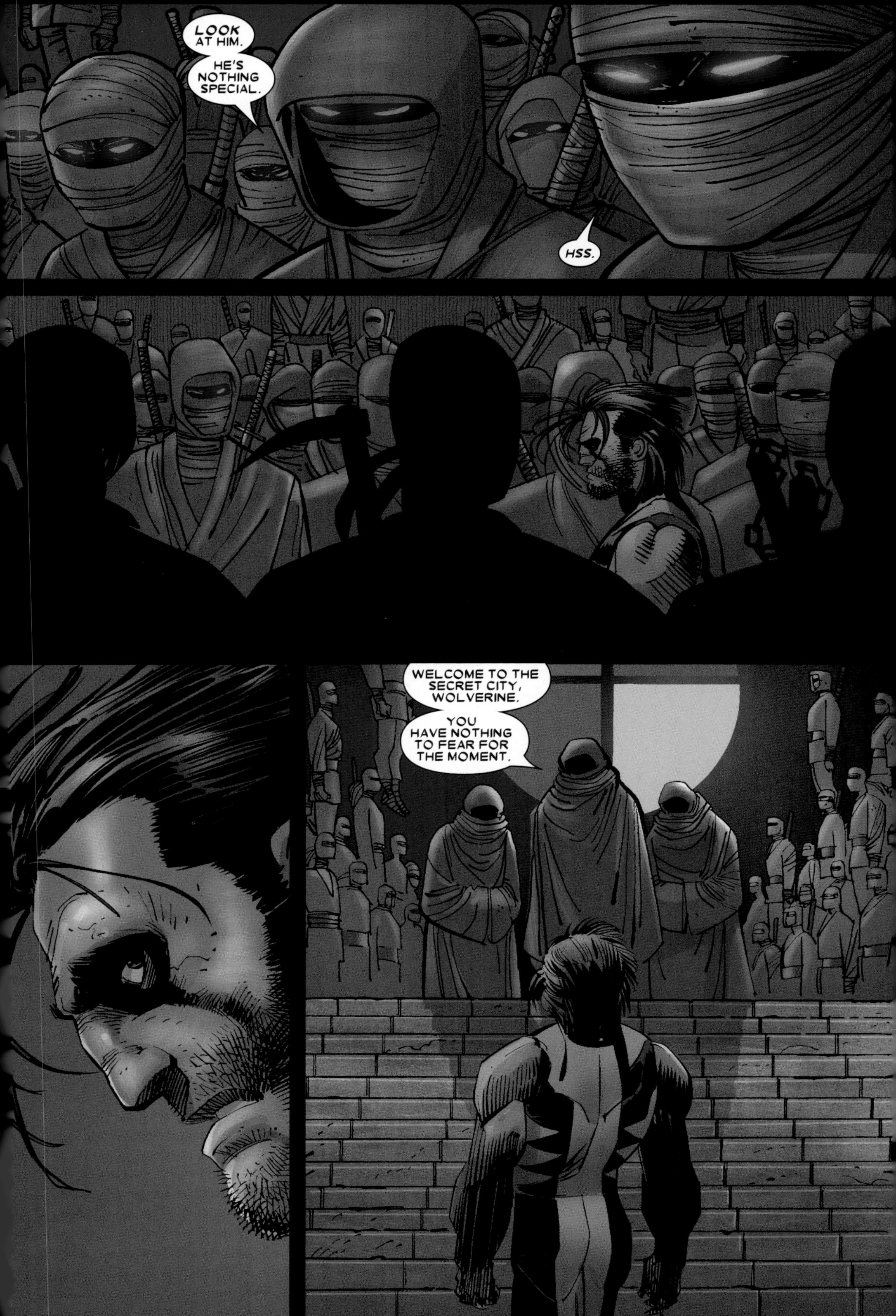
LOOK AT HIM.
HE'S NOTHING SPECIAL.
HSS.
WELCOME TO THE SECRET CITY, WOLVERINE.
YOU HAVE NOTHING TO FEAR FOR THE MOMENT.

MY BROTHERS HAVE FORGOTTEN THE *DESIRE* FOR VOICE, BUT THEIR *EARS* STILL FUNCTION WELL.

WE KNOW WHY YOU ARE HERE AND IT *AMUSES* US.

NOT FOR LONG.

SUCH A *BRAVE* LITTLE FOOL. DO YOU REALLY THINK YOU SHALL SURVIVE THIS EXPERIENCE? WE ARE SICKLY *NOW*, BUT WE ARE *VETERANS* OF *THE OLDEST WAR.*

OUR BATTLE WAS THE STUFF OF *LEGENDS* AND OUR SOLDIERS HERE HAVE EACH BEEN TAUGHT THE *ASPECTS* OF OUR DARKEST TALENTS.

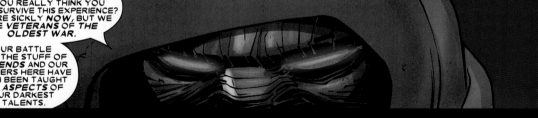

TELL ME WHERE THE GORGON IS AND I'LL ONLY *BURN* THIS PLACE TO THE GROUND.

WITH WHAT? THOSE *TRINKETS* IN YOUR BELT? YOUR TECHNOLOGY MEANS LITTLE TO US, WOLVERINE--

--AND IF YOU WANT THE GORGON--FORMER *HIGH PRIEST OF THE HAND*--YOU NEED LOOK NO FURTHER THAN THE *DEATH* IN YOUR CITIES AND THE *FEAR* ON EVERY FACE.

FORMER?

HE LEADS *HYDRA* NOW, USHERING IN *THE END,* WITH *INFINITE RESOURCES.* BUT THE HAND STILL NEEDS A LEADER...A QUEEN HERE IN OUR INFERNAL PALACE.

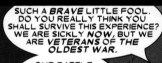

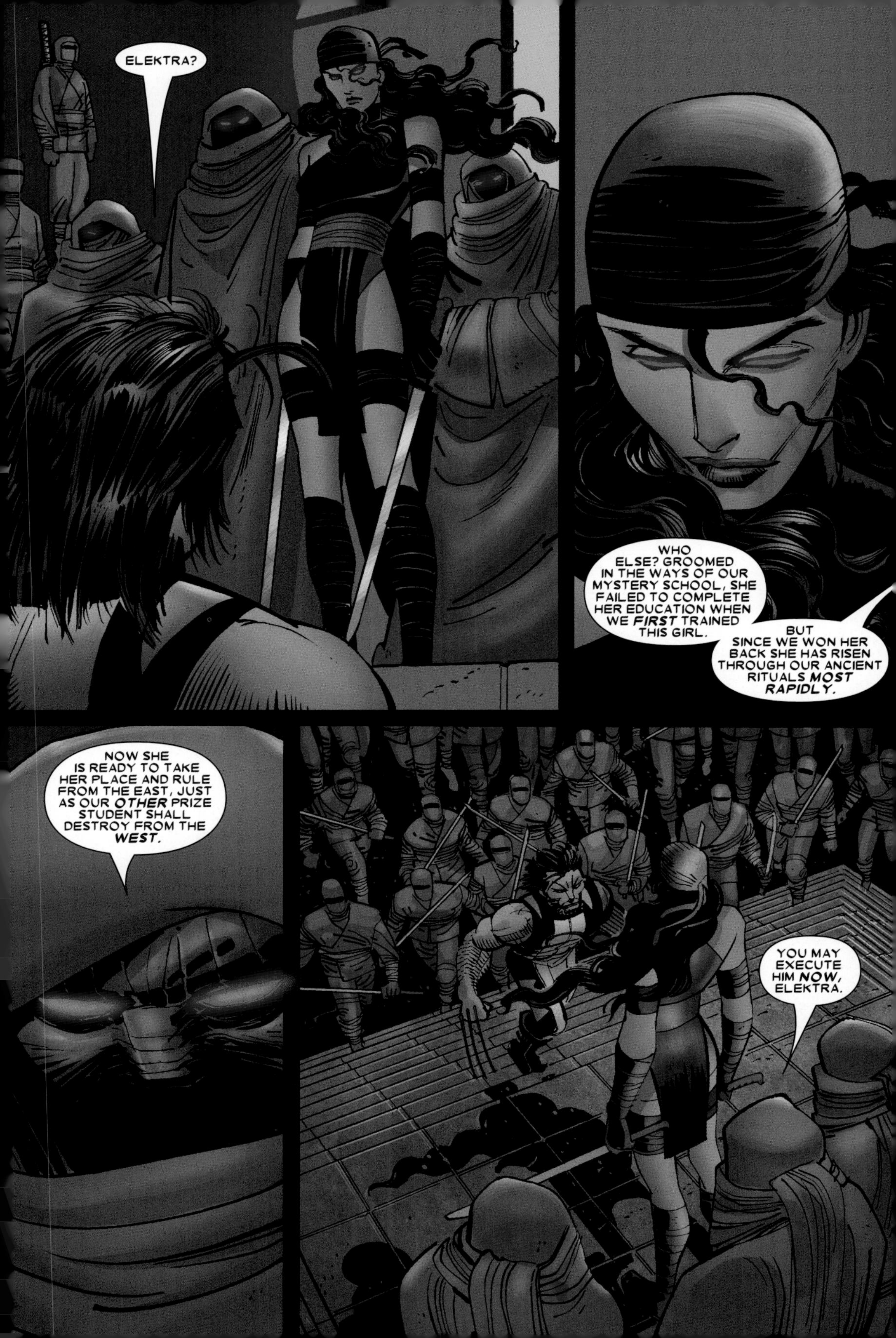
ELEKTRA?
WHO ELSE? GROOMED IN THE WAYS OF OUR MYSTERY SCHOOL, SHE FAILED TO COMPLETE HER EDUCATION WHEN WE FIRST TRAINED THIS GIRL.
BUT SINCE WE WON HER BACK SHE HAS RISEN THROUGH OUR ANCIENT RITUALS MOST RAPIDLY.
NOW SHE IS READY TO TAKE HER PLACE AND RULE FROM THE EAST, JUST AS OUR OTHER PRIZE STUDENT SHALL DESTROY FROM THE WEST.
YOU MAY EXECUTE HIM NOW, ELEKTRA.

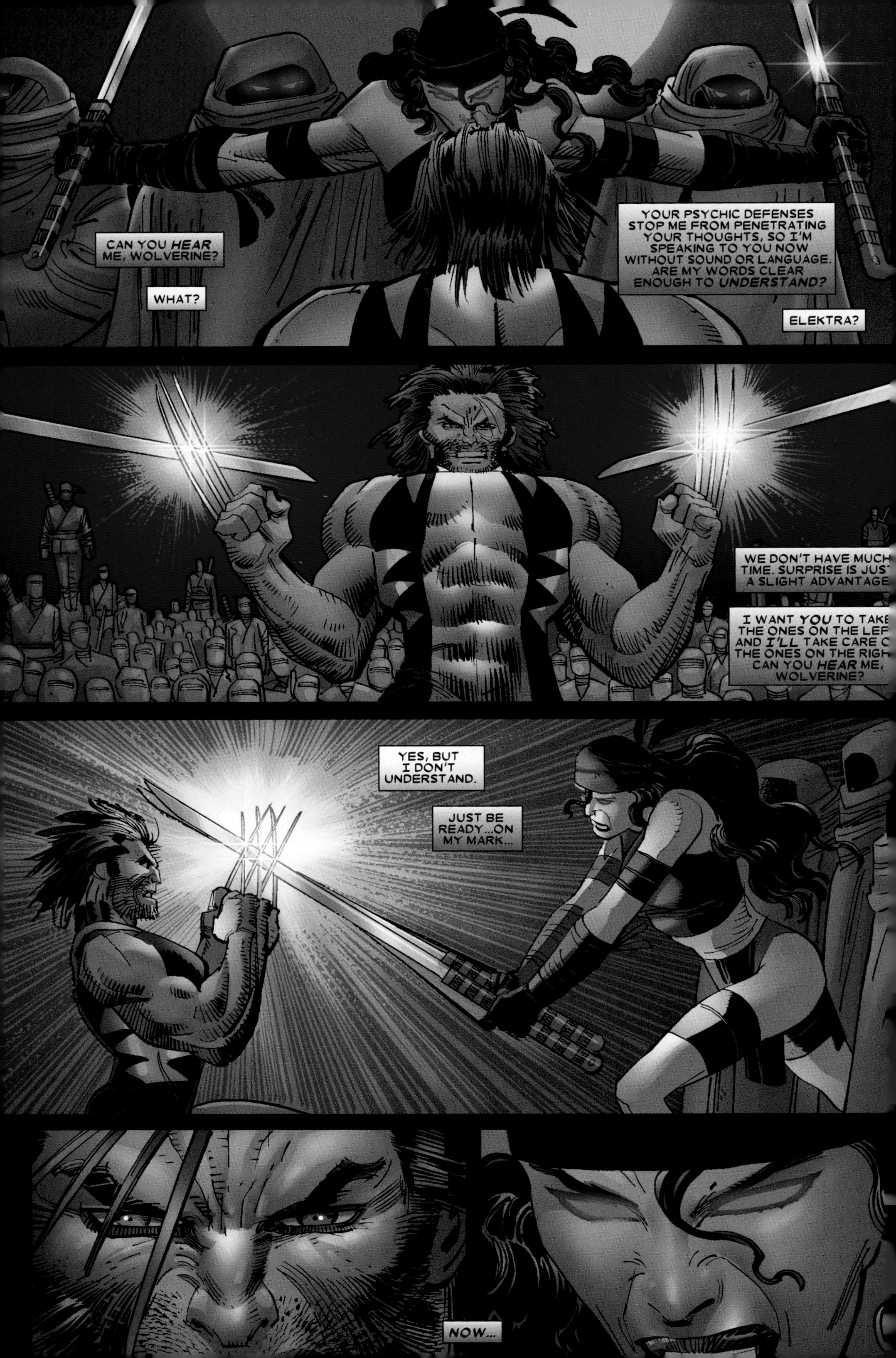
CAN YOU HEAR ME, WOLVERINE?
WHAT?
YOUR PSYCHIC DEFENSES STOP ME FROM PENETRATING YOUR THOUGHTS, SO I'M SPEAKING TO YOU NOW WITHOUT SOUND OR LANGUAGE. ARE MY WORDS CLEAR ENOUGH TO UNDERSTAND?
ELEKTRA?
WE DON'T HAVE MUCH TIME. SURPRISE IS JUST A SLIGHT ADVANTAGE.
I WANT YOU TO TAKE THE ONES ON THE LEFT AND I'LL TAKE CARE OF THE ONES ON THE RIGHT. CAN YOU HEAR ME, WOLVERINE?
YES, BUT I DON'T UNDERSTAND.
JUST BE READY...ON MY MARK...
NOW...

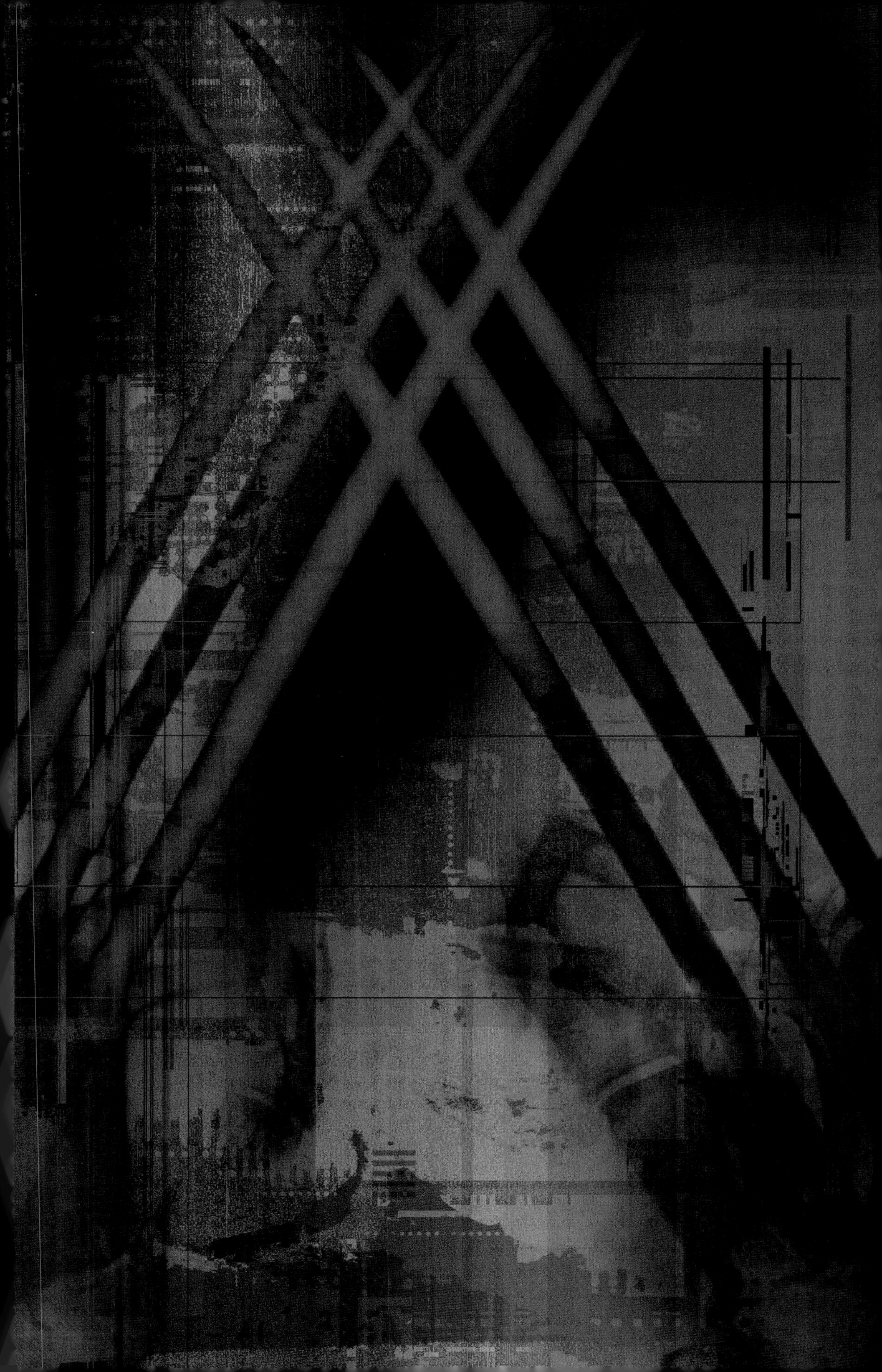

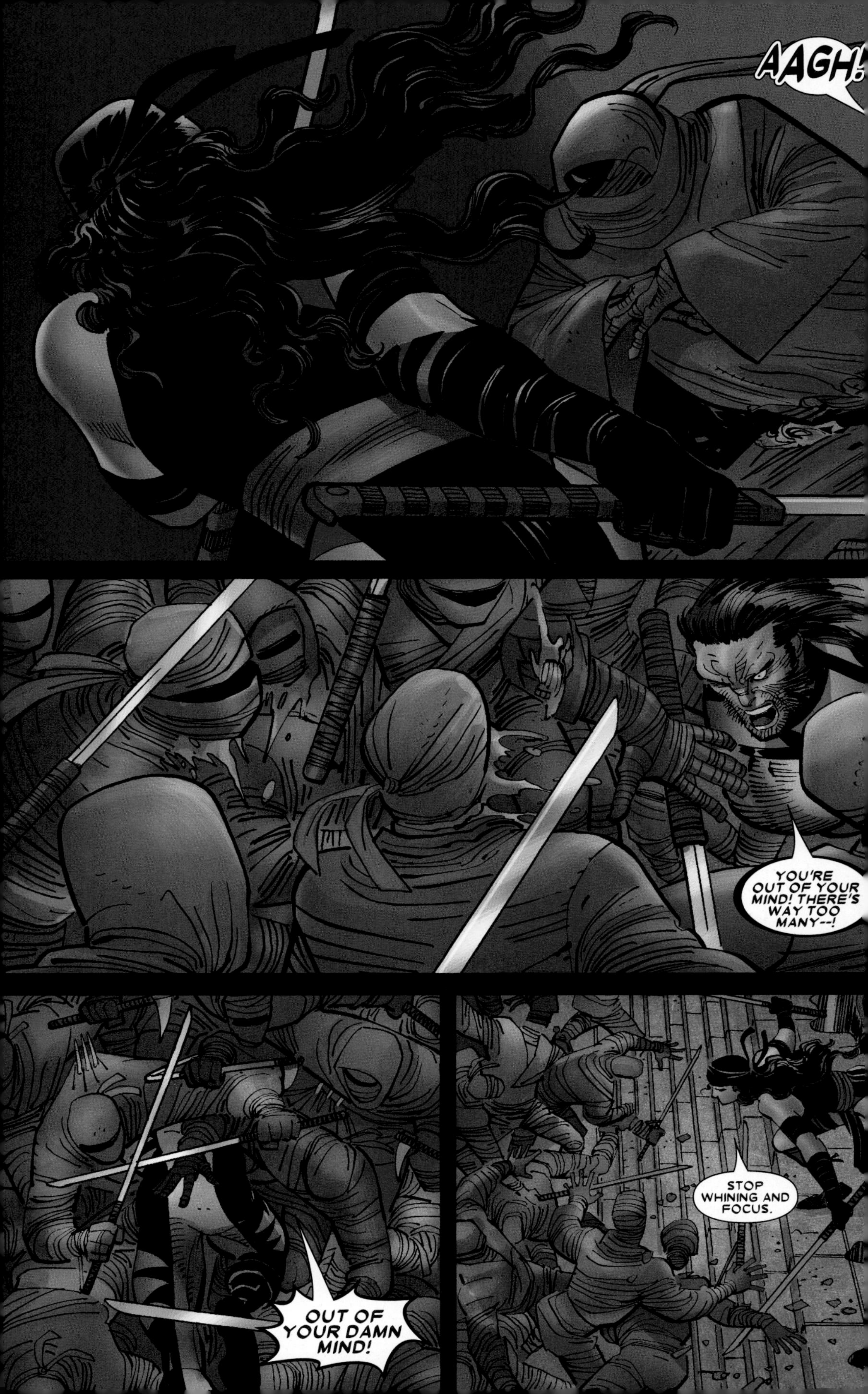
AAGH!
YOU'RE OUT OF YOUR MIND! THERE'S WAY TOO MANY--!
OUT OF YOUR DAMN MIND!
STOP WHINING AND FOCUS.

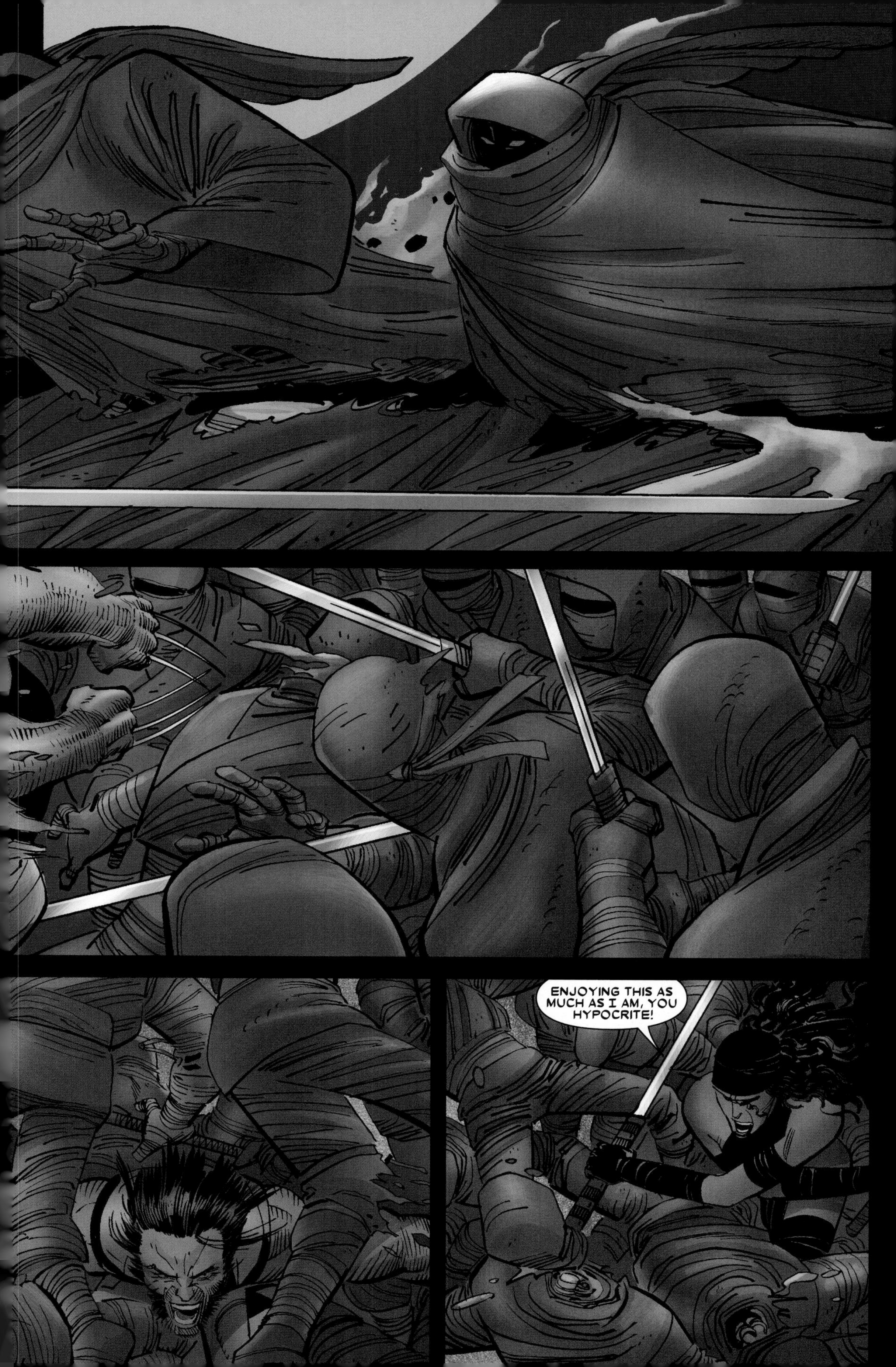
ENJOYING THIS AS MUCH AS I AM, YOU HYPOCRITE!

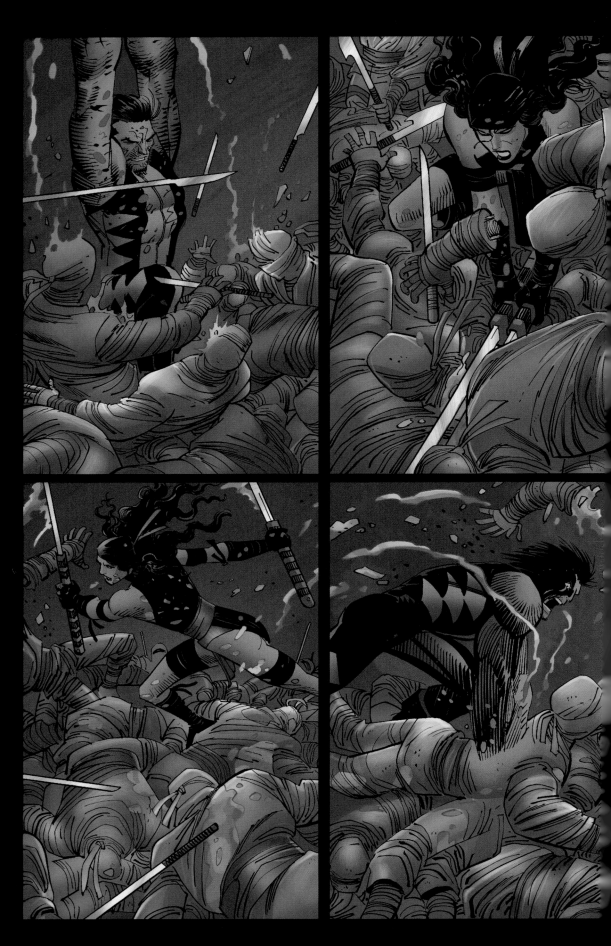

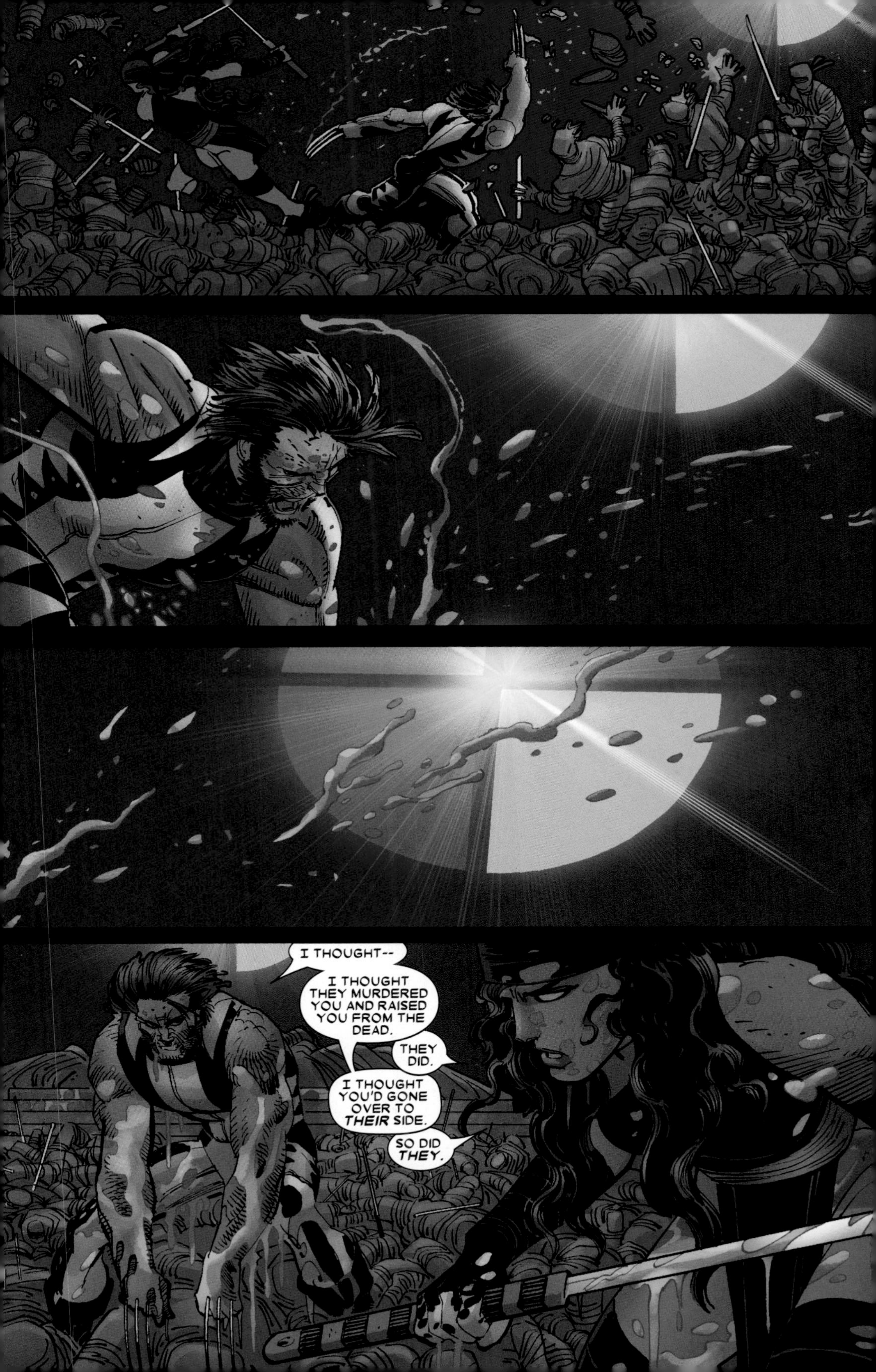
I THOUGHT--
I THOUGHT THEY MURDERED YOU AND RAISED YOU FROM THE DEAD.
THEY DID.
I THOUGHT YOU'D GONE OVER TO *THEIR* SIDE.
SO DID *THEY*.

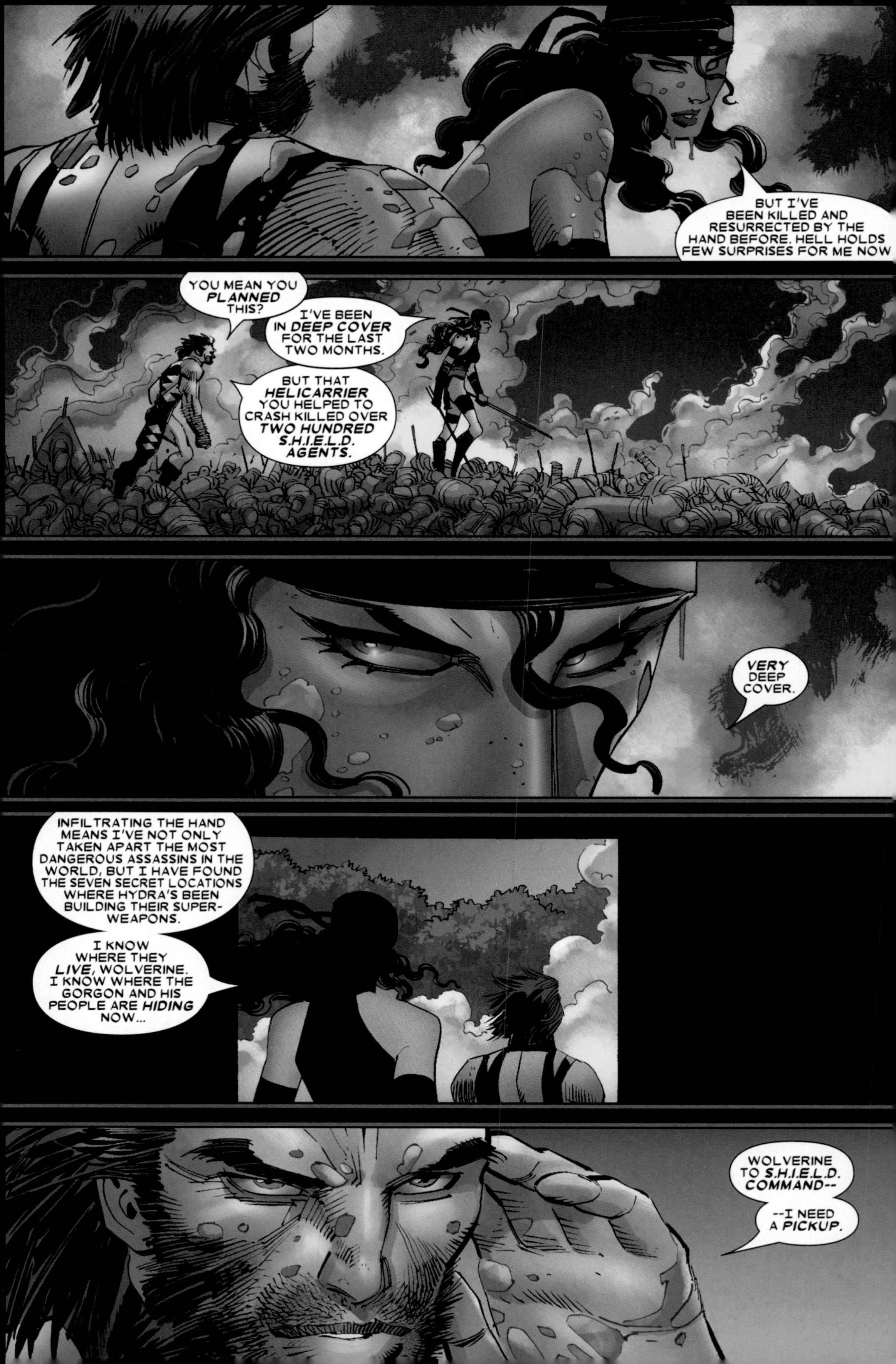
BUT I'VE BEEN KILLED AND RESURRECTED BY THE HAND BEFORE. HELL HOLDS FEW SURPRISES FOR ME NOW
YOU MEAN YOU PLANNED THIS?
I'VE BEEN IN DEEP COVER FOR THE LAST TWO MONTHS.
BUT THAT HELICARRIER YOU HELPED TO CRASH KILLED OVER TWO HUNDRED S.H.I.E.L.D. AGENTS.
VERY DEEP COVER.
INFILTRATING THE HAND MEANS I'VE NOT ONLY TAKEN APART THE MOST DANGEROUS ASSASSINS IN THE WORLD, BUT I HAVE FOUND THE SEVEN SECRET LOCATIONS WHERE HYDRA'S BEEN BUILDING THEIR SUPER-WEAPONS.
I KNOW WHERE THEY LIVE, WOLVERINE. I KNOW WHERE THE GORGON AND HIS PEOPLE ARE HIDING NOW...
WOLVERINE TO S.H.I.E.L.D. COMMAND--
--I NEED A PICKUP.

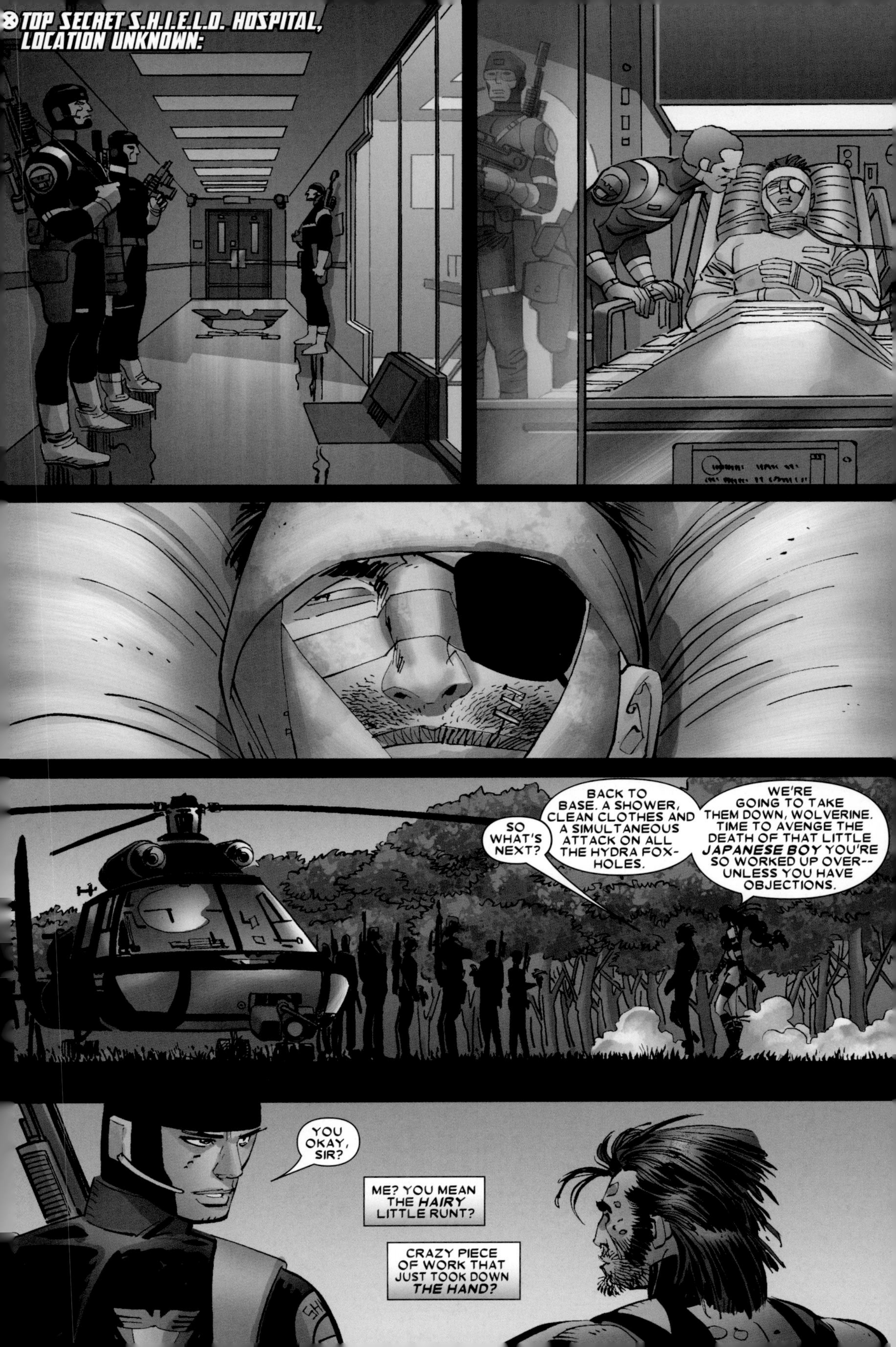
TOP SECRET S.H.I.E.L.D. HOSPITAL, LOCATION UNKNOWN:
SO WHAT'S NEXT?
BACK TO BASE. A SHOWER, CLEAN CLOTHES AND A SIMULTANEOUS ATTACK ON ALL THE HYDRA FOX-HOLES.
WE'RE GOING TO TAKE THEM DOWN, WOLVERINE. TIME TO AVENGE THE DEATH OF THAT LITTLE JAPANESE BOY YOU'RE SO WORKED UP OVER-- UNLESS YOU HAVE OBJECTIONS.
YOU OKAY, SIR?
ME? YOU MEAN THE HAIRY LITTLE RUNT?
CRAZY PIECE OF WORK THAT JUST TOOK DOWN THE HAND?

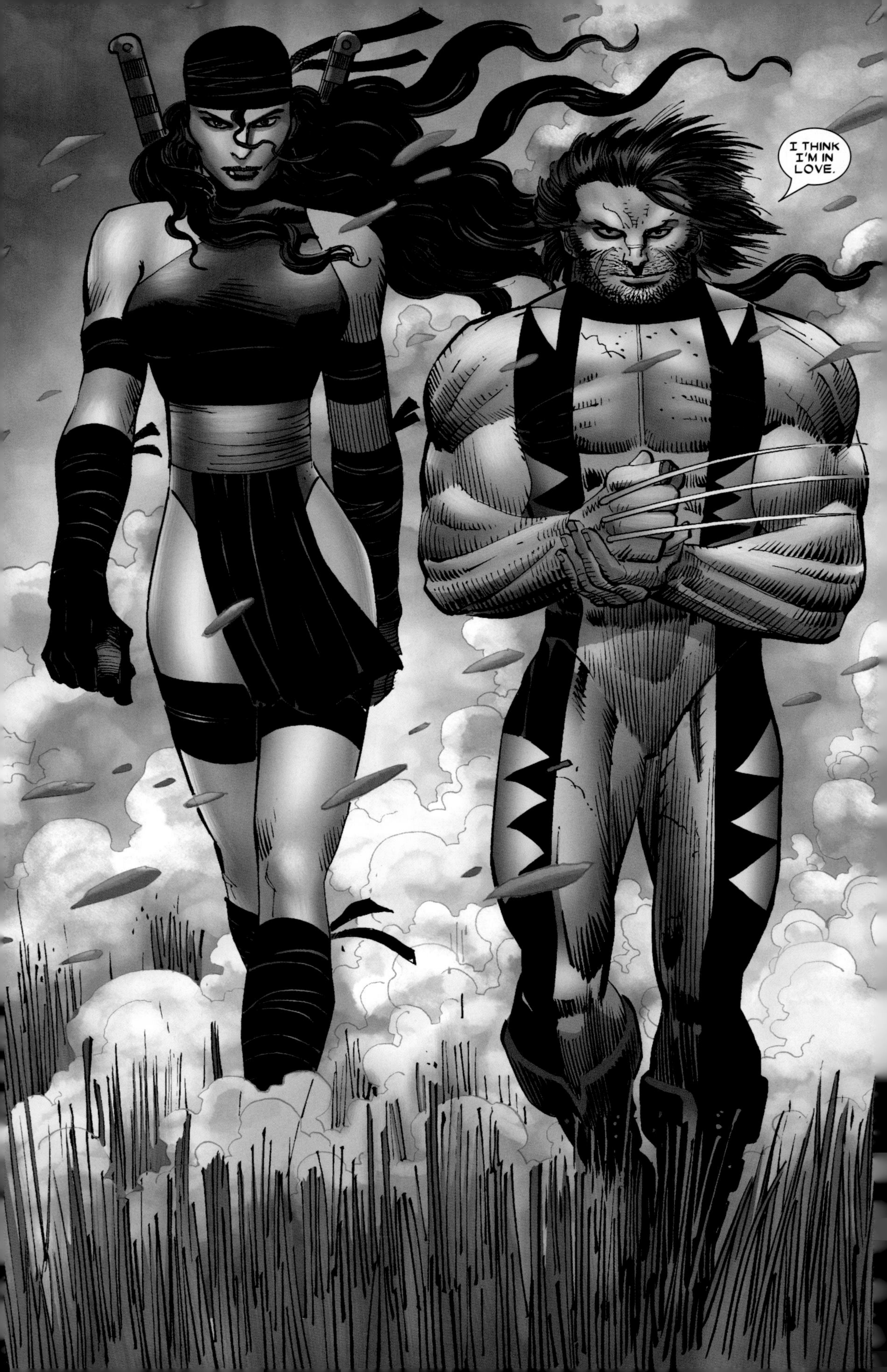
I THINK I'M IN LOVE.

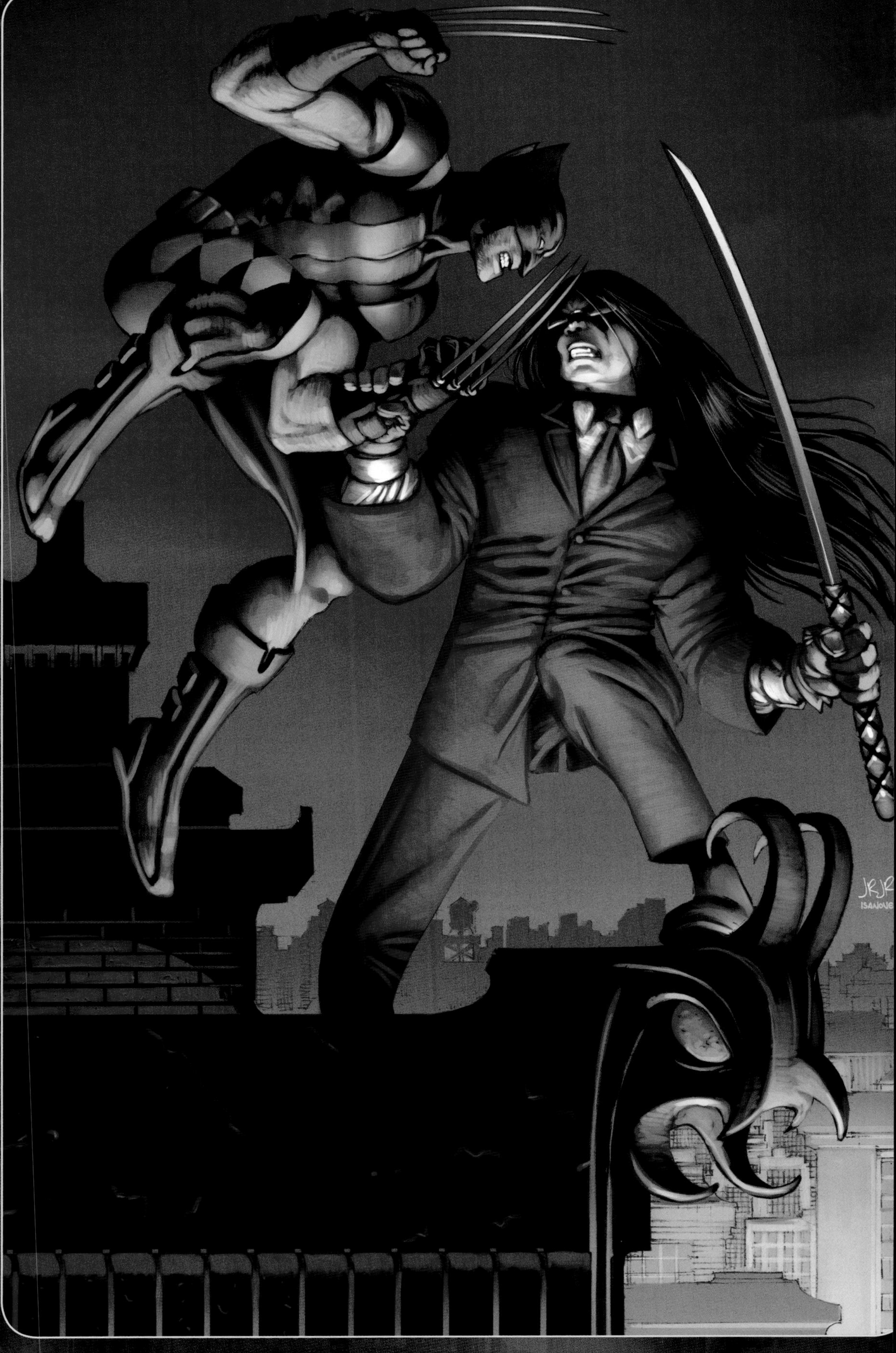

#30

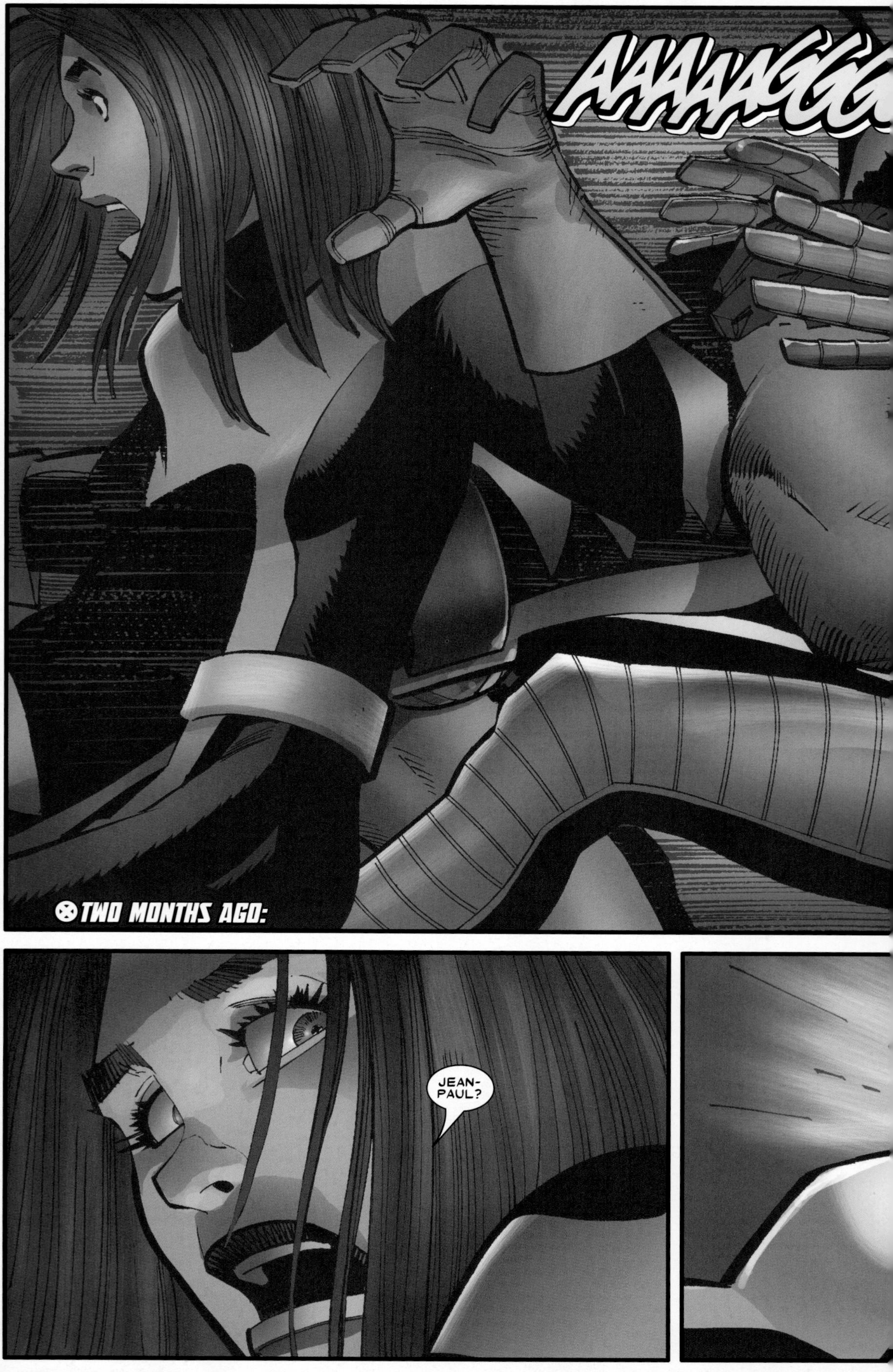
AAAAAGGG
TWO MONTHS AGO:
JEAN-PAUL?

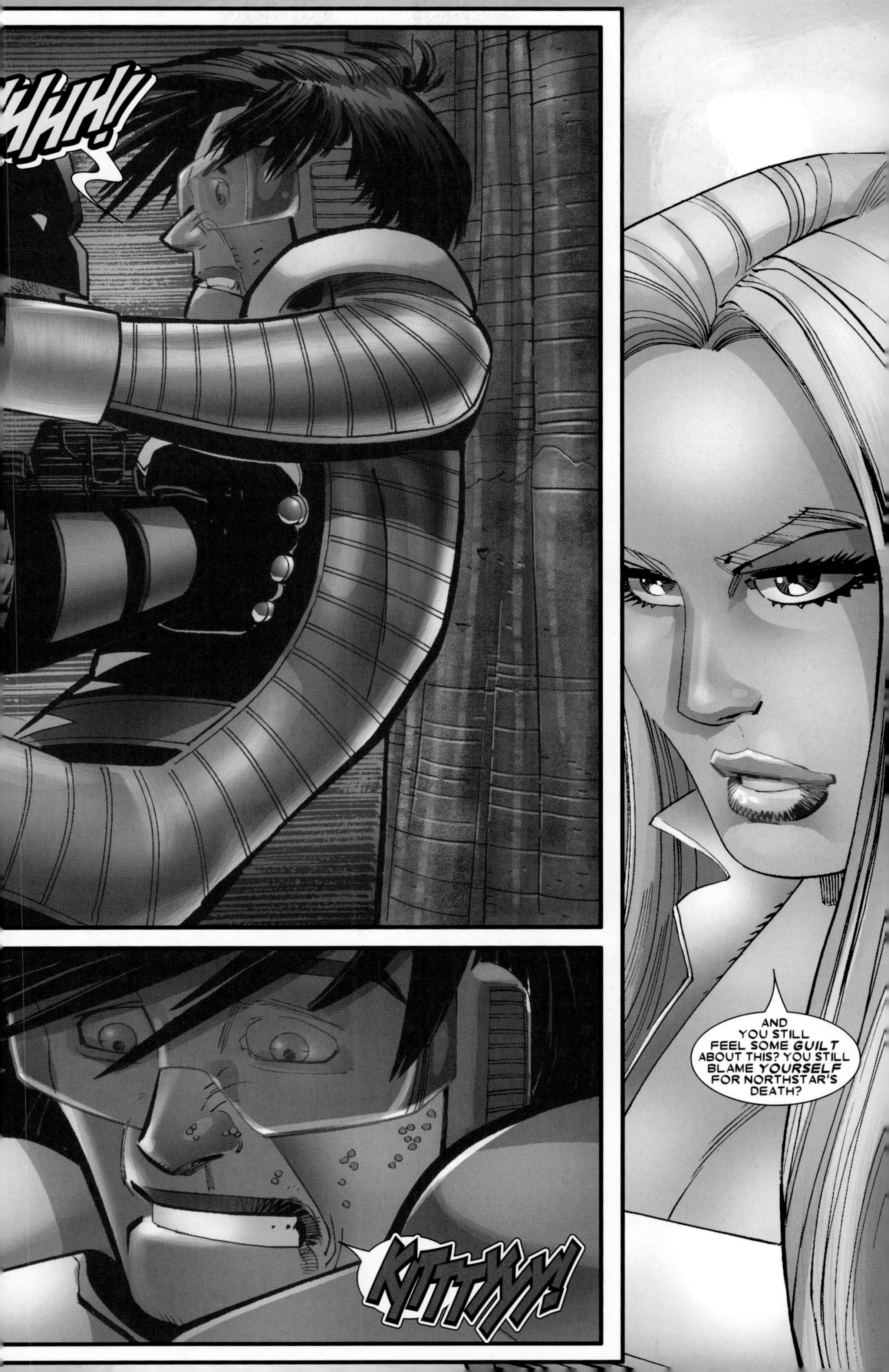
AND YOU STILL FEEL SOME GUILT ABOUT THIS? YOU STILL BLAME YOURSELF FOR NORTHSTAR'S DEATH?
KITTYYY!

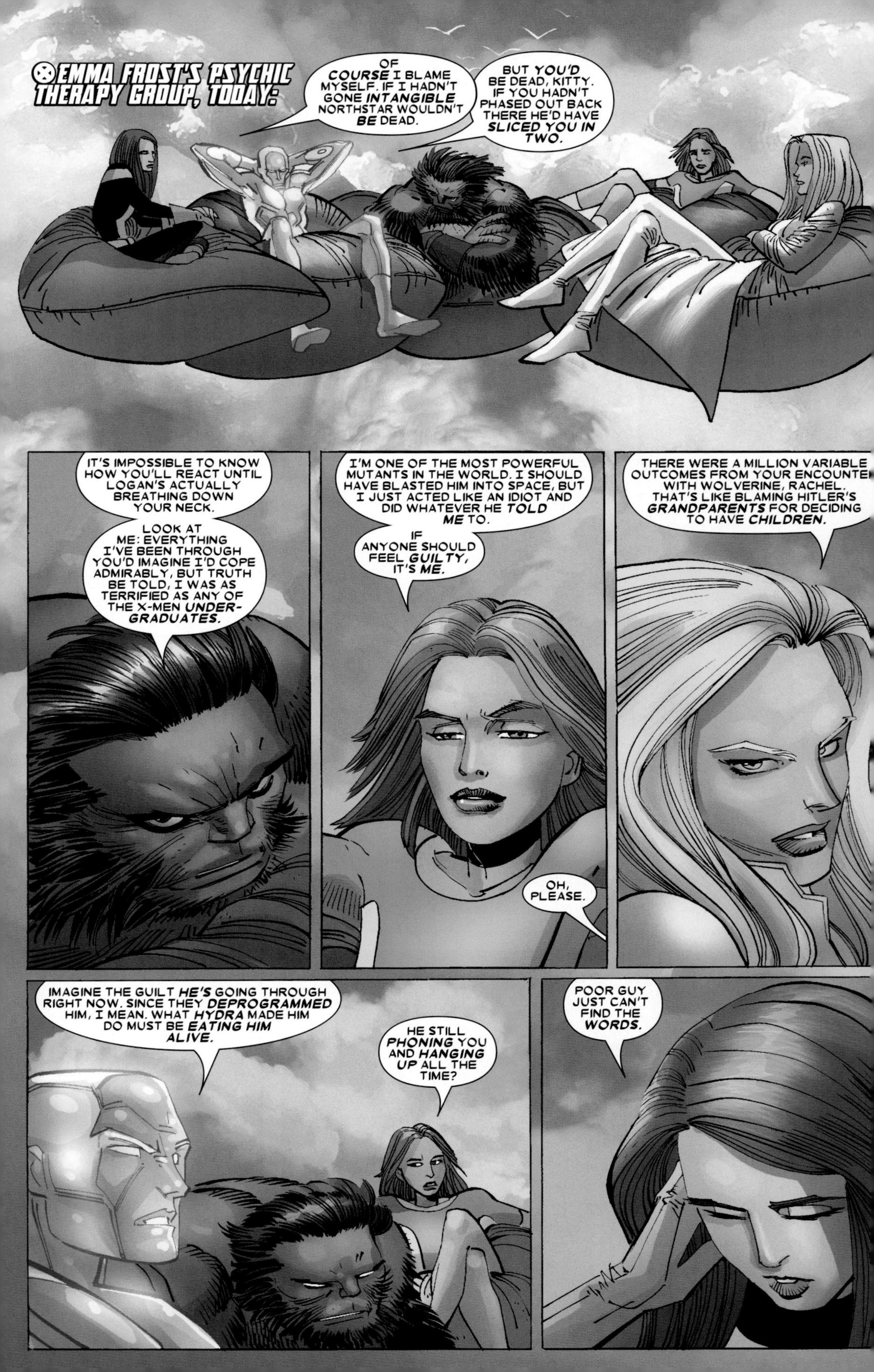

EMMA FROST'S PSYCHIC THERAPY GROUP, TODAY:
OF COURSE I BLAME MYSELF. IF I HADN'T GONE INTANGIBLE NORTHSTAR WOULDN'T BE DEAD.
BUT YOU'D BE DEAD, KITTY. IF YOU HADN'T PHASED OUT BACK THERE HE'D HAVE SLICED YOU IN TWO.
IT'S IMPOSSIBLE TO KNOW HOW YOU'LL REACT UNTIL LOGAN'S ACTUALLY BREATHING DOWN YOUR NECK.
LOOK AT ME: EVERYTHING I'VE BEEN THROUGH YOU'D IMAGINE I'D COPE ADMIRABLY, BUT TRUTH BE TOLD, I WAS AS TERRIFIED AS ANY OF THE X-MEN UNDER-GRADUATES.
I'M ONE OF THE MOST POWERFUL MUTANTS IN THE WORLD. I SHOULD HAVE BLASTED HIM INTO SPACE, BUT I JUST ACTED LIKE AN IDIOT AND DID WHATEVER HE TOLD ME TO.
IF ANYONE SHOULD FEEL GUILTY, IT'S ME.
OH, PLEASE.
THERE WERE A MILLION VARIABLE OUTCOMES FROM YOUR ENCOUNTE WITH WOLVERINE, RACHEL. THAT'S LIKE BLAMING HITLER'S GRANDPARENTS FOR DECIDING TO HAVE CHILDREN.
IMAGINE THE GUILT HE'S GOING THROUGH RIGHT NOW. SINCE THEY DEPROGRAMMED HIM, I MEAN. WHAT HYDRA MADE HIM DO MUST BE EATING HIM ALIVE.
HE STILL PHONING YOU AND HANGING UP ALL THE TIME?
POOR GUY JUST CAN'T FIND THE WORDS.

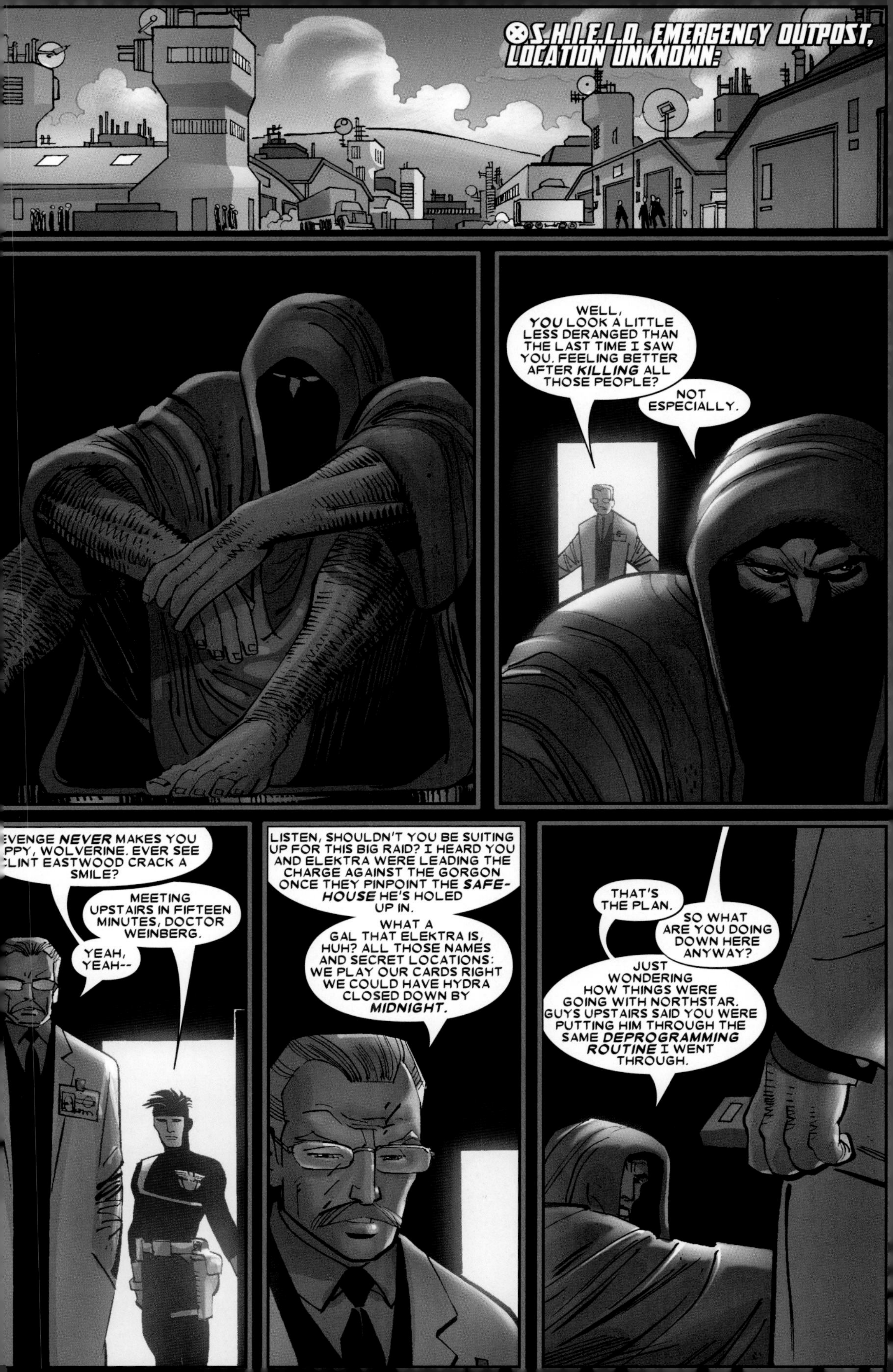
S.H.I.E.L.D. EMERGENCY OUTPOST, LOCATION UNKNOWN:
WELL, YOU LOOK A LITTLE LESS DERANGED THAN THE LAST TIME I SAW YOU. FEELING BETTER AFTER KILLING ALL THOSE PEOPLE?
NOT ESPECIALLY.
EVENGE NEVER MAKES YOU PPY, WOLVERINE. EVER SEE CLINT EASTWOOD CRACK A SMILE?
MEETING UPSTAIRS IN FIFTEEN MINUTES, DOCTOR WEINBERG.
YEAH, YEAH--
LISTEN, SHOULDN'T YOU BE SUITING UP FOR THIS BIG RAID? I HEARD YOU AND ELEKTRA WERE LEADING THE CHARGE AGAINST THE GORGON ONCE THEY PINPOINT THE SAFE-HOUSE HE'S HOLED UP IN.
WHAT A GAL THAT ELEKTRA IS, HUH? ALL THOSE NAMES AND SECRET LOCATIONS: WE PLAY OUR CARDS RIGHT WE COULD HAVE HYDRA CLOSED DOWN BY MIDNIGHT.
THAT'S THE PLAN.
SO WHAT ARE YOU DOING DOWN HERE ANYWAY?
JUST WONDERING HOW THINGS WERE GOING WITH NORTHSTAR. GUYS UPSTAIRS SAID YOU WERE PUTTING HIM THROUGH THE SAME DEPROGRAMMING ROUTINE I WENT THROUGH.

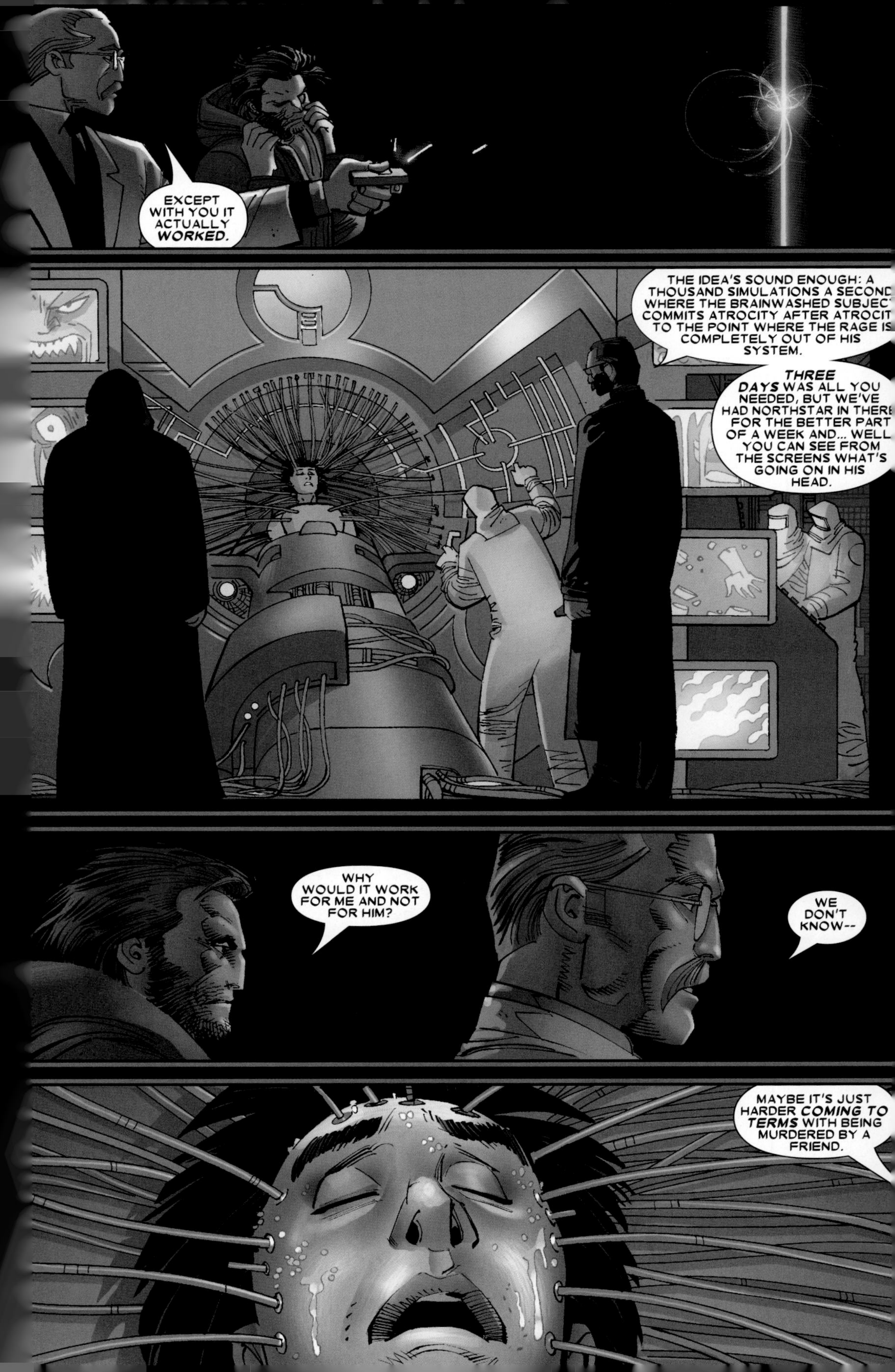
EXCEPT WITH YOU IT ACTUALLY WORKED.
THE IDEA'S SOUND ENOUGH: A THOUSAND SIMULATIONS A SECOND WHERE THE BRAINWASHED SUBJECT COMMITS ATROCITY AFTER ATROCITY TO THE POINT WHERE THE RAGE IS COMPLETELY OUT OF HIS SYSTEM.
THREE DAYS WAS ALL YOU NEEDED, BUT WE'VE HAD NORTHSTAR IN THERE FOR THE BETTER PART OF A WEEK AND... WELL. YOU CAN SEE FROM THE SCREENS WHAT'S GOING ON IN HIS HEAD.
WHY WOULD IT WORK FOR ME AND NOT FOR HIM?
WE DON'T KNOW--
MAYBE IT'S JUST HARDER COMING TO TERMS WITH BEING MURDERED BY A FRIEND.

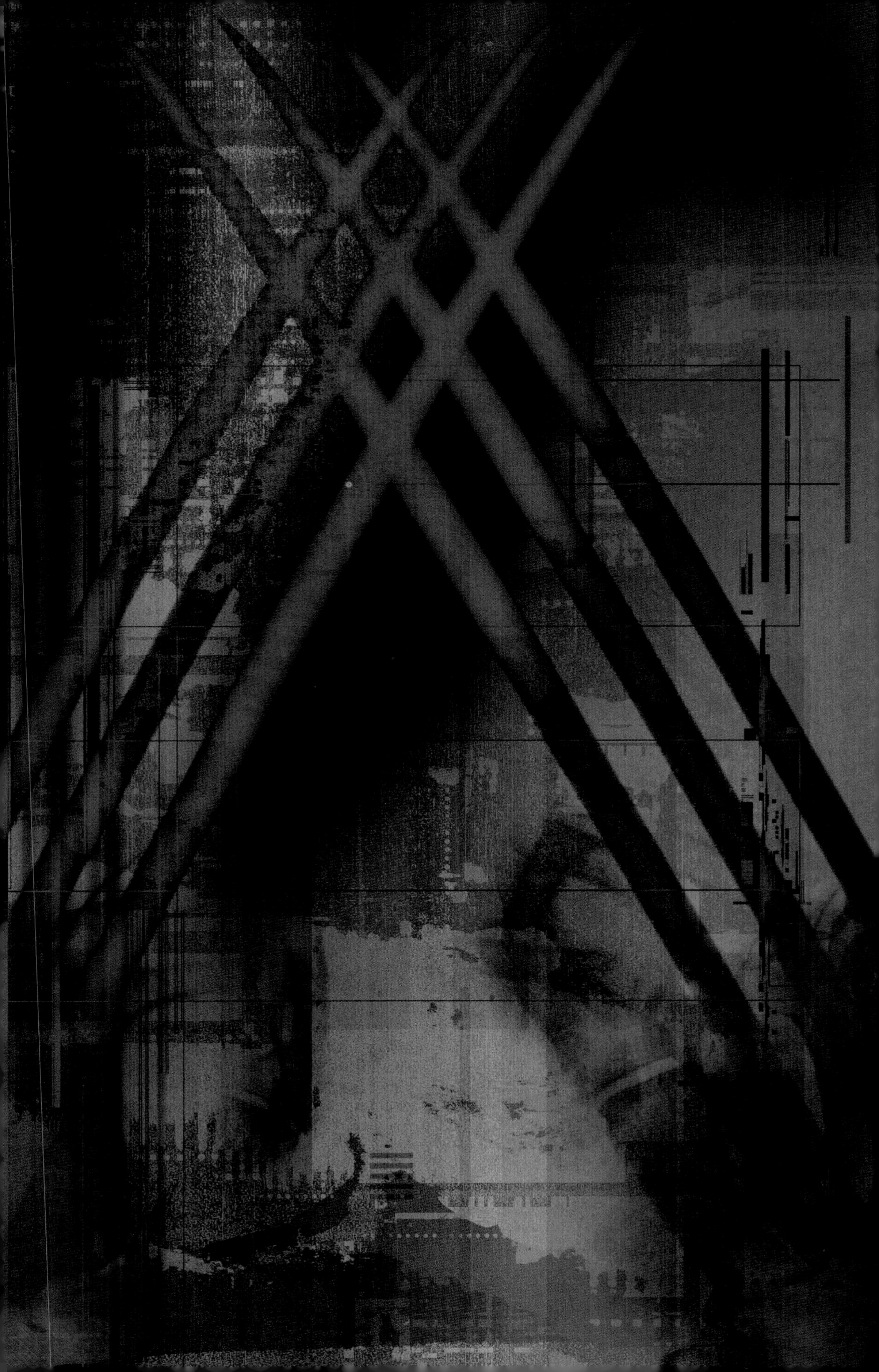

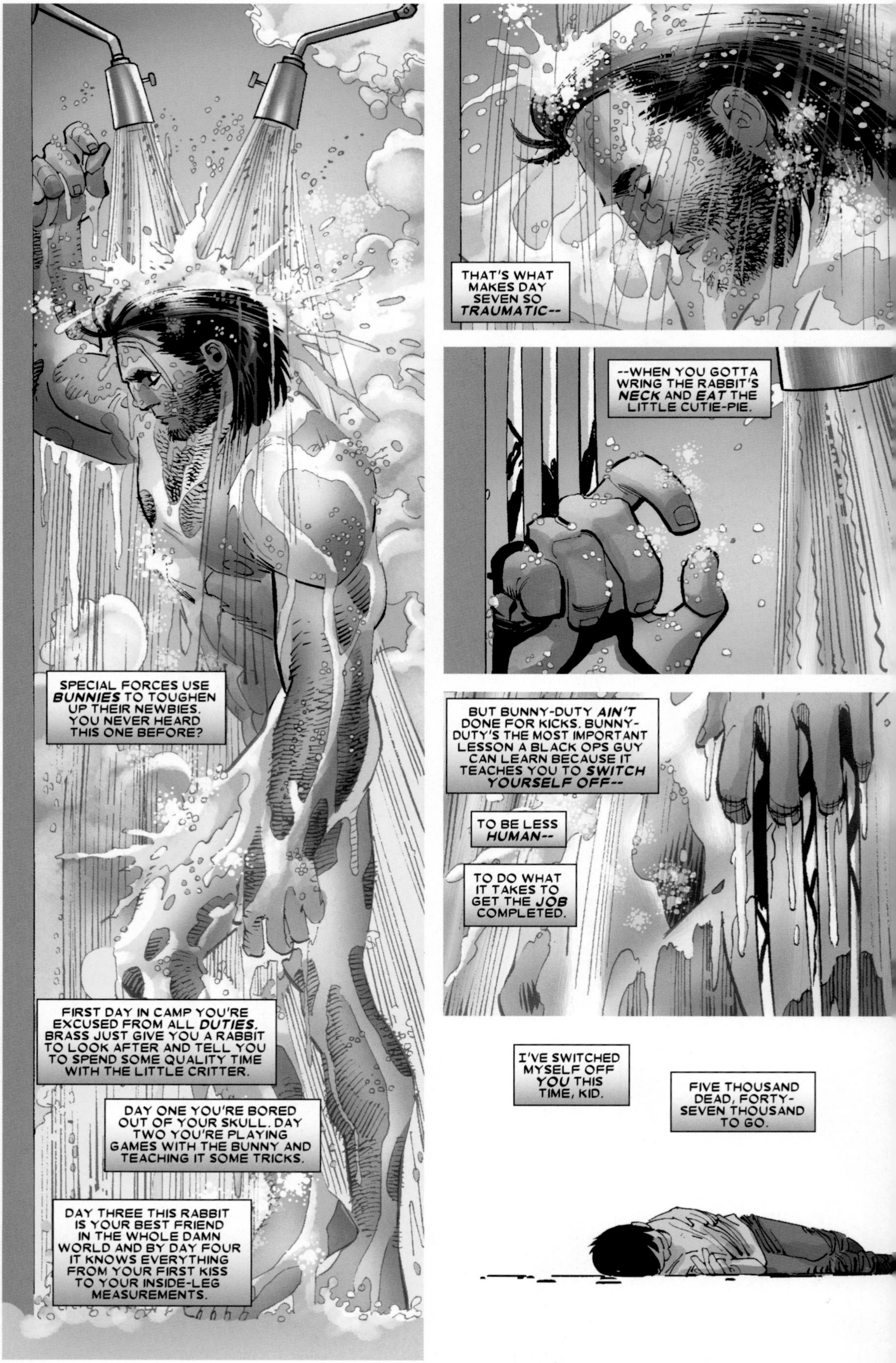
SPECIAL FORCES USE BUNNIES TO TOUGHEN UP THEIR NEWBIES. YOU NEVER HEARD THIS ONE BEFORE?
FIRST DAY IN CAMP YOU'RE EXCUSED FROM ALL DUTIES. BRASS JUST GIVE YOU A RABBIT TO LOOK AFTER AND TELL YOU TO SPEND SOME QUALITY TIME WITH THE LITTLE CRITTER.
DAY ONE YOU'RE BORED OUT OF YOUR SKULL. DAY TWO YOU'RE PLAYING GAMES WITH THE BUNNY AND TEACHING IT SOME TRICKS.
DAY THREE THIS RABBIT IS YOUR BEST FRIEND IN THE WHOLE DAMN WORLD AND BY DAY FOUR IT KNOWS EVERYTHING FROM YOUR FIRST KISS TO YOUR INSIDE-LEG MEASUREMENTS.
THAT'S WHAT MAKES DAY SEVEN SO TRAUMATIC--
--WHEN YOU GOTTA WRING THE RABBIT'S NECK AND EAT THE LITTLE CUTIE-PIE.
BUT BUNNY-DUTY AIN'T DONE FOR KICKS. BUNNY-DUTY'S THE MOST IMPORTANT LESSON A BLACK OPS GUY CAN LEARN BECAUSE IT TEACHES YOU TO SWITCH YOURSELF OFF--
TO BE LESS HUMAN--
TO DO WHAT IT TAKES TO GET THE JOB COMPLETED.
I'VE SWITCHED MYSELF OFF YOU THIS TIME, KID.
FIVE THOUSAND DEAD, FORTY-SEVEN THOUSAND TO GO.

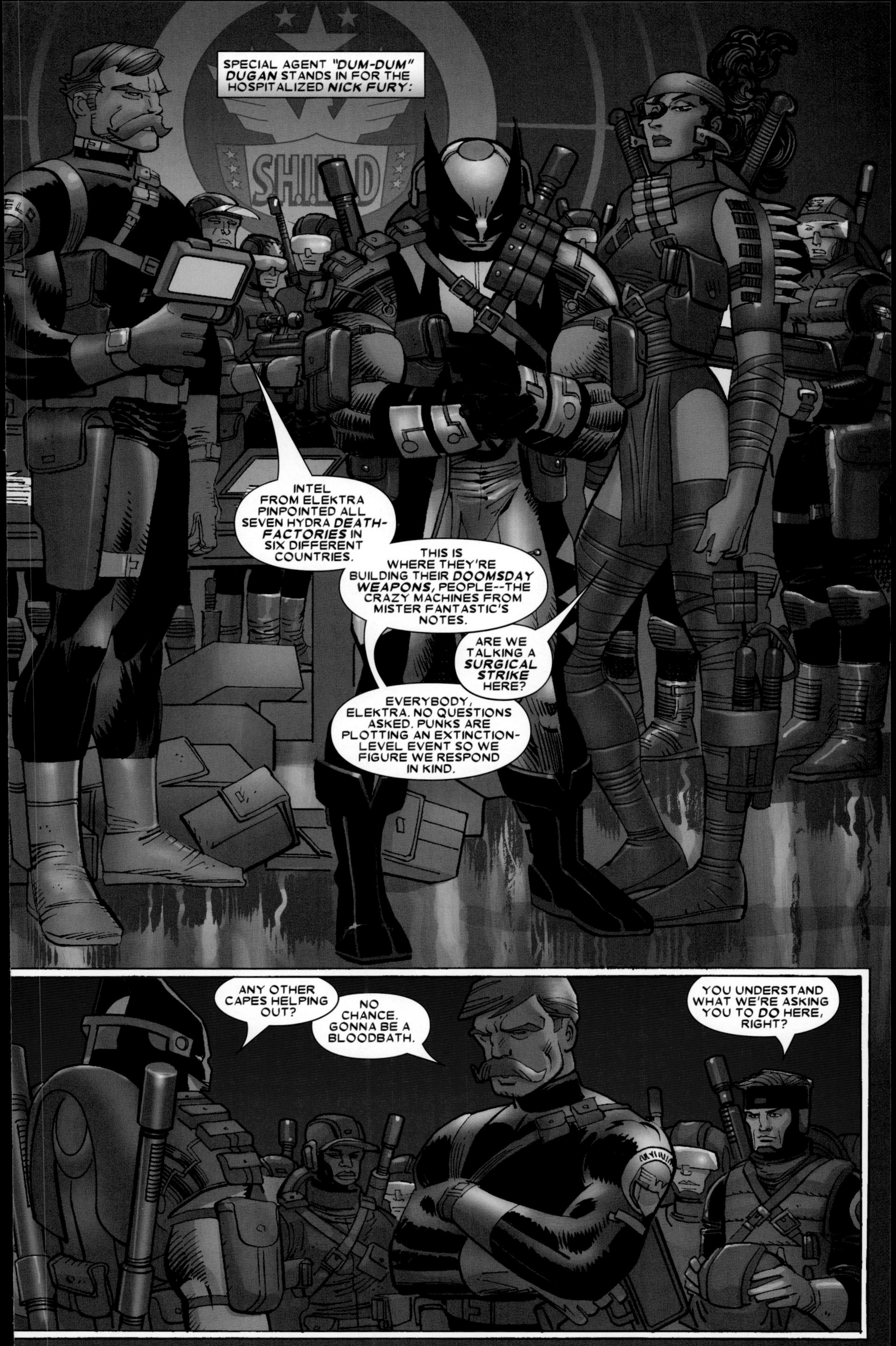
SPECIAL AGENT "DUM-DUM" DUGAN STANDS IN FOR THE HOSPITALIZED NICK FURY:
S.H.I.E.L.D
INTEL FROM ELEKTRA PINPOINTED ALL SEVEN HYDRA DEATH-FACTORIES IN SIX DIFFERENT COUNTRIES.
THIS IS WHERE THEY'RE BUILDING THEIR DOOMSDAY WEAPONS, PEOPLE--THE CRAZY MACHINES FROM MISTER FANTASTIC'S NOTES.
ARE WE TALKING A SURGICAL STRIKE HERE?
EVERYBODY, ELEKTRA. NO QUESTIONS ASKED. PUNKS ARE PLOTTING AN EXTINCTION-LEVEL EVENT SO WE FIGURE WE RESPOND IN KIND.
ANY OTHER CAPES HELPING OUT?
NO CHANCE. GONNA BE A BLOODBATH.
YOU UNDERSTAND WHAT WE'RE ASKING YOU TO DO HERE, RIGHT?

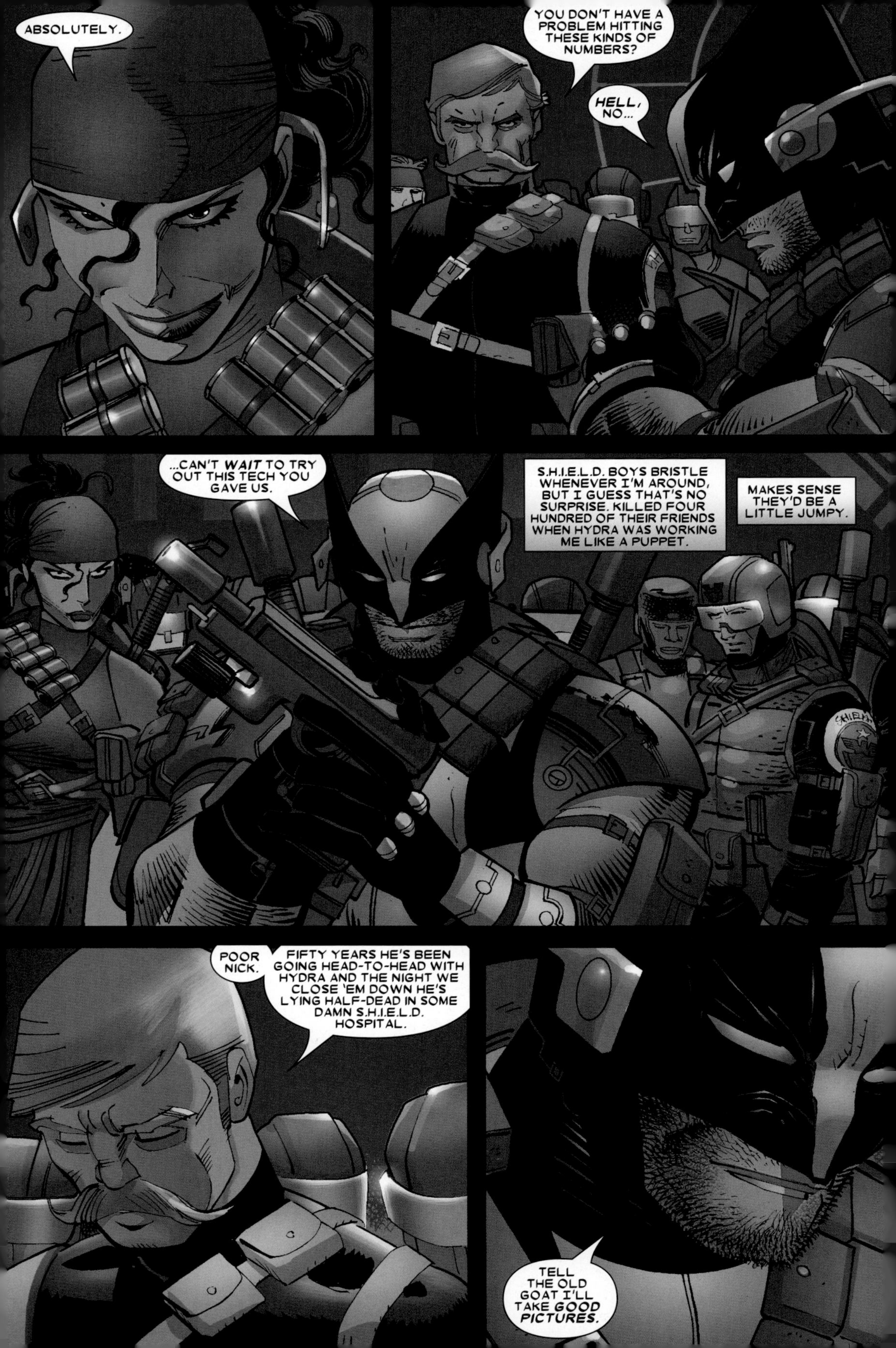
ABSOLUTELY.
YOU DON'T HAVE A PROBLEM HITTING THESE KINDS OF NUMBERS?
HELL, NO...
...CAN'T WAIT TO TRY OUT THIS TECH YOU GAVE US.
S.H.I.E.L.D. BOYS BRISTLE WHENEVER I'M AROUND, BUT I GUESS THAT'S NO SURPRISE. KILLED FOUR HUNDRED OF THEIR FRIENDS WHEN HYDRA WAS WORKING ME LIKE A PUPPET.
MAKES SENSE THEY'D BE A LITTLE JUMPY.
POOR NICK.
FIFTY YEARS HE'S BEEN GOING HEAD-TO-HEAD WITH HYDRA AND THE NIGHT WE CLOSE 'EM DOWN HE'S LYING HALF-DEAD IN SOME DAMN S.H.I.E.L.D. HOSPITAL.
TELL THE OLD GOAT I'LL TAKE GOOD PICTURES.

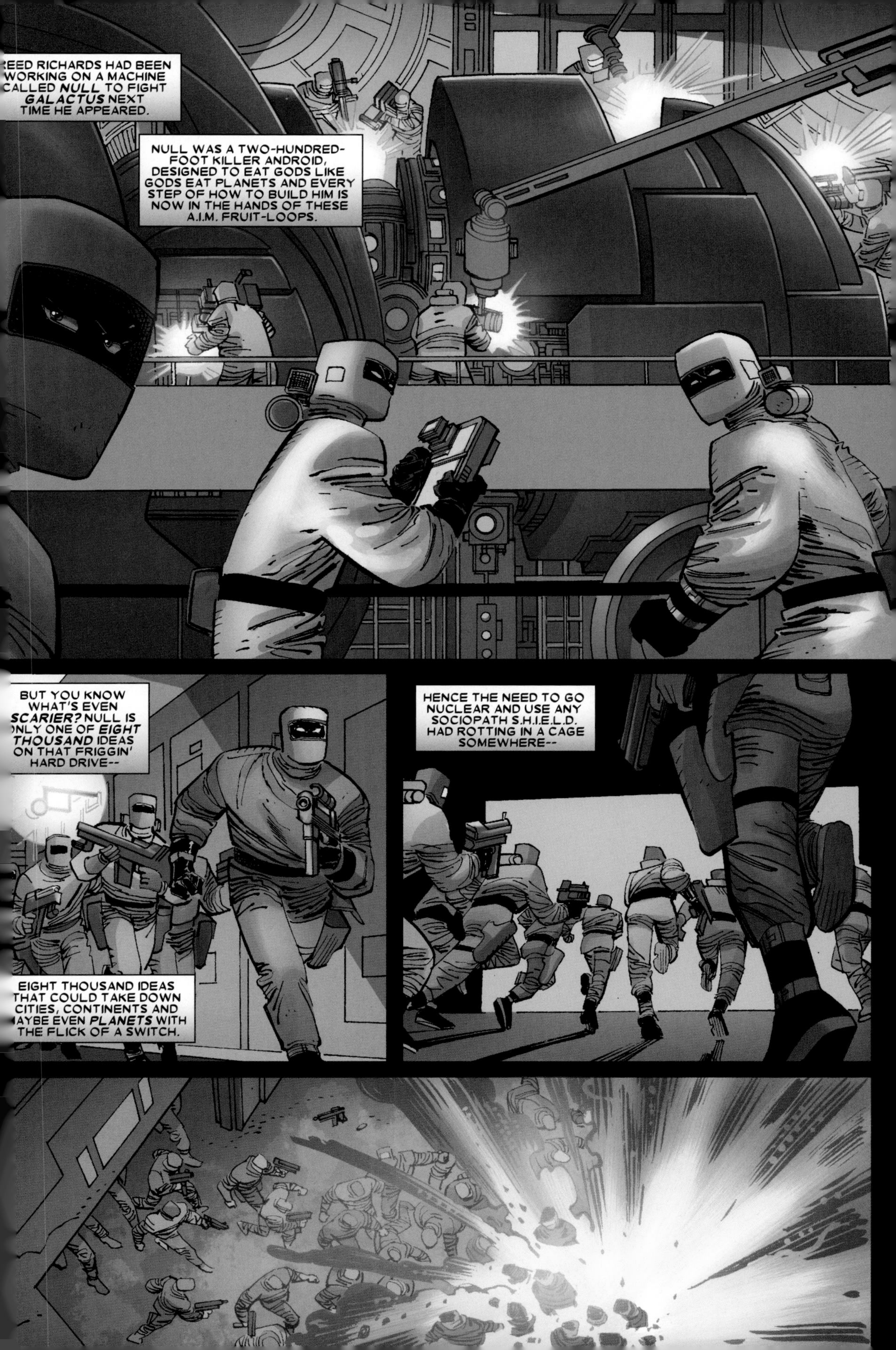
REED RICHARDS HAD BEEN WORKING ON A MACHINE CALLED NULL TO FIGHT GALACTUS NEXT TIME HE APPEARED.
NULL WAS A TWO-HUNDRED-FOOT KILLER ANDROID, DESIGNED TO EAT GODS LIKE GODS EAT PLANETS AND EVERY STEP OF HOW TO BUILD HIM IS NOW IN THE HANDS OF THESE A.I.M. FRUIT-LOOPS.
BUT YOU KNOW WHAT'S EVEN SCARIER? NULL IS ONLY ONE OF EIGHT THOUSAND IDEAS ON THAT FRIGGIN' HARD DRIVE--
EIGHT THOUSAND IDEAS THAT COULD TAKE DOWN CITIES, CONTINENTS AND MAYBE EVEN PLANETS WITH THE FLICK OF A SWITCH.
HENCE THE NEED TO GO NUCLEAR AND USE ANY SOCIOPATH S.H.I.E.L.D. HAD ROTTING IN A CAGE SOMEWHERE--

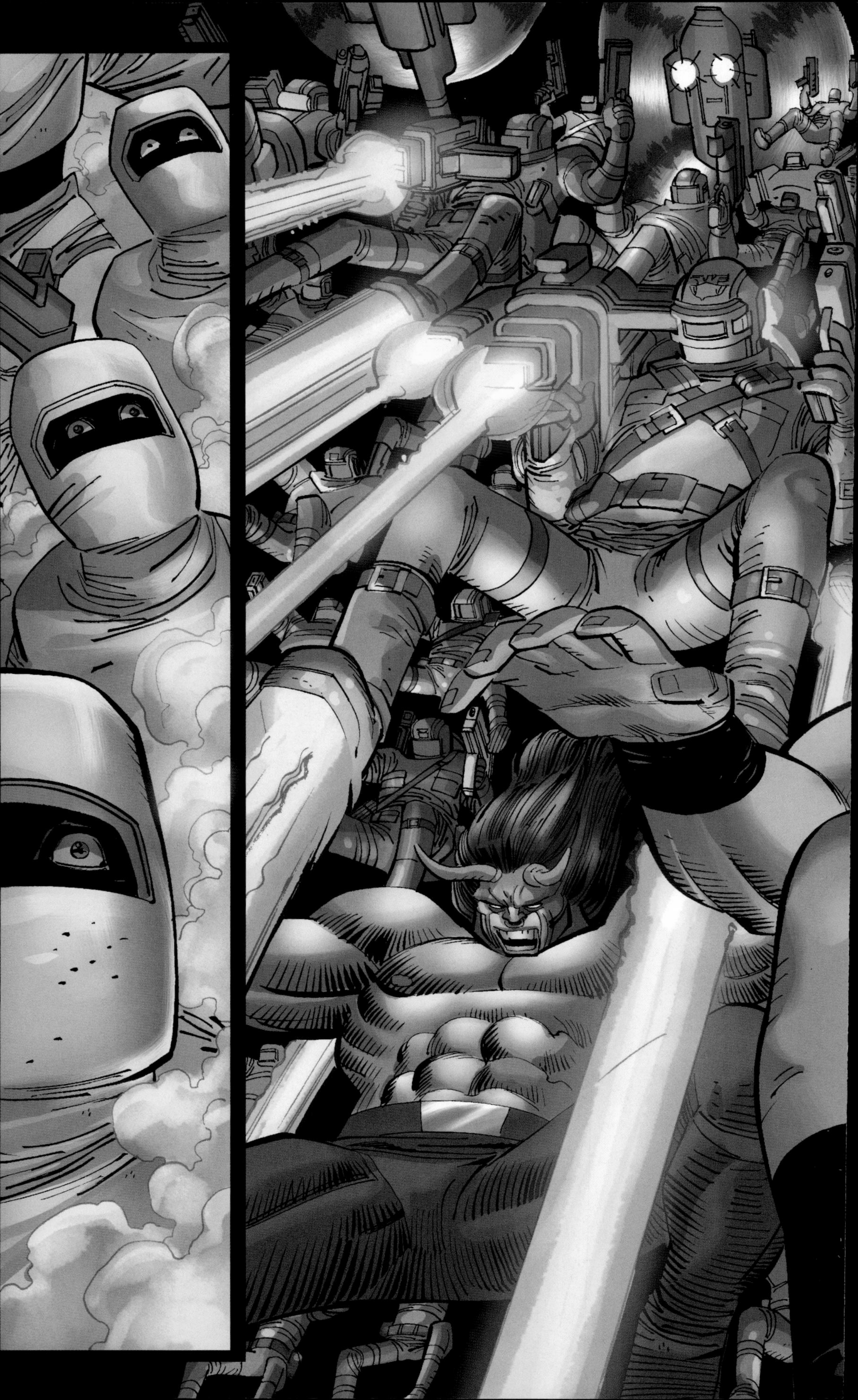

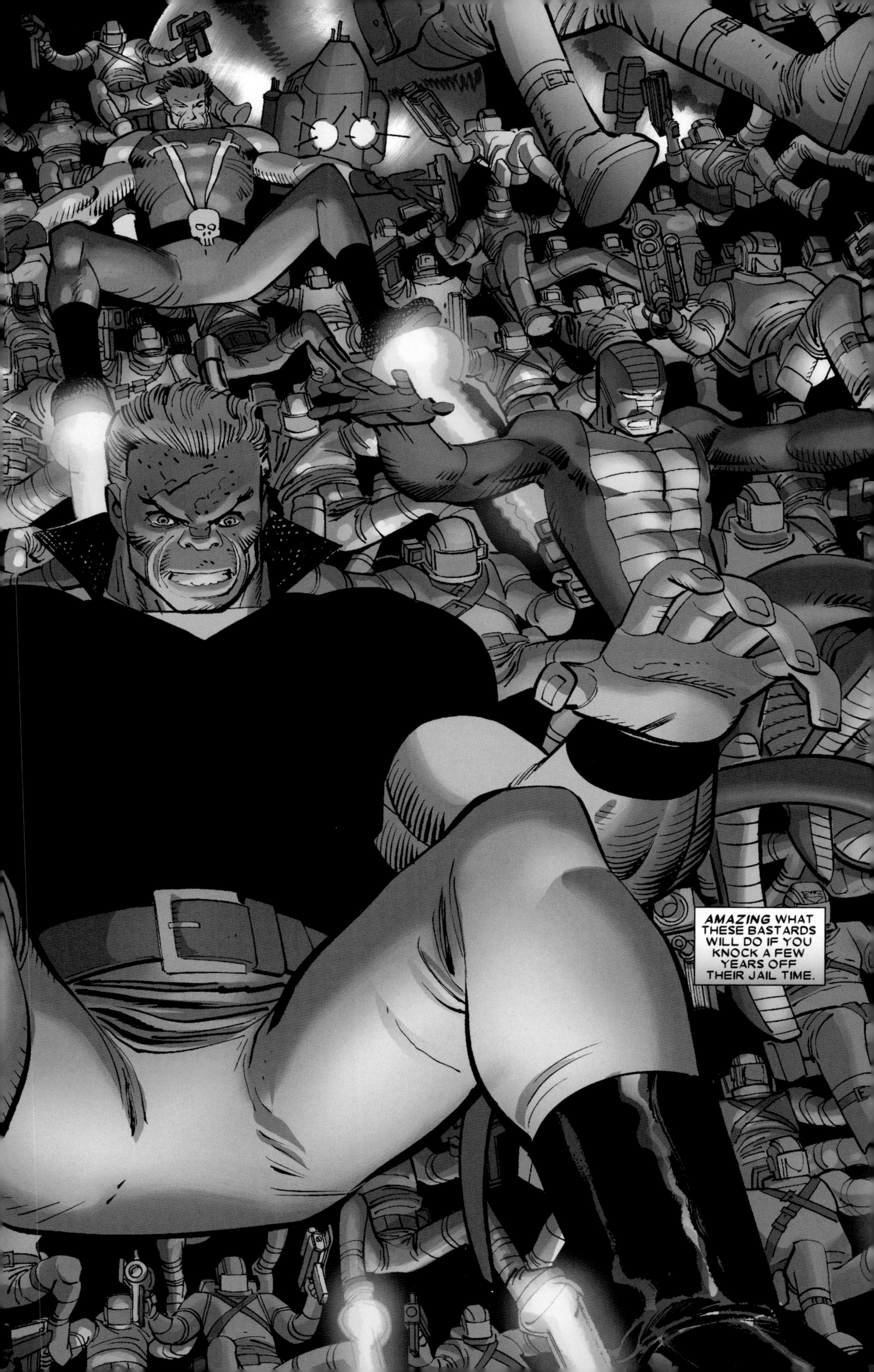
AMAZING WHAT THESE BASTARDS WILL DO IF YOU KNOCK A FEW YEARS OFF THEIR JAIL TIME.

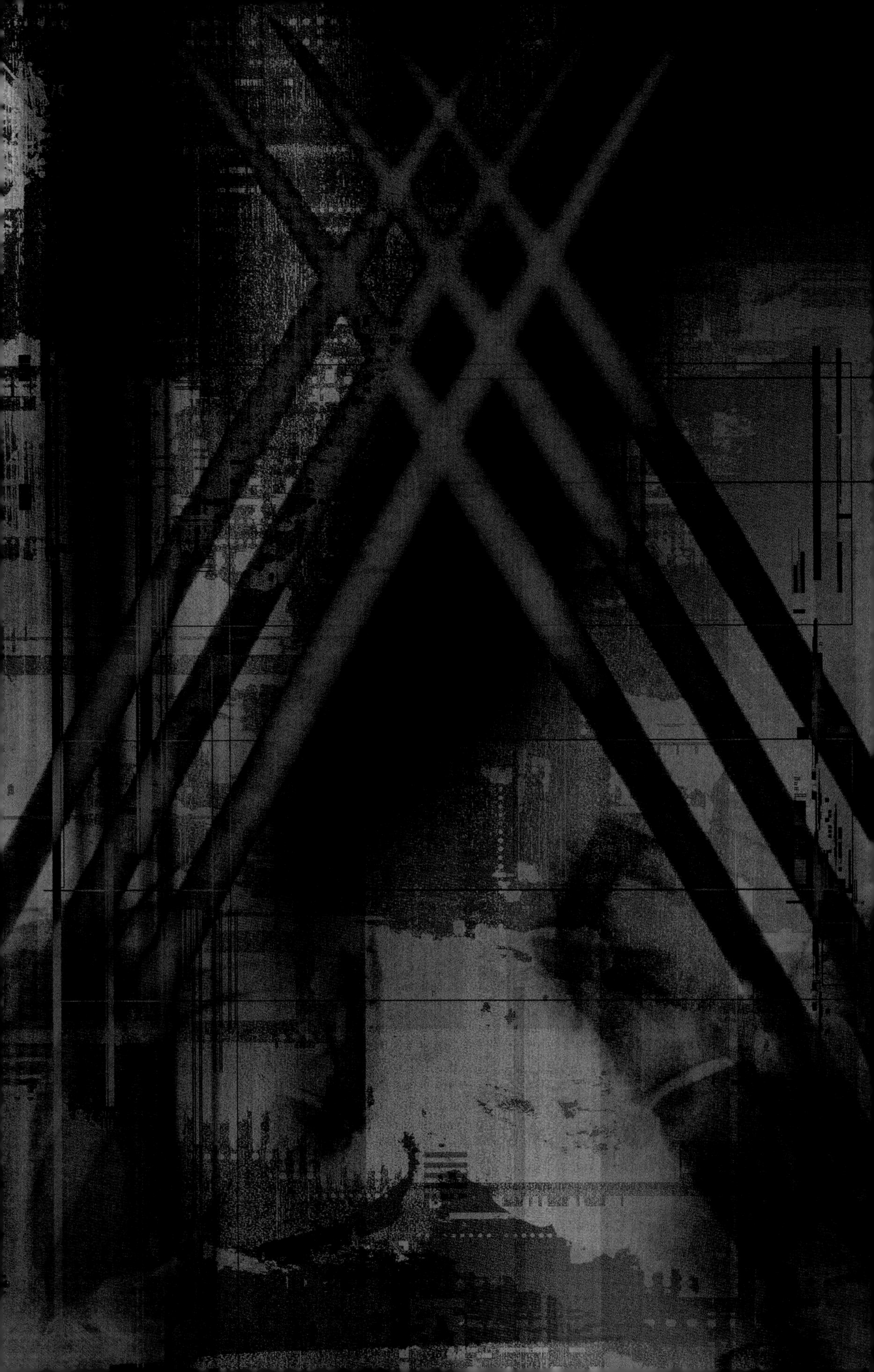

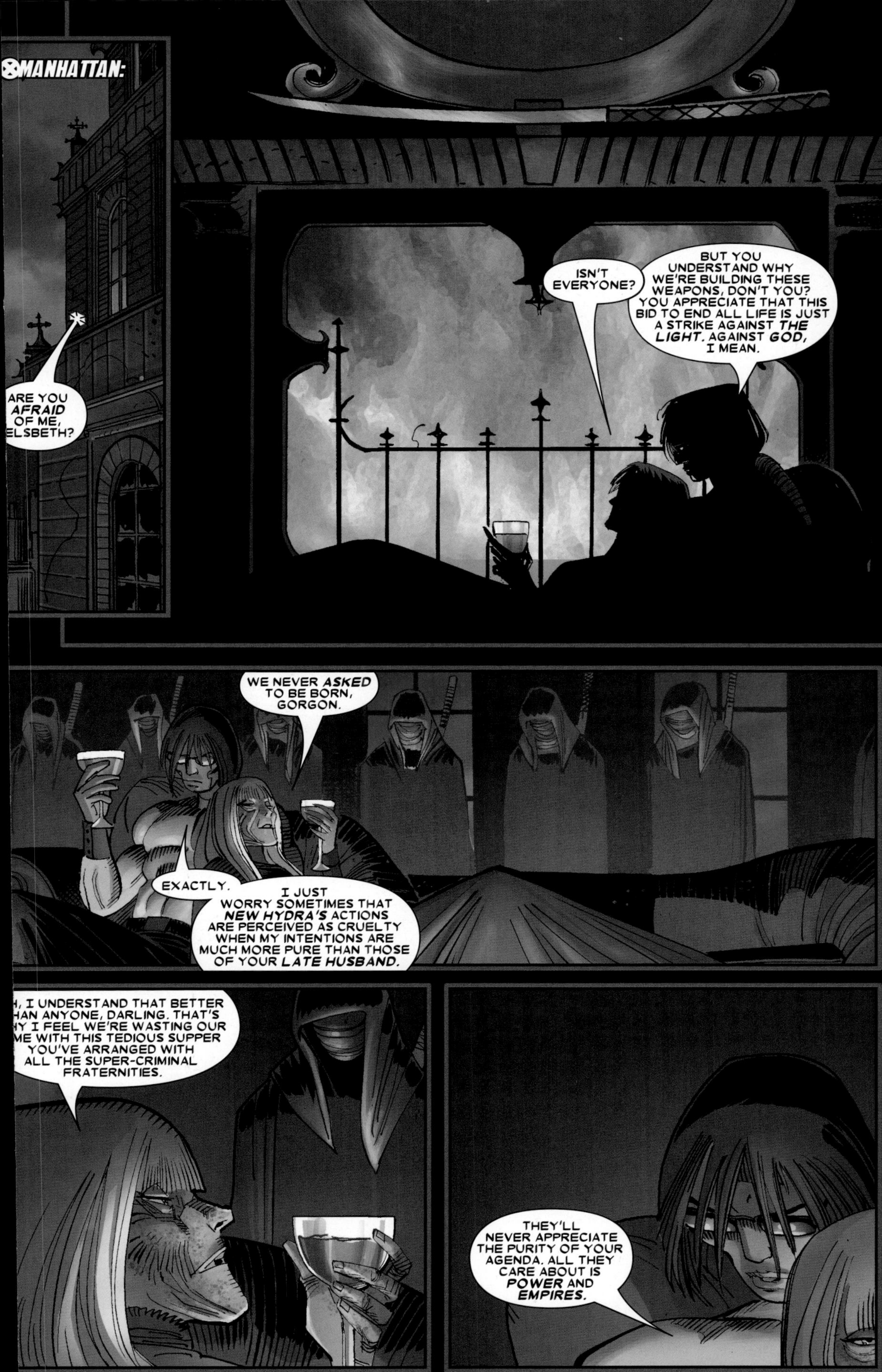
MANHATTAN:
ARE YOU AFRAID OF ME, ELSBETH?
ISN'T EVERYONE?
BUT YOU UNDERSTAND WHY WE'RE BUILDING THESE WEAPONS, DON'T YOU? YOU APPRECIATE THAT THIS BID TO END ALL LIFE IS JUST A STRIKE AGAINST THE LIGHT. AGAINST GOD, I MEAN.
WE NEVER ASKED TO BE BORN, GORGON.
EXACTLY.
I JUST WORRY SOMETIMES THAT NEW HYDRA'S ACTIONS ARE PERCEIVED AS CRUELTY WHEN MY INTENTIONS ARE MUCH MORE PURE THAN THOSE OF YOUR LATE HUSBAND.
H, I UNDERSTAND THAT BETTER HAN ANYONE, DARLING. THAT'S HY I FEEL WE'RE WASTING OUR ME WITH THIS TEDIOUS SUPPER YOU'VE ARRANGED WITH ALL THE SUPER-CRIMINAL FRATERNITIES.
THEY'LL NEVER APPRECIATE THE PURITY OF YOUR AGENDA. ALL THEY CARE ABOUT IS POWER AND EMPIRES.

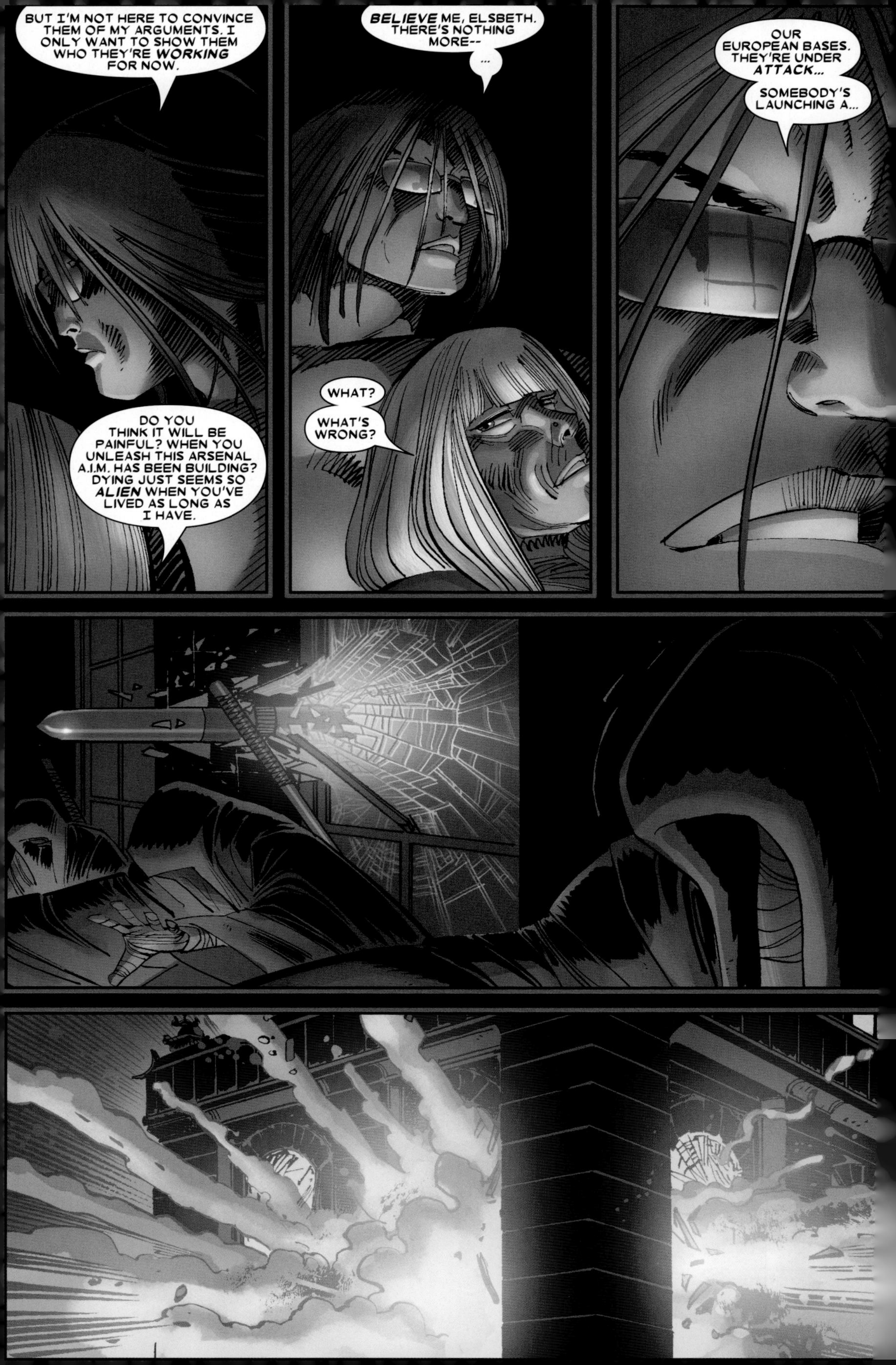
BUT I'M NOT HERE TO CONVINCE THEM OF MY ARGUMENTS. I ONLY WANT TO SHOW THEM WHO THEY'RE WORKING FOR NOW.
DO YOU THINK IT WILL BE PAINFUL? WHEN YOU UNLEASH THIS ARSENAL A.I.M. HAS BEEN BUILDING? DYING JUST SEEMS SO ALIEN WHEN YOU'VE LIVED AS LONG AS I HAVE.
BELIEVE ME, ELSBETH. THERE'S NOTHING MORE--
...
WHAT?
WHAT'S WRONG?
OUR EUROPEAN BASES. THEY'RE UNDER ATTACK...
SOMEBODY'S LAUNCHING A...

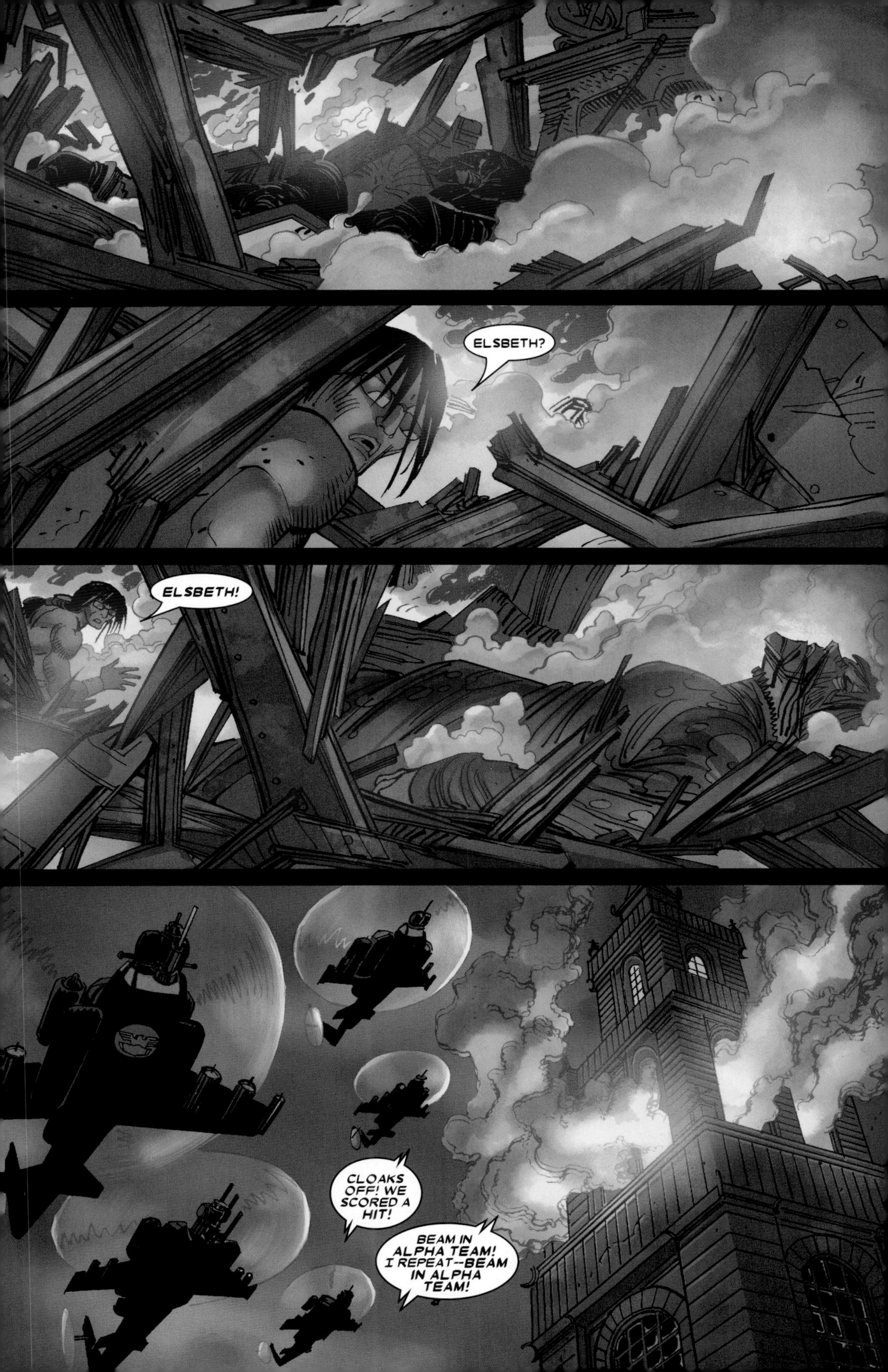
ELSBETH?
ELSBETH!
CLOAKS OFF! WE SCORED A HIT!
BEAM IN ALPHA TEAM! I REPEAT--BEAM IN ALPHA TEAM!

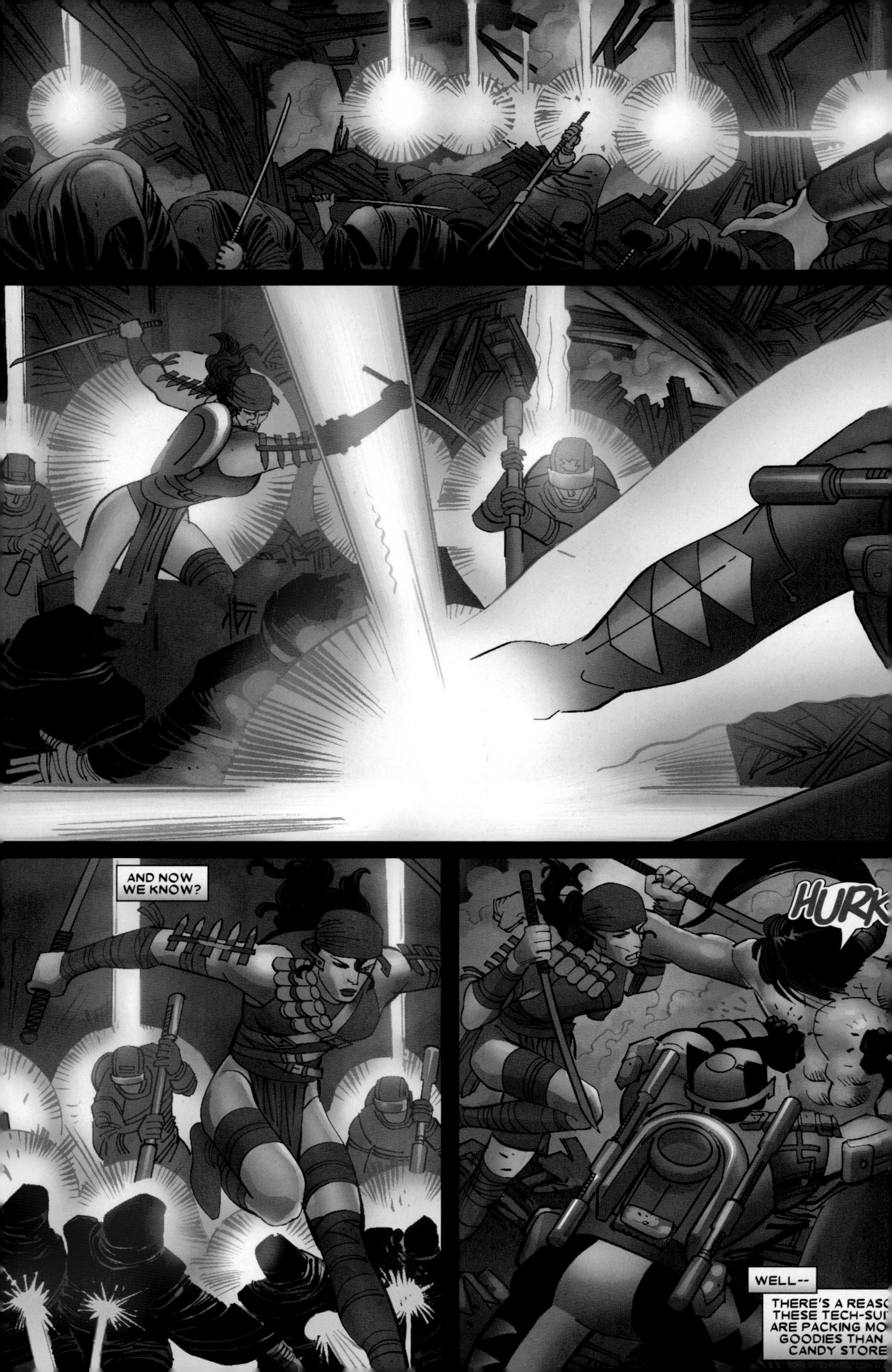
AND NOW WE KNOW?
HURK
WELL--
THERE'S A REASO
THESE TECH-SUI
ARE PACKING MO
GOODIES THAN
CANDY STORE

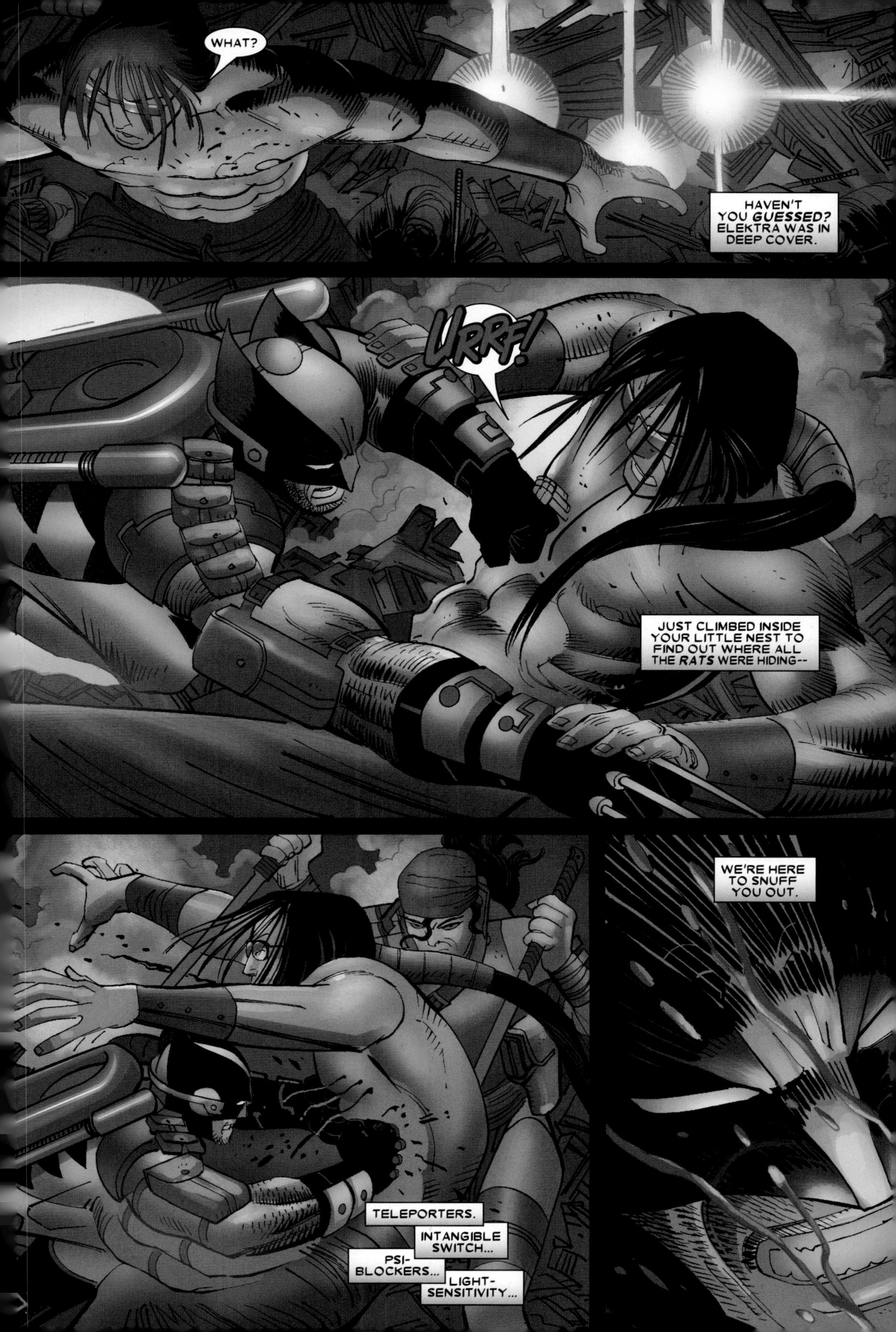
WHAT?
HAVEN'T YOU GUESSED? ELEKTRA WAS IN DEEP COVER.
URRF!
JUST CLIMBED INSIDE YOUR LITTLE NEST TO FIND OUT WHERE ALL THE RATS WERE HIDING--
TELEPORTERS.
INTANGIBLE SWITCH...
PSI-BLOCKERS...
LIGHT-SENSITIVITY...
WE'RE HERE TO SNUFF YOU OUT.

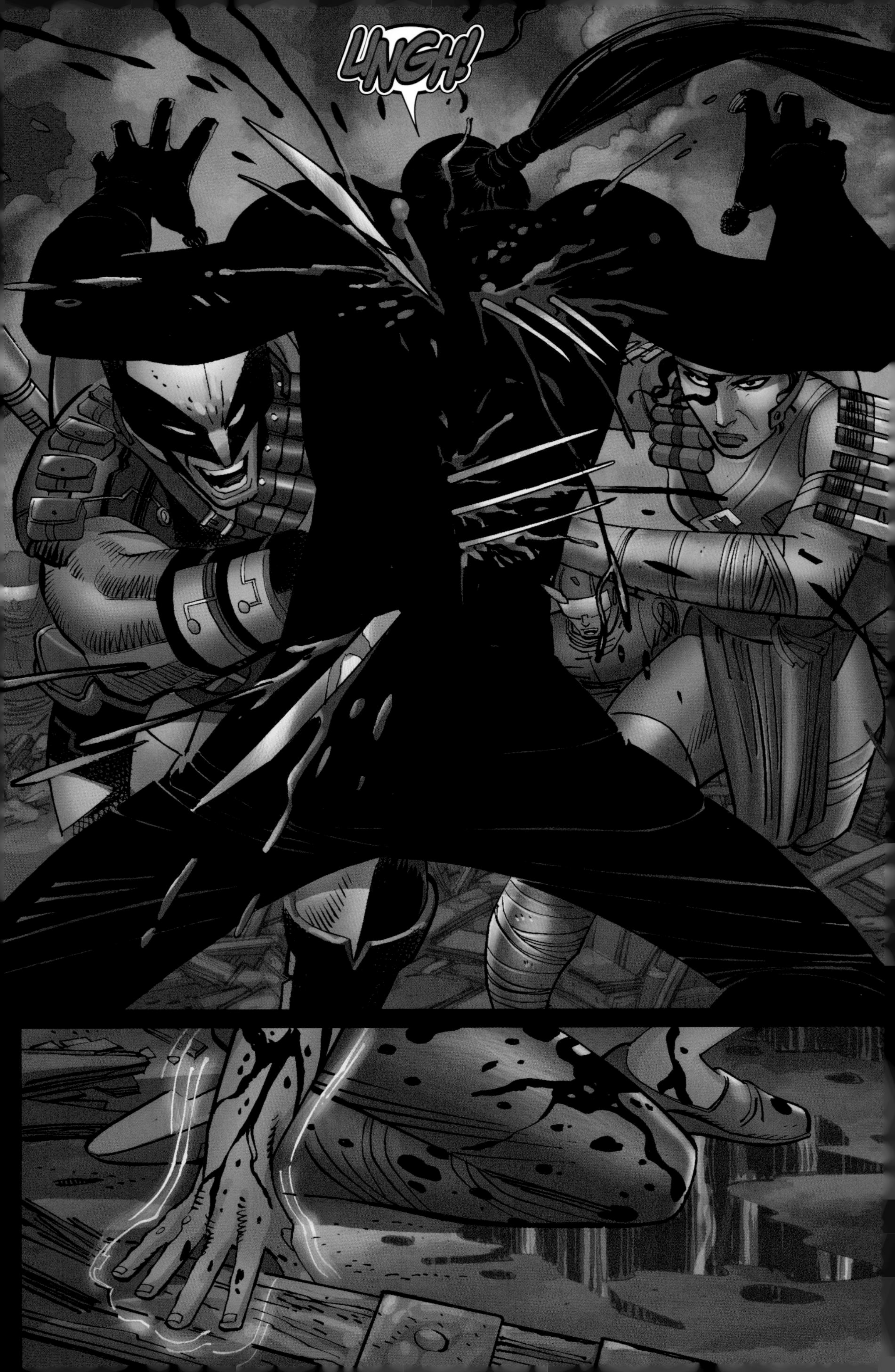
UNGH!

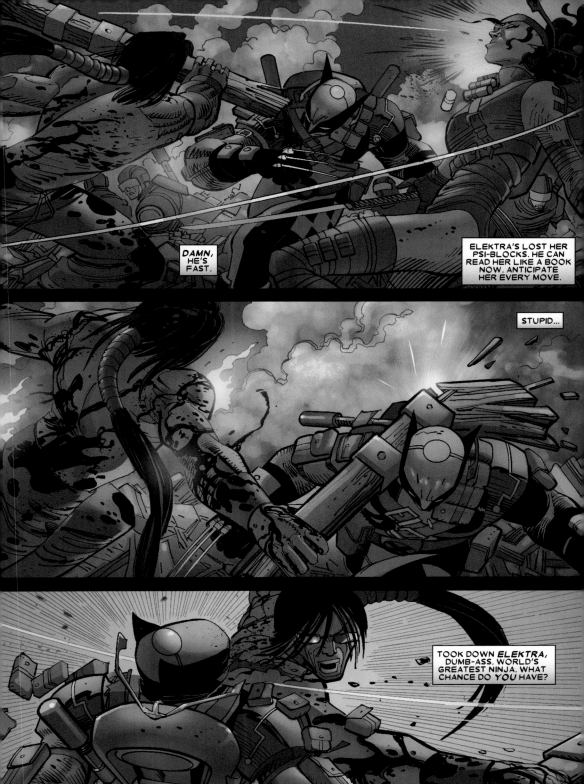

DAMN, HE'S FAST.

ELEKTRA'S LOST HER PSI-BLOCKS. HE CAN READ HER LIKE A BOOK NOW. ANTICIPATE HER EVERY MOVE.

STUPID...

TOOK DOWN *ELEKTRA*, DUMB-ASS. WORLD'S GREATEST NINJA. WHAT CHANCE DO *YOU* HAVE?

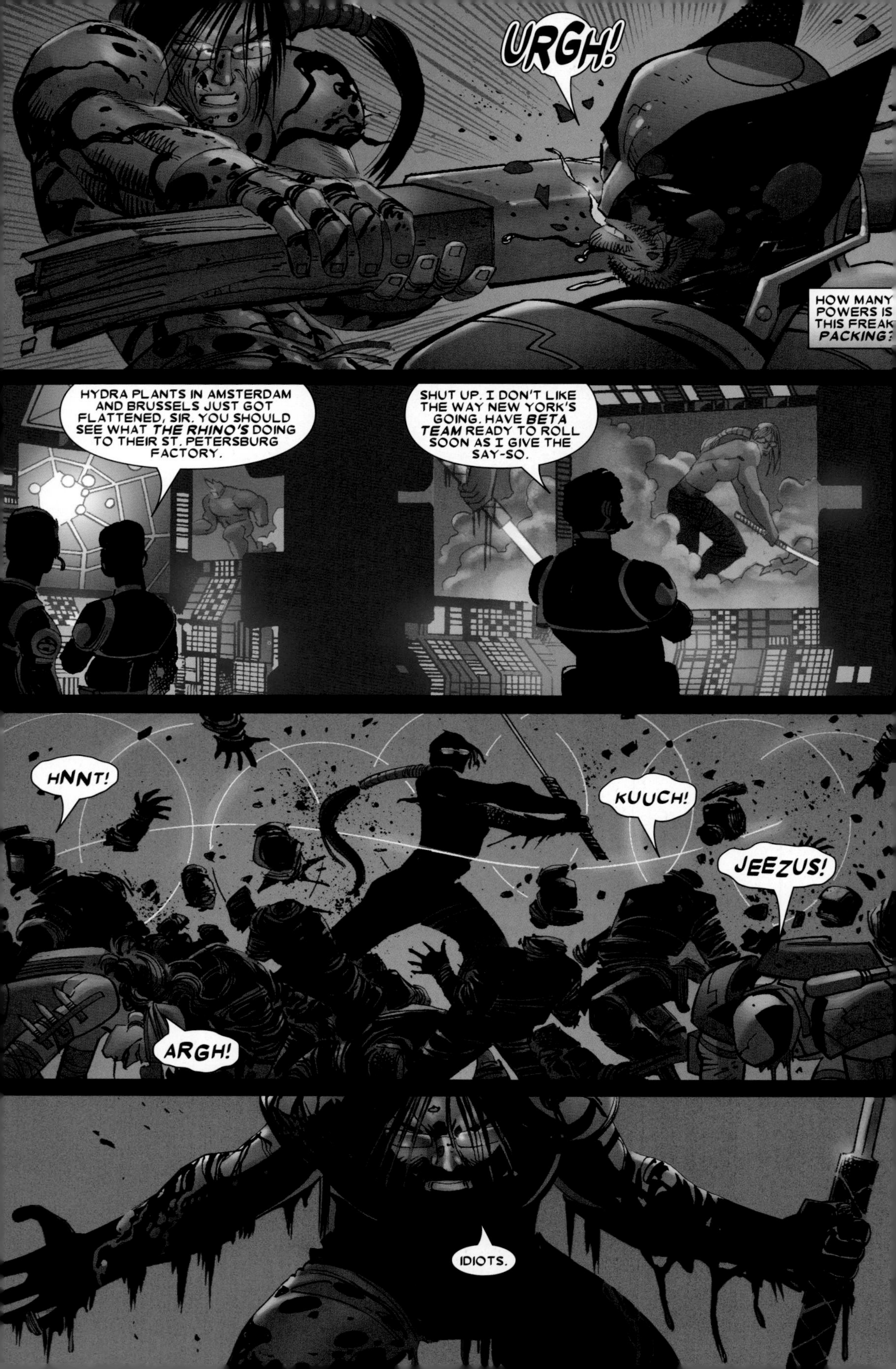
URGH!
HOW MANY POWERS IS THIS FREAK PACKING?
HYDRA PLANTS IN AMSTERDAM AND BRUSSELS JUST GOT FLATTENED, SIR. YOU SHOULD SEE WHAT THE RHINO'S DOING TO THEIR ST. PETERSBURG FACTORY.
SHUT UP. I DON'T LIKE THE WAY NEW YORK'S GOING. HAVE BETA TEAM READY TO ROLL SOON AS I GIVE THE SAY-SO.
HNNT!
KUUCH!
JEEZUS!
ARGH!
IDIOTS.

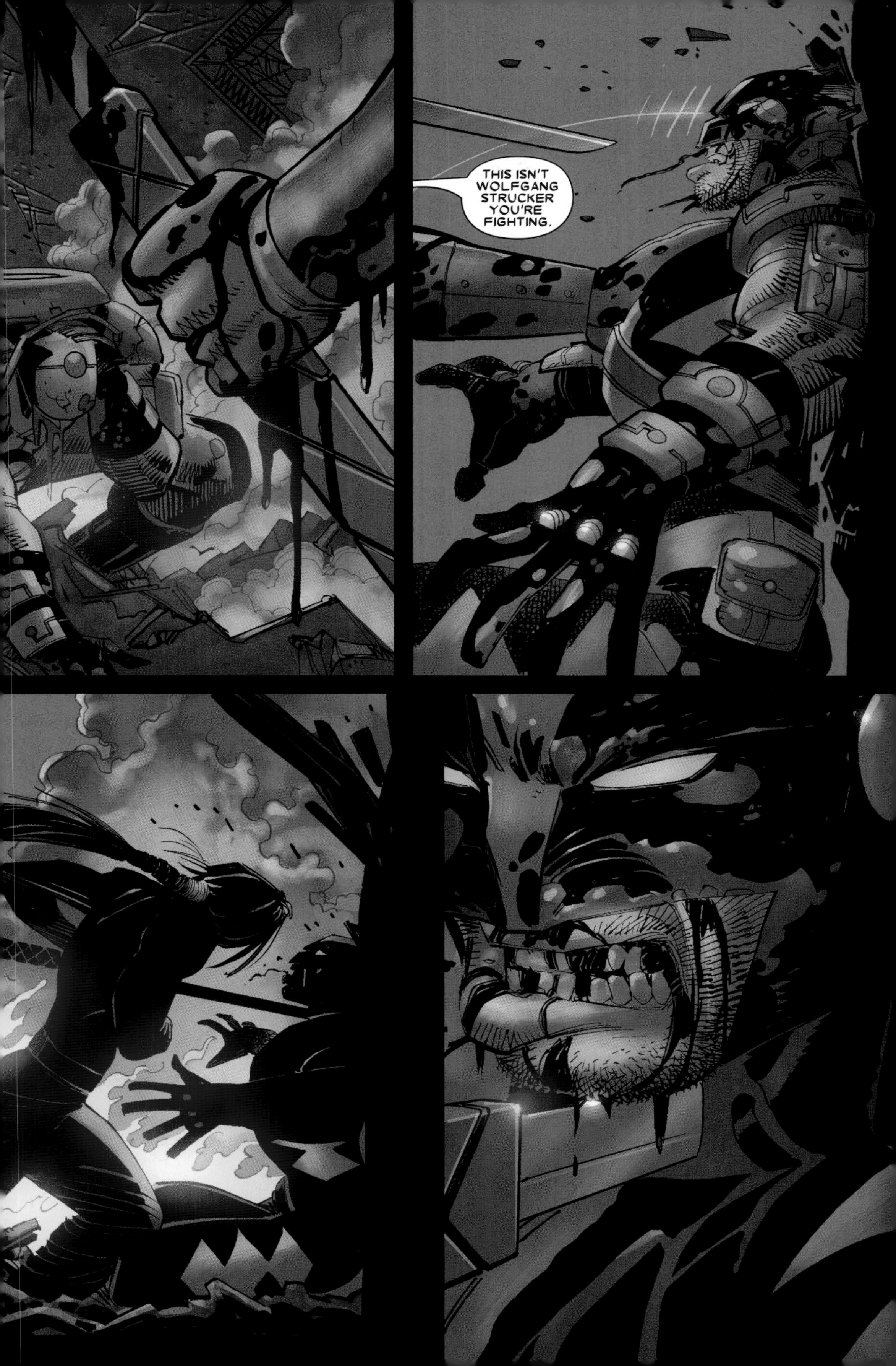
THIS ISN'T WOLFGANG STRUCKER YOU'RE FIGHTING.

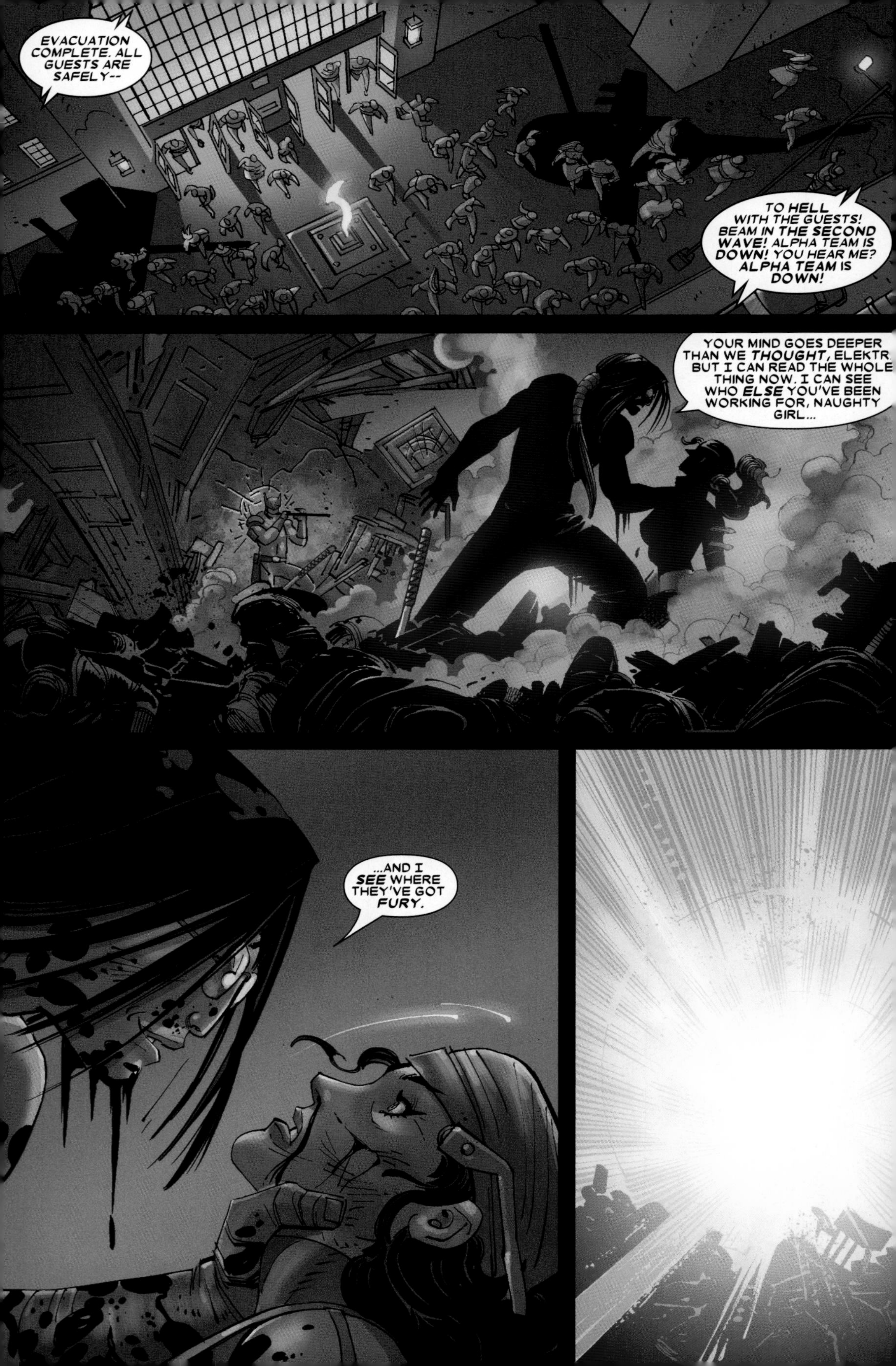
EVACUATION COMPLETE. ALL GUESTS ARE SAFELY--
TO HELL WITH THE GUESTS! BEAM IN THE SECOND WAVE! ALPHA TEAM IS DOWN! YOU HEAR ME? ALPHA TEAM IS DOWN!
YOUR MIND GOES DEEPER THAN WE THOUGHT, ELEKTR BUT I CAN READ THE WHOLE THING NOW. I CAN SEE WHO ELSE YOU'VE BEEN WORKING FOR, NAUGHTY GIRL...
...AND I SEE WHERE THEY'VE GOT FURY.

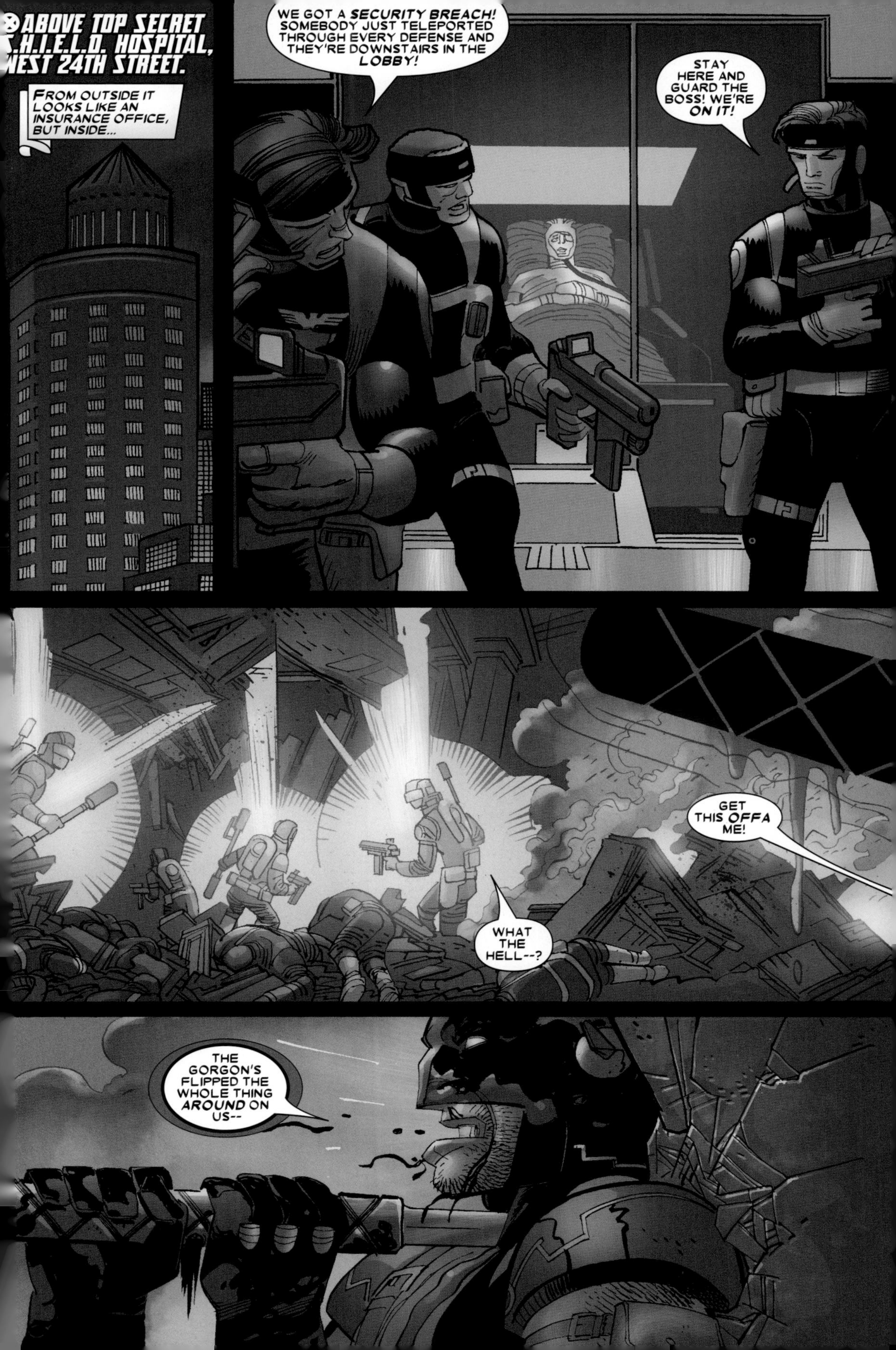
ABOVE TOP SECRET S.H.I.E.L.D. HOSPITAL, WEST 24TH STREET.
FROM OUTSIDE IT LOOKS LIKE AN INSURANCE OFFICE, BUT INSIDE...
WE GOT A SECURITY BREACH! SOMEBODY JUST TELEPORTED THROUGH EVERY DEFENSE AND THEY'RE DOWNSTAIRS IN THE LOBBY!
STAY HERE AND GUARD THE BOSS! WE'RE ON IT!
GET THIS OFFA ME!
WHAT THE HELL--?
THE GORGON'S FLIPPED THE WHOLE THING AROUND ON US--

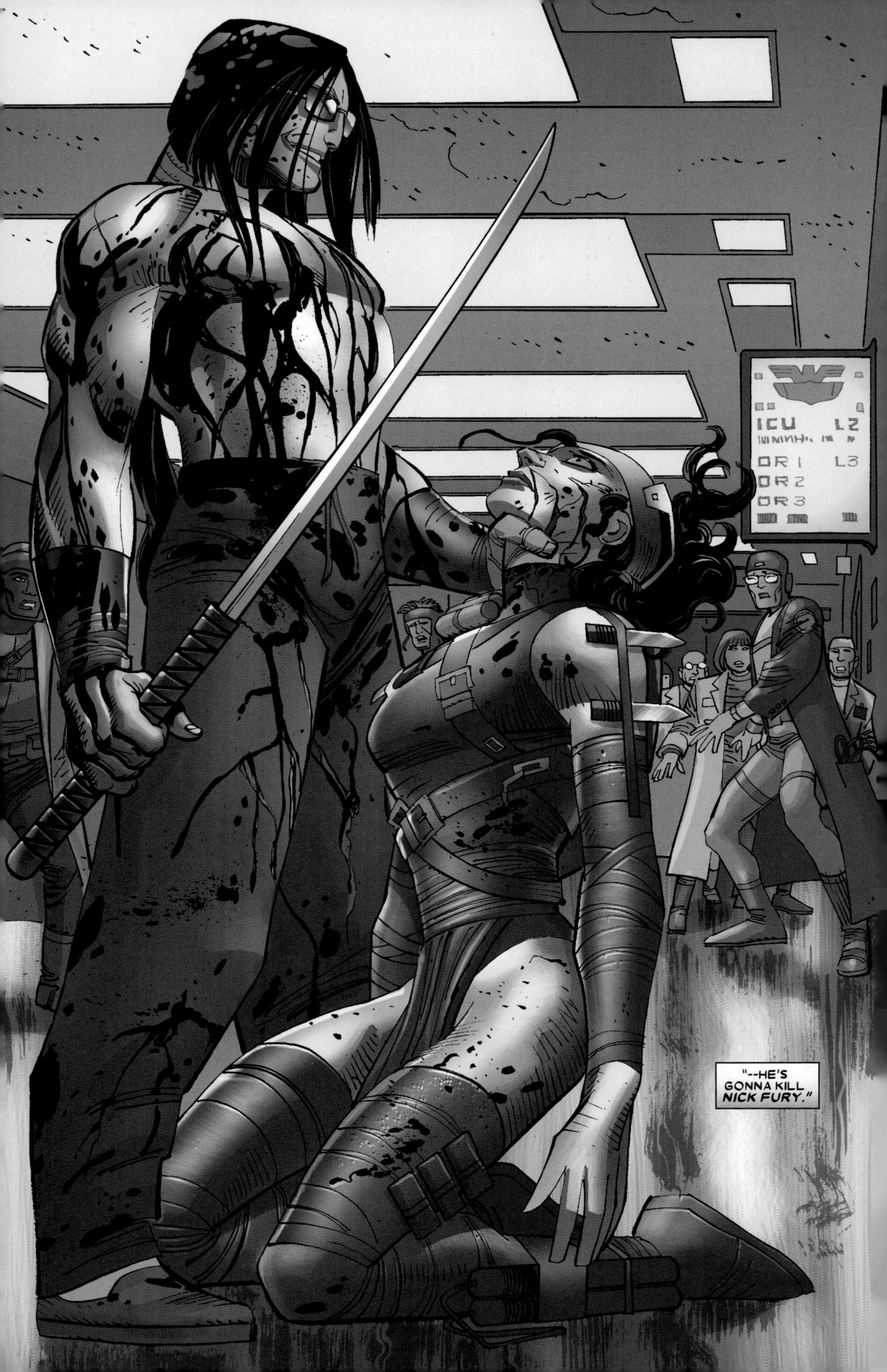
ICU L2
OR 1 L3
OR 2
OR 3
"--HE'S GONNA KILL NICK FURY."

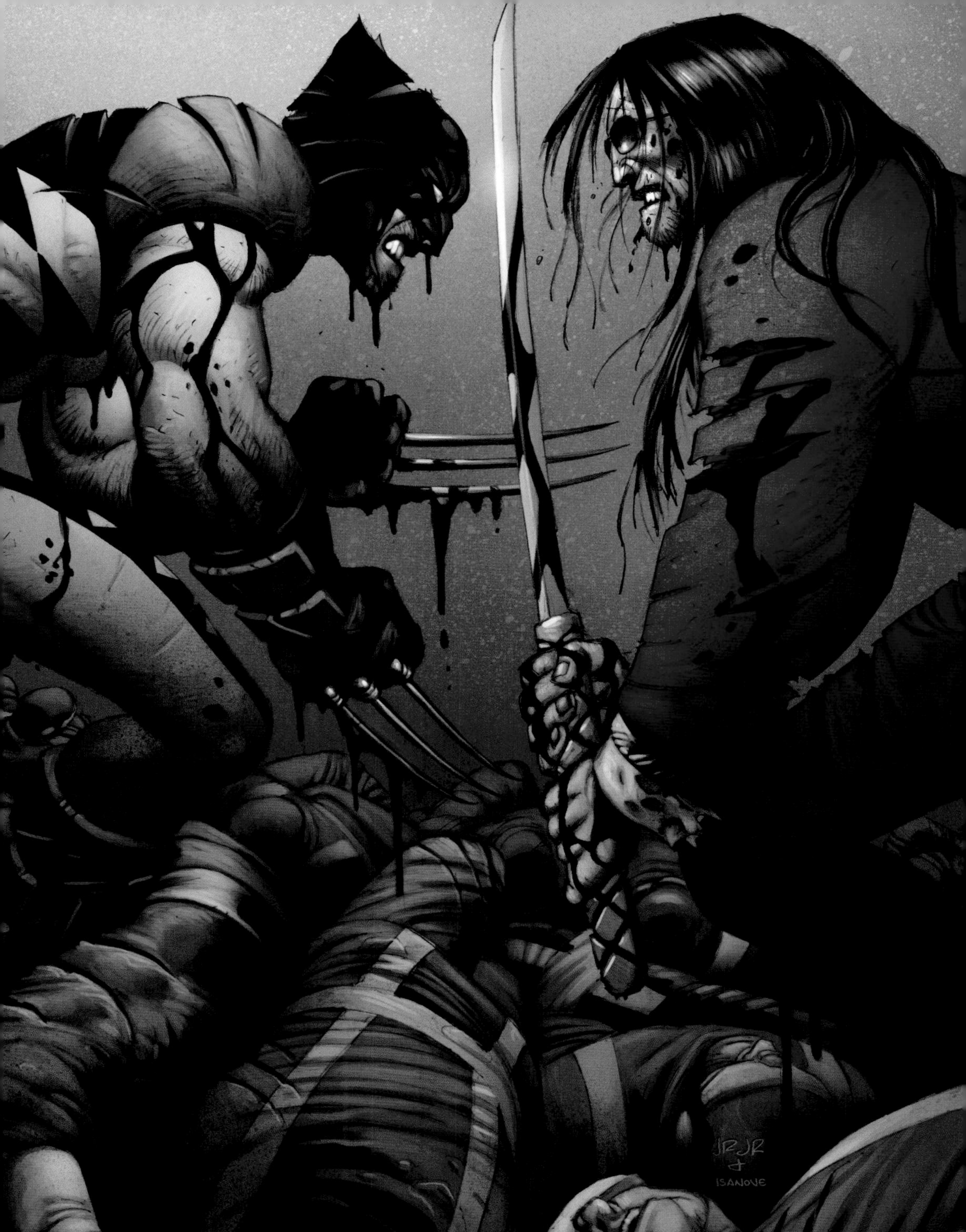
JRJR
&
ISANOVE

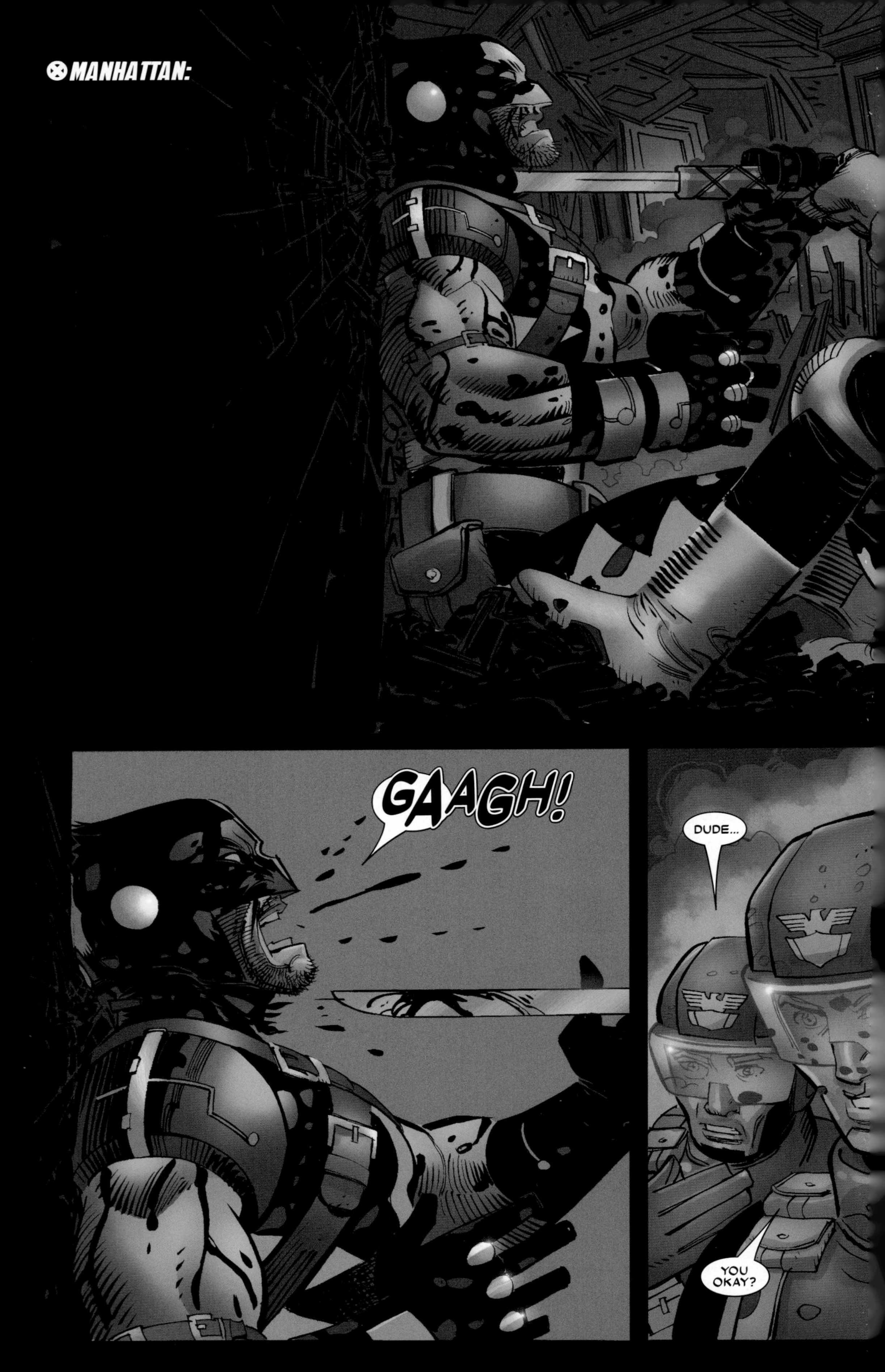
MANHATTAN:
GAAGH!
DUDE...
YOU OKAY?

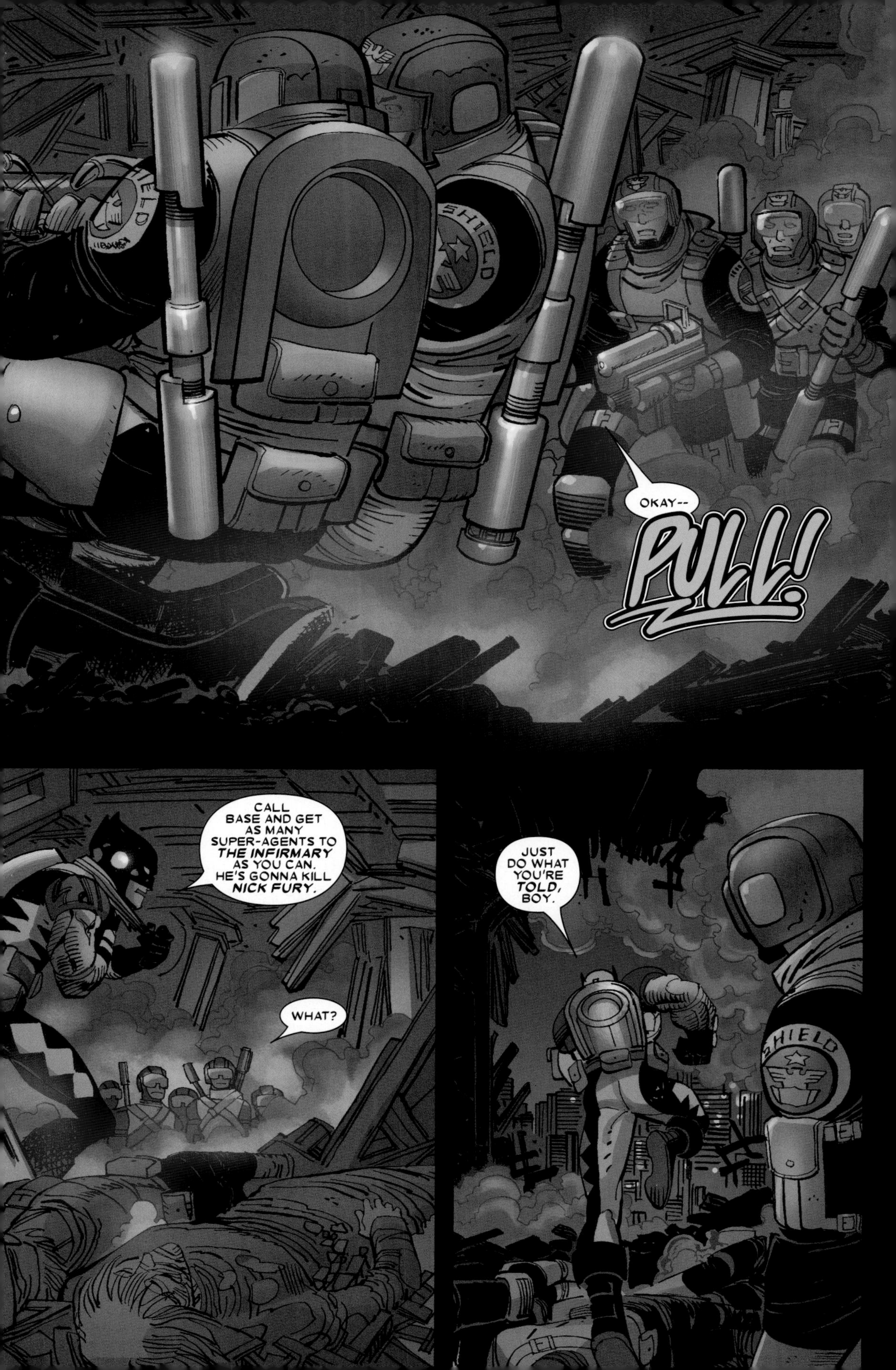
OKAY--
PULL!
CALL BASE AND GET AS MANY SUPER-AGENTS TO *THE INFIRMARY* AS YOU CAN. HE'S GONNA KILL *NICK FURY*.
WHAT?
JUST DO WHAT YOU'RE *TOLD*, BOY.

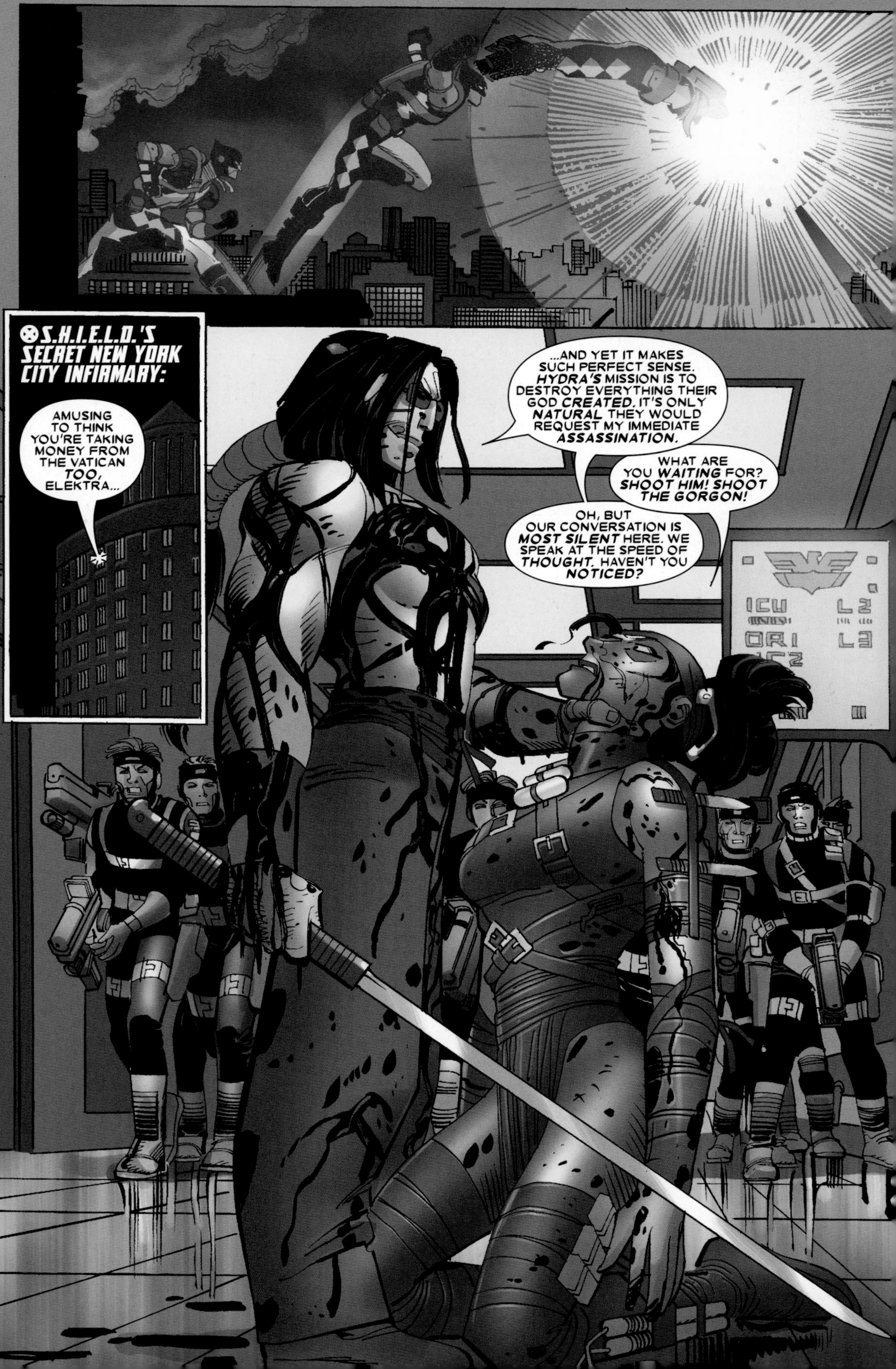
S.H.I.E.L.D.'S SECRET NEW YORK CITY INFIRMARY:
AMUSING TO THINK YOU'RE TAKING MONEY FROM THE VATICAN *TOO*, ELEKTRA...
...AND YET IT MAKES SUCH PERFECT SENSE. *HYDRA'S* MISSION IS TO DESTROY EVERYTHING THEIR GOD *CREATED*. IT'S ONLY *NATURAL* THEY WOULD REQUEST MY IMMEDIATE *ASSASSINATION*.
WHAT ARE YOU *WAITING* FOR? *SHOOT HIM! SHOOT THE GORGON!*
OH, BUT OUR CONVERSATION IS *MOST SILENT* HERE. WE SPEAK AT THE SPEED OF *THOUGHT*. HAVEN'T YOU *NOTICED?*
ICU L2
ORI L3

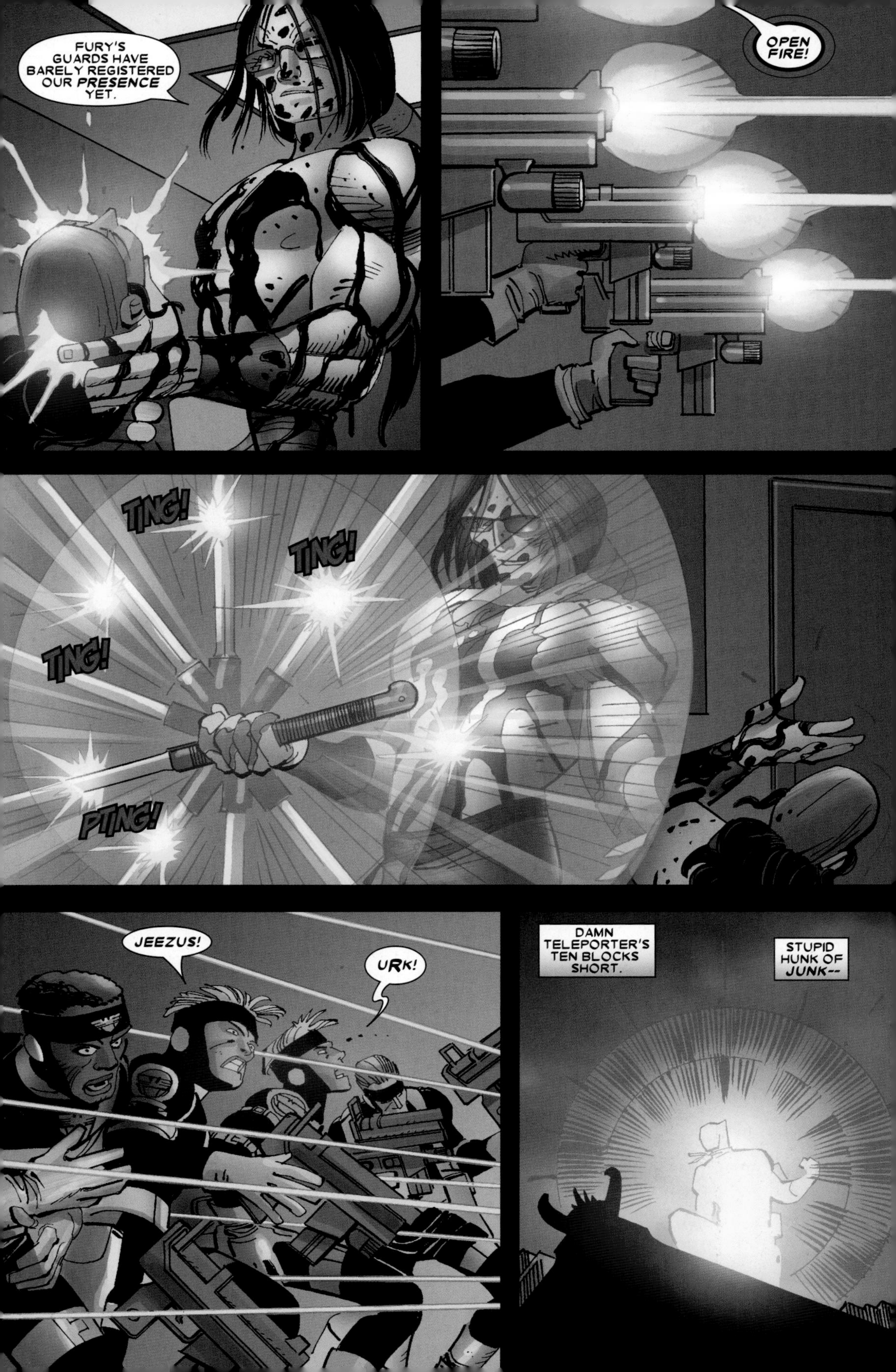
FURY'S GUARDS HAVE BARELY REGISTERED OUR PRESENCE YET.
OPEN FIRE!
TING!
TING!
TING!
PTING!
JEEZUS!
URK!
DAMN TELEPORTER'S TEN BLOCKS SHORT.
STUPID HUNK OF JUNK--

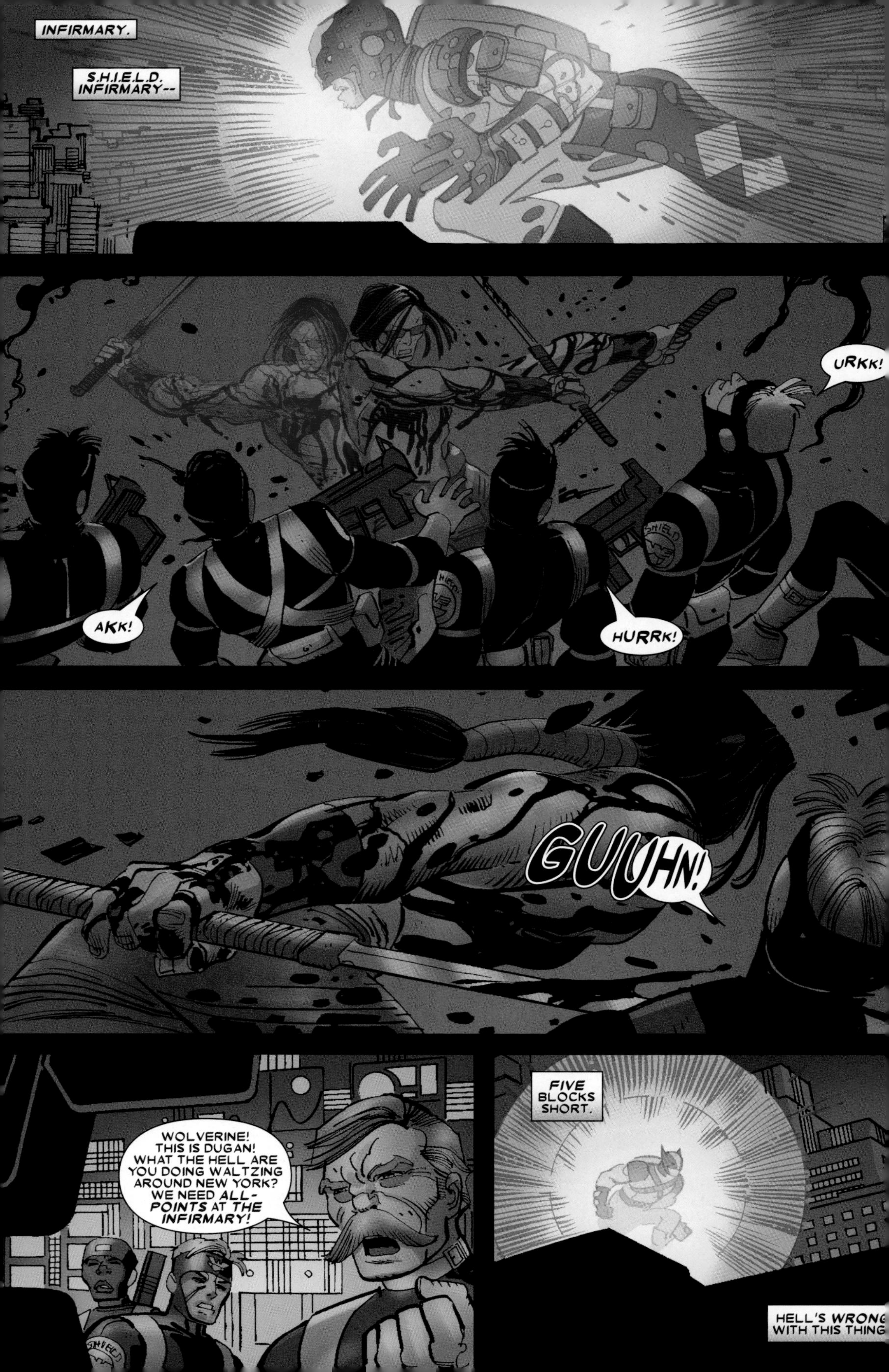
INFIRMARY.
S.H.I.E.L.D. INFIRMARY--
URKK!
AKK!
HURRK!
GUUHN!
WOLVERINE! THIS IS DUGAN! WHAT THE HELL ARE YOU DOING WALTZING AROUND NEW YORK? WE NEED ALL-POINTS AT THE INFIRMARY!
FIVE BLOCKS SHORT.
HELL'S WRONG WITH THIS THING

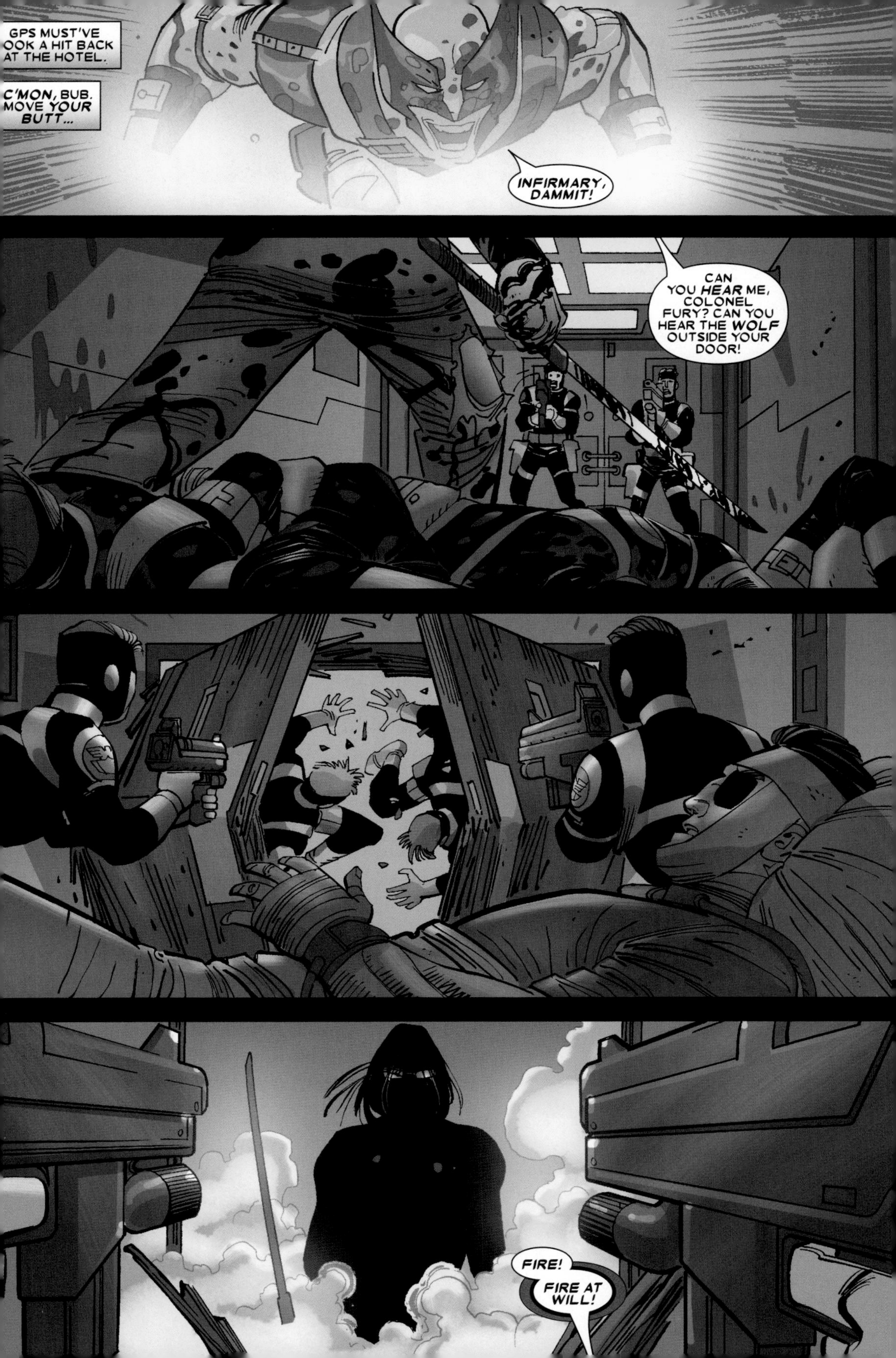
GPS MUST'VE OOK A HIT BACK AT THE HOTEL.
C'MON, BUB. MOVE YOUR BUTT...
INFIRMARY, DAMMIT!
CAN YOU HEAR ME, COLONEL FURY? CAN YOU HEAR THE WOLF OUTSIDE YOUR DOOR!
FIRE!
FIRE AT WILL!

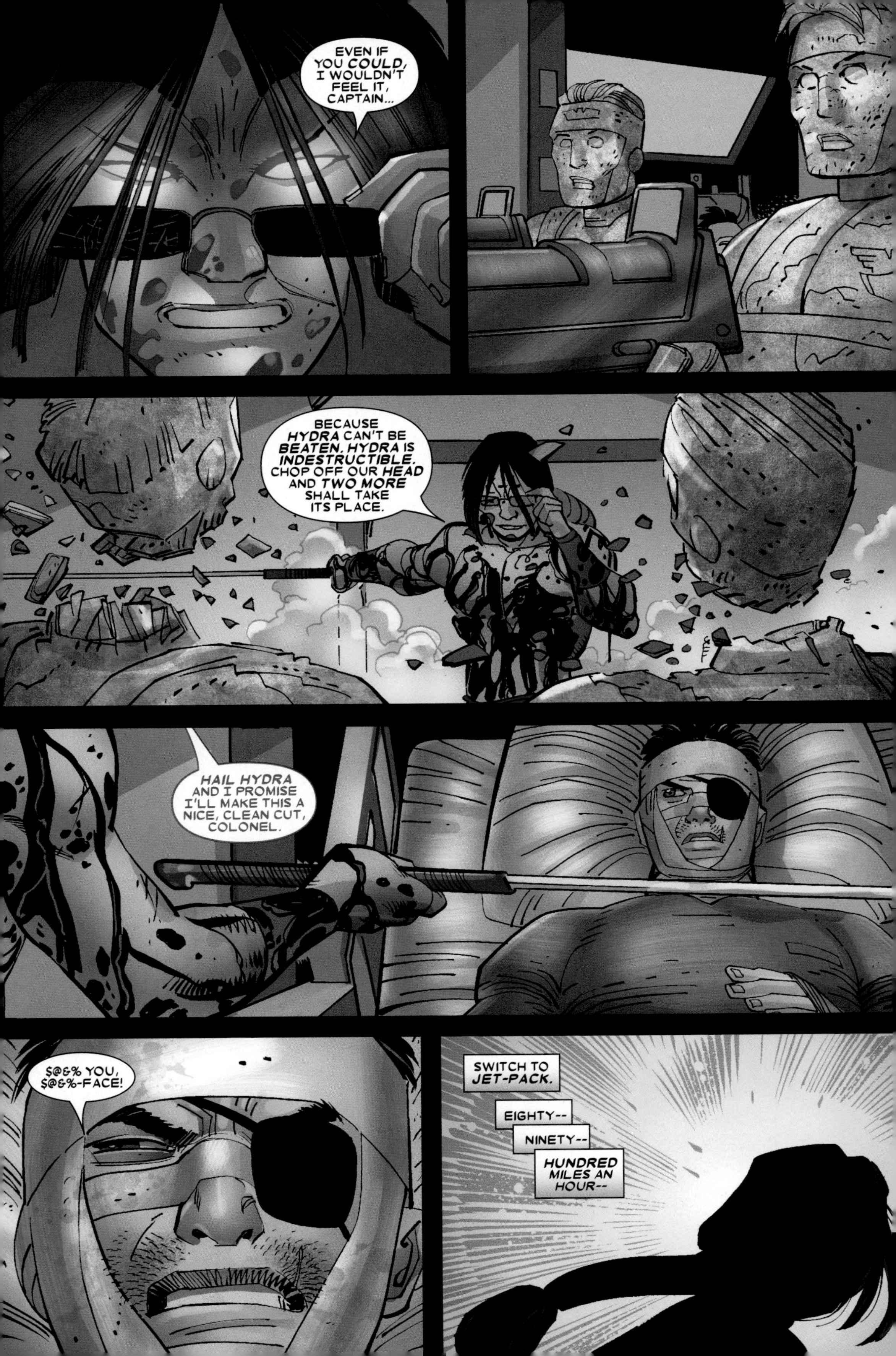
EVEN IF YOU COULD, I WOULDN'T FEEL IT, CAPTAIN...
BECAUSE HYDRA CAN'T BE BEATEN. HYDRA IS INDESTRUCTIBLE. CHOP OFF OUR HEAD AND TWO MORE SHALL TAKE ITS PLACE.
HAIL HYDRA AND I PROMISE I'LL MAKE THIS A NICE, CLEAN CUT, COLONEL.
$@&% YOU, $@&%-FACE!
SWITCH TO JET-PACK.
EIGHTY--
NINETY--
HUNDRED MILES AN HOUR--

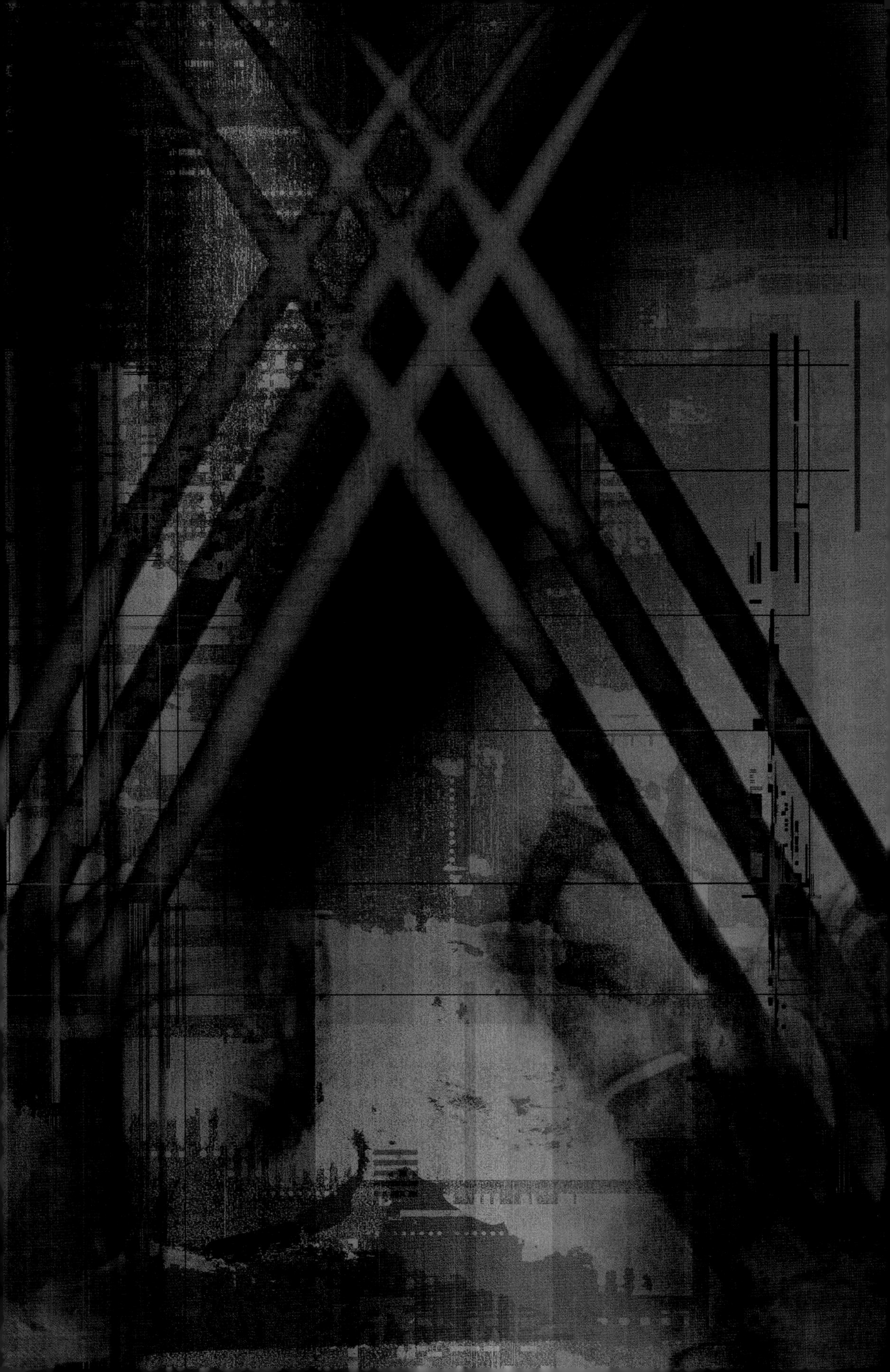

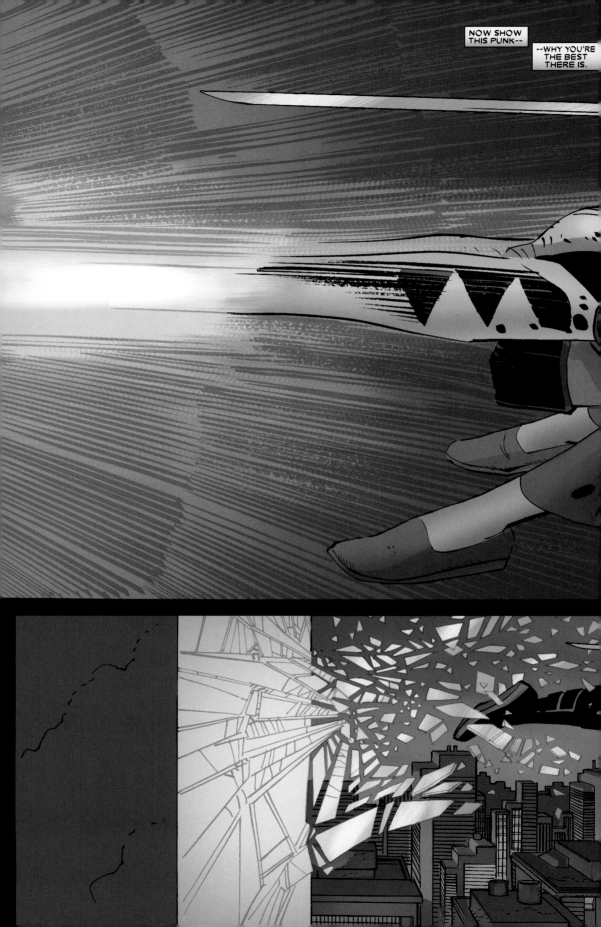

NOW SHOW THIS PUNK--

--WHY YOU'RE THE BEST THERE IS.

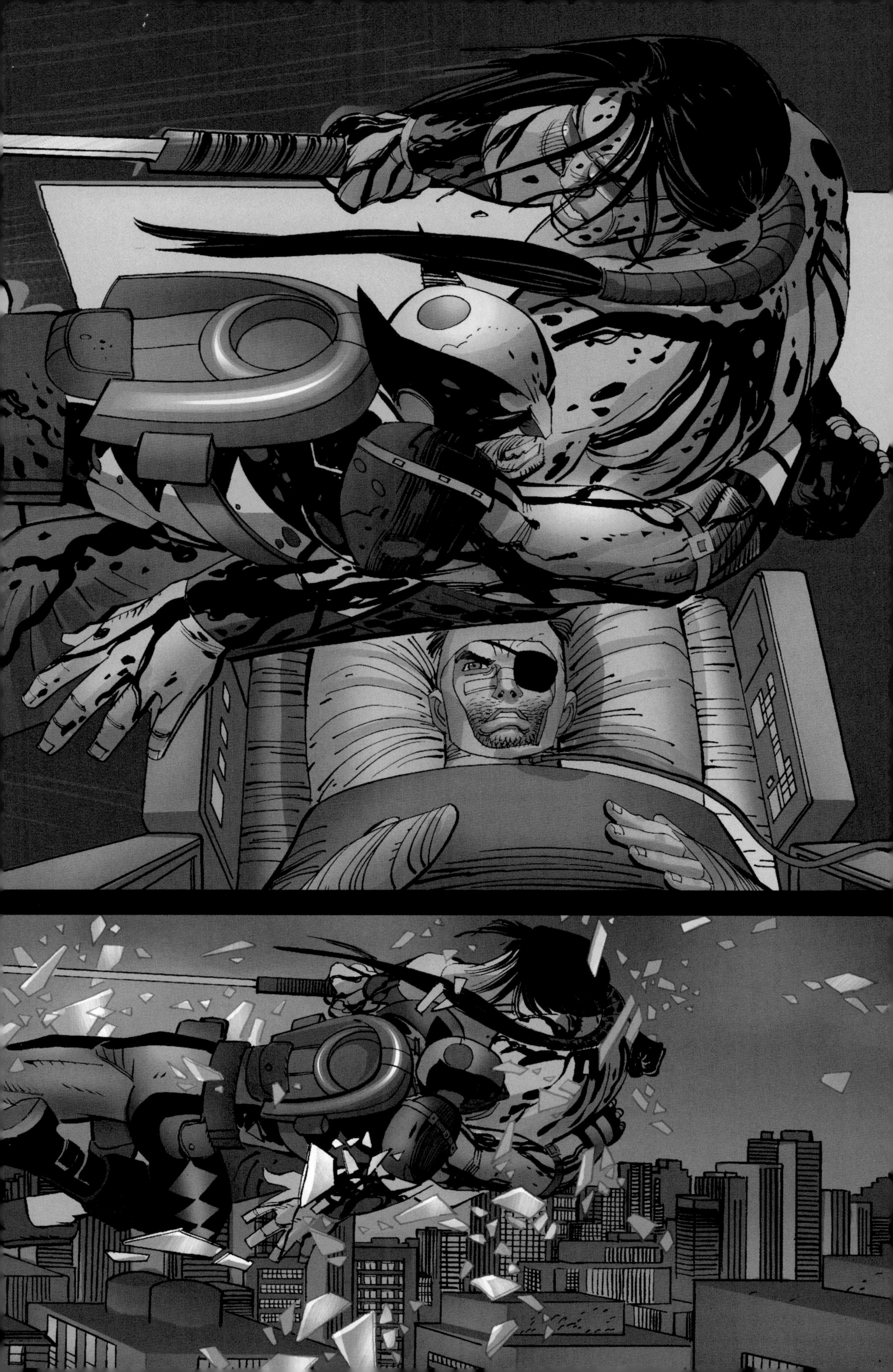

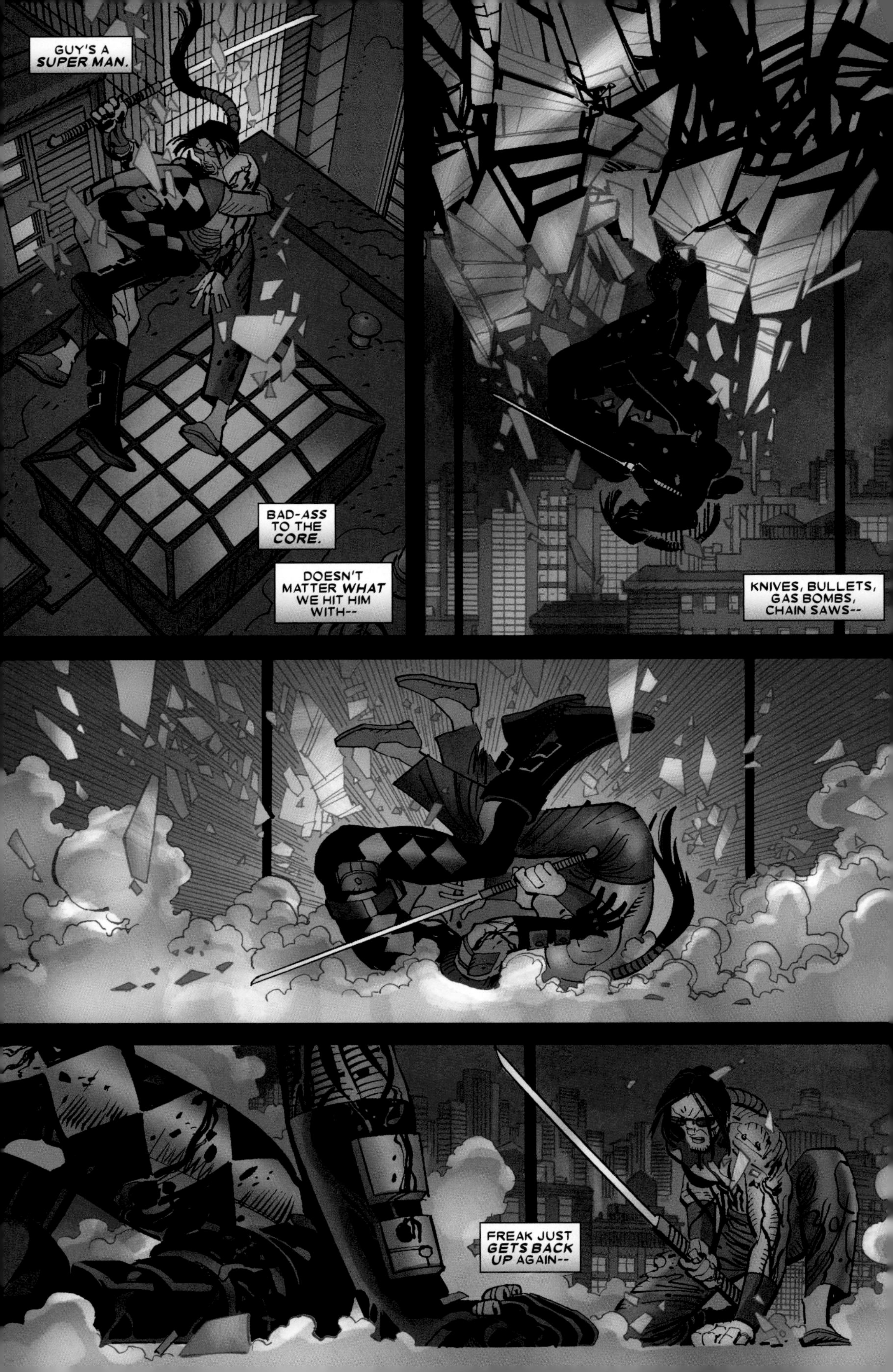
GUY'S A SUPER MAN.
BAD-ASS TO THE CORE.
DOESN'T MATTER WHAT WE HIT HIM WITH--
KNIVES, BULLETS, GAS BOMBS, CHAIN SAWS--
FREAK JUST GETS BACK UP AGAIN--

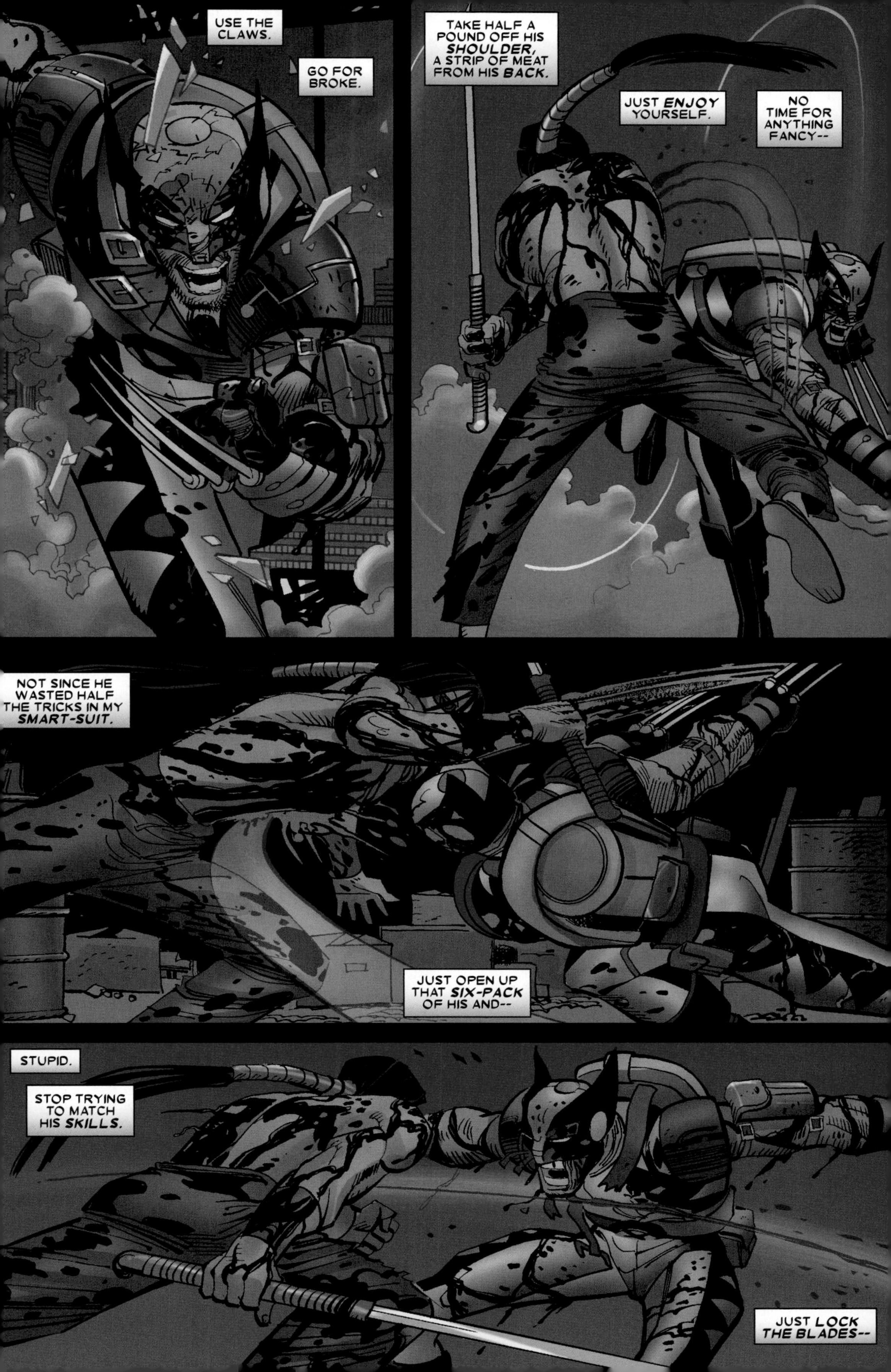
USE THE CLAWS.
GO FOR BROKE.
TAKE HALF A POUND OFF HIS SHOULDER, A STRIP OF MEAT FROM HIS BACK.
JUST ENJOY YOURSELF.
NO TIME FOR ANYTHING FANCY--
NOT SINCE HE WASTED HALF THE TRICKS IN MY SMART-SUIT.
JUST OPEN UP THAT SIX-PACK OF HIS AND--
STUPID.
STOP TRYING TO MATCH HIS SKILLS.
JUST LOCK THE BLADES--

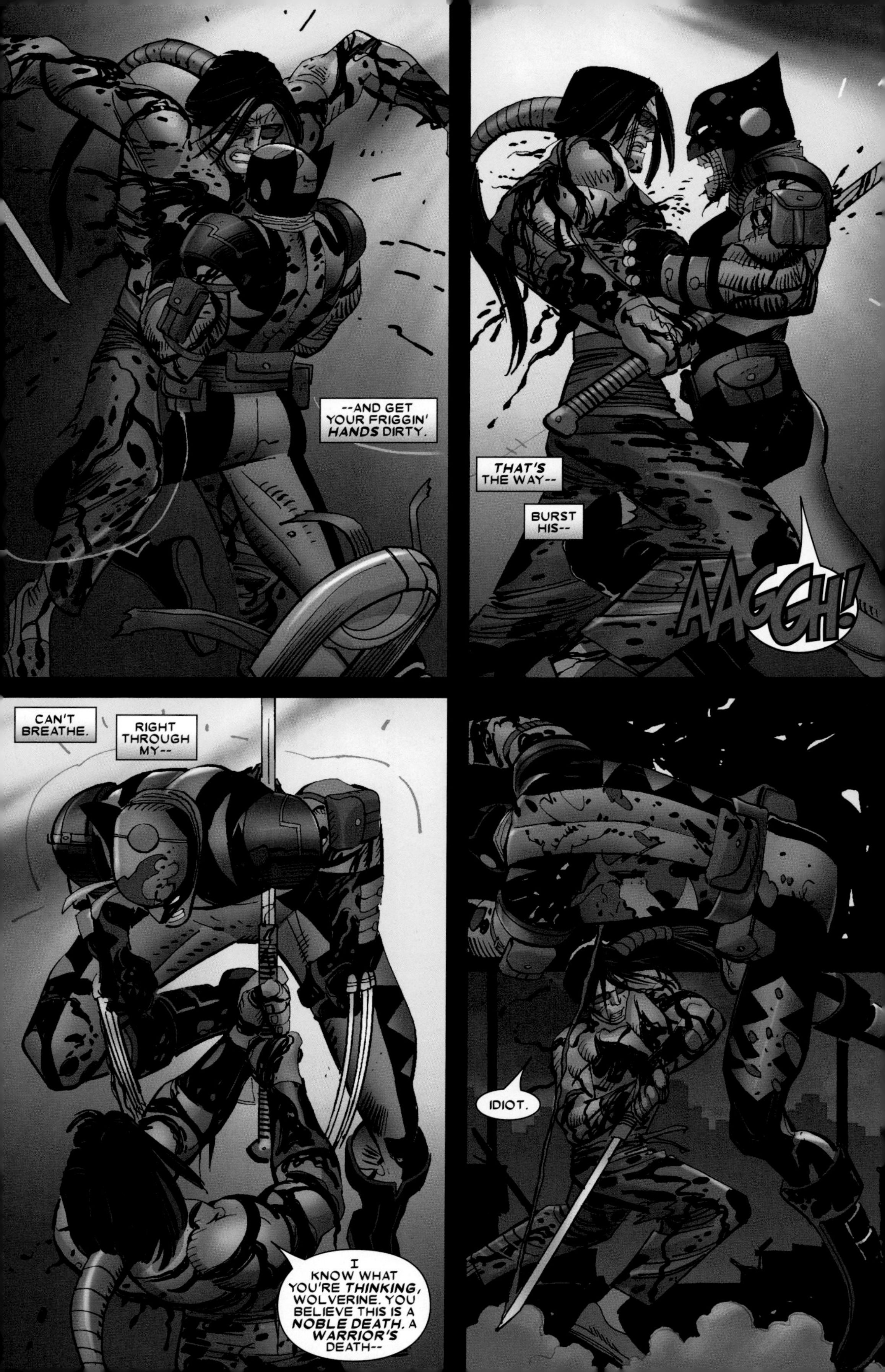

--AND GET YOUR FRIGGIN' HANDS DIRTY.
THAT'S THE WAY--
BURST HIS--
AAGGH!
CAN'T BREATHE.
RIGHT THROUGH MY--
I KNOW WHAT YOU'RE THINKING, WOLVERINE. YOU BELIEVE THIS IS A NOBLE DEATH. A WARRIOR'S DEATH--
IDIOT.

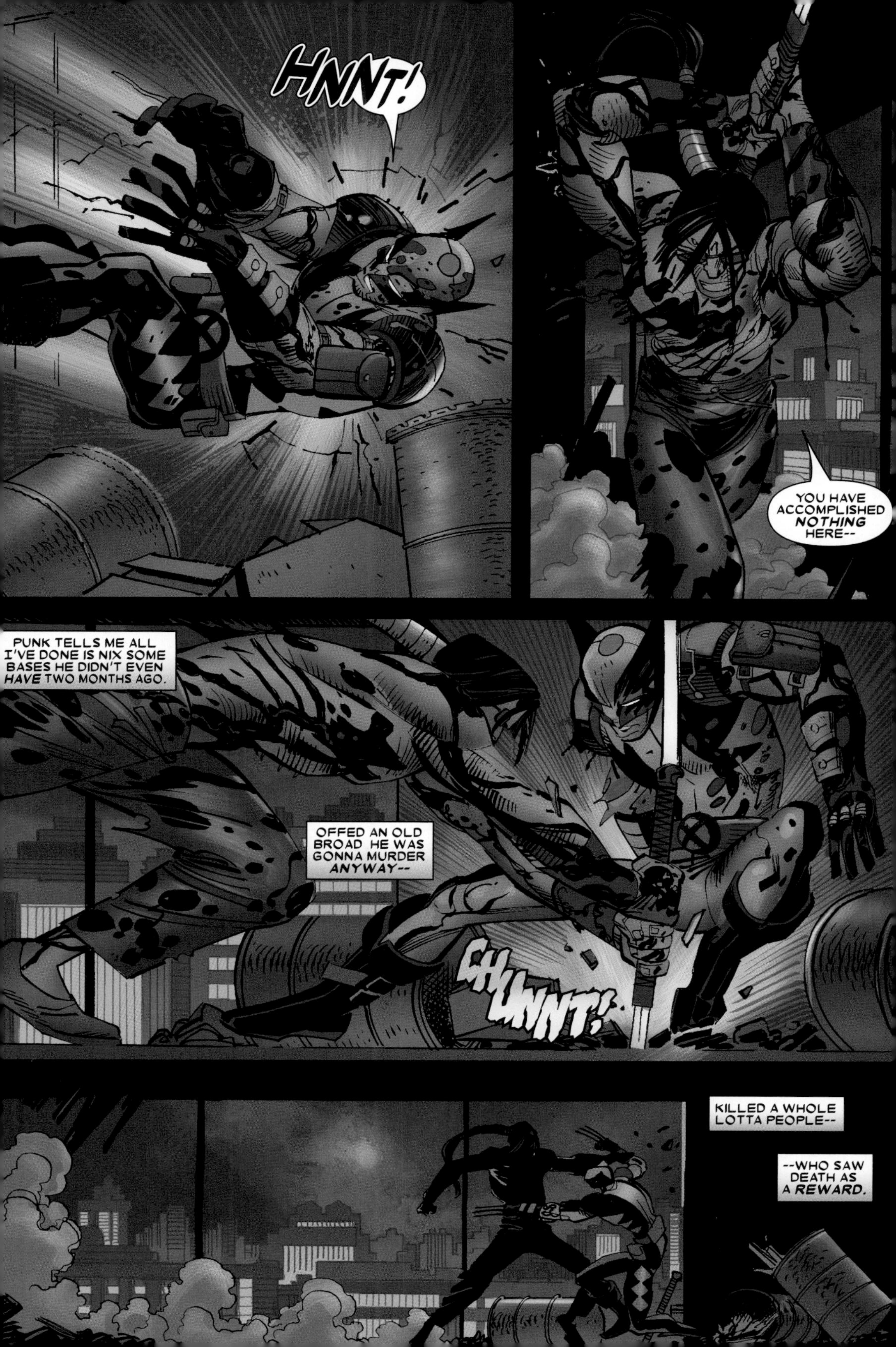
HNNT!
YOU HAVE ACCOMPLISHED NOTHING HERE--
PUNK TELLS ME ALL I'VE DONE IS NIX SOME BASES HE DIDN'T EVEN HAVE TWO MONTHS AGO.
OFFED AN OLD BROAD HE WAS GONNA MURDER ANYWAY--
CHUNNT!
KILLED A WHOLE LOTTA PEOPLE--
--WHO SAW DEATH AS A REWARD.

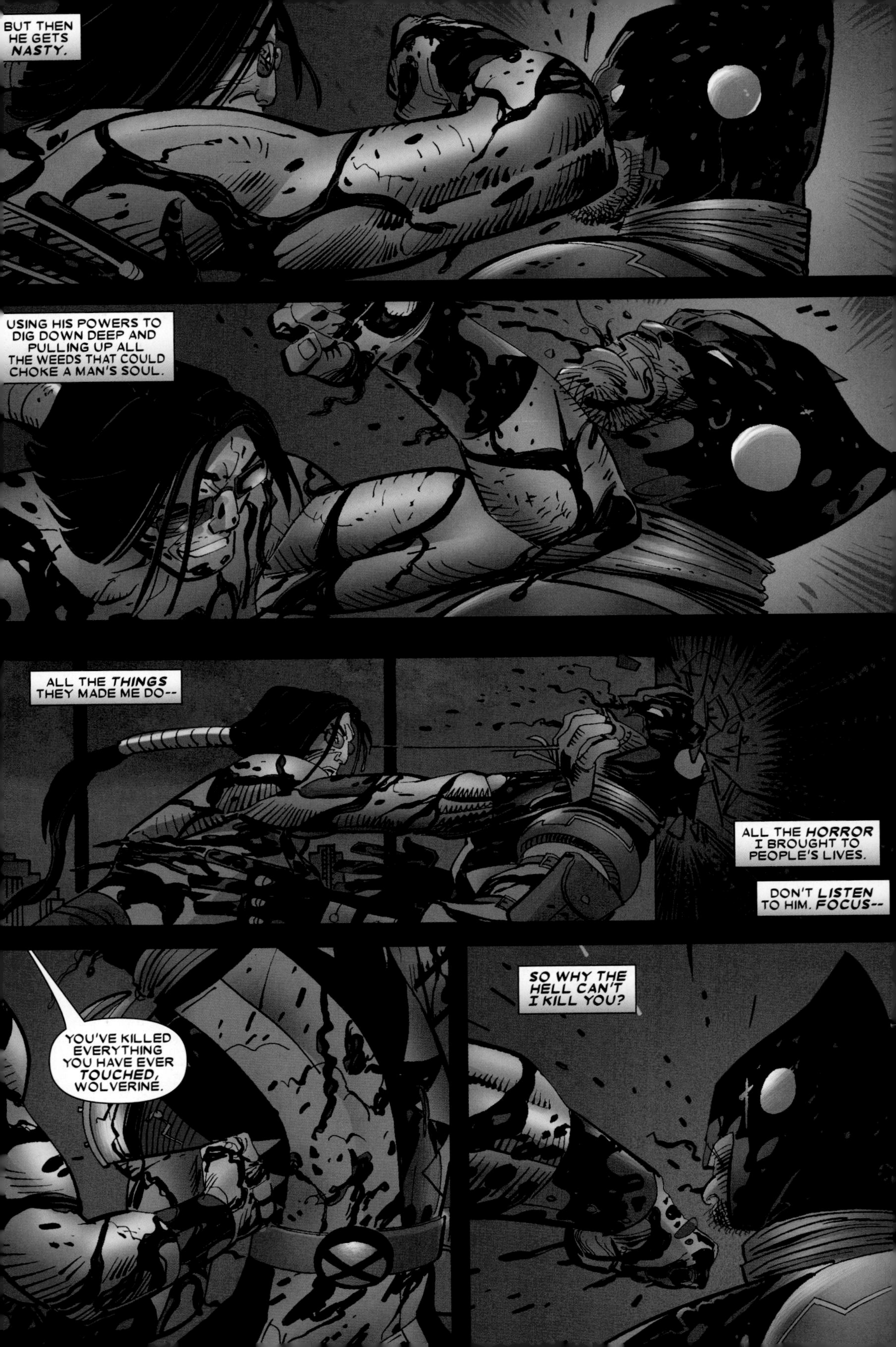

BUT THEN HE GETS *NASTY*.
USING HIS POWERS TO DIG DOWN DEEP AND PULLING UP ALL THE WEEDS THAT COULD CHOKE A MAN'S SOUL.
ALL THE *THINGS* THEY MADE ME DO--
ALL THE *HORROR* I BROUGHT TO PEOPLE'S LIVES.
DON'T *LISTEN* TO HIM. *FOCUS*--
YOU'VE KILLED EVERYTHING YOU HAVE EVER *TOUCHED*, WOLVERINE.
SO WHY THE HELL CAN'T I KILL YOU?

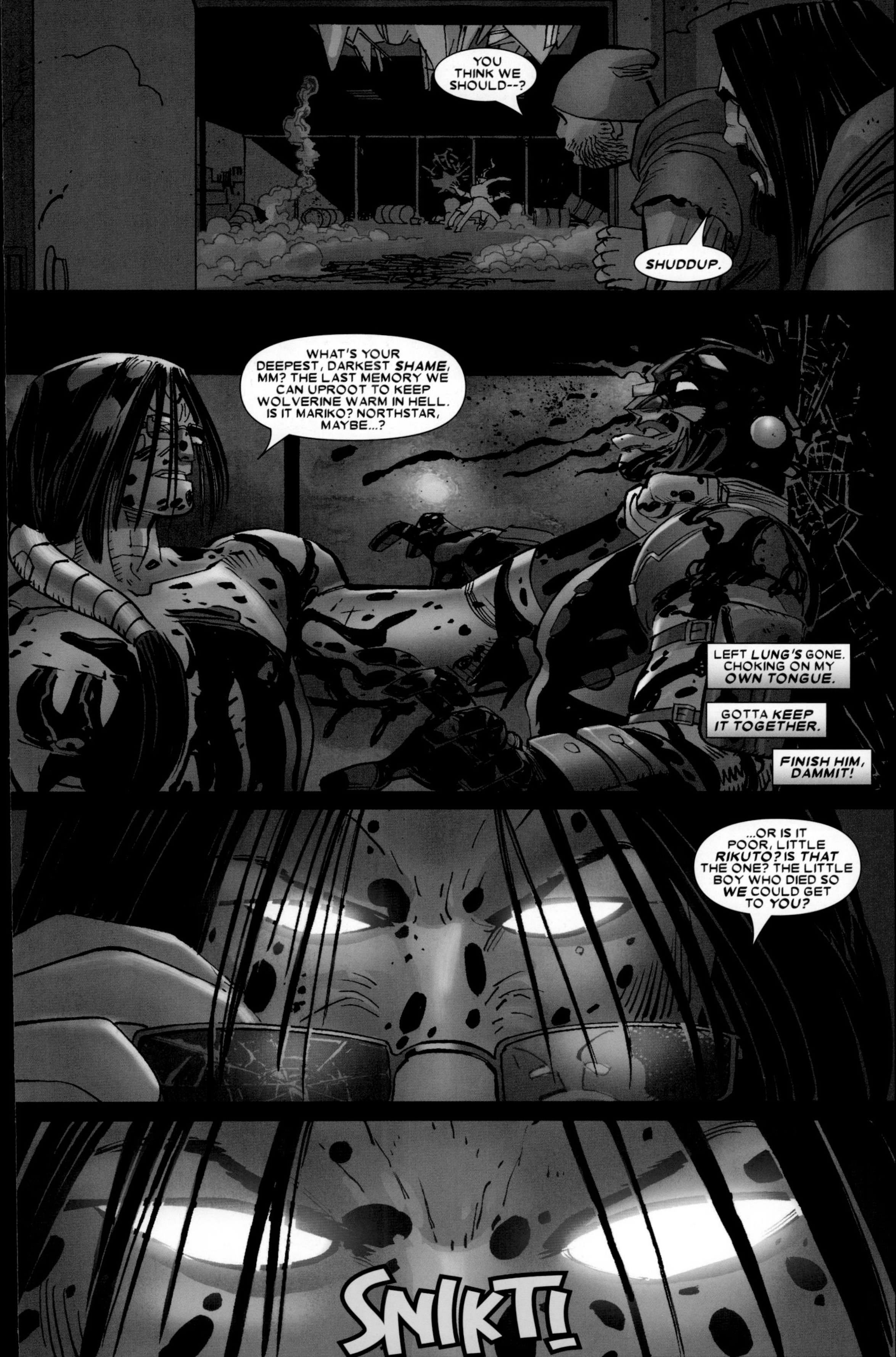
YOU THINK WE SHOULD--?
SHUDDUP.
WHAT'S YOUR DEEPEST, DARKEST SHAME, MM? THE LAST MEMORY WE CAN UPROOT TO KEEP WOLVERINE WARM IN HELL. IS IT MARIKO? NORTHSTAR, MAYBE...?
LEFT LUNG'S GONE. CHOKING ON MY OWN TONGUE.
GOTTA KEEP IT TOGETHER.
FINISH HIM, DAMMIT!
...OR IS IT POOR, LITTLE RIKUTO? IS THAT THE ONE? THE LITTLE BOY WHO DIED SO WE COULD GET TO YOU?
SNIKT!

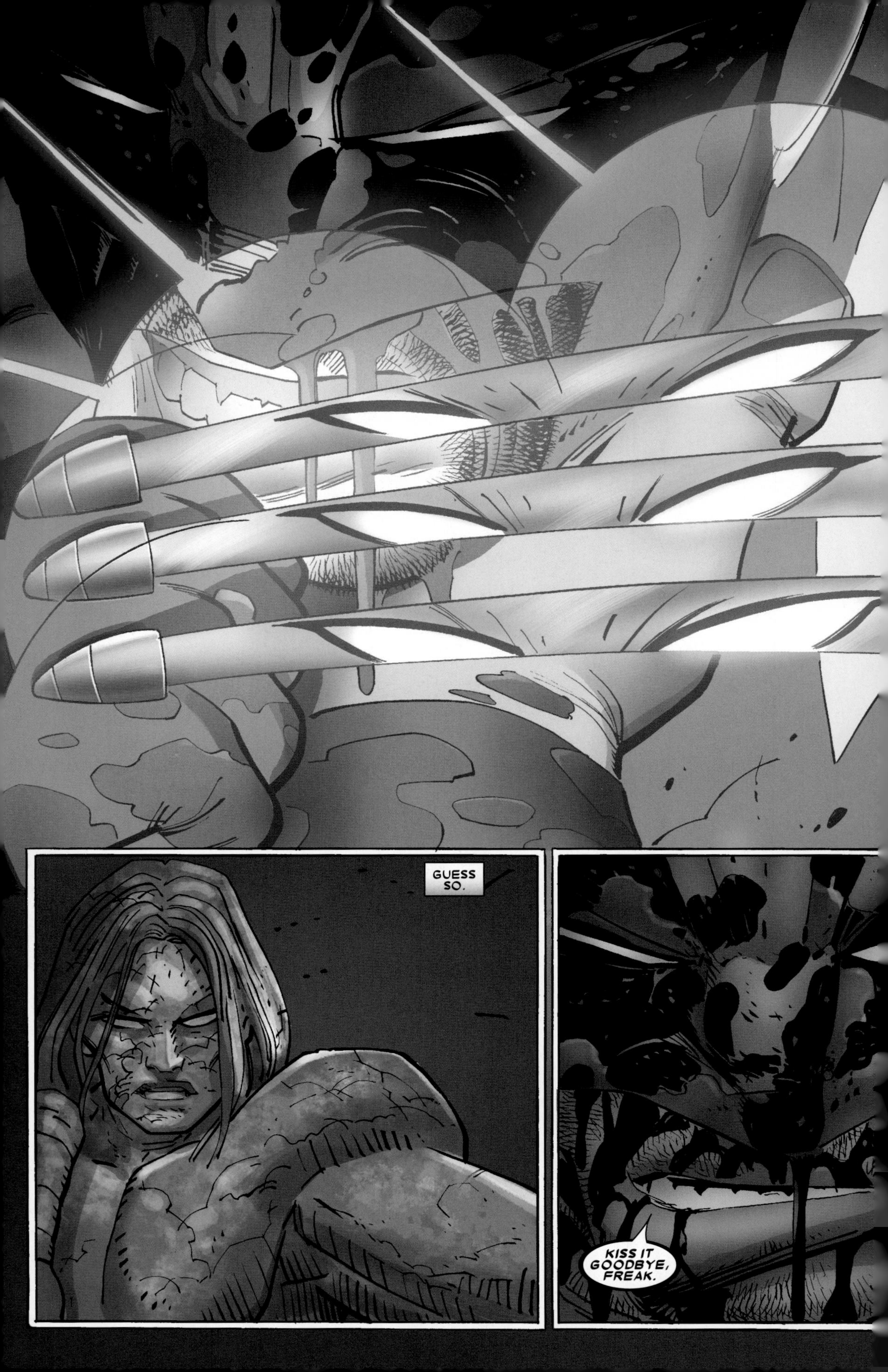
GUESS SO.
KISS IT GOODBYE, FREAK.

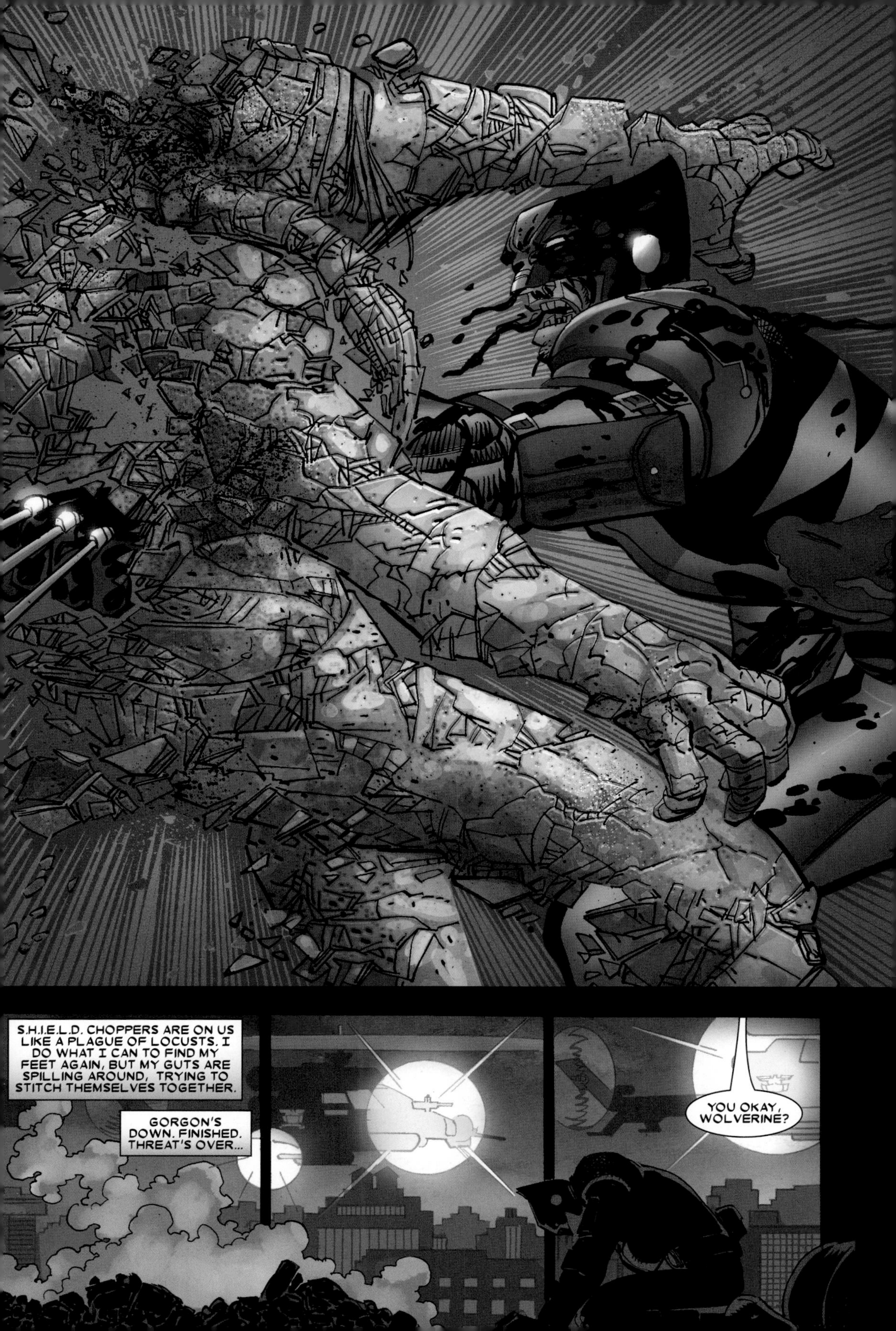
S.H.I.E.L.D. CHOPPERS ARE ON US LIKE A PLAGUE OF LOCUSTS. I DO WHAT I CAN TO FIND MY FEET AGAIN, BUT MY GUTS ARE SPILLING AROUND, TRYING TO STITCH THEMSELVES TOGETHER.
GORGON'S DOWN. FINISHED. THREAT'S OVER...
YOU OKAY, WOLVERINE?

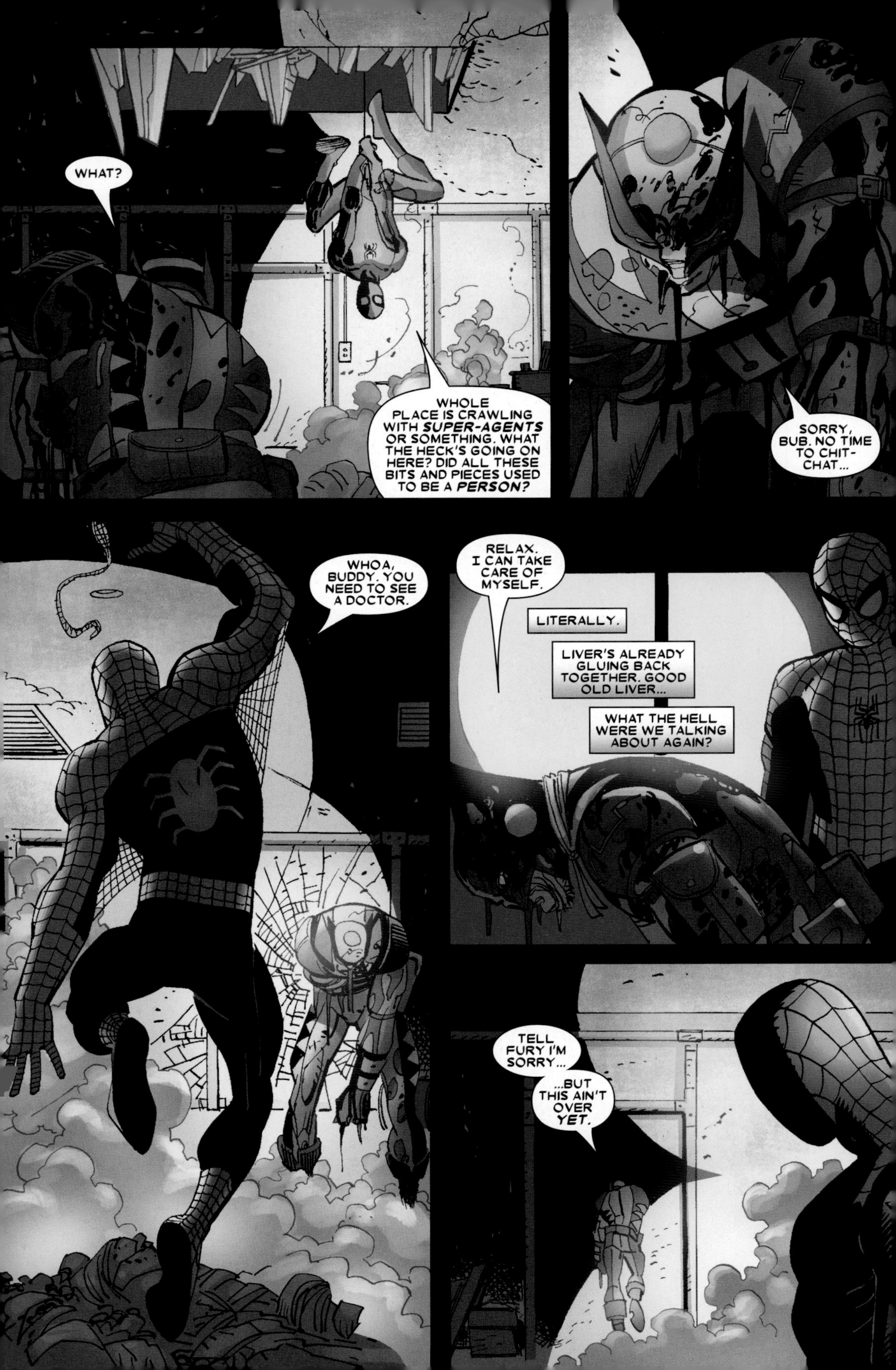
WHAT?
WHOLE PLACE IS CRAWLING WITH SUPER-AGENTS OR SOMETHING. WHAT THE HECK'S GOING ON HERE? DID ALL THESE BITS AND PIECES USED TO BE A PERSON?
SORRY, BUB. NO TIME TO CHIT-CHAT...
WHOA, BUDDY. YOU NEED TO SEE A DOCTOR.
RELAX. I CAN TAKE CARE OF MYSELF.
LITERALLY.
LIVER'S ALREADY GLUING BACK TOGETHER. GOOD OLD LIVER...
WHAT THE HELL WERE WE TALKING ABOUT AGAIN?
TELL FURY I'M SORRY...
...BUT THIS AIN'T OVER YET.

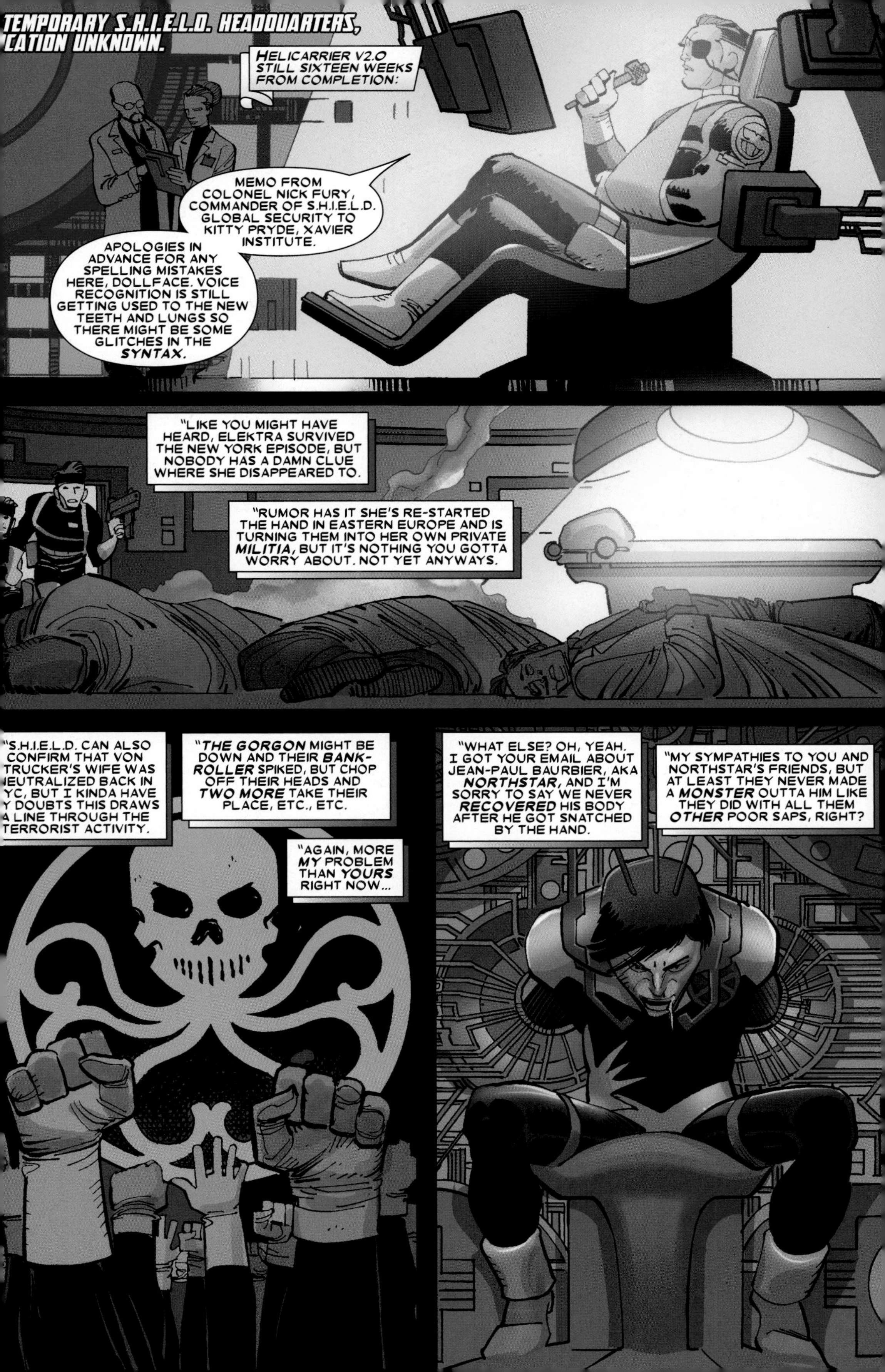
TEMPORARY S.H.I.E.L.D. HEADQUARTERS, CATION UNKNOWN.
HELICARRIER V2.0 STILL SIXTEEN WEEKS FROM COMPLETION:
MEMO FROM COLONEL NICK FURY, COMMANDER OF S.H.I.E.L.D. GLOBAL SECURITY TO KITTY PRYDE, XAVIER INSTITUTE.
APOLOGIES IN ADVANCE FOR ANY SPELLING MISTAKES HERE, DOLLFACE. VOICE RECOGNITION IS STILL GETTING USED TO THE NEW TEETH AND LUNGS SO THERE MIGHT BE SOME GLITCHES IN THE SYNTAX.
"LIKE YOU MIGHT HAVE HEARD, ELEKTRA SURVIVED THE NEW YORK EPISODE, BUT NOBODY HAS A DAMN CLUE WHERE SHE DISAPPEARED TO.
"RUMOR HAS IT SHE'S RE-STARTED THE HAND IN EASTERN EUROPE AND IS TURNING THEM INTO HER OWN PRIVATE MILITIA, BUT IT'S NOTHING YOU GOTTA WORRY ABOUT. NOT YET ANYWAYS.
"S.H.I.E.L.D. CAN ALSO CONFIRM THAT VON TRUCKER'S WIFE WAS IEUTRALIZED BACK IN YC, BUT I KINDA HAVE Y DOUBTS THIS DRAWS A LINE THROUGH THE TERRORIST ACTIVITY.
"THE GORGON MIGHT BE DOWN AND THEIR BANK-ROLLER SPIKED, BUT CHOP OFF THEIR HEADS AND TWO MORE TAKE THEIR PLACE, ETC., ETC.
"AGAIN, MORE MY PROBLEM THAN YOURS RIGHT NOW...
"WHAT ELSE? OH, YEAH. I GOT YOUR EMAIL ABOUT JEAN-PAUL BAURBIER, AKA NORTHSTAR, AND I'M SORRY TO SAY WE NEVER RECOVERED HIS BODY AFTER HE GOT SNATCHED BY THE HAND.
"MY SYMPATHIES TO YOU AND NORTHSTAR'S FRIENDS, BUT AT LEAST THEY NEVER MADE A MONSTER OUTTA HIM LIKE THEY DID WITH ALL THEM OTHER POOR SAPS, RIGHT?

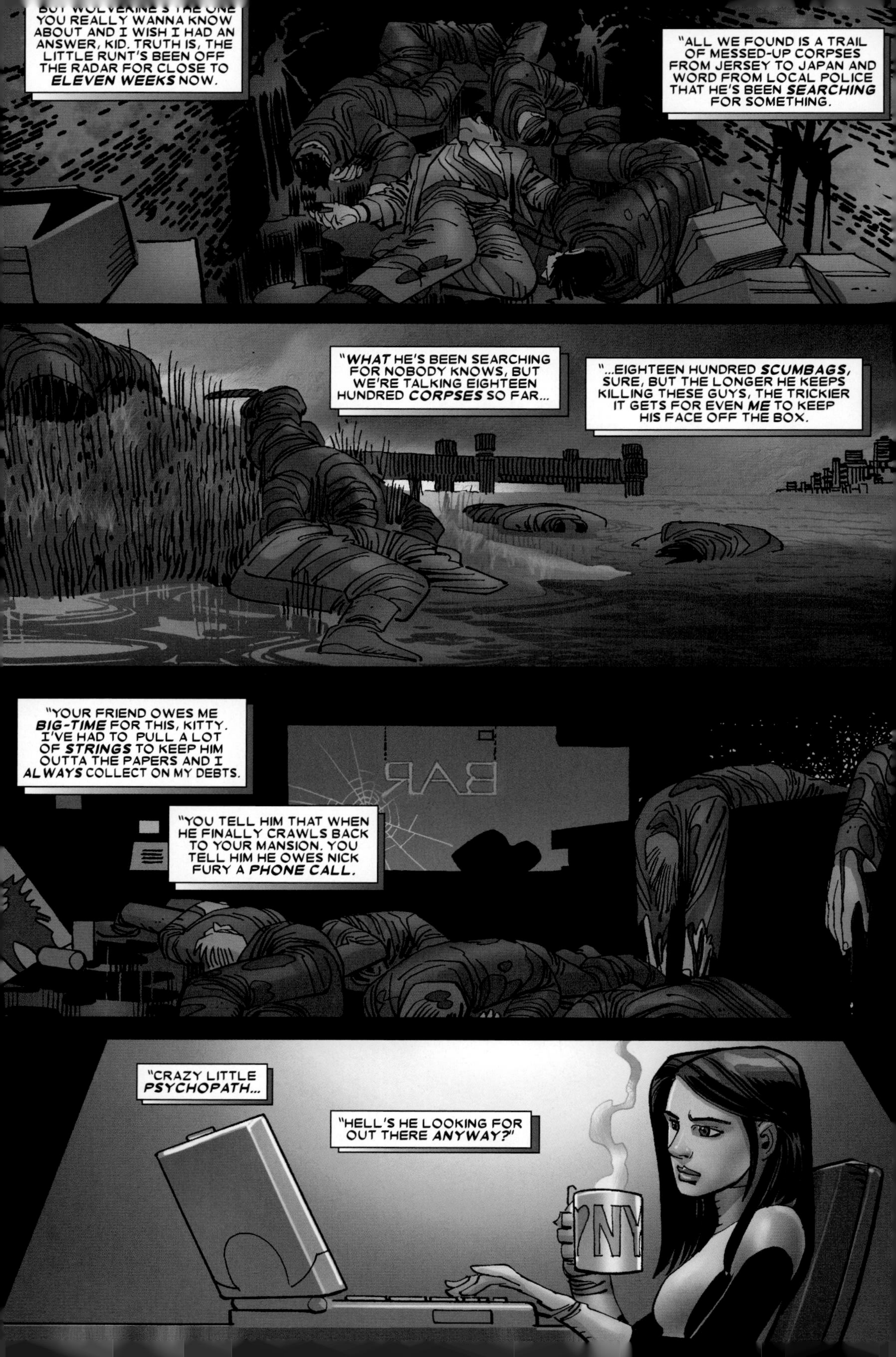
BUT WOLVERINE'S THE ONE YOU REALLY WANNA KNOW ABOUT AND I WISH I HAD AN ANSWER, KID. TRUTH IS, THE LITTLE RUNT'S BEEN OFF THE RADAR FOR CLOSE TO ELEVEN WEEKS NOW.
"ALL WE FOUND IS A TRAIL OF MESSED-UP CORPSES FROM JERSEY TO JAPAN AND WORD FROM LOCAL POLICE THAT HE'S BEEN SEARCHING FOR SOMETHING.
"WHAT HE'S BEEN SEARCHING FOR NOBODY KNOWS, BUT WE'RE TALKING EIGHTEEN HUNDRED CORPSES SO FAR...
"...EIGHTEEN HUNDRED SCUMBAGS, SURE, BUT THE LONGER HE KEEPS KILLING THESE GUYS, THE TRICKIER IT GETS FOR EVEN ME TO KEEP HIS FACE OFF THE BOX.
"YOUR FRIEND OWES ME BIG-TIME FOR THIS, KITTY. I'VE HAD TO PULL A LOT OF STRINGS TO KEEP HIM OUTTA THE PAPERS AND I ALWAYS COLLECT ON MY DEBTS.
"YOU TELL HIM THAT WHEN HE FINALLY CRAWLS BACK TO YOUR MANSION, YOU TELL HIM HE OWES NICK FURY A PHONE CALL.
"CRAZY LITTLE PSYCHOPATH...
"HELL'S HE LOOKING FOR OUT THERE ANYWAY?"

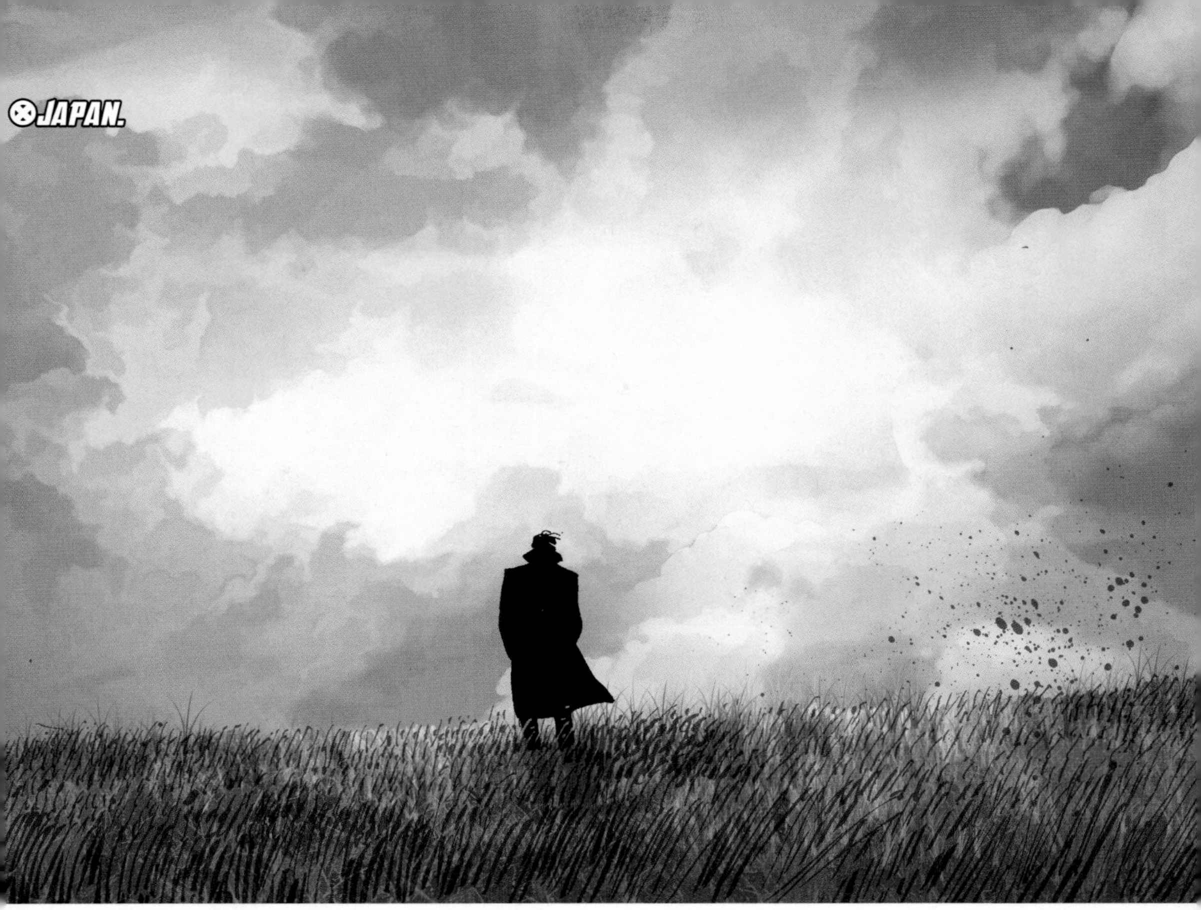
JAPAN.
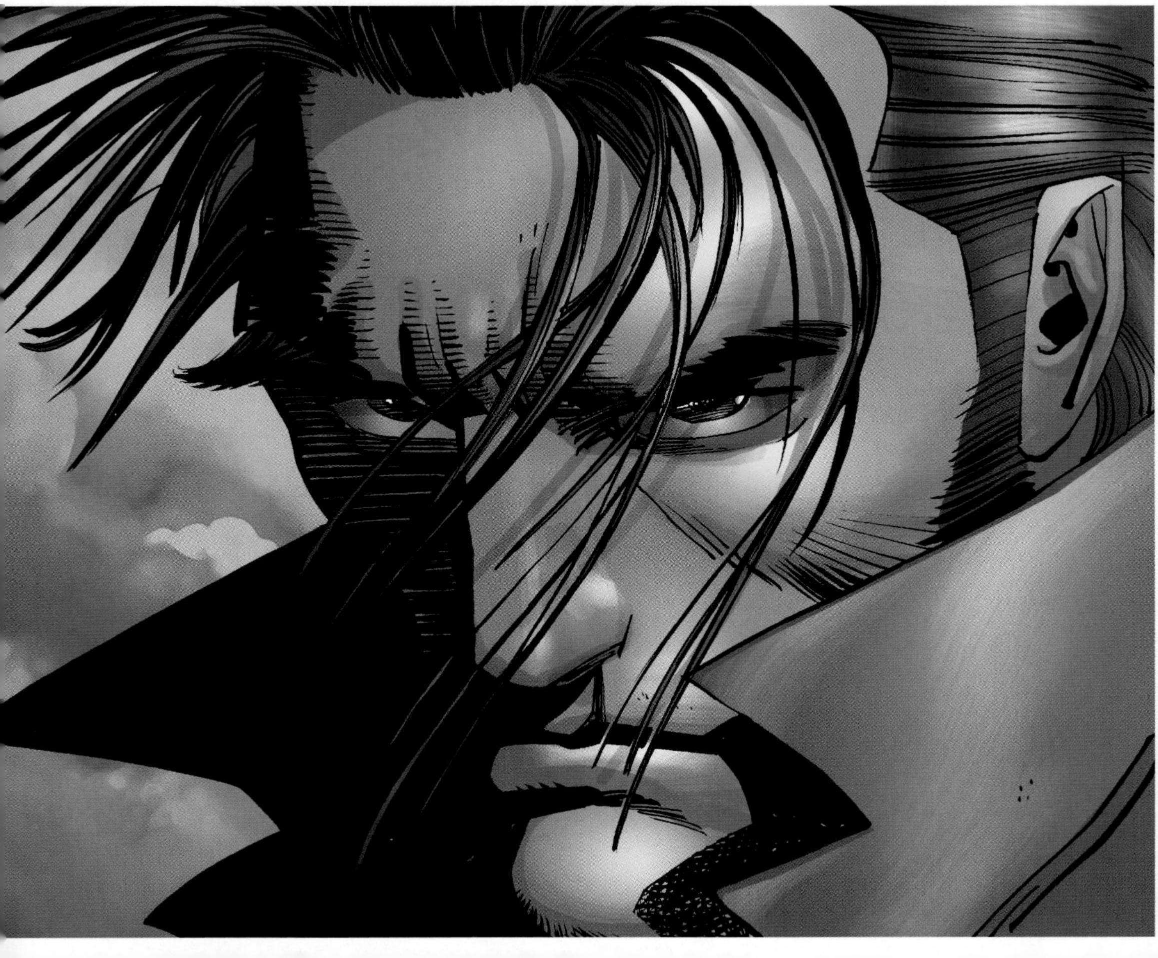

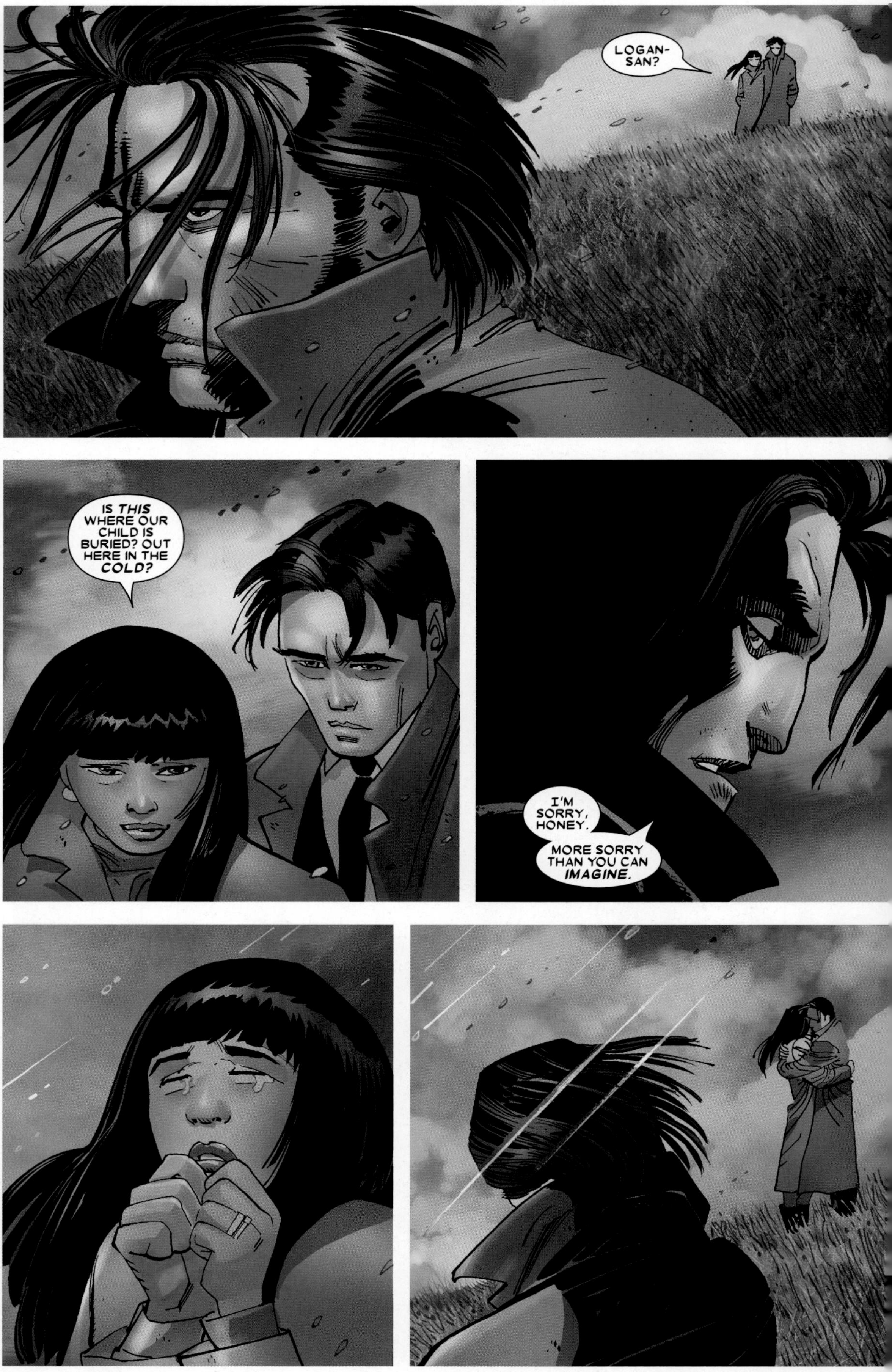
LOGAN-SAN?
IS THIS WHERE OUR CHILD IS BURIED? OUT HERE IN THE COLD?
I'M SORRY, HONEY.
MORE SORRY THAN YOU CAN IMAGINE.

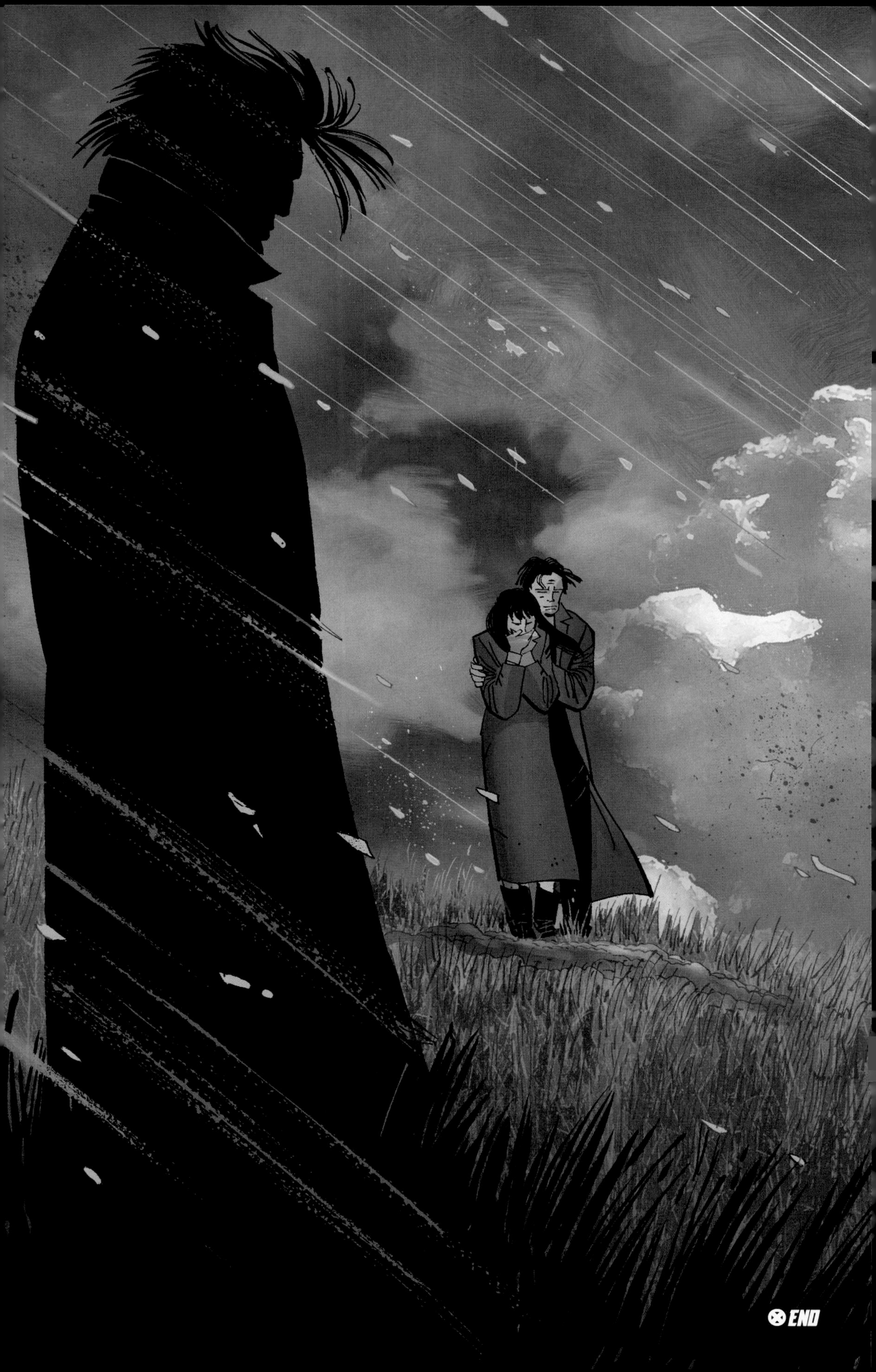
END

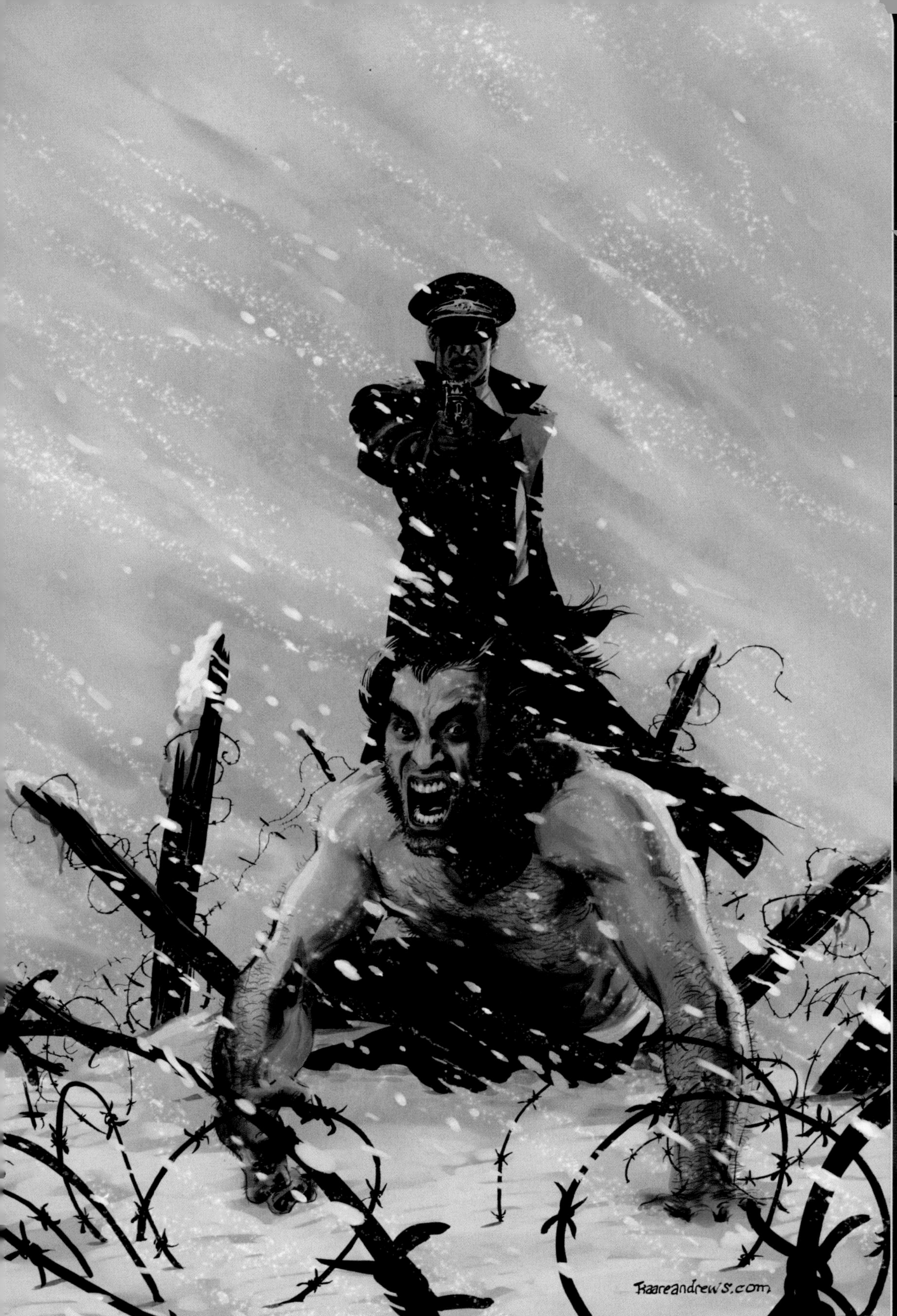
Kaareandrews.com

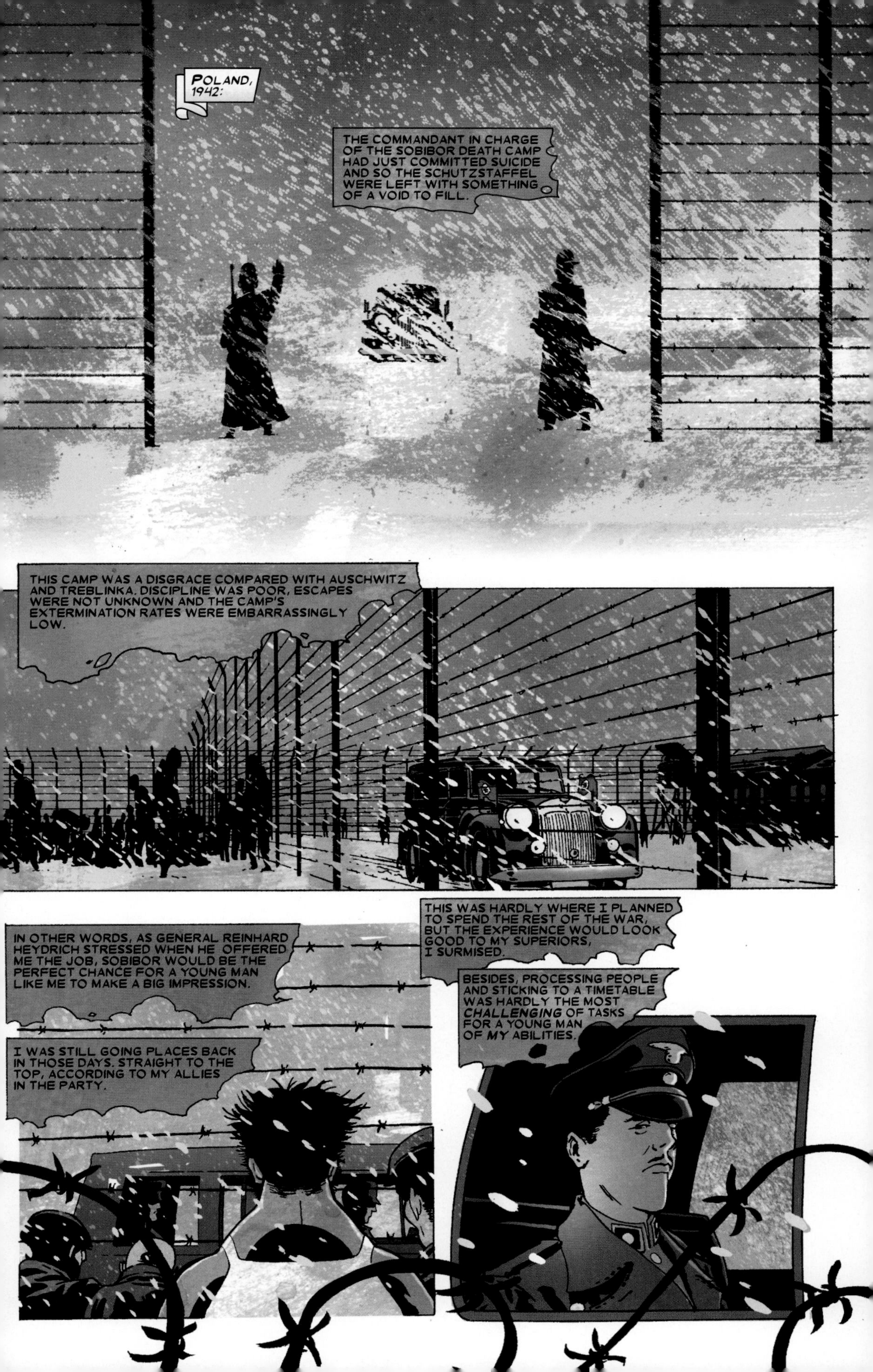
POLAND, 1942:
THE COMMANDANT IN CHARGE OF THE SOBIBOR DEATH CAMP HAD JUST COMMITTED SUICIDE AND SO THE SCHUTZSTAFFEL WERE LEFT WITH SOMETHING OF A VOID TO FILL.
THIS CAMP WAS A DISGRACE COMPARED WITH AUSCHWITZ AND TREBLINKA. DISCIPLINE WAS POOR, ESCAPES WERE NOT UNKNOWN AND THE CAMP'S EXTERMINATION RATES WERE EMBARRASSINGLY LOW.
IN OTHER WORDS, AS GENERAL REINHARD HEYDRICH STRESSED WHEN HE OFFERED ME THE JOB, SOBIBOR WOULD BE THE PERFECT CHANCE FOR A YOUNG MAN LIKE ME TO MAKE A BIG IMPRESSION.
I WAS STILL GOING PLACES BACK IN THOSE DAYS. STRAIGHT TO THE TOP, ACCORDING TO MY ALLIES IN THE PARTY.
THIS WAS HARDLY WHERE I PLANNED TO SPEND THE REST OF THE WAR, BUT THE EXPERIENCE WOULD LOOK GOOD TO MY SUPERIORS, I SURMISED.
BESIDES, PROCESSING PEOPLE AND STICKING TO A TIMETABLE WAS HARDLY THE MOST CHALLENGING OF TASKS FOR A YOUNG MAN OF MY ABILITIES.

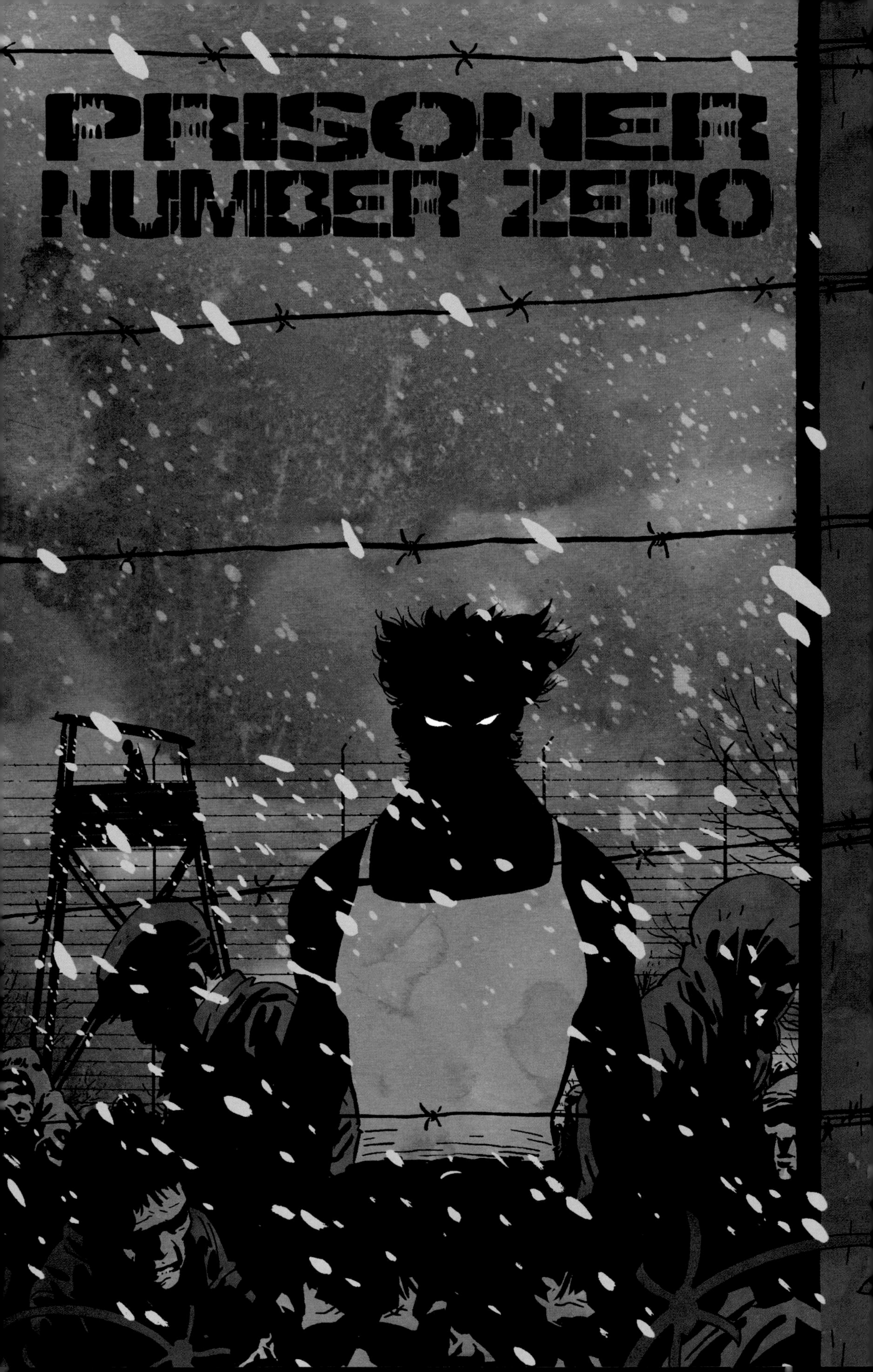
PRISONER
NUMBER ZERO

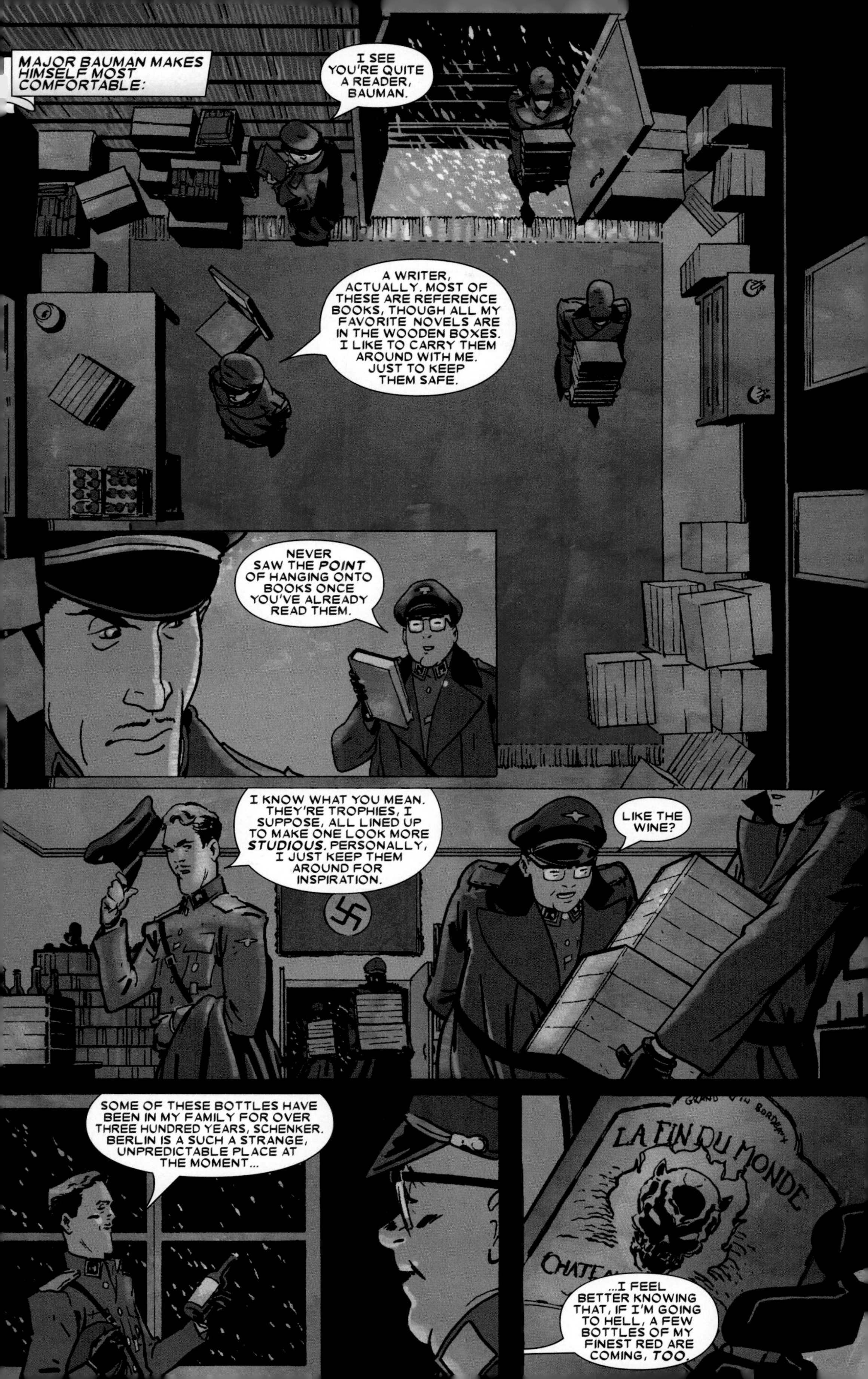
MAJOR BAUMAN MAKES HIMSELF MOST COMFORTABLE:
I SEE YOU'RE QUITE A READER, BAUMAN.
A WRITER, ACTUALLY. MOST OF THESE ARE REFERENCE BOOKS, THOUGH ALL MY FAVORITE NOVELS ARE IN THE WOODEN BOXES. I LIKE TO CARRY THEM AROUND WITH ME. JUST TO KEEP THEM SAFE.
NEVER SAW THE POINT OF HANGING ONTO BOOKS ONCE YOU'VE ALREADY READ THEM.
I KNOW WHAT YOU MEAN. THEY'RE TROPHIES, I SUPPOSE, ALL LINED UP TO MAKE ONE LOOK MORE STUDIOUS. PERSONALLY, I JUST KEEP THEM AROUND FOR INSPIRATION.
LIKE THE WINE?
SOME OF THESE BOTTLES HAVE BEEN IN MY FAMILY FOR OVER THREE HUNDRED YEARS, SCHENKER. BERLIN IS A SUCH A STRANGE, UNPREDICTABLE PLACE AT THE MOMENT...
LA FIN DU MONDE
...I FEEL BETTER KNOWING THAT, IF I'M GOING TO HELL, A FEW BOTTLES OF MY FINEST RED ARE COMING, TOO.

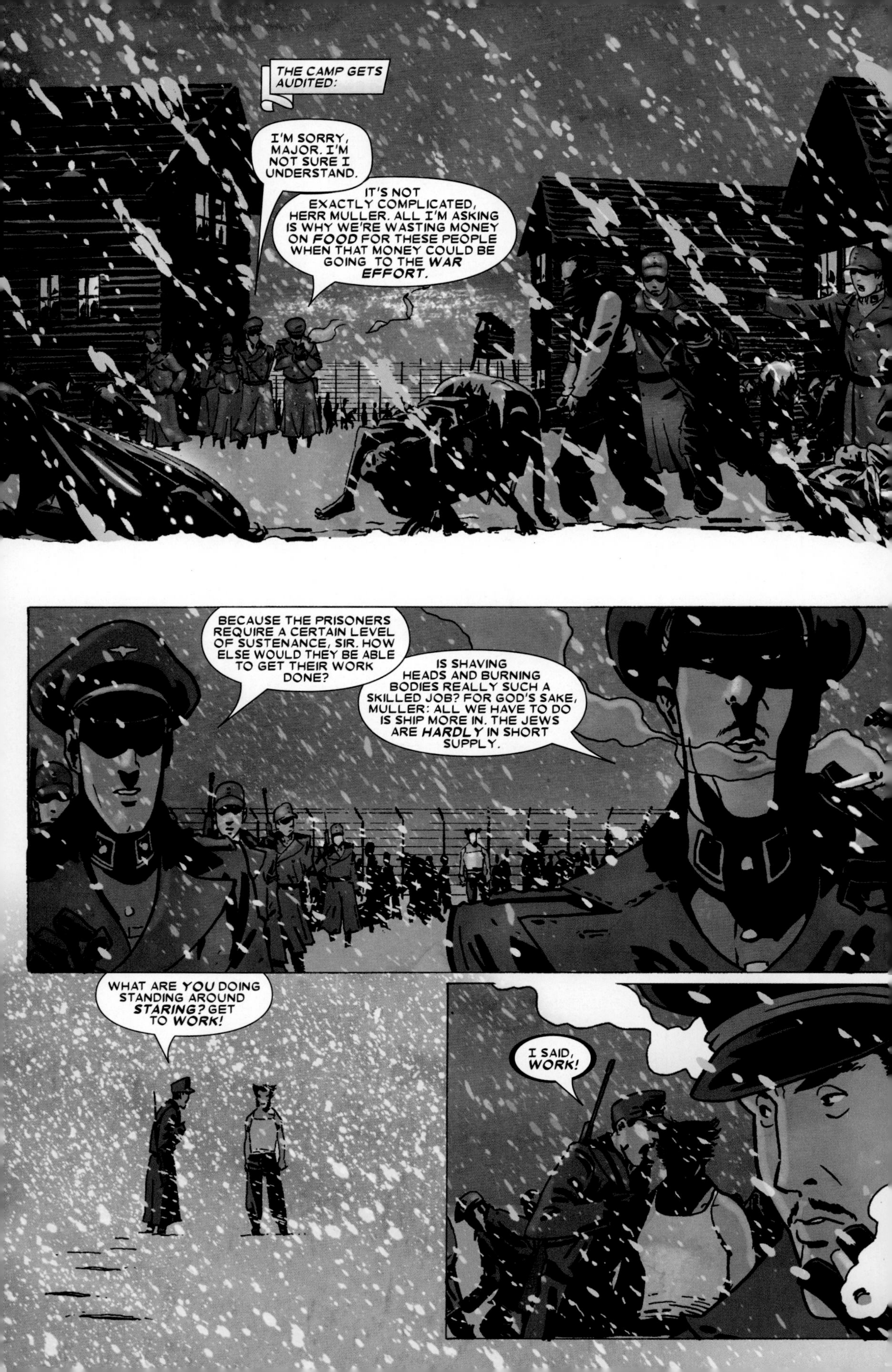
THE CAMP GETS AUDITED:
I'M SORRY, MAJOR. I'M NOT SURE I UNDERSTAND.
IT'S NOT EXACTLY COMPLICATED, HERR MULLER. ALL I'M ASKING IS WHY WE'RE WASTING MONEY ON FOOD FOR THESE PEOPLE WHEN THAT MONEY COULD BE GOING TO THE WAR EFFORT.
BECAUSE THE PRISONERS REQUIRE A CERTAIN LEVEL OF SUSTENANCE, SIR. HOW ELSE WOULD THEY BE ABLE TO GET THEIR WORK DONE?
IS SHAVING HEADS AND BURNING BODIES REALLY SUCH A SKILLED JOB? FOR GOD'S SAKE, MULLER: ALL WE HAVE TO DO IS SHIP MORE IN. THE JEWS ARE HARDLY IN SHORT SUPPLY.
WHAT ARE YOU DOING STANDING AROUND STARING? GET TO WORK!
I SAID, WORK!

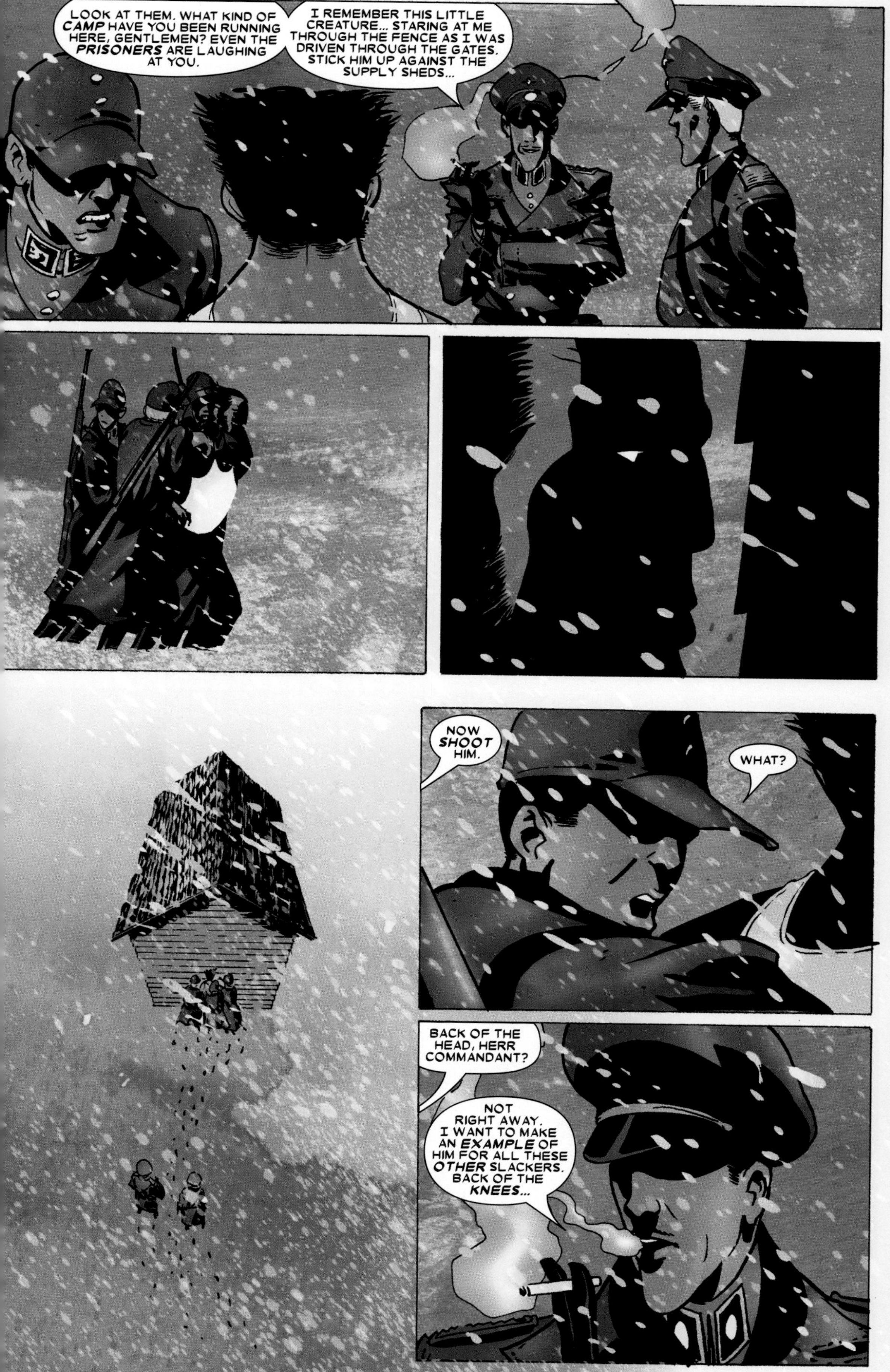
LOOK AT THEM. WHAT KIND OF CAMP HAVE YOU BEEN RUNNING HERE, GENTLEMEN? EVEN THE PRISONERS ARE LAUGHING AT YOU.
I REMEMBER THIS LITTLE CREATURE... STARING AT ME THROUGH THE FENCE AS I WAS DRIVEN THROUGH THE GATES. STICK HIM UP AGAINST THE SUPPLY SHEDS...
NOW SHOOT HIM.
WHAT?
BACK OF THE HEAD, HERR COMMANDANT?
NOT RIGHT AWAY. I WANT TO MAKE AN EXAMPLE OF HIM FOR ALL THESE OTHER SLACKERS. BACK OF THE KNEES...

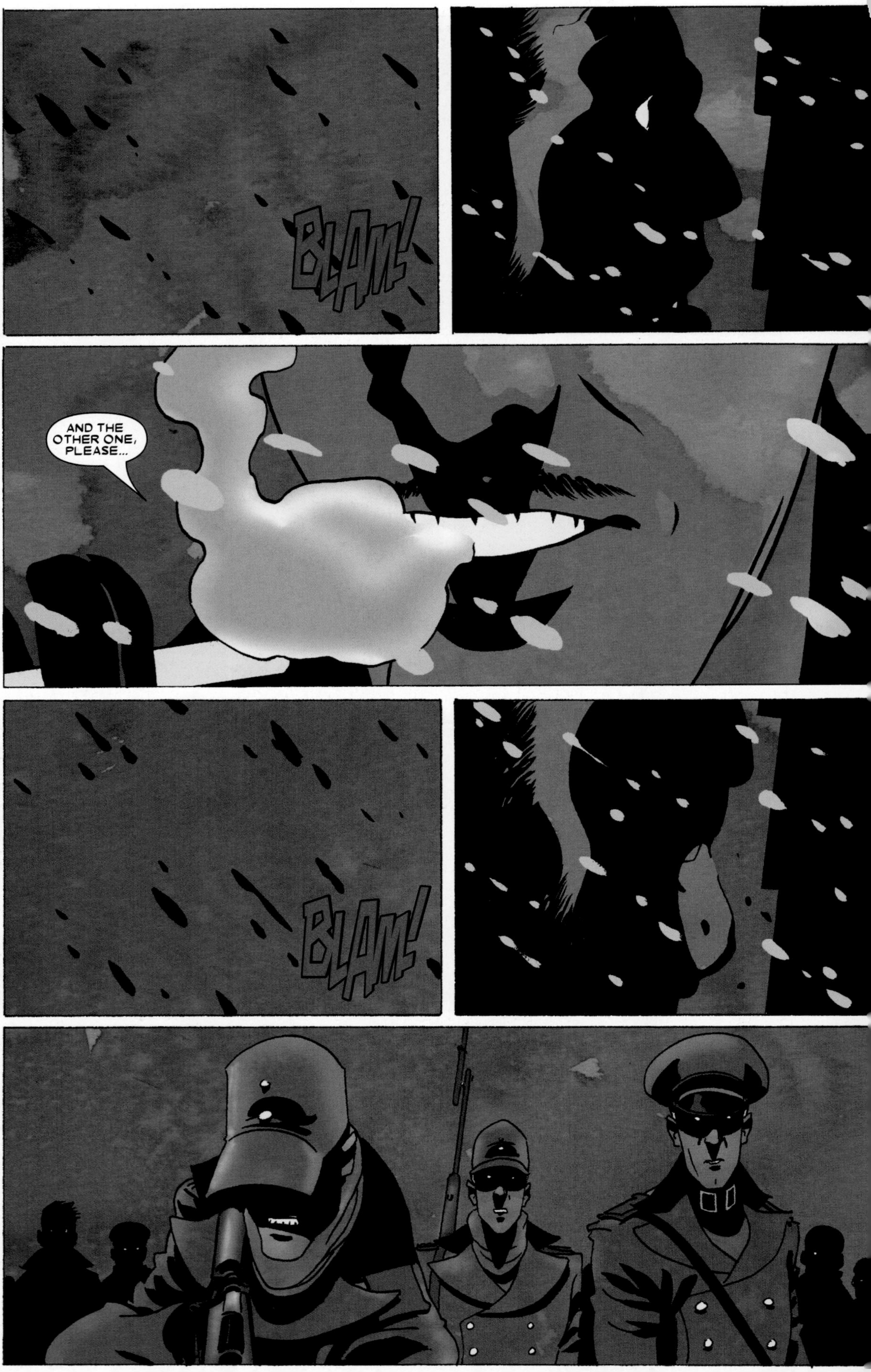
BLAM!
AND THE OTHER ONE, PLEASE...
BLAM!

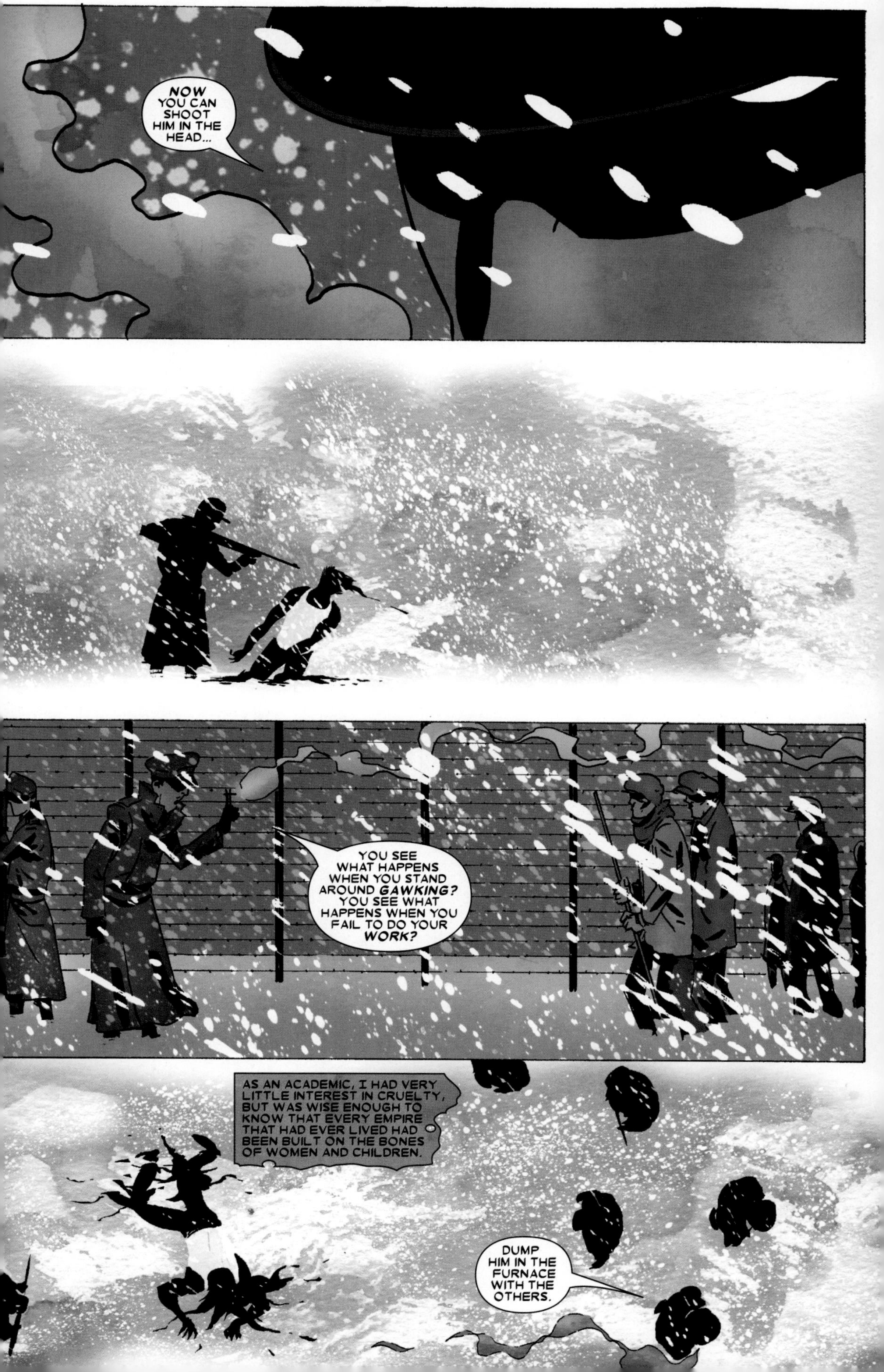
NOW YOU CAN SHOOT HIM IN THE HEAD...
YOU SEE WHAT HAPPENS WHEN YOU STAND AROUND GAWKING? YOU SEE WHAT HAPPENS WHEN YOU FAIL TO DO YOUR WORK?
AS AN ACADEMIC, I HAD VERY LITTLE INTEREST IN CRUELTY, BUT WAS WISE ENOUGH TO KNOW THAT EVERY EMPIRE THAT HAD EVER LIVED HAD BEEN BUILT ON THE BONES OF WOMEN AND CHILDREN.
DUMP HIM IN THE FURNACE WITH THE OTHERS.

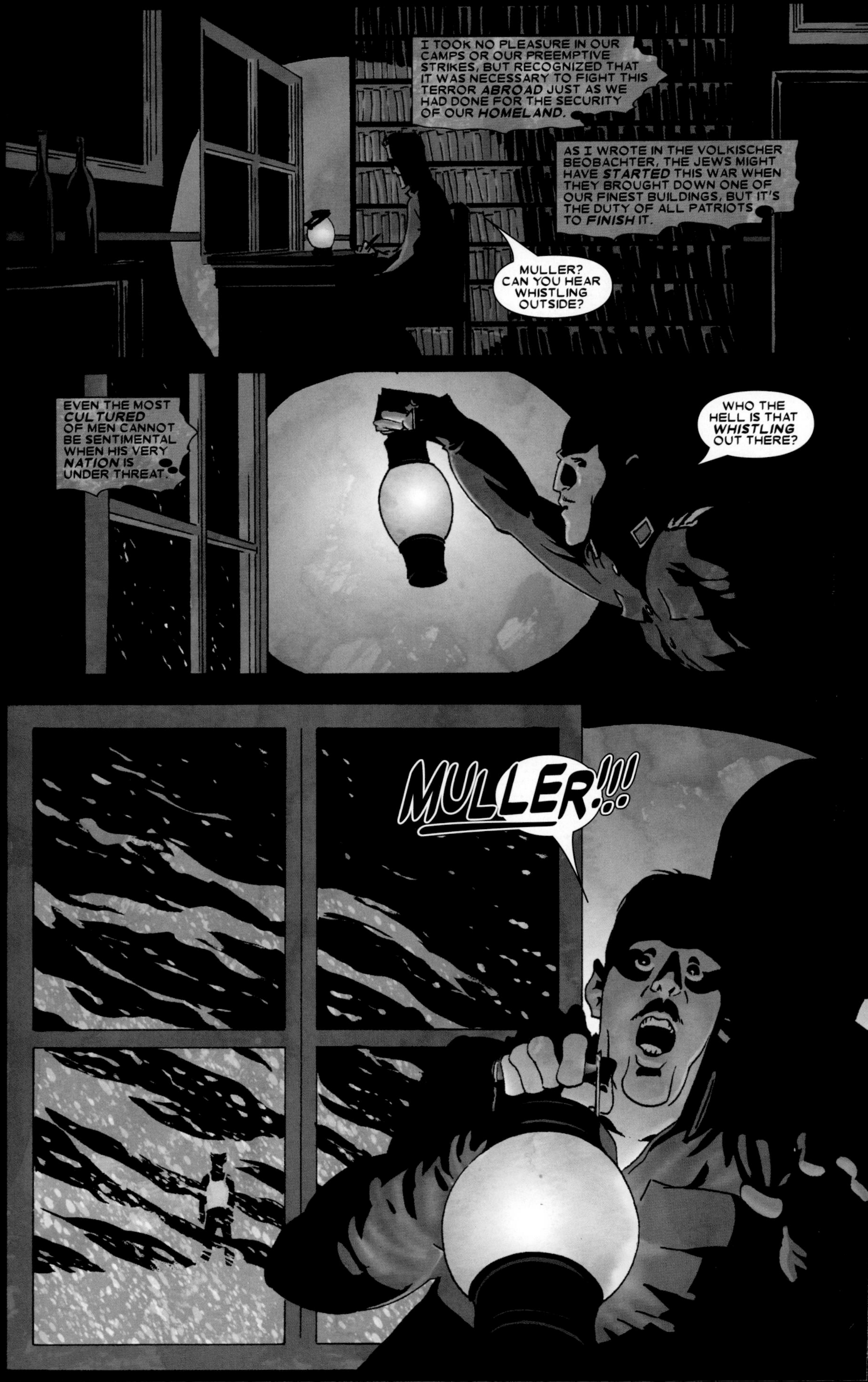
I TOOK NO PLEASURE IN OUR CAMPS OR OUR PREEMPTIVE STRIKES, BUT RECOGNIZED THAT IT WAS NECESSARY TO FIGHT THIS TERROR ABROAD JUST AS WE HAD DONE FOR THE SECURITY OF OUR HOMELAND.
AS I WROTE IN THE VOLKISCHER BEOBACHTER, THE JEWS MIGHT HAVE STARTED THIS WAR WHEN THEY BROUGHT DOWN ONE OF OUR FINEST BUILDINGS, BUT IT'S THE DUTY OF ALL PATRIOTS TO FINISH IT.
MULLER? CAN YOU HEAR WHISTLING OUTSIDE?
EVEN THE MOST CULTURED OF MEN CANNOT BE SENTIMENTAL WHEN HIS VERY NATION IS UNDER THREAT.
WHO THE HELL IS THAT WHISTLING OUT THERE?
MULLER!!!

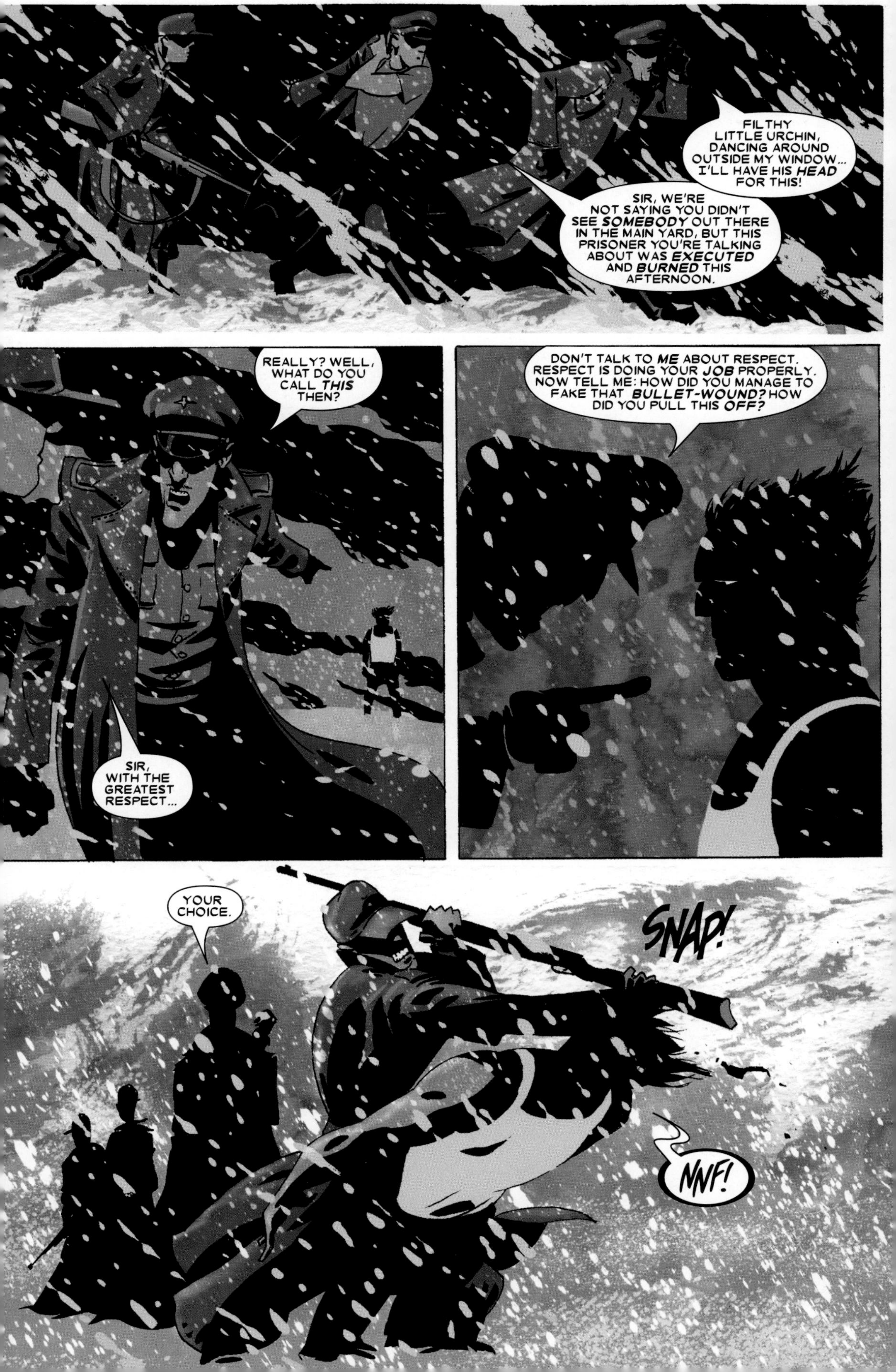
FILTHY LITTLE URCHIN, DANCING AROUND OUTSIDE MY WINDOW... I'LL HAVE HIS *HEAD* FOR THIS!
SIR, WE'RE NOT SAYING YOU DIDN'T SEE *SOMEBODY* OUT THERE IN THE MAIN YARD, BUT THIS PRISONER YOU'RE TALKING ABOUT WAS *EXECUTED* AND *BURNED* THIS AFTERNOON.
REALLY? WELL, WHAT DO YOU CALL *THIS* THEN?
SIR, WITH THE GREATEST RESPECT...
DON'T TALK TO *ME* ABOUT RESPECT. RESPECT IS DOING YOUR *JOB* PROPERLY. NOW TELL ME: HOW DID YOU MANAGE TO FAKE THAT *BULLET-WOUND?* HOW DID YOU PULL THIS *OFF?*
YOUR CHOICE.
SNAP!
NNF!

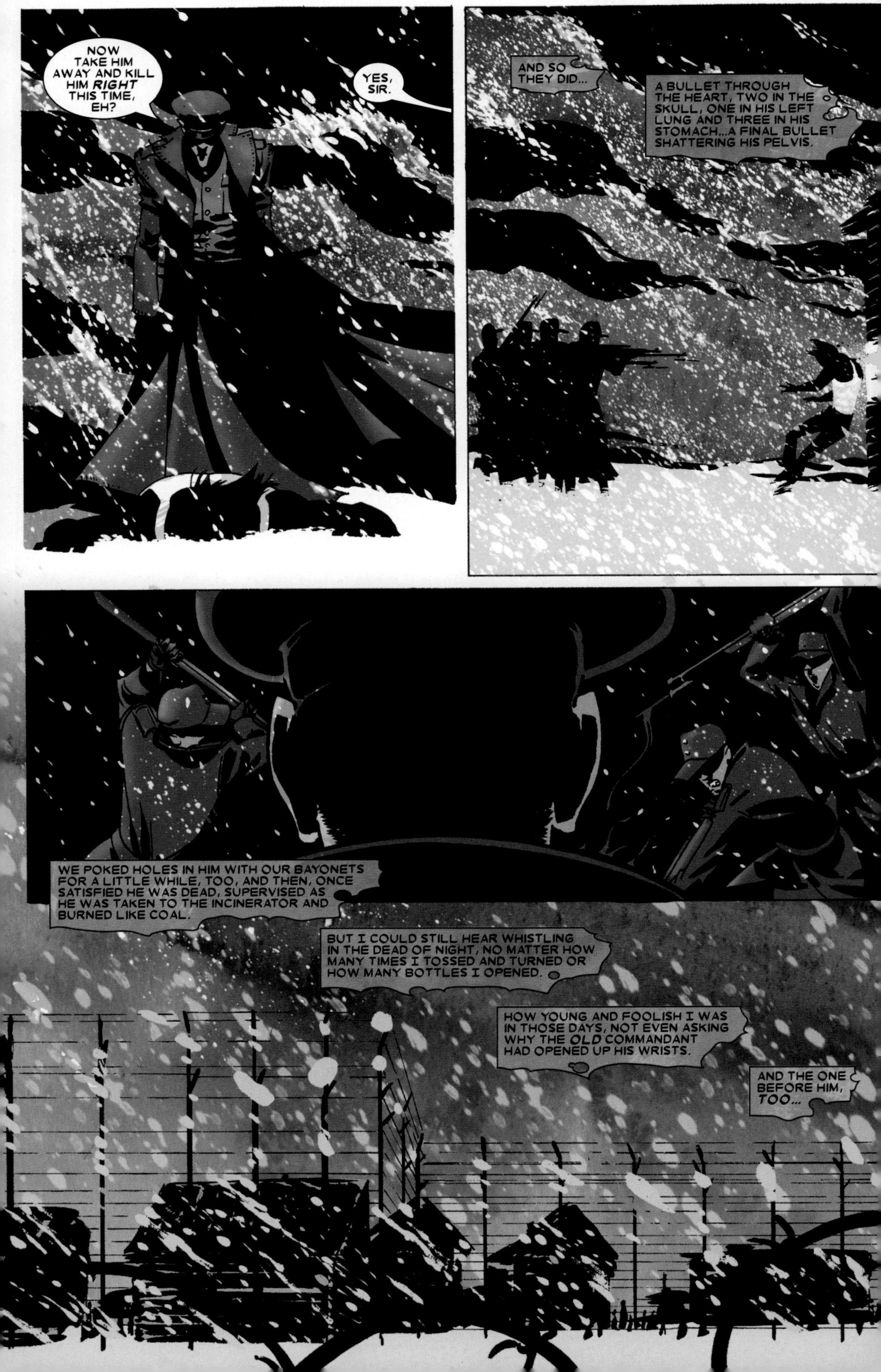
NOW TAKE HIM AWAY AND KILL HIM RIGHT THIS TIME, EH?
YES, SIR.
AND SO THEY DID...
A BULLET THROUGH THE HEART, TWO IN THE SKULL, ONE IN HIS LEFT LUNG AND THREE IN HIS STOMACH...A FINAL BULLET SHATTERING HIS PELVIS.
WE POKED HOLES IN HIM WITH OUR BAYONETS FOR A LITTLE WHILE, TOO, AND THEN, ONCE SATISFIED HE WAS DEAD, SUPERVISED AS HE WAS TAKEN TO THE INCINERATOR AND BURNED LIKE COAL.
BUT I COULD STILL HEAR WHISTLING IN THE DEAD OF NIGHT, NO MATTER HOW MANY TIMES I TOSSED AND TURNED OR HOW MANY BOTTLES I OPENED.
HOW YOUNG AND FOOLISH I WAS IN THOSE DAYS, NOT EVEN ASKING WHY THE OLD COMMANDANT HAD OPENED UP HIS WRISTS.
AND THE ONE BEFORE HIM, TOO...

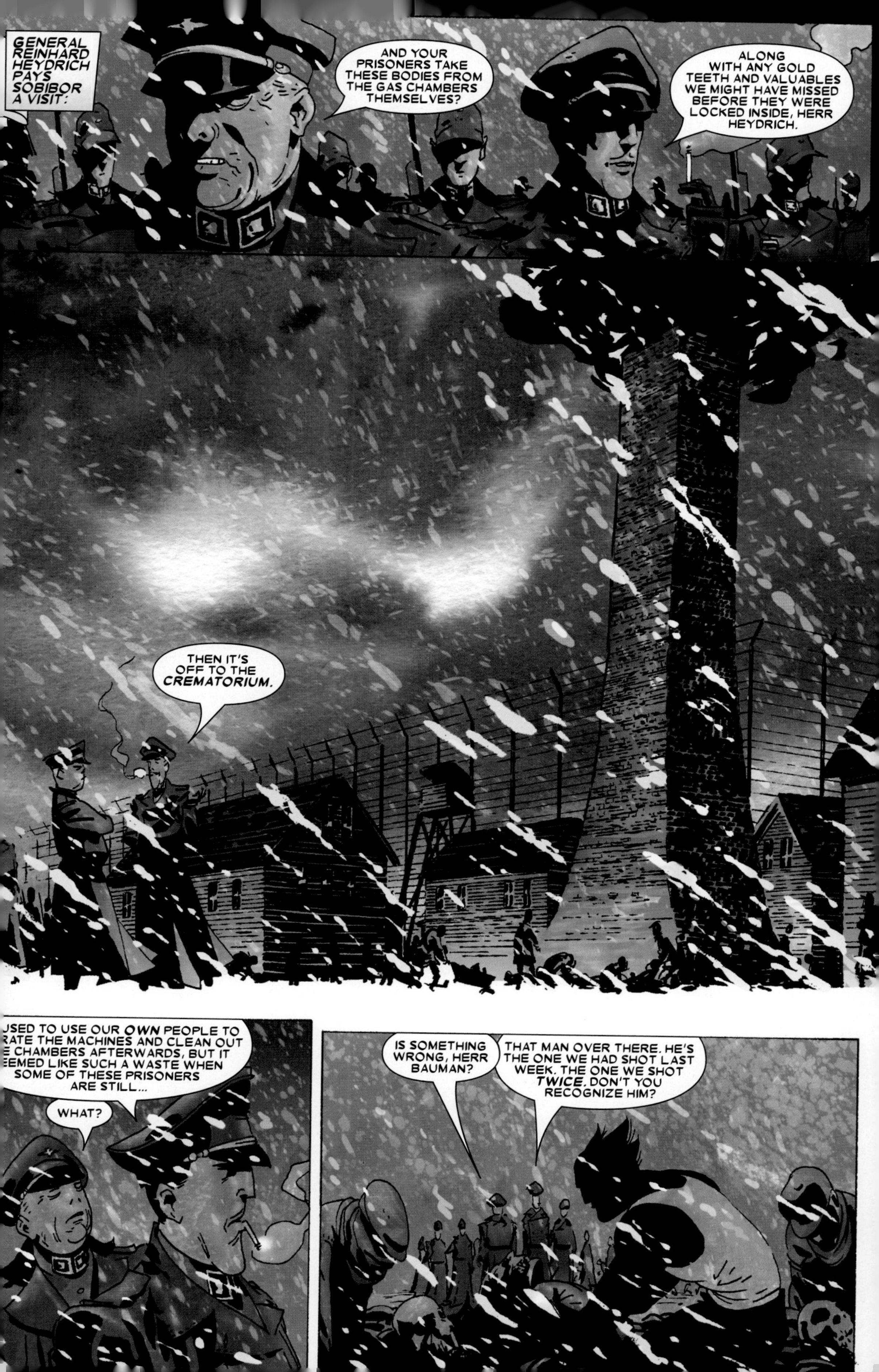
GENERAL REINHARD HEYDRICH PAYS SOBIBOR A VISIT:
AND YOUR PRISONERS TAKE THESE BODIES FROM THE GAS CHAMBERS THEMSELVES?
ALONG WITH ANY GOLD TEETH AND VALUABLES WE MIGHT HAVE MISSED BEFORE THEY WERE LOCKED INSIDE, HERR HEYDRICH.
THEN IT'S OFF TO THE CREMATORIUM.
USED TO USE OUR OWN PEOPLE TO RATE THE MACHINES AND CLEAN OUT E CHAMBERS AFTERWARDS, BUT IT EEMED LIKE SUCH A WASTE WHEN SOME OF THESE PRISONERS ARE STILL...
WHAT?
IS SOMETHING WRONG, HERR BAUMAN?
THAT MAN OVER THERE. HE'S THE ONE WE HAD SHOT LAST WEEK. THE ONE WE SHOT TWICE. DON'T YOU RECOGNIZE HIM?

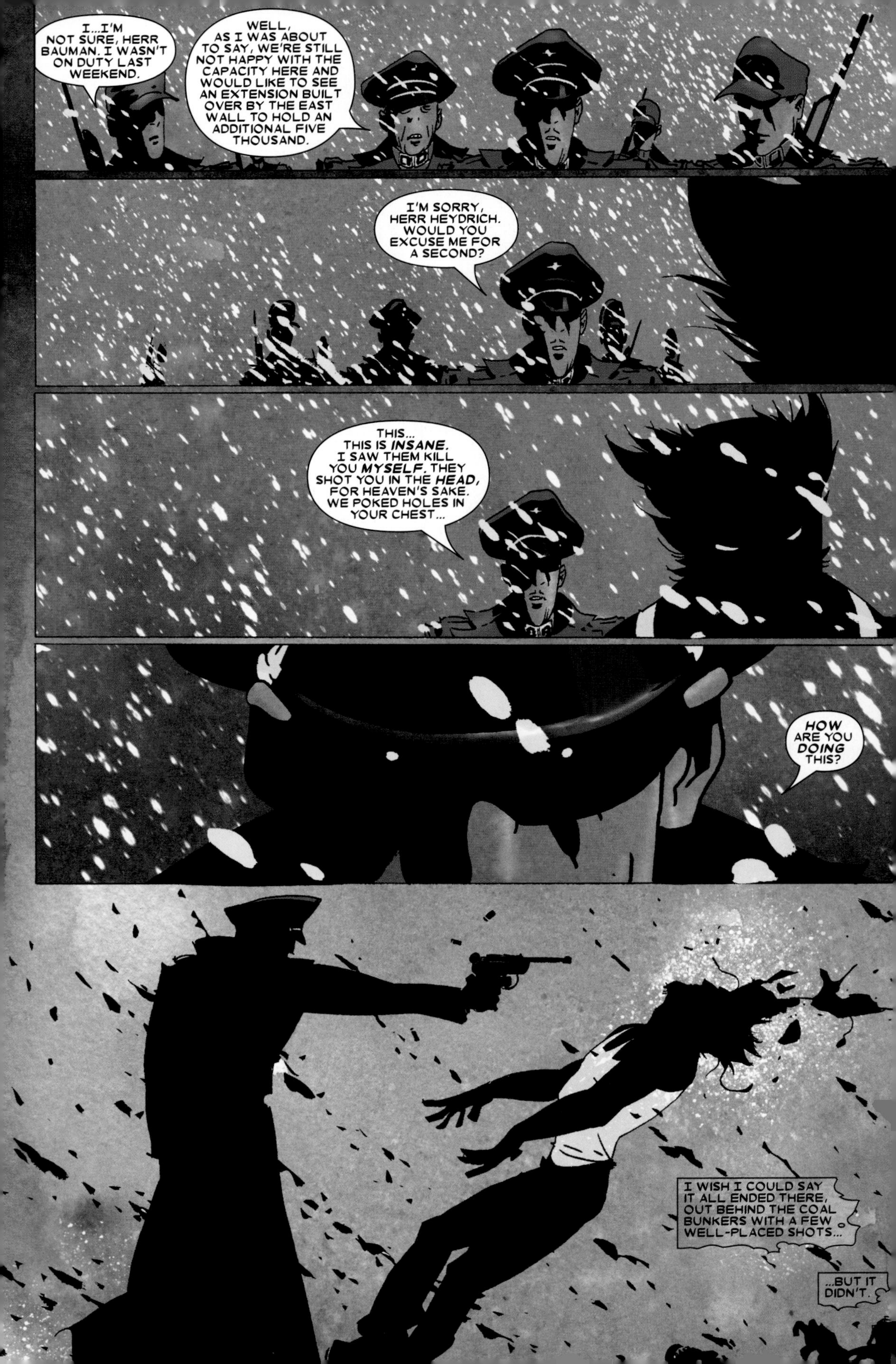
I...I'M NOT SURE, HERR BAUMAN. I WASN'T ON DUTY LAST WEEKEND.
WELL, AS I WAS ABOUT TO SAY, WE'RE STILL NOT HAPPY WITH THE CAPACITY HERE AND WOULD LIKE TO SEE AN EXTENSION BUILT OVER BY THE EAST WALL TO HOLD AN ADDITIONAL FIVE THOUSAND.
I'M SORRY, HERR HEYDRICH. WOULD YOU EXCUSE ME FOR A SECOND?
THIS... THIS IS INSANE. I SAW THEM KILL YOU MYSELF. THEY SHOT YOU IN THE HEAD, FOR HEAVEN'S SAKE. WE POKED HOLES IN YOUR CHEST...
HOW ARE YOU DOING THIS?
I WISH I COULD SAY IT ALL ENDED THERE, OUT BEHIND THE COAL BUNKERS WITH A FEW WELL-PLACED SHOTS...
...BUT IT DIDN'T.

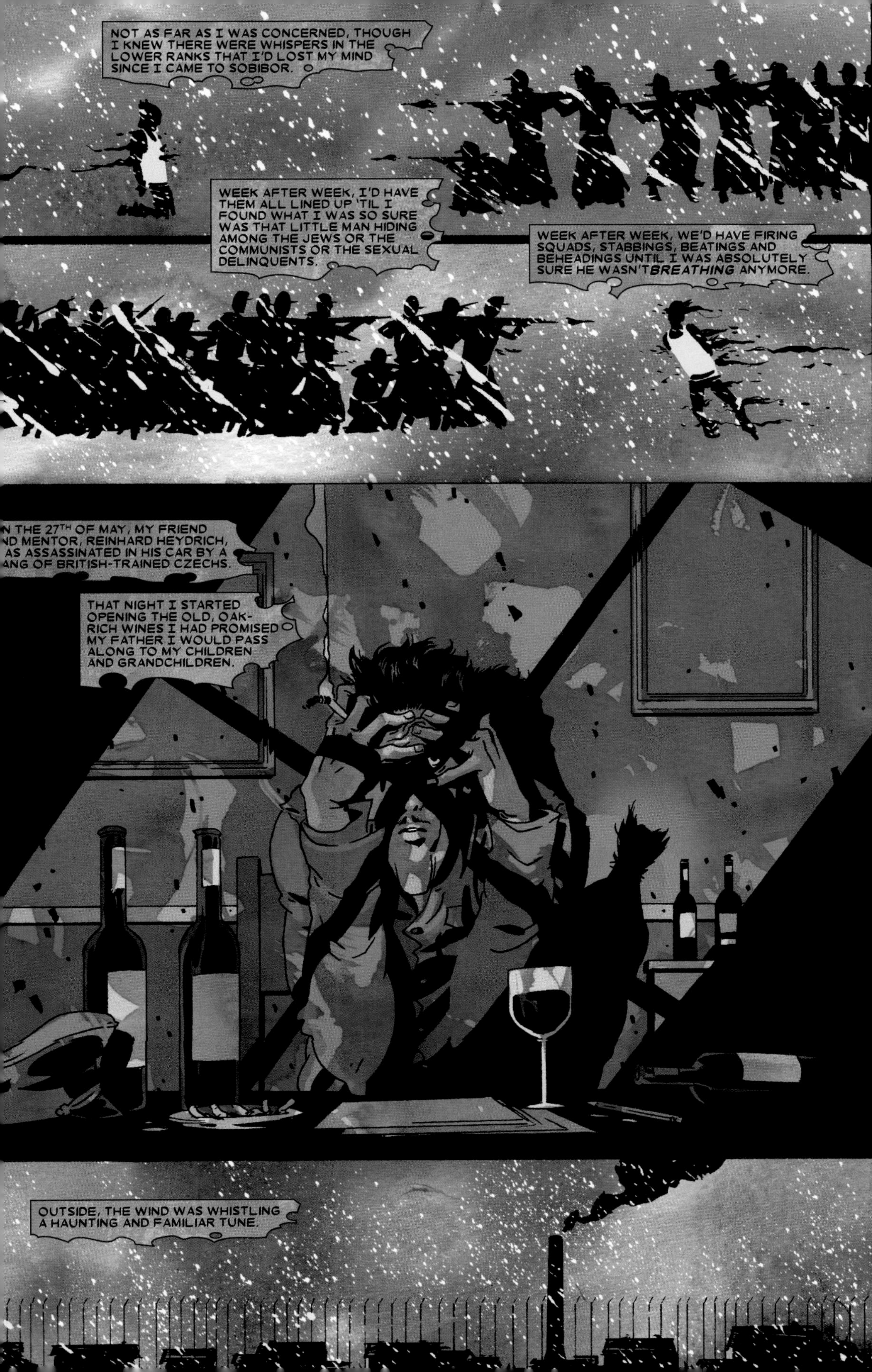
NOT AS FAR AS I WAS CONCERNED, THOUGH I KNEW THERE WERE WHISPERS IN THE LOWER RANKS THAT I'D LOST MY MIND SINCE I CAME TO SOBIBOR.
WEEK AFTER WEEK, I'D HAVE THEM ALL LINED UP 'TIL I FOUND WHAT I WAS SO SURE WAS THAT LITTLE MAN HIDING AMONG THE JEWS OR THE COMMUNISTS OR THE SEXUAL DELINQUENTS.
WEEK AFTER WEEK, WE'D HAVE FIRING SQUADS, STABBINGS, BEATINGS AND BEHEADINGS UNTIL I WAS ABSOLUTELY SURE HE WASN'T *BREATHING* ANYMORE.
N THE 27TH OF MAY, MY FRIEND ND MENTOR, REINHARD HEYDRICH, AS ASSASSINATED IN HIS CAR BY A ANG OF BRITISH-TRAINED CZECHS.
THAT NIGHT I STARTED OPENING THE OLD, OAK-RICH WINES I HAD PROMISED MY FATHER I WOULD PASS ALONG TO MY CHILDREN AND GRANDCHILDREN.
OUTSIDE, THE WIND WAS WHISTLING A HAUNTING AND FAMILIAR TUNE.

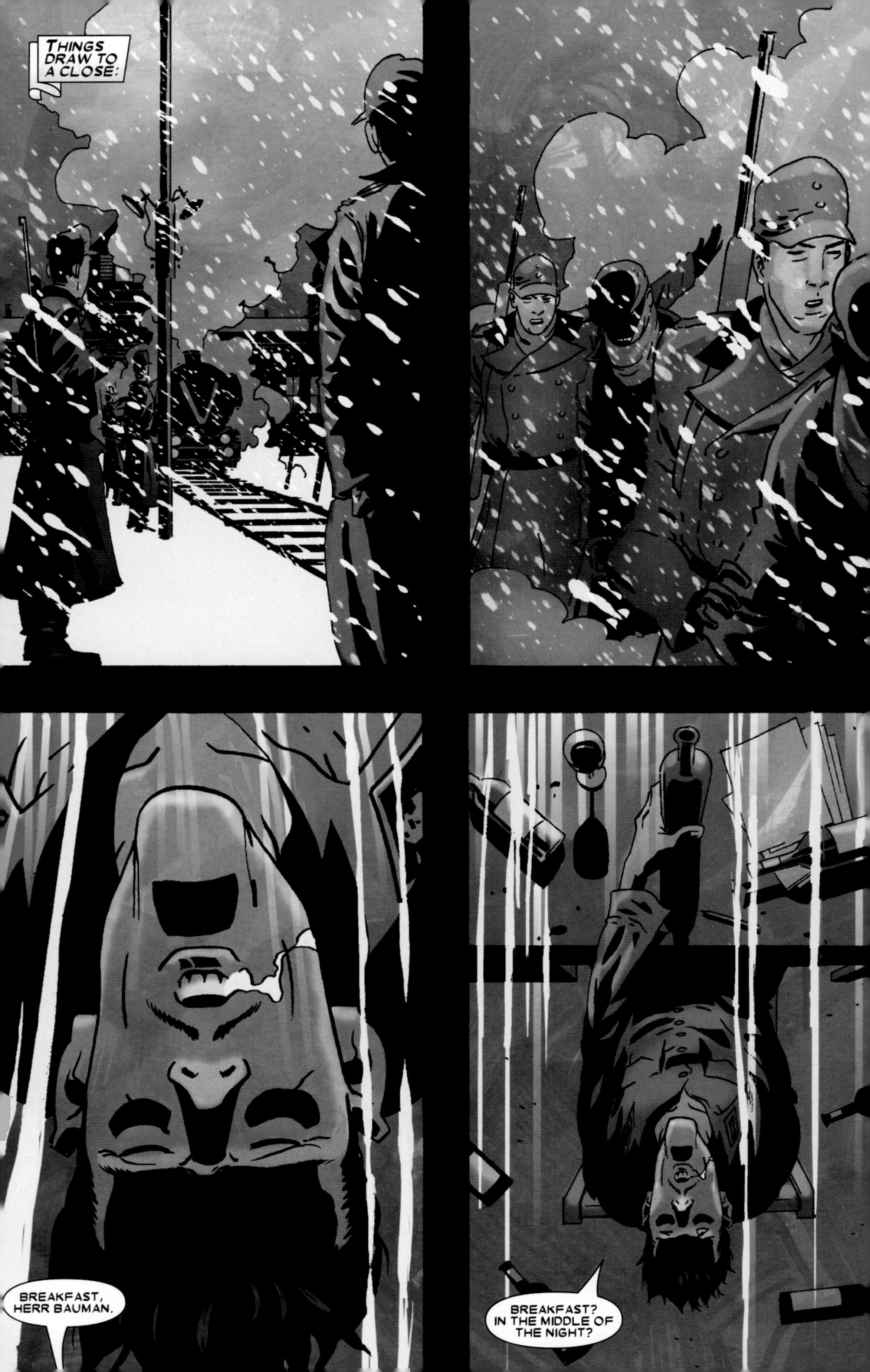
THINGS DRAW TO A CLOSE:
BREAKFAST, HERR BAUMAN.
BREAKFAST? IN THE MIDDLE OF THE NIGHT?

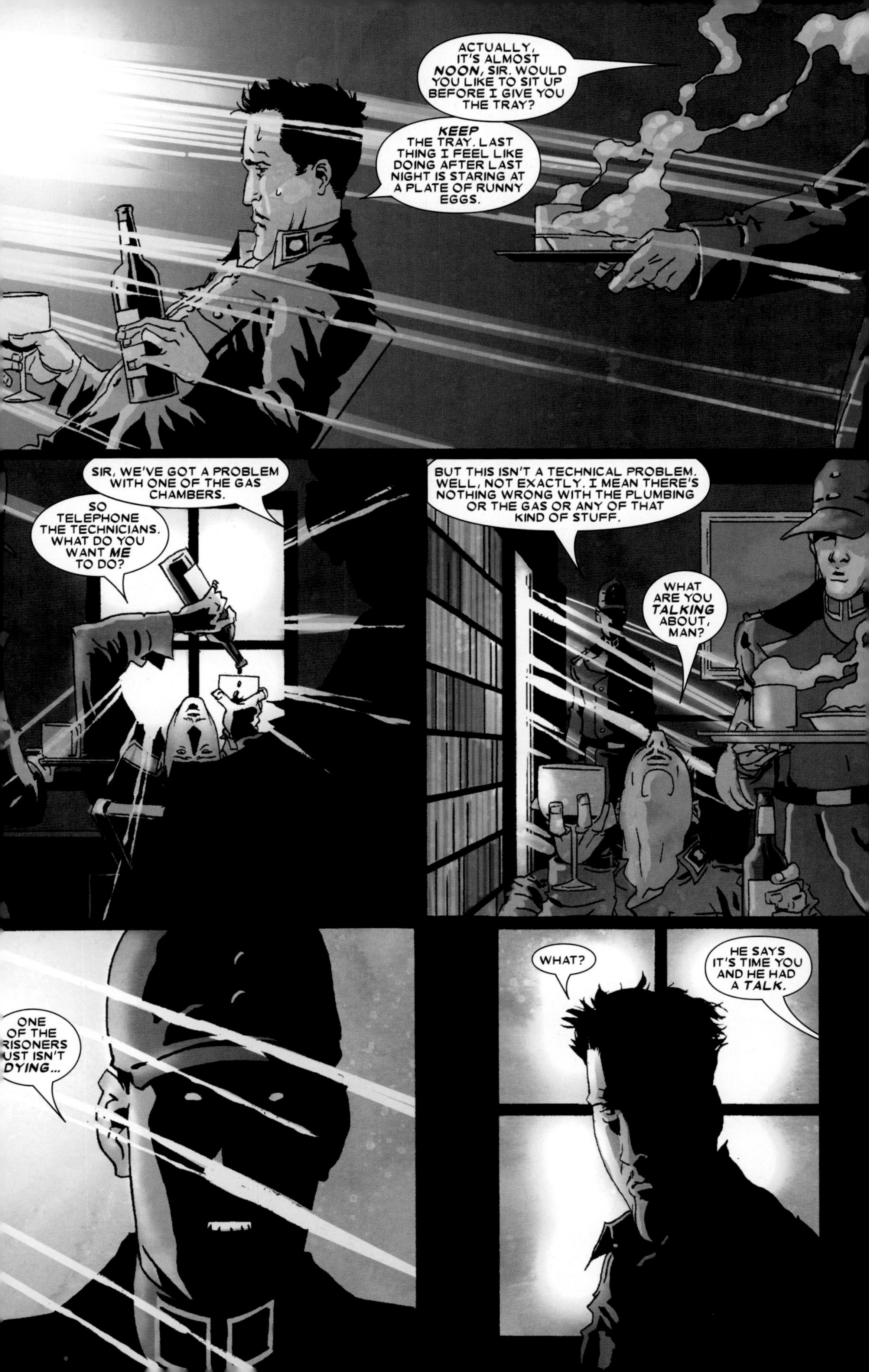
ACTUALLY, IT'S ALMOST NOON, SIR. WOULD YOU LIKE TO SIT UP BEFORE I GIVE YOU THE TRAY?
KEEP THE TRAY. LAST THING I FEEL LIKE DOING AFTER LAST NIGHT IS STARING AT A PLATE OF RUNNY EGGS.
SIR, WE'VE GOT A PROBLEM WITH ONE OF THE GAS CHAMBERS.
SO TELEPHONE THE TECHNICIANS. WHAT DO YOU WANT ME TO DO?
BUT THIS ISN'T A TECHNICAL PROBLEM. WELL, NOT EXACTLY. I MEAN THERE'S NOTHING WRONG WITH THE PLUMBING OR THE GAS OR ANY OF THAT KIND OF STUFF.
WHAT ARE YOU TALKING ABOUT, MAN?
ONE OF THE RISONERS UST ISN'T DYING...
WHAT?
HE SAYS IT'S TIME YOU AND HE HAD A TALK.

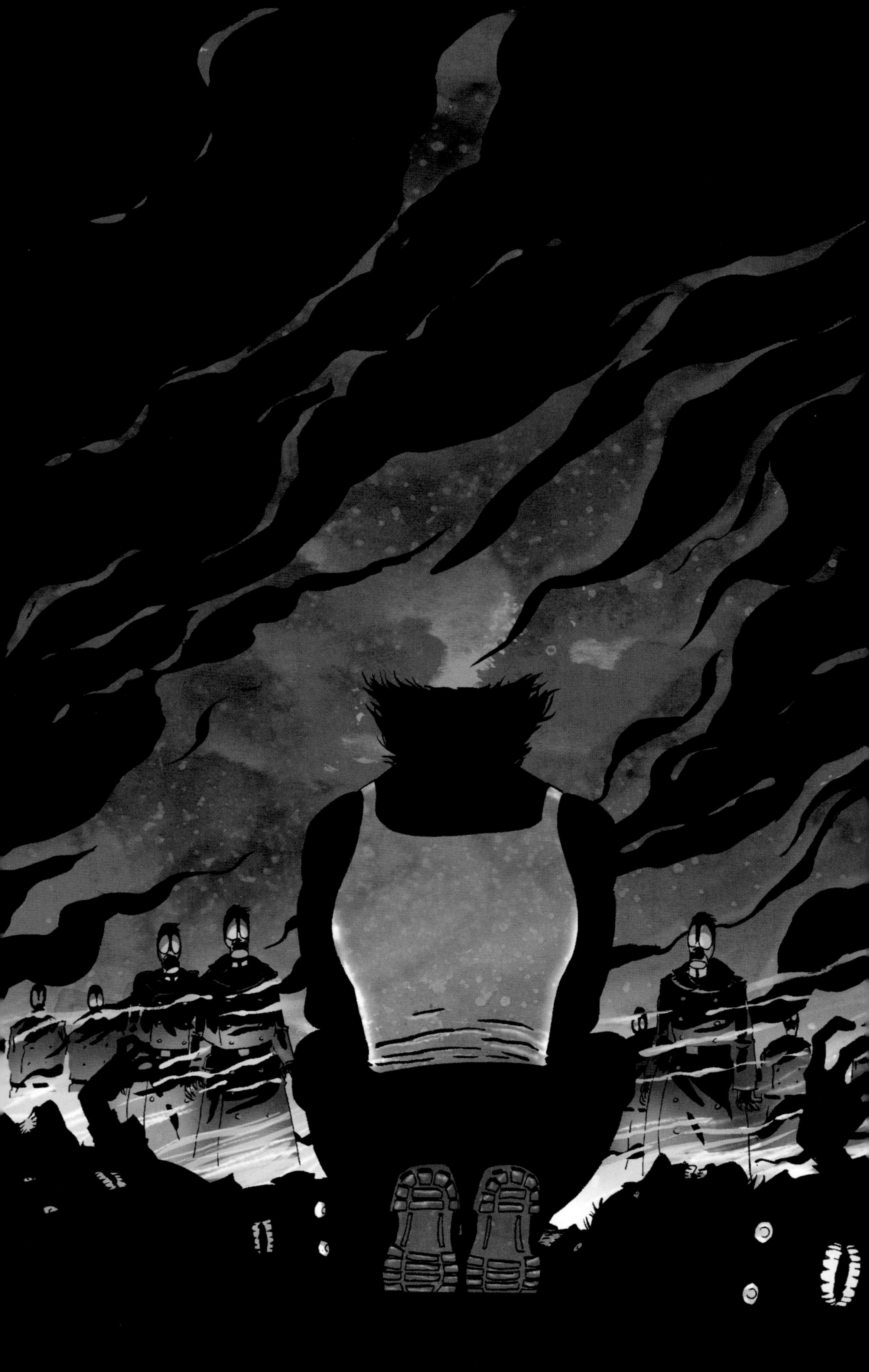

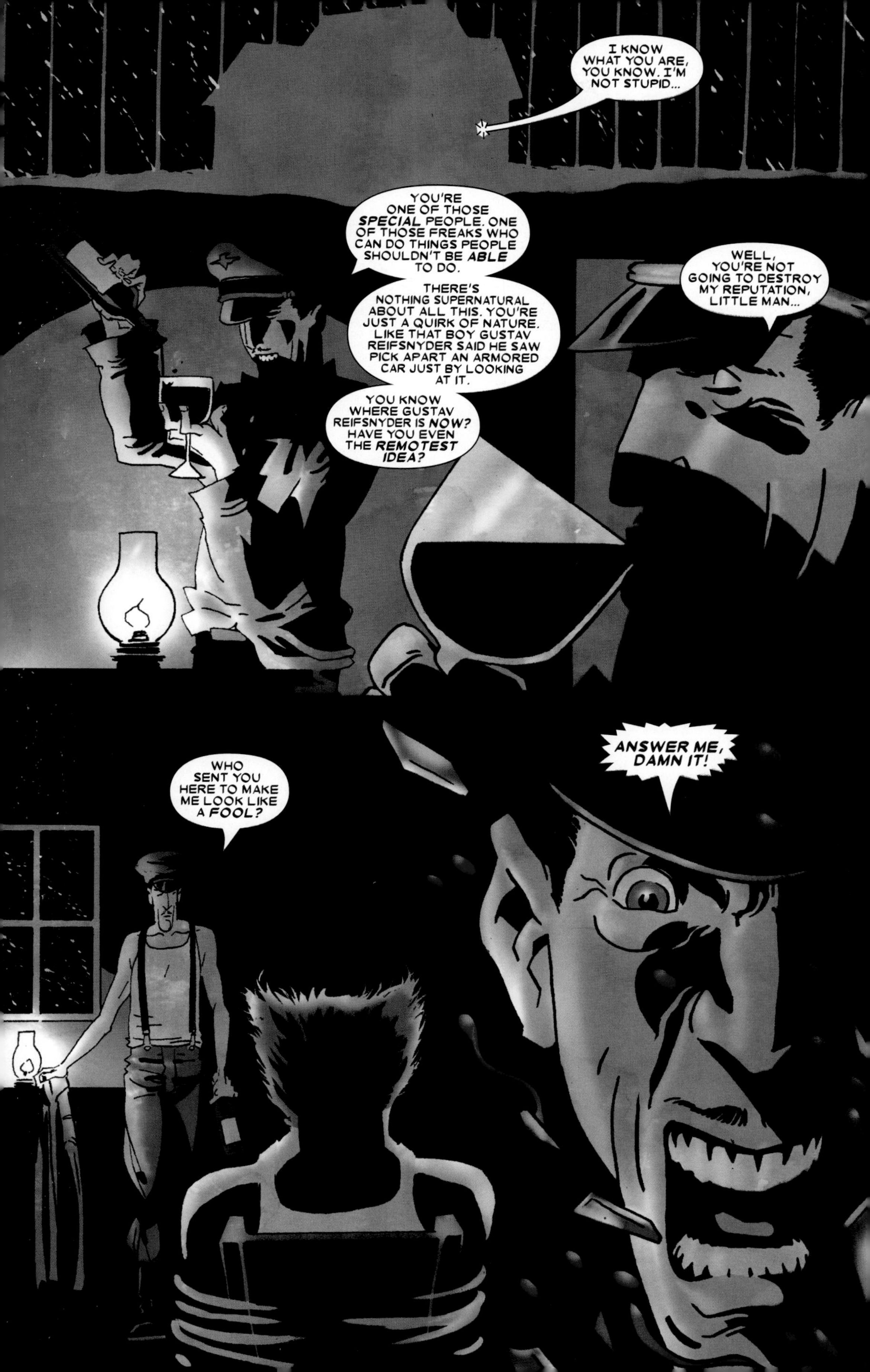
I KNOW WHAT YOU ARE, YOU KNOW. I'M NOT STUPID...
YOU'RE ONE OF THOSE SPECIAL PEOPLE. ONE OF THOSE FREAKS WHO CAN DO THINGS PEOPLE SHOULDN'T BE ABLE TO DO.
THERE'S NOTHING SUPERNATURAL ABOUT ALL THIS. YOU'RE JUST A QUIRK OF NATURE. LIKE THAT BOY GUSTAV REIFSNYDER SAID HE SAW PICK APART AN ARMORED CAR JUST BY LOOKING AT IT.
YOU KNOW WHERE GUSTAV REIFSNYDER IS NOW? HAVE YOU EVEN THE REMOTEST IDEA?
WELL, YOU'RE NOT GOING TO DESTROY MY REPUTATION, LITTLE MAN...
WHO SENT YOU HERE TO MAKE ME LOOK LIKE A FOOL?
ANSWER ME, DAMN IT!

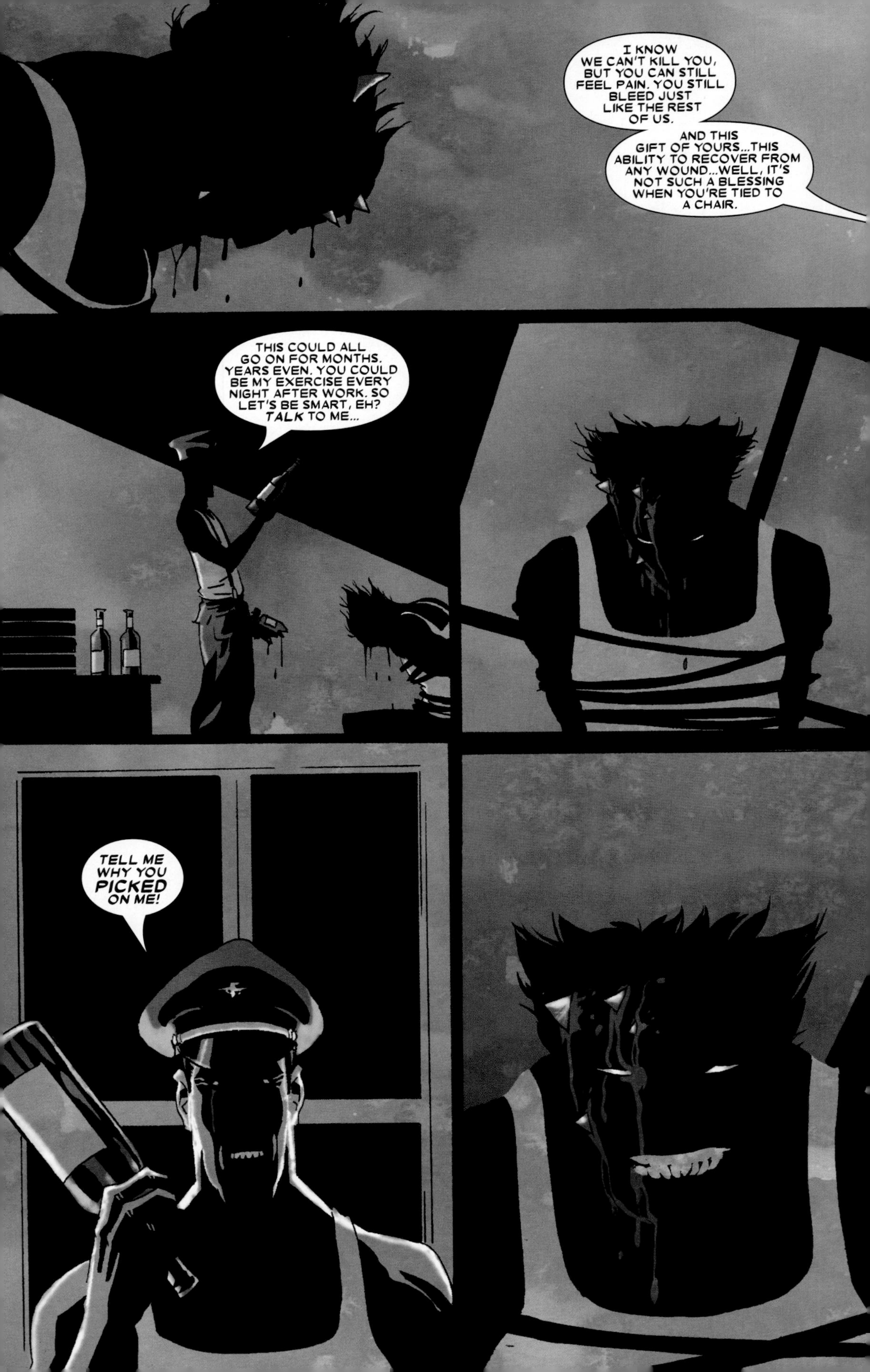
I KNOW WE CAN'T KILL YOU, BUT YOU CAN STILL FEEL PAIN. YOU STILL BLEED JUST LIKE THE REST OF US.
AND THIS GIFT OF YOURS...THIS ABILITY TO RECOVER FROM ANY WOUND...WELL, IT'S NOT SUCH A BLESSING WHEN YOU'RE TIED TO A CHAIR.
THIS COULD ALL GO ON FOR MONTHS. YEARS EVEN. YOU COULD BE MY EXERCISE EVERY NIGHT AFTER WORK. SO LET'S BE SMART, EH? *TALK* TO ME...
TELL ME WHY YOU **PICKED** ON ME!

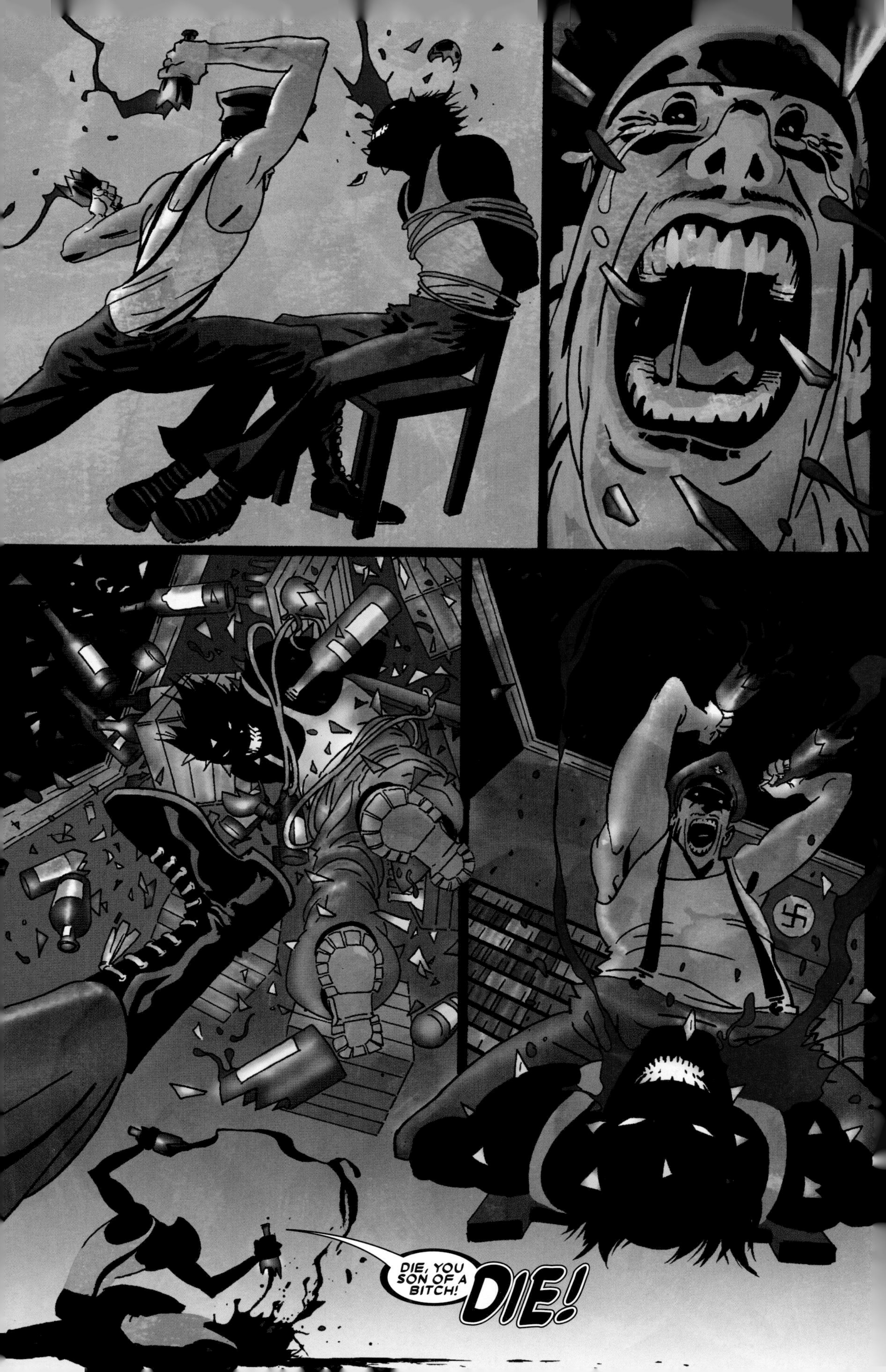
DIE, YOU SON OF A BITCH!
DIE!

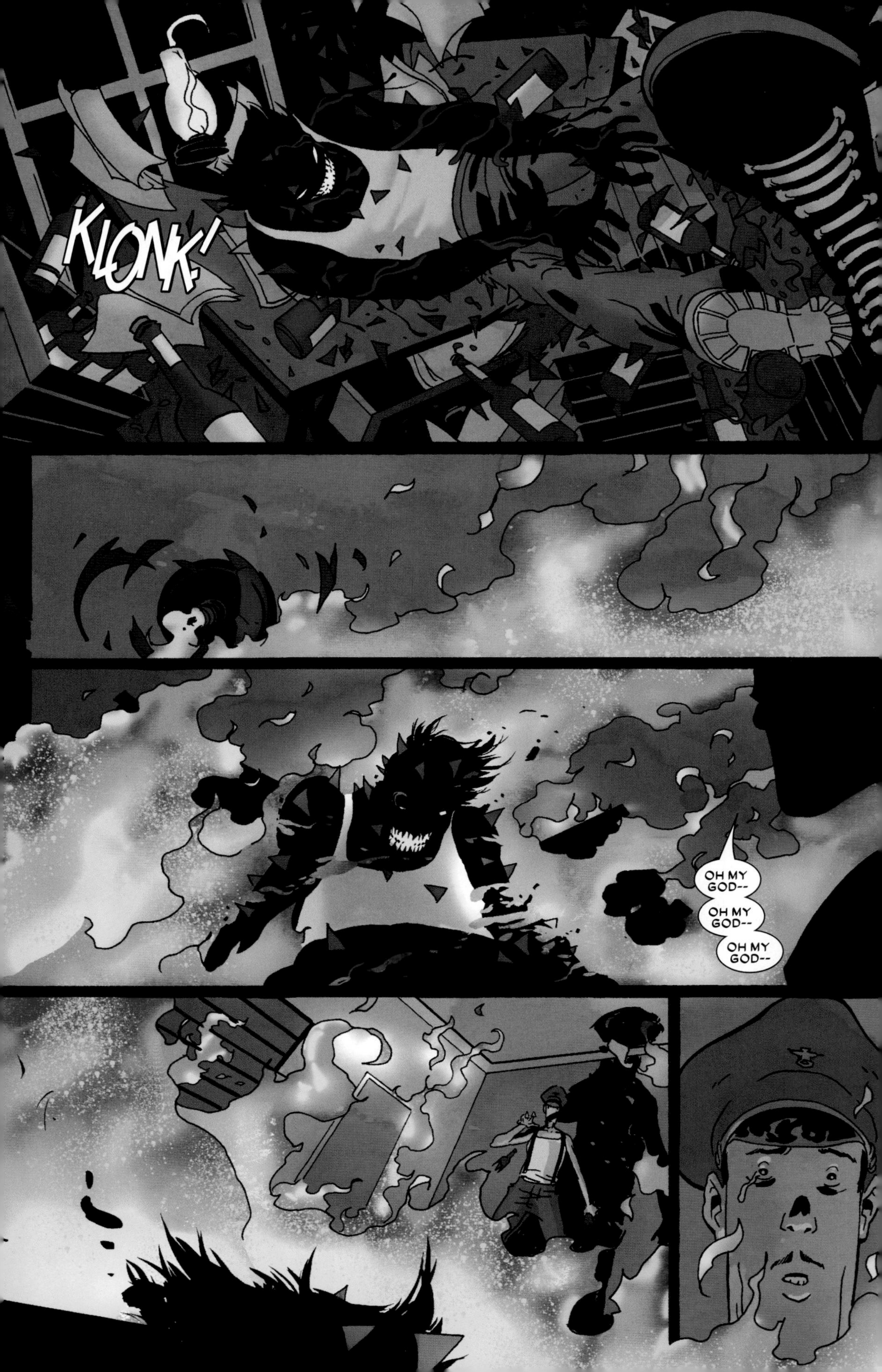
KLONK!
OH MY GOD--
OH MY GOD--
OH MY GOD--

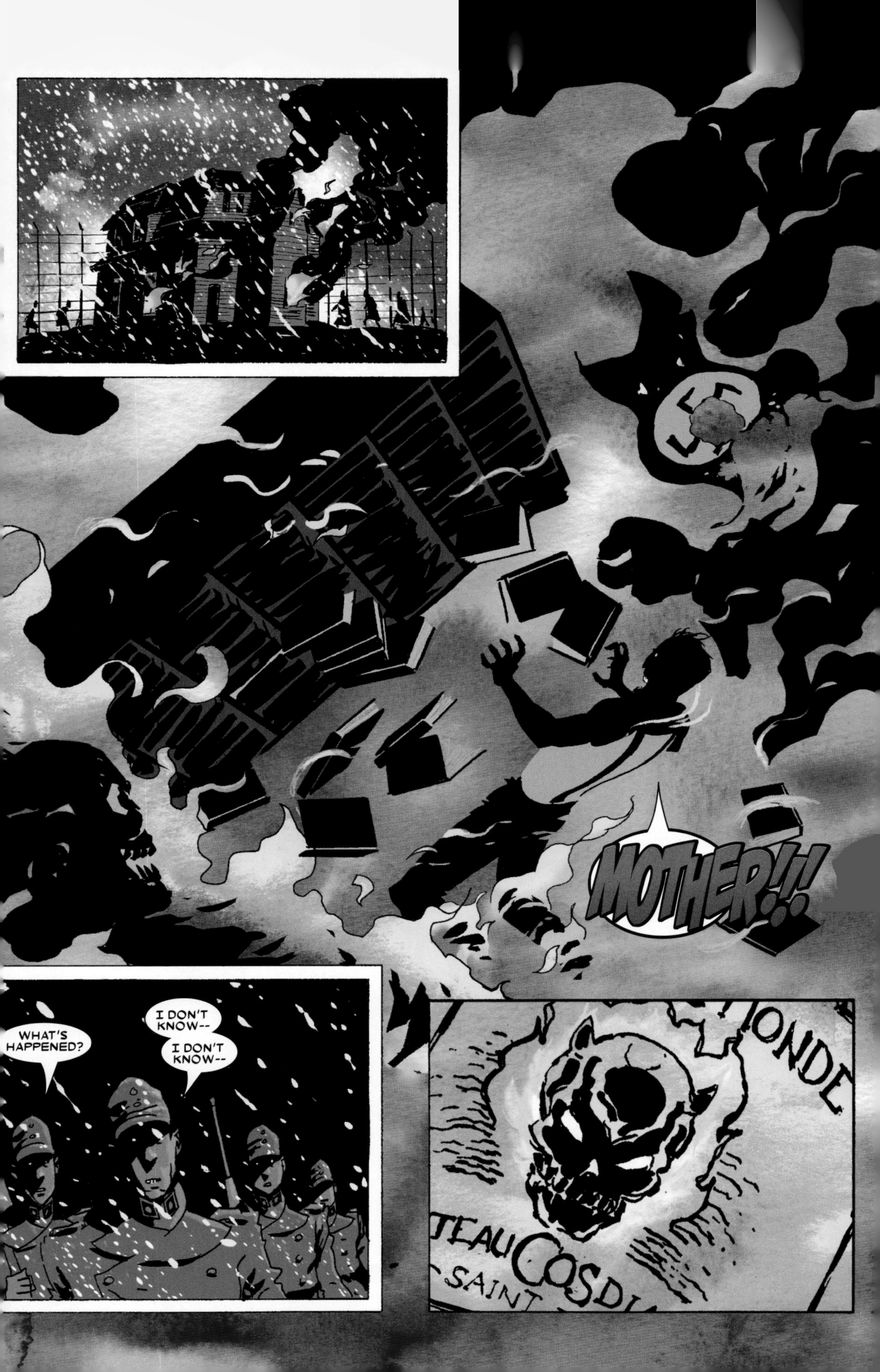
MOTHER!!!
WHAT'S HAPPENED?
I DON'T KNOW--
I DON'T KNOW--
ONDE
TEAU COS DI
SAINT

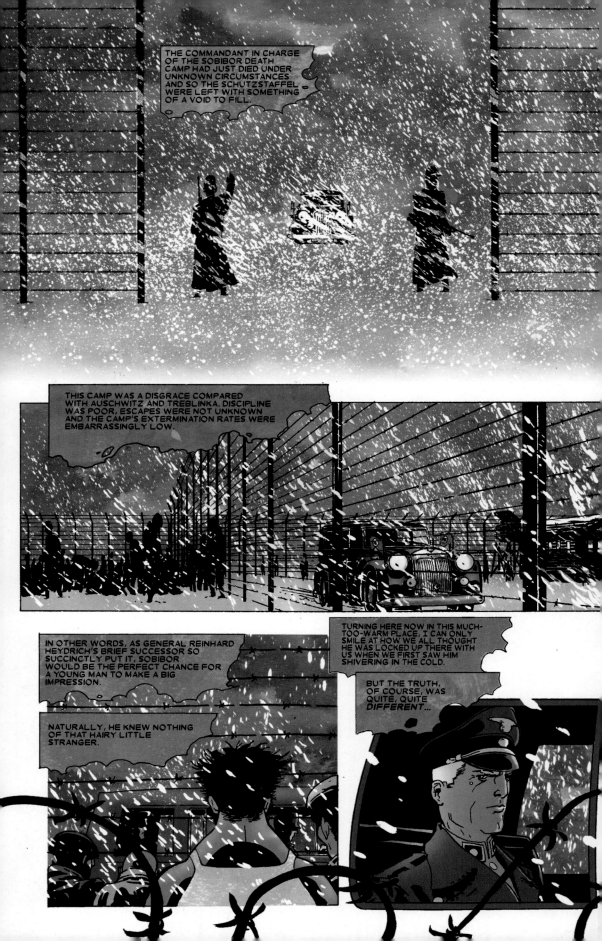

THE COMMANDANT IN CHARGE OF THE SOBIBOR DEATH CAMP HAD JUST DIED UNDER UNKNOWN CIRCUMSTANCES AND SO THE SCHUTZSTAFFEL WERE LEFT WITH SOMETHING OF A VOID TO FILL.

THIS CAMP WAS A DISGRACE COMPARED WITH AUSCHWITZ AND TREBLINKA. DISCIPLINE WAS POOR, ESCAPES WERE NOT UNKNOWN AND THE CAMP'S EXTERMINATION RATES WERE EMBARRASSINGLY LOW.

IN OTHER WORDS, AS GENERAL REINHARD HEYDRICH'S BRIEF SUCCESSOR SO SUCCINCTLY PUT IT, SOBIBOR WOULD BE THE PERFECT CHANCE FOR A YOUNG MAN TO MAKE A BIG IMPRESSION.

NATURALLY, HE KNEW NOTHING OF THAT HAIRY LITTLE STRANGER.

TURNING HERE NOW IN THIS MUCH-TOO-WARM PLACE, I CAN ONLY SMILE AT HOW WE ALL THOUGHT HE WAS LOCKED UP THERE WITH US WHEN WE FIRST SAW HIM SHIVERING IN THE COLD.

BUT THE TRUTH, OF COURSE, WAS QUITE, QUITE *DIFFERENT*...

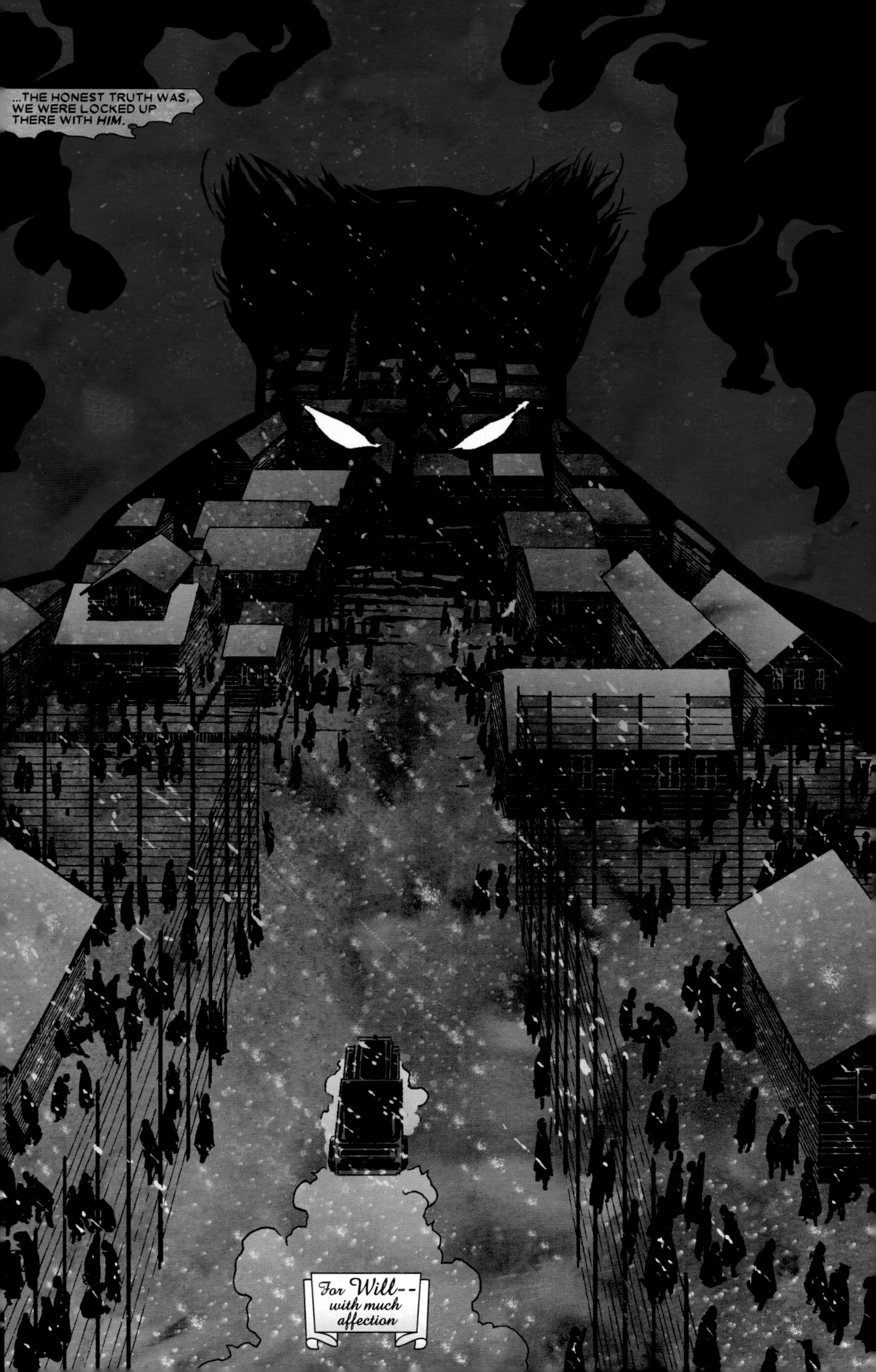
...THE HONEST TRUTH WAS, WE WERE LOCKED UP THERE WITH *HIM*.
For Will-- with much affection

BREAKFAST WITH LOGAN AND WILL

Forget Green Eggs and Ham. The strangest breakfast I ever had was in Barcelona a while back as I munched over a croissant with industry legend Will Eisner and spent an hour talking about Wolverine. But I'm getting a little ahead of myself here.

Will Eisner, as you hopefully know, was one of the greatest comic-book creators of all time. Some say he WAS the greatest, though he tended to laugh off such high praise and remind you that, over sixty years ago, he turned down *Superman* when Siegel and Shuster were hawking the concept from publisher to publisher. He's most famous for his unique and wonderful *Spirit* stories, but the material that impressed me most was the later work he accomplished in the last ten years of his life. When I told him this shortly before his death, he seemed especially pleased because he felt that he'd grown enormously from his Spirit days and I think it's one of the reasons we got along so well.

Another reason is that, quite by accident, I wasn't as in awe of him as most of my peers because I hadn't read the bulk of his work until AFTER we met. In fact, being an idiot, I remember feeling I'd drawn the short straw when I found out that I was seated next to this guy in his eighties at a dinner we were both attending a couple of years back in Spain. It was a brilliant convention and I was already friends with most of the American guests which is why I was a little disappointed to be stuck at the end of the table with a guy I knew next to nothing about.

But what a laugh we had and what a brilliant conversation. All my pals were roaring and screaming as they chewed on their pasta while I chatted to Will and his brilliantly smart wife about everything from the up-coming Presidential election to having Jack Kirby as the kid who makes your morning coffee. This guy's life and career had covered the entire century and he seemed to have first-hand experience in everything I was interested in. Cassaday, Quitely and the rest of the guys took off to a nightclub after the meal and, though drunken debauchery is my normal, natural state, I stunned them by saying I was heading back to the hotel bar with the Eisners and I sat up and chatted with them all night, soaking up story after story.

We spent about a week together in Spain and, though Will had less than no interest in super-hero comics, he asked me what I was working on and I filled him in on the various lucky breaks I'd had like *The Ultimates* and *Superman: Red Son*. I had an idea for a *Wolverine* story I'd been trying to work up, possibly done as a mini-series, and I told him I'd had a lot of problems with it. The story was set in a Nazi concentration camp and the characters and structure were all there, but something about it really annoyed me. I told him I felt weird using what's essentially a cartoon character in something where real people died and I wondered if it was bad taste, even if the story had the best of intentions. He said he knew what I meant, but people died in World War Two and Vietnam and were dying right now over in Iraq. His point was that, following my logic, super heroes couldn't be used in anything where real people had died and there was no need to be so precious. But it still didn't feel right. Wolverine's smart, cool one-liners (hell, even his voice) just seemed too inappropriate. It just pulled me right out of the story and he said he knew what I meant and would think about it.

Cut to breakfast next morning and I'm sitting with my wife and infant daughter and Eisner strides into the room, sits down and smiles, telling me he had the answer to my problem. Even I didn't know what he was talking about at first and my wife just looked at HIS wife as he explained that removing every line of dialogue from Wolverine completely changes the effect of the story and helps give the whole thing more of an EC ghost story vibe. Right away, I knew that he was right. All the "bubs" and so on being surgically removed completely changed the entire tone of the story and his final suggestion (making this a one-off instead of the originally planned mini) was the cherry on the cake. He told me comics should be the maximum amount of information told in as few images as possible and he was absolutely right. Ever since then, I've tried to live by this maxim.

I called him up a while back and told him that I was going to give him a special thank-you for his suggestions and he laughed like a drain, saying that he couldn't pick Wolverine out of a line-up with Spider-Man and Mickey Mouse. But he appreciated the sentiment.

And I appreciated the help.

Thanks, Will.

Mark Millar
Glasgow, Scotland
17th August 2005